7pam

Rethinking Marketing

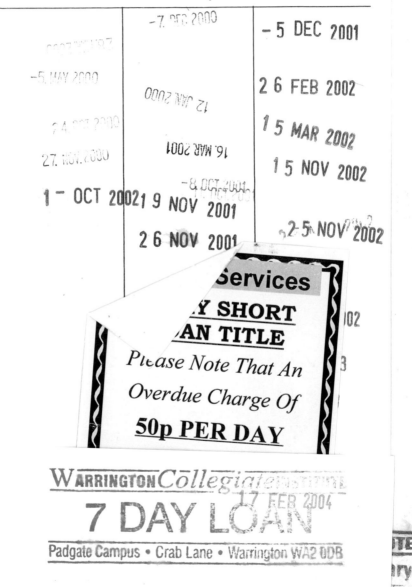

Rethinking Marketing

Towards Critical Marketing Accountings

edited by

Douglas Brownlie, Mike Saren, Robin Wensley and Richard Whittington

SAGE Publications
London • Thousand Oaks • New Delhi

First published 1999

SAGE Publications Ltd
6 Bonhill Street
London EC2A 4PU

SAGE Publications Inc.
2455 Teller Road
Thousand Oaks, California 91320

SAGE Publications India Pvt Ltd
32, M-Block Market
Greater Kailash – I
New Delhi 110 048

British Library Cataloguing in Publication data

A catalogue record for this book is available from
the British Library

ISBN 0 8039 7490 6
ISBN 0 8039 7491 4 (pbk)

Library of Congress catalog card number 98–75047

Typeset by Photoprint, Torquay, Devon
Printed and bound in Great Britain by Athenaeum Press,
Gateshead

Contents

Contributors' Notes

Luis Araujo is currently a Senior Lecturer in Marketing at the Department of Marketing, the Management School, University of Lancaster. He holds a mechanical engineering degree from the University of Porto (Portugal) and an MA and a PhD from the University of Lancaster. His main research interests and publications lie in the area of interorganizational relationships and networks.

Peter Binns, after previous posts at Warwick University, UK – first of all in the Philosophy Department and then as Senior Research Fellow in the Business School – is now a Principal Consultant with Bath Consultancy Group. His main interests are in the design, management and leadership of organizational and cultural change projects, whole-system development and the role of values in organizational learning.

When this volume was first mooted, **Stephen Brown** was mighty of thew, clear of eye, sharp of mind and enthused by the unprincipled principles of postmodernism. Aeons, however, have passed since then. Hemlines have risen and fallen, as have companies, civilizations and entire continents. Stephen is now a decrepit, rheumy-eyed, absent-minded something or other. What's more, he now realizes that, as a modernist trapped inside a postmodernist body of work, he has been living a lie the whole time. He'd like to thank the editors and publishers of *Rethinking Marketing* for giving him the opportunity to own up, tell all and generally unburden himself.

Douglas Brownlie is Professor of Marketing at Stirling University, UK. It recently occurred to him that he'd been talking, reading and writing about this place called 'marketing' for most of his working life, and that he'd settled down there, built a home, furnished it with carefully selected amulets, joined the local neighbourhood watch and taken up gardening. With a chuckle he recalled the ritual teasing of his parents who would always find time to ask at some point during his infrequent visits, 'When are you going to get a *real* job, son?' As an earnest marketing scholar he'd always prefer a staunchly literal reading of this mild jest, avoiding its play on several insecurities, the most obvious being the ontological insecurity of the 'real'. Of course, he'd defend his job zealously, often with the fiery passion and conviction of the patriot. Occasionally the testing would continue with remarks such as, 'Oh, methinks the laddie doth protest a wee bit too much', typically made as barely audible asides, as if to invisible witnesses. They no longer tease him this way; his protests always fell on deaf ears anyway. They taught him the lesson about territorial claims that he needed teaching: you cannot own the land, the land owns you. In a recent aside they observed, 'When you started out on this rethinking marketing book you had a full head of lustrous fair hair. It's mostly gone now.' A modest attribution methinks.

Gibson Burrell is Professor of Organizational Behaviour at the University of Warwick, UK. He is currently working on a book on the subject of 'histories of the concept of organization', and a four-volume series of readings in critical organization studies.

Bernard Cova, Professor at EAP Paris, is endeavouring to renovate current marketing theory and practice. He belongs to the school of marketing known as Postmodern Marketing, which advocates a rehabilitation of marketing in society, preferring tribal marketing and societing to traditional approaches. For 10 years he has worked on the development of a marketing approach to assist companies specializing in project and systems selling. He is considered by European marketers and researchers to be the leading expert in the field of project marketing.

Sally Dibb is a Senior Lecturer in Marketing and Strategic Management at the Warwick Business School, University of Warwick, UK. She is co-author of the best-selling *Marketing: Concepts and Strategy* textbook. Other recent books include *The Marketing Casebook*, *The Marketing Planning Workbook* and *The Market Segmentation Workbook*. Her research, teaching and consultancy interests focus on marketing segmentation, marketing planning and buyer behaviour. She has published extensively in these areas, including articles in the *European Journal of Marketing*, *Industrial Marketing Management*, *International Journal of Advertising*, *Journal of Service Industry Management*, *Journal of Strategic Marketing*, *Long Range Planning*, *OMEGA* and others.

Richard Elliott is Professor of Marketing and Consumer Research in the School of Business and Economics, University of Exeter, UK. Prior to this he was University Reader in Marketing at Oxford University and a fellow of St Anne's College. His current research interests focus on the social consequences of consumer culture, the oral history of brand consciousness and critical discourse analysis of representations of consumption. His work has been published in the *International Journal of Advertising*, *British Journal of Social Psychology*, *International Journal of Research in Marketing*, *Journal of Consumer Policy*, *Journal of the Market Research Society*, *British Journal of Management*, *European Journal of Marketing*, *Advances in Consumer Research*, *Psychology and Marketing* and *Journal of Marketing Management*.

Päivi Eriksson is Professor of Strategy at the School of Business Administration, University of Tampere, Finland. Prior to this appointment, she was a Senior Research Fellow at the Academy of Finland and worked at the Helsinki School of Economics and Business Administration in Finland, Stanford University in the USA and Warwick Business School in the UK. Her teaching and research areas include strategic management, marketing management and qualitative research methodologies. Her articles appear in the *Scandinavian Journal of Management*, *European Journal of Marketing* and others.

Stephen Fineman is Professor of Organizational Behaviour in the School of Management, Bath University, UK. His work includes introducing emotion to organizational theory, research on the 'greening' of corporations and critical approaches towards stress. Recent books include *Emotions in Organizations*, *Experiencing Organizations* and *Organizing and Organizations*.

Notable for his progress from 'New Blood' in the *European Journal of Marketing* (N.C. Smith, ed.; 1987, 21 (9)) to academic footnote (O'Dono-hoe, 'Postmodern poachers: young adult experiences of advertising', unpublished PhD thesis, University of Edinburgh, 1994: ix) without an intervening career, **Robert Grafton Small** is now equally at ease with the opportunities of early retirement. His pastimes currently involve doctors' waiting rooms, backstreet bookshops and, in recognition of his honorary readership at Keele University, a long-term immersion in the everyday affairs of Glasgow and Glaswegians.

William P. Hetrick is Assistant Professor of Business in the Division of Social Science at Bethel College, Tennessee, USA. His research interests focus on consumer research and critical social theory. He has published articles in the *Journal of Consumer Research*, *Rethinking Marxism* and the *Journal of Organizational Change Management*. Additionally, he has participated in many conferences and symposia in the USA and abroad.

Morris B. Holbrook is the W.T. Dillard Professor of Marketing in the Graduate School of Business at Columbia University, New York, USA. Holbrook received his MBA and PhD in Marketing from Columbia University. Since 1975, he has taught courses at the Columbia Business School in such areas as marketing strategy, sales management, research methods, consumer behaviour, and commercial communication in the culture of consumption. His research has covered a wide variety of topics in marketing and consumer behaviour, with a special focus on issues related to communication in general and to aesthetics, semiotics, art, entertainment and stereography in particular.

David Knights is Professor of Organizational Analysis and Head of the School of Management at Keele University, UK. He obtained his master's and doctorate at Manchester University and has previously held chairs in the University of Nottingham Business School and the Manchester School of

Management, UMIST. His current research, largely funded by ESRC grants, is in innovation, education, BPR, virtual markets and bank fraud. He is co-editor of the international journal *Gender, Work and Organization* and is on the editorial board of several journals. Recent books include *Managers Divided: Organisational Politics and Information Technology Management* (with F. Murray, 1994), *Regulation and Deregulation in European Financial Services* (with G. Morgan (eds), 1997) and *Financial Service Institutions and Social Transformations: International Studies of a Sector in Transition* (with T. Tinker (eds), 1997).

Gilles Laurent is Professor of Marketing at Groupe HEC, a leading business school in France. He received his PhD from MIT, in Management Science. He has published papers in the *Journal of Marketing Research*, *Management Science*, *Marketing Science*, *International Journal of Research in Marketing* and other outlets. He is a former editor of the *International Journal of Research in Marketing*. He has been a guest editor for special issues of *Recherche et Applications en Marketing*, *Decisions Marketing*, *International Journal of Research in Marketing* and *Marketing Letters*. He has published three books, the most recent being *Research Traditions in Marketing*, edited with Gary Lilien and Bernard Pras, which is a basis for the contribution in this volume. His research interests are diverse and his publications relate to maths programming, consumer involvement, awareness scores, loyalty, and (too) many other topics.

Hector R. Lozada (PhD, University of Kentucky, USA) is Assistant Professor of Marketing at Seton Hall University. He teaches undergraduate Consumer Behavior and Marketing Research, and graduate International Marketing and Marketing Strategies. His research focuses on three main areas: consumer research, marketing strategy and innovation, and green marketing. He has published articles in the *Journal of Consumer Research*, *Journal of Managerial Issues*, *Journal of Business & Industrial Marketing*, and *Journal of Euromarketing*. Additionally, he has presented papers in various conferences and symposia in the USA and elsewhere.

Pamela Odih (PhD, University of Manchester Institute of Science and Technology, UK) is a Research Associate at Nottingham University Business School, UK. Her research focuses on four main areas: consumer research, gender studies, media and culture studies and postmodernity. Gendered time and its bearing on consumption and wider gender relations is her specialist area. Recent publications include 'Gendered time in the age of deconstruction', *Time and Society*, Spring 1999.

Bernard Pras is Professor and Director of the Research Centre DMSP at the University of Paris Dauphine, and Professor at Essec, France. He holds a DBA degree from Indiana University, USA, and a PhD in economics from the University of Paris, France. He is the founding President of the French

Marketing Association (Association Française du Marketing). His fields of interest are consumer behaviour and international marketing. He has published several books and articles in major journals.

Mike Saren is Professor of Marketing at the University of Strathclyde. He is currently working on a number of research projects including an EC funded investigation into new product development processes. His other research interests cover the areas of the strategic marketing of technology, relational approaches to marketing, and marketing theory. In the past he has secured research funding from both public and private sectors including the EC, ICL, ESRC and SERC. His work has been published in many academic management journals in the UK, Europe and the USA, including the *International Journal of Research in Marketing, Omega, British Journal of Management* and *Industrial Marketing Management.*

Philip Stern is Lecturer in Marketing and Strategic Management at Warwick Business School, UK. His research and consulting are focused on the pharmaceutical industry and he is particularly interested in the prescribing perceptions and behaviours of general practitioners. He has worked in new product development and production management for Unilever and spent an enlightening period as a European Category Merchandiser for Avon Products.

Michael J. Thomas was appointed Professor of Marketing at Strathclyde University in January 1987. He is a consultant to the Know-How Fund (British overseas aid programme) and the United Nations Development Programme. He is particularly interested in the future of the marketing profession (and was National Chairman of the Chartered Institute of Marketing in 1995) and the role of marketing in economic development (he is a frequent visitor to Poland, Singapore, Hong Kong and Sri Lanka, as well as to the USA). He is the author of the *Pocket Guide to Marketing, Gower Handbook of Marketing* (4th edition) and *CIM Handbook of Marketing Strategy.* He sits on the editorial boards of the *Journal of Marketing Management, Journal of International Marketing, Journal of Brand Management, International Marketing Review, Journal of Marketing Practice* and he also edits *Marketing Intelligence & Planning.* He was recently awarded the Commanders Cross of the Order of Merit of Poland for his contribution to the economic transformation process in Poland. He is a member of the Board of Directors of the Alliance of Universities for Democracy.

Robin Wensley is Professor of Strategic Management and Marketing at the Warwick Business School, UK, and was elected Chair of Faculty of Social Studies in 1997. He is a member of the Senate of the Chartered Institute of Marketing. He has been involved with consultancy and management development with many major companies including British Telecom, Philips NV, ICL, IBM, Glaxo, Nestlé, Dynacast and Jardine Pacific. His research and consultancy interests include marketing strategy and planning, investment decision making and the assessment of competitive advantage. He is on the editorial board of the *International Journal of Research in Marketing*. His work has appeared in the *Harvard Business Review*, *Journal of Marketing* and *Strategic Management Journal*. He has twice won the annual Alpha Kappa Psi award for the most influential article in the US *Journal of Marketing*.

Hugh Willmott is Professor of Organizational Analysis in the Manchester School of Management at UMIST, UK. He is currently working on a number of projects whose common theme is the changing organization and management of work, including a project in the ESRC Virtual Society programme and an ICAEW funded study of strategic reorientation. His most recent books include *Skill and Consent* (1992, co-edited), *Making Quality Critical* (1995, co-edited) and *Managing Change, Changing Managers* (1995, co-authored). *Making Sense of Management: A Critical Introduction* (co-authored with Mats Alvesson) was published in 1996. *Management Lives* (co-authored with David Knights) is to appear in 1999. Hugh currently has served on the editorial boards of *Administrative Science Quarterly*, *Organization*, *Organization Studies and Accounting*, and *Organizations and Society*.

Richard Whittington is a fellow of New College, Oxford and Reader in Strategy and Deputy Director (MBA) of the Said Business School, University of Oxford, UK. His publications include *Corporate Strategies in Recession and Recovery* and *What is Strategy – And Does it Matter?* He is Associate Editor of the *British Journal of Management* and is on the editorial board of *Organization Studies*. He is currently involved in international research projects on strategy and structure in post-war Europe, and new organizational forms around the world. He has previously taught at the University of Warwick and Imperial College, London, and has been Visiting Professor at Groupe HEC, Paris.

Gerald Zaltman is the Joseph C. Wilson Professor of Business Administration at Harvard University, USA. His major research interests focus on buyer behaviour and on how managers use information in learning about markets. He has developed a new market research tool (ZMET), which is now being used by corporations for understanding the mental models underlying customer and manager thinking and behaviour. He has published widely in such journals as the *Journal of Marketing Research*, *Journal of Marketing*, *Journal of Advertising Research*, *Knowledge*, *American Behavioral Scientist* and *Industrial Marketing Management*. He is the co-author (with V. Barabba) of *Hearing the Voice of the Customer*.

Acknowledgements

The editors would like to thank Rosemary Nixon and Hans Lock at Sage for their help, support and general tolerance in the preparation of this manuscript. We would also like to acknowledge the encouragement and support of Sue Jones, as well for the thoughtful contribution she made to the Rethinking Marketing Symposium. Warwick Business School also provided funding to support the initial symposium. To Geoff Easton and Luis Araujo we must say thanks for providing the facilities and hospitality of the University of Lancaster during our periodic progress meetings at a place halfway between Glasgow and Birmingham. As Luis himself remarked, he will be glad, as we will too, to finally have a copy of the famous book to hand, having some idea of how many sandwiches, bananas, coffee, orange juice, and other items were consumed to get it into print.

1 Marketing Disequilibrium: On Redress and Restoration

Douglas Brownlie, Mike Saren, Robin Wensley and Richard Whittington

If we know in what way society is unbalanced, we must do what we can to add weight to the lighter scale ... we must have formed a conception of equilibrium and be ever ready to change sides like justice, 'that fugitive from the camp of conquerors'.

(Weil, 1963: 151)

What is it like to think new thoughts; to come face to face with the strangeness of the familiar; to undo the fragile web of assumption that binds us to common sense? What does it take to render new images of the familiar; to look anew at the world we already know; to see the ordinary and everyday from a fresh perspective; to see them as others see them; to see yourself as others see you? When did you last feel the sharp slap of confusion and doubt, or the unexpected rush of foresight that accompanies defamiliarization and disorientation? What remains when a pantheon of ideas begins to collapse in on itself and loosen its grip on the imagination? What do we turn to when we see that our answers to the question 'what manner of men are these?' (Geertz, 1973: 16) sets others in the frame of our own banalities? What manner of men could it be that would not ask of others 'what manner of men are we?' How can we 'show the text as it cannot know itself' (Eagleton, 1976: xx)? What can we do to 'invent allusions to the conceivable which cannot be presented' (Lyotard, 1984: 81)? What can be done to disturb the marketing 'gaze' so that what is 'always before our eyes' no longer routinely escapes remark (Wittgenstein, 1968)? How is it possible to render the familiar strange, the comfortable uncomfortable, the understood misunderstood, the predictable unpredictable, the ingenuous disingenuous, the normal abnormal, the transparent opaque, the intimate alien, the settled unsettled, the acceptable unacceptable, the taken-for-granted problematic, the balanced unbalanced, the thinkable unthinkable; the thought rethought?

Of what can we speak when the mythic plane is defrocked and new masks have yet to arrive (Hughes, 1997: xi)?

Thoughts on rethinking the underimagined and overdetermined

The poetry of difference inspires this reflexive interrogation. It also gives expression to concerns for the myopia and intolerance that can feed off conformity while nourishing it too. Those high-minded concerns led to the original Rethinking Marketing Symposium in July 1993. The symposium attracted an international group of participants who shared an interest in exploring new ways of thinking about marketing and the conditions that might make new perspectives possible. The chapters which appear here were developed from among original contributions that were made to the symposium. They reveal that a wide range of provocative ideas and perspectives were brought to a variety of contemporary marketing topics (Brownlie et al., 1993; 1994).

The ongoing project of rethinking marketing has also been inspired by the more profane ambition of contributing to the nascent stream of critical marketing scholarship which is striving for impetus, visibility and impact on the mainstream from the margins (cf. Arnold and Fisher, 1996; Benton, 1987; Brownlie and Saren, 1992; Dholakia, 1988; Dholakia and Firat, 1980; Dholakia et al., 1987; Dixon, 1992; Hetrick and Lozada, 1994; Larsen and Wright, 1993; Marion, 1993; Monieson, 1988; Murray and Ozanne, 1991; Murray et al., 1994). Because of the permeable boundaries of marketing there are a number of perspectives which are not part of the orthodox mainstream, including 'critical' perspectives. The aim of the symposium was to provide a platform for the discussion of such perspectives, exploring new ways of thinking about marketing as a way of 'doing particular social relations' (Morgan, 1992: 136). The symposium also set out to release creative potential that might otherwise remain dormant or denied, for as Hopper et al. observe, the value of a critical perspective 'resides in its capacity to reveal some of the basic assumptions and theoretical deficiencies of [conventional] approaches' (1987: 438).

In this text we now set out to insert these new ideas not only into the written record of the discipline, but into its imaginative record too. In this sense we are attempting to show how a critical approach to the development of marketing thought can reveal new pathways for marketing scholarship, perhaps helping to prepare well-trodden paths for the fact of change. However, we are attempting to draw attention not merely to 'new' marketing phenomena, but to the conditions of possibility of 'new' phenomena: how we might render different images of what we have already decided is knowable; and the kinds of things it would be possible to say or not to say about those images. In this regard we are also calling for a more historicized and reflexive understanding of the discipline (cf. Holbrook, 1997) for, as Grey comments,

The history of management studies, like the history of all disciplines, is one in which the contributions of some are recognised while those of others are occluded

We were originally brought to an attenuated sense of wonder by a shared feeling that, after 20 years of unheeded disquisition on the benefits of a market orientation and suchlike, the tide was at last turning marketing's way: the perennial battles for recognition and legitimacy were being won; and with our rather blunted rhetoric we were now pressing against open doors. Marketing as a discipline, a practice and an ideology was coming of age (Whittington and Whipp, 1992). An important text had just been published as a showcase for the work of a major programme of empirical research into marketing and competitiveness which was funded by the UK government's Economic and Social Research Council (Saunders, 1994). Marketing's star was in the ascendancy and its ambitions were sweeping, heroic and, some would say, immodest (cf. Alvesson and Willmott, 1996; Knights et al., 1994; Wensley, 1990).

Indeed, in many ways the 1990s have become the decade of marketing. Its ideas and rhetoric have been widely used to legitimize change in organizations in the public and private sectors, in profit and non-profit organizations, in services and manufacturing, in consumer and business markets, with regional and global operations (du Gay and Salaman, 1992; du Gay et al., 1996; Whittington and Whipp, 1992; Whittington et al., 1994). In the East as well as the West, markets are offered as the solution to the challenges of whole societies. The entire process of consumption itself is central and pervasive in these (post) modern times where 'all ideologies have been defeated: in the end their dogmas were unmasked as illusions and people stopped taking them seriously' (Kundera, 1991: 127).

And so it might seem that our concerns for imbalance might sound rather measured and well rehearsed, especially if you agree that marketing is an eclectic and progressive scientific subject: that its institutions facilitate a self-conscious critical approach; that those institutions help promote a wider recognition for the expertise that marketing contributes to society; that marketing is a creative subject which is already capable of regenerating itself; and that all this is evidenced by the application of marketing technology to an ever widening range of organizational, social and political contexts. You might then wonder why we should bother thinking about rethinking marketing anyway, when there is so much 'business as usual' to be done (Hunt, 1994: 13; Saunders, 1994). Shelby Hunt put this particular point very succinctly at the final plenary discussion of the symposium when he asked the participants 'should we?': that is, why should we rethink marketing?

Participants shared a sneaking feeling that 'business as usual' was not enough and that marketing's underlying framework of theory and concepts required critical attention. This view has gathered momentum since the symposium, as the contributions to this volume will reveal. Others have previously taken a similar line of thought, arguing that the creativity and growth of the discipline, and the profession, were in danger of being stifled by the overwhelming tendency to take fixed positions of agreement on those important statements about the character of marketing knowledge and its

or marginalised. Although this may have an aspect of chance, more obviously it reflects distinct patterns of inequality. Thus those voices which are generally marginal in society are likely to be written out of any specific history. (1997: 593)

Working within the fields of marketing and strategy, we sense the potential for new perspectives which could contribute to the development of mainstream forms of theory and research and the popular representations of practice they have to offer. We also feel that marketing is becoming too much of an important part of everyday social organization to be left solely to the technocratic rhetoric and representations of managerialist thinking, where a narrow focus on means–ends relationships is predominant. It is also our aim to contribute to the renewal of what Habermas (1971; 1974) understands as the emancipatory impulse, in our case of marketing. Importantly, Bartels (1976) reminds us that marketing has its origins as a discipline in studies of the impact of the monopsonistic buying power of intermediaries on the operations of agricultural markets of the Midwestern states of the USA during the late nineteenth century. Indeed at the turn of that century the 'marketing problem', as it was then known, referred to the 'suspected manipulation of prices for farm products by middlemen to the detriment of producers and consumers alike' (Benton, 1987: 422). The discipline of marketing emerged from studies of what steps could be taken to provide a civic framework within which markets would operate more effectively in the interest of producers and consumers too. And in this sense the early development of the discipline could be seen as contributing to the social good of society through exposing what Alvesson and Willmott refer to as 'how structures of domination and exploitation shape and mediate [exchange] relationships' (1996: 120).

The contribution of critical perspectives to management-related disciplines is perhaps most clearly developed within accounting (Power and Laughlin, 1992). In their lucid critique of research in management accounting, Hopper et al. (1987) discuss the 'failure to theorise accounting as a fully social practice', drawing attention to its narrow base in social science methodology. They question a number of features of mainstream management accounting research, prominent among them being: its theoretical and methodological base in neo-classical economics and functionalist organizational theory; the widely held image of the organization as a unitary and integrated system where resource allocation decisions are a matter of information provision; the conventional representation of management accounting as a politically neutral, technical information service that can be abstracted from fundamental issues of ownership and control; and the widespread acceptance of the authority of managerialist assumptions. They go on to isolate a number of important problems in the discipline, including: the failure to develop the idea that accounting is a set of practices which are both the medium and outcome of the politico-economic context in which accounting is embedded; the failure to consider the role of language in shaping accounting theory and practice; the failure to analyse the historical and cultural specificity of accounting practices and knowledge; and the growing evidence that 'conventional accounting knowledge is often not used in practice; and that when it is, it can induce undesirable and unsought consequences' (1987: 438).

The Rethinking Marketing project drew (and draws) inspiration from this deft piece of critical observation which we argue directly applies to marketing management too. Hopper et al. (1987) not only reveal the potential of critical thinking to contribute to the development of research and theory within management accounting: for their pathfinding work also suggests the potential of critical thinking to contribute to the development of several disciplines which share the basic assumptions of management accounting, including marketing. It is clear then, that as Sawchuck comments, '[marketing] is a fecund terrain for critical thinking' (1994: 95); and that as Alvesson and Willmott advise, 'a critical theory approach to marketing can bring fresh insights and provide a more penetrating appreciation of its ethical and social significance' (1996: 128).

Through revisiting the emancipatory impulse of marketing, we also hope to remind ourselves of the discipline's wider constituency of the managed, consumers and citizens alike, as well as the value of thinking historically (Jameson, 1991) about marketing thought (Fullerton, 1988; Hollander and Rassuli, 1993; Vink, 1992). It does seem as if the discipline has lost something of its early direct involvement in the wider affairs of the community through its relentless pursuit of scientific respectability and narrow technical focus on the bottom line. In our view there is an imbalance in marketing scholarship which critical perspectives could hold in check, if redress and restoration is not available. We take the view that it is possible to reconcile more than one identity for marketing scholarship. The challenge is to be in two minds about things: to be able to engage with more than one perspective; to have a repertoire of more than one way of representing your knowledge; to recognize when the undecidable is being rendered decidable and for what purposes; and to privilege ideas knowingly. Towards this end there is an important role for critical thinking, as Eagleton advises: '[The task of criticism] is not to redouble the text's self-understanding, to collude with its object in a conspiracy of silence. The task is to show the text as it cannot know itself' (1976).

Tilting scales

The Rethinking Marketing Symposium was an attempt not simply to put things right, but to generate a setting in which to contemplate the excitements and transformations which new perspectives can bring. It was an attempt to stir the marketing imagination from its apparent lethargy and to frustrate the easy complacency of mainstream thought on a variety of marketing topics. For a couple of days we could afford to be drawn by our enthusiasm to disobey the gravitational pull of mainstream marketing

thought and to engage in what Alvesson and Willmott refer to as 'reconstruction and critique' (1996: 15), where reconstruction 'mobilizes critical reason to diagnose prevailing conditions' (1996: 15) and 'critique "entails a process of self-reflection . . . designed to achieve liberation from the domination of past constraints" ' (Connerton, 1976: 20, quoted in Alvesson and Willmott, 1996).

Symposium discussions compared various accounts of the imbalance in marketing scholarship and mulled over imaginary scenes in which it had been 'defrocked, with new masks yet to arrive' (cf. Alvesson, 1993; du Gay, 1993; Knights, 1992; Knights and Morgan, 1991; Morgan, 1992). We wondered what form those new masks might take if redress and restoration were to be possible and if we were to contribute to the growing body of knowledge that takes marketing processes as social phenomena worthy of serious critical examination. We found directions to important work in cognate disciplines (cf. Alvesson and Willmott, 1992a; Arrington and Francis, 1989; Berg, 1989; Burrell, 1988; Burrell and Morgan, 1979; Chia, 1995; Cooper, 1989; Cooper and Burrell, 1988; du Gay, 1994; Linstead and Grafton-Small, 1992; Miller and O'Leary, 1987; Parker, 1992; Reed, 1989; Reed and Hughes, 1992; Watson, 1994; Willmott, 1993). But we could not find a poetry sufficient to the task of unpicking our knotted imaginations; of helping us recapture a sense of wonder about the lost continents of the everyday; of rediscovering the marvellous as we once had known it.

On understanding what it takes to think new thoughts, to render the familiar strange, we have now got as far as agreeing that to make 'rethinking' possible, we must first consider what makes the thinkable possible. Giddens argues that 'modern institutions are unthinkable without systematic and informed reflection upon the conditions of social activity' (1993: 15). You could say then that marketing thought calls for such systematic reflection upon the conditions of social activity within its gaze; and marketing rethought calls for the discipline to interrogate this normalizing gaze and to confront the strangeness of the familiar. Rethinking then can be seen as an exercise in the surveillance of meaning (Baudrillard, 1983; 1990), a considered reflexivity which Mills argues is an important component of what he calls 'intellectual craftsmanship' (1959: 196). In a similar vein of reflexivity Cooper and Burrell observe that 'In order to see the ordinary with a fresh vision, we have to make it "extraordinary", i.e. to break with the habits of organized routine and see the world "as though for the first time"; it is necessary to free ourselves of normalized ways of thinking which blind us to the strangeness of the familiar' (1988: 101).

But then again, on second thoughts . . .

Come, sir, arise, away! I'll teach you differences.

Shakespeare, *King Lear*, I.iv (Fraser, 1963: 63)

institutions (cf. Anderson, 1983; American Marketing Association, 1988; Arndt, 1980; 1985; Axelsson and Easton, 1992; Deshpande, 1983; Dholakia and Arndt, 1985; Dholakia et al., 1987; Firat, 1992; Firat et al., 1987; Hunt, 1992; Mattson, 1985; Peter, 1992).

Drawing inspiration from Giddens (1993) we understood that marketing theory is not just a way to frame meaning, it also 'constitutes a moral intervention in the social life whose conditions of existence the theory seeks to clarify'. In this sense what passes for marketing theory requires vigilant interrogation through the critical engagement of dialogic critique. Giddens sees this as 'the very life blood of fruitful conceptual development in social theory' (1993: 1), while Alvesson and Willmott (1996: 119) see it as contributing to the 'challenging and removal of discourses and practices that are incompatible with the development of greater autonomy and responsibility'. Easton and Araujo (1997: 104) have also asserted the importance of critical debate and reflexivity in marketing, suggesting that the purpose of such scrutiny is not to establish definitive interpretations, but to 'look beyond the received view on content, by examining the literary form and style of argumentation' by means of which authors attempt to accomplish the effect of 'truth' through their writing.

In step with escapees

> Strange how things in the offing, once they're sensed, convert to things foreknown; and how what's come upon is manifest, only in the light of what has been gone through.
>
> (Heaney, 1991: 108)

Kundera (1991: 128) discusses how reality was once stronger than ideology; how the imagology of those who now shape public opinion has gained a historic victory over ideology; and how the power of imagology, of the circulation of representations, has now surpassed reality, which for many has ceased to be what they say it once was. You could say that we live in an age when reality is only a support for the packaging; when signs of the real replace the real; when what people buy is not simply objects, but the sign system of objects that imbues these functional objects with both status and signification; when the chicken we buy is not 'real' or 'natural', but 'a culturally manipulated foodstuff . . . an extension of the producer's [or retailer's] marketing strategy' (Sawchuck, 1994: 104). As Sawchuck remarks:

> marketing history has developed the following discourse on its own practice: marketing records ostensibly inherent desires, then creates new products (or repackages old ones) that ostensibly satisfy these desires. In doing so there is a

shift in the level of abstraction. One does not sell a specific product, such as a tampon, one sells 'sanitary protection', of which a tampon is one profitable solution. (1994: 100)

This marketing discourse constructs a particular view of society and markets, organizations, consumers and consumption objects within it (Brownlie and Saren, 1997). As Morgan observes, marketing can be understood as 'a set of practices and discourses which help to constitute and shape social relations in modern Western societies' (1992: 137). Marketing discourse is then a central part of a process whereby 'a particular form of society is constructed, one in which human beings are treated as things' (1992: 154). The marketing gaze constructs consumers as objects, as rational, sovereign, self-actualizing actors whose identity is reduced to the 'ownership of commodities and all social relations are conceived in market terms'. Framed in this way, consumers are seeking 'to maximise the worth of their existence to themselves through personalised acts of choice in a world of goods and services' (du Gay and Salaman, 1992: 623). The social and cultural properties of material things then provide one of the key axes of signification in contemporary societies and marketing can be located within processes through which individual identity is constructed (Appadurai, 1986; Bourdieu, 1984; Douglas, 1992; Douglas and Isherwood, 1979; du Gay et al., 1997; Miller, 1987; 1995; 1997).

Marketing can indeed be understood as the engine of a vast panoptic system of observation and social control by means of which it tracks, traces and seduces unknowing consumers into participation in its processes (Alvesson, 1993; Alvesson and Willmott, 1996: 124; Packard, 1960). Many of the declared woes of contemporary consumer society can, if you choose, be laid at the door of marketing as the conspiring footman of a voracious neo-capitalism (Frank and Weiland, 1997). In the estimation of Alvesson and Willmott (1996) these woes would include pollution, crime and social division and exclusion, as well as the emptiness and ennui of pampered consumers who, without the careful percipience of those authors and others like them, would be incapable of realizing that they are caught in a 'narrow and distorted process of communication and self-formation' (1996: 125); and that this 'inhibits opportunities for autonomy, clarification of genuine needs and wants, and thus greater and lasting satisfaction' (Alvesson and Willmott, 1992a: 435).

A non-critical marketing would document and trace how marketing discourse locates us within this system, either as merchants of the fast moving current generalizations (FMCGs) of marketing knowledge and practice (Brownlie and Saren, 1995), or as compliant consumers of them. It would speak of the constitutive effects of marketing discourse without offering a critique of the existing social arrangements that make the privilege of this perspective possible. It would sidestep the issue of how objects are made meaningful in the processes and practices of their consumption. It would be silent on the idea that consumption encompasses many different activities and that different people are situated differently in relation to those activities (du Gay et al., 1997: 96). It would be silent on the idea that consumption not only marks social difference, but represents an important means through which we relate to each other and, as Belk remarks 'weave the web of culture' (1995: 69). It would be blind to the different ways in which material possessions, as signs and symbols, are used to create and sustain social bonds or distinctions, or how social relations and experiences are mediated (Giddens, 1991: 5) by institutional circumstances. It would be silent on consumption as a socially structured practice in which the meanings attached to or coded into goods and services are contingent and provisional and situated through the practice of everyday living (de Certeau, 1984). It would choose to assume, for the sake of accomplishing the rhetorical effect of critique, that although goods and services are inscribed with meaning through their production and delivery, this is the only meaning that they may come to have: thereby being blind to the notion that consumption can be seen as an active process involving signifying practices which put to use the ' "polysemic quality of commodities" as signs' (du Gay et al., 1997: 104). It would be blind to the active and creative part consumers play in constructing the meaning of objects. It would conveniently assume that consumers follow a pre-written script, or that goods have a preordained meaning and that we can read off various cultural, social and political effects from these assumed meanings (1997: 94–5), rather than explore the different uses made of goods in the practices of the everyday lives of consumers and consumed. It would be unable to recognize emancipation anywhere but in its officially sanctioned showplaces. It would be blind to the possibility that the ardent claims of academics and other wide-eyed, well-scrubbed children of the suburbs are more a symbol of the contemporary culture machine's authority than an agent of resistance (Frank, 1997: 154). It would be silent in the face of its own unspoken claims to authority and privilege.

The aim of Rethinking Marketing was not merely to articulate criticism, but to explore the potential liberatory aspects of 'the tensions between current marketing thinking and criticisms of it' (Roslender, 1997). Furthermore, it was not merely to reproduce the 'strong version' of Alvesson and Willmott's (1992a: 453) critical theory, with its totalizing attack on management ideology and promises of emancipation from false consciousness and 'frozen social relations'. Following Alvesson and Willmott's (1992a: 453) revealing attempt to reformulate the idea of emancipation in management and organization studies, we suggest a more modest form of engagement with the discipline and its representations of the everyday practices of consumers or managers and the institutions that produce and mediate those practices. We too favour an eclectic framework of critique which leaves space for many voices other than those of card-carrying critical theorists. There is indeed much to be learned from letting consumers or managers speak for themselves, even if critical ethnographers have difficulty 'hearing' what is being said, for there is much to commend Lilley's view that 'managers and critical management researchers may be playing similar games, with similar rules, for different teams' (1997: 51).

A critical marketing would then reassert the part to be played by active consumers and managers. It would of course seek to problematize the assumption that marketing managers and consumers act as the carriers of an impartial marketized rationality. It would show how marketing technology cannot provide a neutral way of looking at the world, irrespective of the intentions behind its deployment. It would raise awareness of how marketing discourse constitutes its object of analysis, consumers and managers, and is implicated in the production and reproduction of the existing social arrangements which constitute its domain of research (Morgan, 1992: 152). As Alvesson and Willmott suggest, it would also be motivated by 'an effort to discredit and ideally eliminate forms of management and organization that have institutionalized the opposition between the purposefulness of individuals and the seeming givenness and narrow instrumentality of work–process relationships' (1992b: 4), where, after Baudrillard (1975), we can consider markets as work organizations, consumption as a form of work, and consumers as an occupational group. As Morgan advises, it would develop a 'critique of existing social arrangements as much as a critique of marketing itself' (1992: 154). And it would seek to do so through developing a critique of the existing social arrangements that constitute the privilege and authority of critical perspectives. Rather than seeing 'emancipation' as a final end in itself, it would see it as an ongoing process, a state of mind that needs to be nurtured and sustained: for one person's emancipation is surely another's imprisonment, just as one person's totalizing ideology is another's free-thinking (Eagleton, 1991: 4); just as one person's convoluted dressage is another's straight talking; just as one person's alternative music is another's derivative product of the rebel ideology that fuels music industry marketing; just as the protestation of one person's counterculture is another's repackaged ritual stomping. It would carefully consider the possibility of critique and how any critique could possibly be framed (Bauman, 1994; Grey, 1997; Parker, 1995) given a context in which the primary business of business is no longer producing goods or services, or exploiting labour, but manufacturing culture (Frank, 1997: 157).

A critical marketing would subject the 'truth claims' of the powerful to careful and consistent scrutiny. And when Hunt claims that 'relativism implies nihilism – the belief that we can never have genuine knowledge about anything, that no one else can know anything' (1994: 20), we would understand the rhetorical value of 'nihilism' as a threat, a scapegoat, which seeks to disguise a strategy of fiery polemics (Brown, 1997: 230). Aside from the recent work of Brown (1995; 1997) there is little evidence to show that, were authoritarian bombast to arouse critical suspicion and disbelief, it could also find a voice in a senior marketing journal. Yet, without this possibility the angry catechisms of the privileged will continue to go by uninterrogated; and to slide by as a neutral, or worse, 'natural' part of our collective unconsciousness (Duncombe, 1997: 109). Isn't it interesting that someone can or marginalised. Although this may have an aspect of chance, more obviously it reflects distinct patterns of inequality. Thus those voices which are generally marginal in society are likely to be written out of any specific history. (1997: 593)

Working within the fields of marketing and strategy, we sense the potential for new perspectives which could contribute to the development of mainstream forms of theory and research and the popular representations of practice they have to offer. We also feel that marketing is becoming too much of an important part of everyday social organization to be left solely to the technocratic rhetoric and representations of managerialist thinking, where a narrow focus on means–ends relationships is predominant. It is also our aim to contribute to the renewal of what Habermas (1971; 1974) understands as the emancipatory impulse, in our case of marketing. Importantly, Bartels (1976) reminds us that marketing has its origins as a discipline in studies of the impact of the monopsonistic buying power of intermediaries on the operations of agricultural markets of the Midwestern states of the USA during the late nineteenth century. Indeed at the turn of that century the 'marketing problem', as it was then known, referred to the 'suspected manipulation of prices for farm products by middlemen to the detriment of producers and consumers alike' (Benton, 1987: 422). The discipline of marketing emerged from studies of what steps could be taken to provide a civic framework within which markets would operate more effectively in the interest of producers and consumers too. And in this sense the early development of the discipline could be seen as contributing to the social good of society through exposing what Alvesson and Willmott refer to as 'how structures of domination and exploitation shape and mediate [exchange] relationships' (1996: 120).

The contribution of critical perspectives to management-related disciplines is perhaps most clearly developed within accounting (Power and Laughlin, 1992). In their lucid critique of research in management accounting, Hopper et al. (1987) discuss the 'failure to theorise accounting as a fully social practice', drawing attention to its narrow base in social science methodology. They question a number of features of mainstream management accounting research, prominent among them being: its theoretical and methodological base in neo-classical economics and functionalist organizational theory; the widely held image of the organization as a unitary and integrated system where resource allocation decisions are a matter of information provision; the conventional representation of management accounting as a politically neutral, technical information service that can be abstracted from fundamental issues of ownership and control; and the widespread acceptance of the authority of managerialist assumptions. They go on to isolate a number of important problems in the discipline, including: the failure to develop the idea that accounting is a set of practices which are both the medium and outcome of the politico-economic context in which accounting is embedded; the failure to consider the role of language in shaping accounting theory and practice; the failure to analyse the historical and cultural specificity of accounting practices and knowledge; and the growing evidence that 'conventional accounting knowledge is often not used in practice; and that when it is, it can induce undesirable and unsought consequences' (1987: 438).

The Rethinking Marketing project drew (and draws) inspiration from this deft piece of critical observation which we argue directly applies to marketing management too. Hopper et al. (1987) not only reveal the potential of critical thinking to contribute to the development of research and theory within management accounting: for their pathfinding work also suggests the potential of critical thinking to contribute to the development of several disciplines which share the basic assumptions of management accounting, including marketing. It is clear then, that as Sawchuck comments, '[marketing] is a fecund terrain for critical thinking' (1994: 95); and that as Alvesson and Willmott advise, 'a critical theory approach to marketing can bring fresh insights and provide a more penetrating appreciation of its ethical and social significance' (1996: 128).

Through revisiting the emancipatory impulse of marketing, we also hope to remind ourselves of the discipline's wider constituency of the managed, consumers and citizens alike, as well as the value of thinking historically (Jameson, 1991) about marketing thought (Fullerton, 1988; Hollander and Rassuli, 1993; Vink, 1992). It does seem as if the discipline has lost something of its early direct involvement in the wider affairs of the community through its relentless pursuit of scientific respectability and narrow technical focus on the bottom line. In our view there is an imbalance in marketing scholarship which critical perspectives could hold in check, if redress and restoration is not available. We take the view that it is possible to reconcile more than one identity for marketing scholarship. The challenge is to be in two minds about things: to be able to engage with more than one perspective; to have a repertoire of more than one way of representing your knowledge; to recognize when the undecidable is being rendered decidable and for what purposes; and to privilege ideas knowingly. Towards this end there is an important role for critical thinking, as Eagleton advises: '[The task of criticism] is not to redouble the text's self-understanding, to collude with its object in a conspiracy of silence. The task is to show the text as it cannot know itself' (1976).

Tilting scales

The Rethinking Marketing Symposium was an attempt not simply to put things right, but to generate a setting in which to contemplate the excitements and transformations which new perspectives can bring. It was an attempt to stir the marketing imagination from its apparent lethargy and to frustrate the easy complacency of mainstream thought on a variety of marketing topics. For a couple of days we could afford to be drawn by our enthusiasm to disobey the gravitational pull of mainstream marketing thought and to engage in what Alvesson and Willmott refer to as 'reconstruction and critique' (1996: 15), where reconstruction 'mobilizes critical reason to diagnose prevailing conditions' (1996: 15) and 'critique "entails a process of self-reflection . . . designed to achieve liberation from the domination of past constraints" ' (Connerton, 1976: 20, quoted in Alvesson and Willmott, 1996).

Symposium discussions compared various accounts of the imbalance in marketing scholarship and mulled over imaginary scenes in which it had been 'defrocked, with new masks yet to arrive' (cf. Alvesson, 1993; du Gay, 1993; Knights, 1992; Knights and Morgan, 1991; Morgan, 1992). We wondered what form those new masks might take if redress and restoration were to be possible and if we were to contribute to the growing body of knowledge that takes marketing processes as social phenomena worthy of serious critical examination. We found directions to important work in cognate disciplines (cf. Alvesson and Willmott, 1992a; Arrington and Francis, 1989; Berg, 1989; Burrell, 1988; Burrell and Morgan, 1979; Chia, 1995; Cooper, 1989; Cooper and Burrell, 1988; du Gay, 1994; Linstead and Grafton-Small, 1992; Miller and O'Leary, 1987; Parker, 1992; Reed, 1989; Reed and Hughes, 1992; Watson, 1994; Willmott, 1993). But we could not find a poetry sufficient to the task of unpicking our knotted imaginations; of helping us recapture a sense of wonder about the lost continents of the everyday; of rediscovering the marvellous as we once had known it.

On understanding what it takes to think new thoughts, to render the familiar strange, we have now got as far as agreeing that to make 'rethinking' possible, we must first consider what makes the thinkable possible. Giddens argues that 'modern institutions are unthinkable without systematic and informed reflection upon the conditions of social activity' (1993: 15). You could say then that marketing thought calls for such systematic reflection upon the conditions of social activity within its gaze; and marketing rethought calls for the discipline to interrogate this normalizing gaze and to confront the strangeness of the familiar. Rethinking then can be seen as an exercise in the surveillance of meaning (Baudrillard, 1983; 1990), a considered reflexivity which Mills argues is an important component of what he calls 'intellectual craftsmanship' (1959: 196). In a similar vein of reflexivity Cooper and Burrell observe that 'In order to see the ordinary with a fresh vision, we have to make it "extraordinary", i.e. to break with the habits of organized routine and see the world "as though for the first time"; it is necessary to free ourselves of normalized ways of thinking which blind us to the strangeness of the familiar' (1988: 101).

But then again, on second thoughts . . .

> Come, sir, arise, away! I'll teach you differences.
>
> Shakespeare, *King Lear*, I.iv (Fraser, 1963: 63)

We were originally brought to an attenuated sense of wonder by a shared feeling that, after 20 years of unheeded disquisition on the benefits of a market orientation and suchlike, the tide was at last turning marketing's way: the perennial battles for recognition and legitimacy were being won; and with our rather blunted rhetoric we were now pressing against open doors. Marketing as a discipline, a practice and an ideology was coming of age (Whittington and Whipp, 1992). An important text had just been published as a showcase for the work of a major programme of empirical research into marketing and competitiveness which was funded by the UK government's Economic and Social Research Council (Saunders, 1994). Marketing's star was in the ascendancy and its ambitions were sweeping, heroic and, some would say, immodest (cf. Alvesson and Willmott, 1996; Knights et al., 1994; Wensley, 1990).

Indeed, in many ways the 1990s have become the decade of marketing. Its ideas and rhetoric have been widely used to legitimize change in organizations in the public and private sectors, in profit and non-profit organizations, in services and manufacturing, in consumer and business markets, with regional and global operations (du Gay and Salaman, 1992; du Gay et al., 1996; Whittington and Whipp, 1992; Whittington et al., 1994). In the East as well as the West, markets are offered as the solution to the challenges of whole societies. The entire process of consumption itself is central and pervasive in these (post) modern times where 'all ideologies have been defeated: in the end their dogmas were unmasked as illusions and people stopped taking them seriously' (Kundera, 1991: 127).

And so it might seem that our concerns for imbalance might sound rather measured and well rehearsed, especially if you agree that marketing is an eclectic and progressive scientific subject: that its institutions facilitate a self-conscious critical approach; that those institutions help promote a wider recognition for the expertise that marketing contributes to society; that marketing is a creative subject which is already capable of regenerating itself; and that all this is evidenced by the application of marketing technology to an ever widening range of organizational, social and political contexts. You might then wonder why we should bother thinking about rethinking marketing anyway, when there is so much 'business as usual' to be done (Hunt, 1994: 13; Saunders, 1994). Shelby Hunt put this particular point very succinctly at the final plenary discussion of the symposium when he asked the participants 'should we?': that is, why should we rethink marketing?

Participants shared a sneaking feeling that 'business as usual' was not enough and that marketing's underlying framework of theory and concepts required critical attention. This view has gathered momentum since the symposium, as the contributions to this volume will reveal. Others have previously taken a similar line of thought, arguing that the creativity and growth of the discipline, and the profession, were in danger of being stifled by the overwhelming tendency to take fixed positions of agreement on those important statements about the character of marketing knowledge and its institutions (cf. Anderson, 1983; American Marketing Association, 1988; Arndt, 1980; 1985; Axelsson and Easton, 1992; Deshpande, 1983; Dholakia and Arndt, 1985; Dholakia et al., 1987; Firat, 1992; Firat et al., 1987; Hunt, 1992; Mattson, 1985; Peter, 1992).

Drawing inspiration from Giddens (1993) we understood that marketing theory is not just a way to frame meaning, it also 'constitutes a moral intervention in the social life whose conditions of existence the theory seeks to clarify'. In this sense what passes for marketing theory requires vigilant interrogation through the critical engagement of dialogic critique. Giddens sees this as 'the very life blood of fruitful conceptual development in social theory' (1993: 1), while Alvesson and Willmott (1996: 119) see it as contributing to the 'challenging and removal of discourses and practices that are incompatible with the development of greater autonomy and responsibility'. Easton and Araujo (1997: 104) have also asserted the importance of critical debate and reflexivity in marketing, suggesting that the purpose of such scrutiny is not to establish definitive interpretations, but to 'look beyond the received view on content, by examining the literary form and style of argumentation' by means of which authors attempt to accomplish the effect of 'truth' through their writing.

In step with escapees

> Strange how things in the offing, once they're sensed, convert to things foreknown; and how what's come upon is manifest, only in the light of what has been gone through.
>
> (Heaney, 1991: 108)

Kundera (1991: 128) discusses how reality was once stronger than ideology; how the imagology of those who now shape public opinion has gained a historic victory over ideology; and how the power of imagology, of the circulation of representations, has now surpassed reality, which for many has ceased to be what they say it once was. You could say that we live in an age when reality is only a support for the packaging; when signs of the real replace the real; when what people buy is not simply objects, but the sign system of objects that imbues these functional objects with both status and signification; when the chicken we buy is not 'real' or 'natural', but 'a culturally manipulated foodstuff . . . an extension of the producer's [or retailer's] marketing strategy' (Sawchuck, 1994: 104). As Sawchuck remarks:

> marketing history has developed the following discourse on its own practice: marketing records ostensibly inherent desires, then creates new products (or repackages old ones) that ostensibly satisfy these desires. In doing so there is a

shift in the level of abstraction. One does not sell a specific product, such as a tampon, one sells 'sanitary protection', of which a tampon is one profitable solution. (1994: 100)

This marketing discourse constructs a particular view of society and markets, organizations, consumers and consumption objects within it (Brownlie and Saren, 1997). As Morgan observes, marketing can be understood as 'a set of practices and discourses which help to constitute and shape social relations in modern Western societies' (1992: 137). Marketing discourse is then a central part of a process whereby 'a particular form of society is constructed, one in which human beings are treated as things' (1992: 154). The marketing gaze constructs consumers as objects, as rational, sovereign, self-actualizing actors whose identity is reduced to the 'ownership of commodities and all social relations are conceived in market terms'. Framed in this way, consumers are seeking 'to maximise the worth of their existence to themselves through personalised acts of choice in a world of goods and services' (du Gay and Salaman, 1992: 623). The social and cultural properties of material things then provide one of the key axes of signification in contemporary societies and marketing can be located within processes through which individual identity is constructed (Appadurai, 1986; Bourdieu, 1984; Douglas, 1992; Douglas and Isherwood, 1979; du Gay et al., 1997; Miller, 1987; 1995; 1997).

Marketing can indeed be understood as the engine of a vast panoptic system of observation and social control by means of which it tracks, traces and seduces unknowing consumers into participation in its processes (Alvesson, 1993; Alvesson and Willmott, 1996: 124; Packard, 1960). Many of the declared woes of contemporary consumer society can, if you choose, be laid at the door of marketing as the conspiring footman of a voracious neo-capitalism (Frank and Weiland, 1997). In the estimation of Alvesson and Willmott (1996) these woes would include pollution, crime and social division and exclusion, as well as the emptiness and ennui of pampered consumers who, without the careful percipience of those authors and others like them, would be incapable of realizing that they are caught in a 'narrow and distorted process of communication and self-formation' (1996: 125); and that this 'inhibits opportunities for autonomy, clarification of genuine needs and wants, and thus greater and lasting satisfaction' (Alvesson and Willmott, 1992a: 435).

A non-critical marketing would document and trace how marketing discourse locates us within this system, either as merchants of the fast moving current generalizations (FMCGs) of marketing knowledge and practice (Brownlie and Saren, 1995), or as compliant consumers of them. It would speak of the constitutive effects of marketing discourse without offering a critique of the existing social arrangements that make the privilege of this perspective possible. It would sidestep the issue of how objects are made meaningful in the processes and practices of their consumption. It would be silent on the idea that consumption encompasses many different activities and that different people are situated differently in relation to those activities (du Gay et al., 1997: 96). It would be silent on the idea that consumption not only marks social difference, but represents an important means through which we relate to each other and, as Belk remarks 'weave the web of culture' (1995: 69). It would be blind to the different ways in which material possessions, as signs and symbols, are used to create and sustain social bonds or distinctions, or how social relations and experiences are mediated (Giddens, 1991: 5) by institutional circumstances. It would be silent on consumption as a socially structured practice in which the meanings attached to or coded into goods and services are contingent and provisional and situated through the practice of everyday living (de Certeau, 1984). It would choose to assume, for the sake of accomplishing the rhetorical effect of critique, that although goods and services are inscribed with meaning through their production and delivery, this is the only meaning that they may come to have: thereby being blind to the notion that consumption can be seen as an active process involving signifying practices which put to use the ' "polysemic quality of commodities" as signs' (du Gay et al., 1997: 104). It would be blind to the active and creative part consumers play in constructing the meaning of objects. It would conveniently assume that consumers follow a pre-written script, or that goods have a preordained meaning and that we can read off various cultural, social and political effects from these assumed meanings (1997: 94–5), rather than explore the different uses made of goods in the practices of the everyday lives of consumers and consumed. It would be unable to recognize emancipation anywhere but in its officially sanc-tioned showplaces. It would be blind to the possibility that the ardent claims of academics and other wide-eyed, well-scrubbed children of the suburbs are more a symbol of the contemporary culture machine's authority than an agent of resistance (Frank, 1997: 154). It would be silent in the face of its own unspoken claims to authority and privilege.

The aim of Rethinking Marketing was not merely to articulate criticism, but to explore the potential liberatory aspects of 'the tensions between current marketing thinking and criticisms of it' (Roslender, 1997). Further-more, it was not merely to reproduce the 'strong version' of Alvesson and Willmott's (1992a: 453) critical theory, with its totalizing attack on manage-ment ideology and promises of emancipation from false consciousness and 'frozen social relations'. Following Alvesson and Willmott's (1992a: 453) revealing attempt to reformulate the idea of emancipation in management and organization studies, we suggest a more modest form of engagement with the discipline and its representations of the everyday practices of consumers or managers and the institutions that produce and mediate those practices. We too favour an eclectic framework of critique which leaves space for many voices other than those of card-carrying critical theorists. There is indeed much to be learned from letting consumers or managers speak for themselves, even if critical ethnographers have difficulty 'hearing' what is being said, for there is much to commend Lilley's view that 'managers and critical management researchers may be playing similar games, with similar rules, for different teams' (1997: 51).

A critical marketing would then reassert the part to be played by active consumers and managers. It would of course seek to problematize the assumption that marketing managers and consumers act as the carriers of an impartial marketized rationality. It would show how marketing technology cannot provide a neutral way of looking at the world, irrespective of the intentions behind its deployment. It would raise awareness of how marketing discourse constitutes its object of analysis, consumers and managers, and is implicated in the production and reproduction of the existing social arrangements which constitute its domain of research (Morgan, 1992: 152). As Alvesson and Willmott suggest, it would also be motivated by 'an effort to discredit and ideally eliminate forms of management and organization that have institutionalized the opposition between the purposefulness of individuals and the seeming givenness and narrow instrumentality of work–process relationships' (1992b: 4), where, after Baudrillard (1975), we can consider markets as work organizations, consumption as a form of work, and consumers as an occupational group. As Morgan advises, it would develop a 'critique of existing social arrangements as much as a critique of marketing itself' (1992: 154). And it would seek to do so through developing a critique of the existing social arrangements that constitute the privilege and authority of critical perspectives. Rather than seeing 'emancipation' as a final end in itself, it would see it as an ongoing process, a state of mind that needs to be nurtured and sustained: for one person's emancipation is surely another's imprisonment, just as one person's totalizing ideology is another's free-thinking (Eagleton, 1991: 4); just as one person's convoluted dressage is another's straight talking; just as one person's alternative music is another's derivative product of the rebel ideology that fuels music industry marketing; just as the protestation of one person's counterculture is another's repackaged ritual stomping. It would carefully consider the possibility of critique and how any critique could possibly be framed (Bauman, 1994; Grey, 1997; Parker, 1995) given a context in which the primary business of business is no longer producing goods or services, or exploiting labour, but manufacturing culture (Frank, 1997: 157).

A critical marketing would subject the 'truth claims' of the powerful to careful and consistent scrutiny. And when Hunt claims that 'relativism implies nihilism – the belief that we can never have genuine knowledge about anything, that no one else can know anything' (1994: 20), we would understand the rhetorical value of 'nihilism' as a threat, a scapegoat, which seeks to disguise a strategy of fiery polemics (Brown, 1997: 230). Aside from the recent work of Brown (1995; 1997) there is little evidence to show that, were authoritarian bombast to arouse critical suspicion and disbelief, it could also find a voice in a senior marketing journal. Yet, without this possibility the angry catechisms of the privileged will continue to go by uninterrogated; and to slide by as a neutral, or worse, 'natural' part of our collective unconsciousness (Duncombe, 1997: 109). Isn't it interesting that someone can make assertions about relativism and nihilism, perhaps as part of a kinship ritual, and yet complex processes of interaction in the discipline are accomplished everyday, anew?

What is of interest in the implied threat of nihilism is that the practice of making such assertions is itself an accomplishment that is not considered worthy of investigation by the marketing discipline. Yet the domain of its social practice is located here: and thus does the marketing discipline not very well understand itself, as McCloskey (1985) has previously observed of economics. Silverman writes that 'ethnomethodology [cf. Garfinkel, 1967] shocks us by pointing to the logical impossibility and yet the routine achievement of a stable, ordered world' (1997: 250). It thus seems that there are different paths available by means of which to undermine the taken-for-granted status of marketing discourse and practice. The path of ironic demonstration favoured by critical theory is but one way of seeing new things in the familiar. The perspectives of ethnomethodology also have the potential to contribute to a more modest and reflexive understanding of the social construction of marketing. As Silverman suggests, both theoretical approaches can be 'deployed to reveal new facts and, slowly and cautiously, to build systematic bodies of knowledge' (1997: 250).

What price critical commodification?

> When you read that the Consumers' Price Index has gone up, it is Fisher you have partly to thank. He pioneered in the development of index numbers and also in mathematical economics. Though mathematical economics has not yet taught us everything about the economy, it has proved a valuable way of keeping economists *occupied*.
>
> (Galbraith, 1977: 192; added emphasis)

We live in an era when it is no longer possible to critique marketing simply on the basis of representation as it is traditionally conceived, i.e. according to the truth claims of the image in relation to some external referent (Baudrillard, 1990). In the era of imagology, there is no sovereign 'real' against which to measure the model, or the copy, the fake, the representation. And although some may take it upon themselves to be the guardians of the 'real', the emancipation of marketing cannot be based solely on the declared idea of an absolute reality against which to judge the imprisonment of others.

Perhaps then it is not so strange that, at a time of expansion and bullish optimism, an international group of marketing and management academics can be brought together by an invitation to rethink the discipline, to share second thoughts or be in two minds about what is happening and where it is heading to. We sense the coming importance of a more modest discipline (Alvesson and Willmott, 1992a, 1992b; Law, 1994: 9) which confronts doubt surrounding a number of precepts which are often taken for granted: doubt that marketing knowledge must always have a useful outcome for managers; that marketing theory and practice can be developed without being sensitive to the social, historical and political context; that the problems of developing the profession can be understood without reference to the wider institutional framework within which knowledge is constructed and knowledge claims are legitimized; that marketing technologies can be utilized through processes involving the scientifically rational, calculable and efficient application of knowledge; that its technologies of governance are politically neutral; that logical positivism should continue to inform so much empirical work undertaken in marketing; that it is an applied discipline focusing on measurement and objectivity; that by continuing to hone the toolkit of sophisticated marketing technology, we widen the range of problems to which it can be applied; that nihilism is the inevitable consequence of relativism in marketing thought; that there is tolerance of methodological pluralism in the development and dissemination of marketing knowledge; that there is an inclination to reflect on the basis of marketing knowledge and the social interaction it seeks to offer accounts of; that methodological pathology provides the only basis of critique in marketing; and doubt that marketing discourse can articulate its own conditions of possibility.

Begrudgery, some will say. Yet what brings us together is not the prospect of unfettered sniping and declamation, but rather a common sense of wonder at the accelerating momentum of our discipline. We share an uneasy feeling that something important is happening which embraces yet transcends marketing: reshaping its conditions of possibility, dissolving its ideology into the onward rush of the everyday (Berman, 1983: 91). We can see that marketing as a way of doing social relations has escaped the gravitational pull of the academy and is itself already in circulation as commodity and sign vehicle (Sawchuck, 1994: 111), despite the foundational view of knowledge widely promoted in the academy. Perhaps these developments are outlining a defining moment in the evolution of marketing discourse. Or perhaps we are just witnessing the double hermeneutic at play, one consequence of which is, as Giddens suggests, 'that original ideas and findings in social science tend to "disappear" to the degree to which they are incorporated within the familiar components of practical activities' (1993: 15). And as Knights trenchantly observes, 'once knowledge of the social world enters the public domain, the human conditions which rendered it possible are changed, thus undermining the original validity of such knowledge' (1992: 514). As Brownlie and Saren (1995: 620) observe, the language and concepts of marketing have somehow entered the public imagination and can be widely heard in everyday vernacular.

We are caught in the ordering of the social that we seek to analyse (Law, 1994: 2). And with the growing 'marketization' of social relations, we consider that the internalization and naturalization of a complex set of practices will provide new forms of common sense, self-evident experience and personal identity which the discipline is not equipped to interrogate, denaturalize, or otherwise tease from underneath the stone of our collective unconscious (Deetz, 1992: 37). Generating a marketing gaze sufficient to this task of revelation offers several opportunities to enrich and strengthen the discipline's contribution to social theory at a time when its limited knowledge base is being stretched thinly across many demanding areas of 'application' (Brownlie et al., 1994: 7). Unpacking the metaphor of 'marketization' suggests the following pathways to what may become 'alternative' marketing phenomena:

- that marketing discourse is widely deployed by scholars and managers outwith marketing, to legitimize privilege regarding the installation of technical apparatus by means of which to govern labour processes of many different hues (Knights et al., 1994; Whittington and Whipp, 1992)
- that the discourse of human relations is similarly being mobilized within marketing to rehumanize markets, and to emancipate customers from the alienation of transactional exchanges, towards the bonding and lasting fulfilment of relationship marketing, performed through the simulation of authentic (governable) human relations
- that the pace of circulation of information about ideas is greatly accelerating and the traditional boundaries between knowledge, information, text and interpretation are breaking down (Brownlie and Saren, 1995: 619)
- that the circulation of discourses between management disciplines is accelerating, and the disciplines are themselves passing into the realm of simulation and sign value with the erasure of origins, causes and the mirror of reality (Baudrillard, 1990: 12)
- that disciplinary space is being created for new pliable and differentiated forms of knowledge (Brownlie and Saren, 1995: 619)
- that consumption is a contemporary form of work in which individuals organize their experience and invest it with meaning (Baudrillard, 1975) with consumers being paid to work, to 'spend and save'
- that consumers can be understood as an occupational community (Van Maanen and Barley, 1984) who will seek to organize themselves so as to protect their interests, using the threat to withdraw their labour as a direct form of intervention in marketing processes
- that the discipline of the market, with its subtle architecture of consumer surveillance, regulated information provision and constrained choice, can be seen as the new panopticon, a revitalized metaphor for a new disciplinary mode of domination
- that marketing processes can be understood as the accomplishments of everyday practice (Whittington, 1996)
- that our teaching should reflect this (Chia, 1996; Watson, 1997; Whittington, 1996)
- that the discipline's heady cocktail of naive scientism and bottom-line recipes can no longer be understood as a bridge between theory and practice, as a guarantee of relevance (Brownlie and Saren, 1997; Wensley, 1997)

- that markets, organizations and consumers are called into being by language (Parker, 1992) so that the representational practices of the discipline should be problematized and brought to the fore, not 'reality' (Brownlie, 1998).

Between the horizon and the dictionary

Reverting to anecdote, it seems that for many years we laboured within a culture that was not sympathetic to marketing and had evolved a repertoire of rhetorical devices which, in anticipating resistance to our edicts, made space for its realization. Then, within a few short years marketing practices had been taken to heart; the rising enterprise culture pressing them into service towards the 'marketization' of many walks of life (Baudrillard, 1998; du Gay, 1993; du Gay and Salaman, 1992; Marcuse, 1991; Ritzer, 1996). We are concerned not that the inflated rhetoric of marketing might be punctured, but that its very success only seems to highlight a paradoxical failure. As a discipline, the sophisticated tools of academic marketing are often ignored and its professional status lags behind that of accountancy and engineering (Doyle, 1987). Despite its own claims to the status of an applied discipline (Hunt, 1994; Saunders, 1994), the 'relevance' of its technology to practice is widely called into question, as is revealed in the debate between Wensley (1995; 1996) and Saunders (1995) concerning the status of market segmentation. Indeed, as Roslender (1997) observes, the lessons of the critical accounting project remain to be successfully carried over into marketing.

Yet, many marketing academics are busy gathering data with the aim of getting closer to the apparent 'needs' of the managerial community; and this effort is being spread very thinly over a wide range of problems without very much appreciation for the limits of marketing ideas in contexts for which they were not originally conceived. Furthermore, this effort remains firmly wedded to an 'ideological method' (Durkheim, 1982: 82) at the core of which is the disputed marketing 'concept' (Benton, 1987; Brownlie and Saren, 1992; Dixon, 1992; Wensley, 1990). Through placing singular emphasis on the use of 'facts' to govern the derivation of theory, in the belief that facts mirror 'reality', this method can only provide inadequate accounts of the pre-understandings that make it possible to identify an issue, let alone pass judgement upon it (Eagleton, 1991: 3). It also assumes the natural world and the social world are ontologically continuous (Willmott, Chapter 16 in this volume). In doing so this method is silent on how behaviour and beliefs are historically and culturally conditioned. It also disregards how research methodology and instrumentation are involved in producing and sustaining a particular construction of reality (Alvesson and Willmott, 1992a: 435).

Our understanding of the principles around which society organized itself is changing and this offers the opportunity to rethink marketing's fixation with the bottom line; to develop a more reflexive understanding of its processes as a discipline and a professional practice; to seek to (re)forge interdisciplinary links with areas of contemporary social theorizing, even if, as Knights and Willmott declare, 'the culture and career ladders of academia endorse a defensive kind of disciplinary closure that inhibits critical self-reflection' (1997: 10); and to release the marketing imaginary from the treadmill of empiricism and its mimetic mode of representation. We share a view that the metaphor of the marketplace is a useful way of thinking about how society organized itself. Marketing in a broad social sense could then be seen as a way of thinking about how our lives were organized around doing particular forms of social relations in particular ways. As Burrell (1997: 1) observes, the symbolic ordering of our lives takes place textually on the page or the screen, but is laid out in very, very particular ways.

And so it seems that the norms of marketing scholarship cannot be divorced from techniques of normalization which structure thought and discourse into mutually exclusive categories. In this book we offer one attempt to develop a bigger picture of the social space which marketing occupies and the taken-for-granted ideas which occupy it. We hope it offers suggestions about what marketing can speak of when the mythic plane is defrocked and new masks have yet to arrive. That rethinking marketing is an ongoing process which needs nurturing is not in doubt. For although we may share a common identity as members of the marketing tribe, we do not need to believe in the same myths about its past and present; and future past and future present.

Organization of the book

This volume brings together a collection of eleven chapters which address the relevance of marketing and propose new ways forward for the discipline and the profession. The material is organized into six parts and each presents contrasting views on key issues in contemporary marketing thought and teaching. Each pair of related chapters receives a short commentary (in one case, two commentaries) from a distinguished figure in the field, with a short introduction from the editors of this text.

The material opens in Part I with a typically challenging and penetrating exposition by Stephen Brown. His chapter addresses the debate about the conventions which govern the production and dissemination of accredited marketing knowledge. Stephen provides a critical assessment of the ideas contributed by traditional positivist styles of thought, including those of leading contributors to debates about marketing philosophy (cf. Hunt, 1994). He brings to his discussion of epistemology and methodology the ideas of postmodern marketing (cf. Brown, 1995; 1997) and the critical relativism that inhabits it.

Various new images and symbolic styles of thinking are emerging to help us redefine how we view markets. Each time we rethink the fundamental metaphor of markets we also rethink the way information is organized textually about markets, constraining or liberating our ability to envisage sets of other possibilities. Part II presents two new systems of codes for thinking about markets. In his chapter Bernard Cova argues that the firm's markets should be analysed as a socio-economic phenomenon embedded in a wider societal context. Luis Araujo views markets as networks of relationships with variable degrees of continuity: hence his emphasis on the temporal aspects of markets compared with traditional exchange theory which forms the basis of most marketing analyses.

As a discipline marketing is anchored around a set of ideas which focus on understanding consumers and their consumption processes in a wide variety of contexts. Recent developments in social theory have shown that our understanding of how consumers behave and what they consume is inadequate. Part III contributes to the development of new perspectives by presenting two chapters which address aspects of consumer theory from two different subject positions within contemporary social theory. Richard Elliott employs the discourse of postmodern critique to explore consumption in terms of its symbolic meaning. He then discusses the implications of this for rethinking marketing and consumer research. David Knights and Pam Odih use the example of financial services marketing to question some of the marketing discipline's cherished nostrums about the nature of consumer needs and their sovereignty. They develop the view that marketing fails to appreciate the historical, socially constructed nature of consumer needs, seeing them as essential to human nature, rather than as a manifestation of the structure of social relations constitutive of them.

The ethics of marketing are increasingly being called into question from various quarters, yet normative marketing theory avoids any analysis of value judgements. Part IV presents two chapters which explore new pathways of thought on marketing ethics. In his chapter Robert Grafton Small examines the interrelationships between trade, morality and the marketplace. He approaches the subject not by viewing ethics as isolated matters of concern to be taken out of social context, but as integral parts of the everyday routines of ordinary working lives. In contrast to this ethnomethodological approach, William Hetrick and Hector Lozada argue that we should examine ethics and marketing phenomena from the perspectives of critical theory and postmodern social theory. Their informative and provocative chapter illuminates the potential of those perspectives to reveal the subtle ways in which marketing discourse is inscribed on the material flow of the discipline. The arguments they propose are set against the ethically complacent and calculative character of much marketing scholarship as they portray it.

As a technique for establishing a point of departure, that of claiming Cinderella status for a topic is popular in some areas of marketing writing. Clearly, it is not beneath us to invoke it when we say that Part V looks at an area to which little attention is paid in the marketing literature. And this is not merely a rhetorical device, as a search for literature on the professionalization of marketing will quickly reveal. The area seeks answers to some important questions about the standing of marketing as a profession and its development as an occupational group with its own distinctive culture. Many would be interested to know why marketing's standing is not on a par with other business professions, particularly accountancy, and how it should develop in the light of this. Päivi Eriksson's chapter presents the findings of an empirical study of the development of the marketing profession in Finnish companies over 40 years and compares this with the development of the Finnish engineering profession. On a penetratingly critical note, Hugh Willmott teases out some of the hype and bluster of marketing's high-minded claims to professional status. He argues that marketing should develop a more self-critical approach to its professional practice and be more modest in its attempts to colonize other disciplinary fields.

In the final part of the book we turn our attention to another important yet often overlooked domain of the discipline's professional practice, i.e. teaching. There is a compelling argument for paying greater attention to our teaching practice as an area for detailed research, study and training. Such activity is one of the hallmarks of a mature professional discipline and provides opportunities for improving our understanding of the processes and culture of our discipline. Teaching is a drama in which we are called upon to perform our marketing knowledge: to give it character and voice through the devices of rhetoric and enactment; to weave a web of discourse that engages the imagination of the audience. Our teaching practice is performed in a wide range of theatres, from the undergraduate tutorial to the boardroom seminar. In those different settings it draws on a variety of skills and devices, each of which needs careful rehearsal and nurturing. Yet, surprisingly, much of the craft of teaching we acquire through experience. For many readers of this book the term 'teaching practice' will recall anxious and exhilarating moments when students, through seeking to demonstrate their learning, have helped us realize the strengths and weaknesses of our ideas and how we put them across. In this way teaching practice can contribute to the development of the discipline's knowledge base. With this in mind, Part VI presents two chapters on the problems of teaching marketing. In their chapter Sally Dibb and Phil Stern take the example of market segmentation theory to illustrate the advantages of achieving a more balanced view between research, rhetoric and reality. They go on to show how such a balanced view can be taken more generally to the teaching of marketing theory. The final chapter by Gilles Laurent and Bernard Pras outlines some key areas of development in marketing research and their implications for the future of the subject.

References

Alvesson, M. (1993) 'Critical theory and consumer marketing', *Scandinavian Journal of Marketing*, 10 (3): 291–313.

Alvesson, M. and Willmott, H. (1992a) 'On the idea of emancipation in management and organization studies', *Academy of Management Review*, 17 (3): 432–64.

Alvesson, M. and Willmott, H. (eds) (1992b) *Critical Management Studies*. London: Sage.

Alvesson, M. and Willmott, H. (1996) *Making Sense of Management: A Critical Introduction*. London: Sage.

American Marketing Association (1988) AMA Task Force on the Development of Marketing Thought, 'Developing, disseminating and utilizing marketing knowledge', *Journal of Marketing*, 52 (Fall): 1–25.

Anderson, P. (1983) 'Marketing, scientific progress and scientific method', *Journal of Marketing*, 47 (Fall): 18–31.

Appadurai, A. (1986) *The Social Life of Things: Commodities in Cultural Perspective*. Cambridge: Cambridge University Press.

Arndt, J. (1980) 'Perspectives for a theory of marketing', *Journal of Business Research*, 8: 389–402.

Arndt, J. (1985) 'On making marketing science more scientific: the role of observations, paradigms, metaphors and puzzle solving', *Journal of Marketing*, 49: 11–23.

Arnold, M. and Fisher, J. (1996) 'Counterculture, criticisms, and crisis: assessing the effect of the sixties on marketing thought', *Journal of Macromarketing*, Spring: 118–33.

Arrington, C. and Francis, J. (1989) 'Letting the chat out of the bag: deconstruction, privilege and accounting research', *Accounting, Organizations and Society*, 14 (1/2): 1–25.

Axelsson, B. and Easton, G. (1992) *Industrial Networks: A New View of Reality*. London: Routledge.

Bartels, R. (1976) *The History of Marketing Thought*, 2nd edn. Columbus, OH: Grid.

Baudrillard, J. (1975) *The Mirror of Production*. St Louis, MO: Telos.

Baudrillard, J. (1983) 'The ecstacy of communication', in H. Foster (ed.), *The Anti-Aesthetic: Essays on Postmodern Culture*. Port Townsend, WA: Bay Press.

Baudrillard, J. (1990) *Fatal Strategies*. New York: Semiotext(e).

Baudrillard, J. (1998) *The Consumer Society: Myths and Structures*. London: Sage.

Bauman, Z. (1994) *Postmodern Ethics*. Cambridge: Polity.

Belk, R. (1995) 'Studies in the new consumer behaviour', in *Acknowledging Consumption: A Review of New Studies*. London: Sage. pp. 58–95.

Benton, R. (1987) 'The practical domain of marketing: the notion of a "free" enterprise economy as a guise for institutionalized marketing power', *American Journal of Economics*, 46 (4): 415–30.

Berg, P. (1989) 'Postmodern management? From facts to fiction in theory and practice', *Scandinavian Journal of Management*, 5 (3): 201–17.

Berman, M. (1983) *All That Is Solid Melts into Air: The Experience of Modernity*. London: Verso.

Bourdieu, P. (1984) *Distinction: A Social Critique of the Judgement of Taste*. London: Routledge & Kegan Paul.

Brown, S. (1995) *Postmodern Marketing*. London: Routledge.

Brown, S. (1997) *Postmodern Marketing 2: Telling Tales*. London: International Thomson Press.

Brownlie, D. (1998) 'Interpretation as composition: debating modes of representation in marketing research'. Mimeo, University of Stirling.

Brownlie, D. and Saren, M. (1992) 'The four Ps of the marketing concept: prescriptive, polemical, permanent and problematical', *European Journal of Marketing*, 26 (4): 34–47.

Brownlie, D. and Saren, M. (1995) 'On the commodification of marketing knowledge: opening themes', in D. Brownlie and M. Saren (eds), *The Commodification of Marketing Knowledge*, *Journal of Marketing Management*, Special issue, 11 (7): 619–27.

Brownlie, D. and Saren, M. (1997) 'Beyond the one-dimensional marketing manager: the discourse of theory, practice and relevance', *International Journal of Research in Marketing*, 14: 147–61.

Brownlie, D., Saren, M., Wensley, R. and Whittington, R. (1993) *Rethinking Marketing: New Perspectives on the Discipline and the Profession.* Coventry: Warwick Business School.

Brownlie, D., Saren, M., Wensley, R. and Whittington, R. (eds) (1994) *The New Marketing Myopia: Critical Perspectives on Theory and Research in Marketing. European Journal of Marketing*, Special Issue, 28 (3).

Burrell, G. (1988) 'Modernism, post modernism and organizational analysis 2: the contribution of Michel Foucault', *Organization Studies*, 9 (2): 221–35.

Burrell, G. (1997) *Pandemonium: Towards a Retro-Organization Theory.* London: Sage.

Burrell, G. and Morgan, G. (1979) *Sociological Paradigms and Organizational Analysis.* London: Heinemann.

Chia, R. (1995) 'From modern to postmodern organizational analysis', *Organization Studies*, 16 (4): 579–604.

Chia, R. (1996) 'Teaching paradigm shift in management education: university business schools and the entrepreneurial imagination', *Journal of Management Studies*, 33 (4): 409–28.

Connerton, P. (1976) *Critical Sociology.* Harmondsworth: Penguin.

Cooper, R. (1989) 'Modernism, post modernism and organizational analysis 3: the contribution of Jacques Derrida', *Organization Studies*, 10 (4): 479–502.

Cooper, R. and Burrell, G. (1988) 'Modernism, postmodernism and organizational analysis: an introduction', *Organization Studies*, 9 (1): 91–112.

de Certeau (1984) *The Practice of Everyday Life.* Berkeley, CA: University of California Press.

Deetz, S. (1992) 'Disciplinary power in the modern corporation', in M. Alvesson and H. Willmott (eds), *Critical Management Studies.* London: Sage. pp. 21–45.

Deshpande, R. (1983) 'Paradigms lost: on theory and method in research in marketing', *Journal of Marketing*, 47 (Fall): 101–10.

Dholakia, N. (1988) 'Interpreting Monieson: creative and destructive tensions', *Journal of Macromarketing*, Fall: 11–14.

Dholakia, N. and Arndt, J. (1985) *Changing the Course of Marketing: Alternative Paradigms for Widening Marketing Theory.* Greenwich, CT: JAI Press.

Dholakia, N. and Firat, F. (1980) 'A critical view of the research enterprise in marketing', in R. Bagozzi et al. (eds) *Marketing in the 80s: Changes and Challenges.* Chicago: American Marketing Association. pp. 316–19.

Dholakia, N., Firat, F. and Bagozzi, R. (1987) 'Rethinking marketing', in F. Firat, N. Dholakia and R. Bagozzi (eds), *Philosophical and Radical Thought in Marketing.* Lexington, MA: Heath.

Dixon, D. (1992) 'Consumer sovereignty, democracy and the marketing concept: a macromarketing perspective', *Canadian Journal of Administrative Science*, 9 (2): 116–25.

Douglas, M. (1992) *Objects and Objections.* Toronto: Toronto Semiotic Circle.

Douglas, M. and Isherwood, B. (1979) *The World of Goods.* London: Allen Lane.

Doyle, P. (1987) 'Marketing and the British chief executive', *Journal of Marketing Management*, 3 (2): 121–32.

du Gay, P. (1993) ' "Numbers and souls": retailing and the de-differentiation of economy and culture', *British Journal of Sociology*, 44 (4): 563–87.

du Gay, P. (1994) 'Colossal immodesties and hopeful monsters: pluralism and organizational conduct', *Organization*, 1 (1): 125–48.

du Gay, P. and Salaman, G. (1992) 'The cult(ure) of the customer', *Journal of Management Studies*, 29 (5): 616–33.

du Gay, P., Salaman, G. and Rees, B. (1996) 'The conduct of management and the management of conduct: contemporary managerial discourse and the constitution of the competent manager', *Journal of Management Studies*, 33 (3): 263–82.

du Gay, P., Hall, S., Janes, L., Mackay, H. and Negus, K. (1997) *Doing Cultural Studies: The Story of the Sony Walkman*. London: Sage.

Duncombe, S. (1997) 'I've seen the future – and it's a Sony!', in T. Frank and M. Weiland (eds), *Commodify Your Dissent: Salvos from the Baffler*. London: Norton. pp. 99–111.

Durkheim, E. (1982) *The Rules of Sociological Method*. London.

Eagleton, T. (1976) *Criticism and Ideology: A Study in Marxist Literary Theory*. London: New Left Books.

Eagleton, T, (1991) *Ideology: An Introduction*. London: Verso.

Easton, G. and Araujo, L. (1997) 'Management research and literary criticism', *British Journal of Management*, 8: 99–106.

Firat, F. (1992) 'Postmodernism and the marketing organization', *Journal of Organizational Change*, 5 (1): 79–83.

Firat, F., Dholakia, N. and Bagozzi, R. (eds) (1987) *Philosophical and Radical Thought in Marketing*. Lexington, MA: Heath.

Frank, T. (1997) 'Alternative to what?', in T. Frank and M. Weiland (eds), *Commodify Your Dissent: Salvos from the Baffler*. London: Norton. pp. 145–61.

Frank, T. and Weiland, M. (eds) (1997) *Commodify Your Dissent: Salvos from the Baffler*. London: Norton.

Fraser, R. (1963) *William Shakespeare: The Tragedy of King Lear*. New York: Signet.

Fullerton, R. (1988) 'How modern is modern marketing? Marketing's evolution and the myth of the production Era', *Journal of Marketing*, 52: 108–25.

Galbraith, J. (1977) *The Age of Uncertainty*. London: BBC.

Garfinkel, H. (1967) *Studies in Ethnomethodology*. Englewood Cliffs, NJ: Prentice-Hall.

Geertz, C. (1973) *The Interpretation of Cultures*. New York: Basic Books.

Giddens, A. (1991) *Modernity and Identity*. Cambridge: Polity.

Giddens, A. (1993) *New Rules of Sociological Method*, 2nd edn. Cambridge: Polity.

Grey, C. (1997) 'Towards a critique of managerialism: the contribution of Simone Weil', *Journal of Management Studies*, 34 (3): 591–611.

Habermas, J. (1971) *Toward a Rational Society*. London: Heinemann.

Habermas, J. (1974) *Theory and Practice*. London: Heinemann.

Heaney, S. (1991) *Seeing Things*. London: Faber and Faber.

Hetrick, W. and Lozada, H. (1994) 'Construing the critical imagination: comments and necessary diversions', *Journal of Consumer Research*, 21: 548–58.

Holbrook, M. (1997) 'Looking back on looking backward: a retrospective review of Edward Bellamy's macromarketing classic', *Journal of Macromarketing*, Spring: 145–51.

Hollander, S. and Rassuli, K. (eds) (1993) *Marketing*. Vol. 6 in the International Library of Critical Writings in Business History. Cheltenham: Edward Elgar.

Hopper, T., Storey, J. and Willmott, H. (1987) 'Accounting for accounting: towards the development of a dialectical view', *Accounting, Organizations and Society*, 12 (5): 437–56.

Hughes, T. (1997) *Tales from Ovid*. London: Faber and Faber.

Hunt, S. (1992) 'For reason and realism in marketing', *Journal of Marketing*, 56 (April): 89–102.

Hunt, S. (1994) 'On rethinking marketing: our discipline, our practice, our methods', in D. Brownlie, M. Saren, R. Wensley and R. Whittington (eds) (1994) *The New Marketing Myopia: Critical Perspectives on Theory and Research in Marketing*, *European Journal of Marketing*, Special Issue, 28 (3).

Jameson, F. (1991) *Postmodernism, or, the Cultural Logic of Late Capitalism.* London: Verso.

Knights, D. (1992) 'Changing spaces: the disruptive impact of a new epistemological location for the study of management', *Academy of Management Review*, 17 (3): 514–36.

Knights, D. and Morgan, G. (1991) 'Corporate strategy, organizations and subjectivity: a critique', *Organisation Studies*, 12 (2): 251–73.

Knights, D. and Willmott, H. (1997) 'The hype and hope of interdisciplinary management studies', *British Journal of Management*, 8: 9–22.

Knights, D., Sturdy, A. and Morgan, G. (1994) 'The consumer rules? An examination of the rhetoric and "Reality" of marketing in financial services', in D. Brownlie, M. Saren, R. Wensley and R. Whittington (eds), *The New Marketing Myopia: Critical Perspectives on Theory and Research in Marketing*, European *Journal of Marketing*, Special Issue, 28 (3).

Kundera, M. (1991) *Immortality.* London: Faber and Faber.

Larsen, V. and Wright, N. (1993) 'A critique of critical theory: response to Murray and Ozanne's "The critical imagination"', *Advances in Consumer Research*, 20: 439–43.

Law, J. (1994) *Organizing Modernity.* Oxford: Blackwell.

Lilley, S. (1997) 'Stuck in the middle with you?', *British Journal of Management*, 8: 51–9.

Linstead, S. and Grafton-Small, R. (1992) 'On reading organizational culture', *Organization Studies*, 13 (3): 331–55.

Lyotard, J.-F. (1984) *The Postmodern Condition: A Report on Knowledge.* Manchester: Manchester University Press.

Marcuse, H. (1991) *One-Dimensional Man*, 2nd edn. London: Routledge.

Marion, G. (1993) 'The marketing management discourse: what's new since the 1960s?', in M.J. Baker (ed.), *Perspectives on Marketing Management.* London: Wiley. Chapter 7.

Mattson, L.-G. (1985) 'An application of the network approach to marketing', in N. Dholakia and J. Arndt (eds), *Changing the Course of Marketing: Alternative Paradigms for Widening Marketing Theory.* Greenwich, CT: JAI Press.

McCloskey, D. (1985) 'The rhetoric of economics', *The Journal of Economic Literature*, 21: 481–517.

Miller, D. (1987) *Material Culture and Mass Consumption.* Oxford: Blackwell.

Miller, D. (ed.) (1995) *Acknowledging Consumption: A Review of New Studies.* London: Routledge.

Miller, D. (1997) 'Consumption and its consequences', in H. Mackay (ed.), *Consumption and Everyday Life.* London: Sage. pp. 14–50.

Miller, P. and O'Leary, T. (1987) 'Accounting and the construction of the governable person', *Accounting, Organizations and Society*, 12 (3): 235–65.

Mills, C. Wright (1959) *The Sociological Imagination.* Oxford: Oxford University Press.

Monieson, D. (1988) 'Intellectualisation in macromarketing: a world disenchanted', *Journal of Macromarketing*, 4–10.

Morgan, G. (1992) 'Marketing discourse and practice: towards a critical analysis', in M. Alvesson and H. Willmott (eds), *Critical Management Studies.* London: Sage. pp. 136–58.

Murray, J. and Ozanne, J. (1991) 'The critical imagination: emancipatory interests in consumer research', *Journal of Consumer Research*, 18: 129–44.

Murray, J., Ozanne, J. and Shapiro, J. (1994) 'Revitalizing the critical imagination: unleashing the crouched tiger', *Journal of Consumer Research*, 21: 559–65.

Packard, V. (1960) *The Hidden Persuaders.* Harmondsworth: Penguin.

Parker, M. (1992) 'Postmodern organizations or postmodern organization theory?', *Organization Studies*, 13 (1): 1–17.

Parker, M. (1995) 'Critique in the name of what? Postmodernism and critical approaches to organization', *Organization Studies*, 16 (4): 553–64.

Peter, J. (1992) 'Realism or relativism for marketing theory and research: a comment on Hunt's scientific realism', *Journal of Marketing*, 56 (April): 72–9.

Power, M. and Laughlin, R. (1992) 'Critical theory and accounting', in M. Alvesson and H. Willmott (eds), *Critical Management Studies*. London: Sage. pp. 113–35.

Reed, M. (1989) *The Sociology of Management*. Hemel Hempstead: Harvester Wheatsheaf.

Reed, M. and Hughes, M. (1992) *Rethinking Organization*. London: Sage.

Ritzer, G. (1996) *The McDonaldization of Society: An Investigation into the Changing Character of Contemporary Social Life*. Thousand Oaks, CA: Pine Forge.

Roslender, R. (1997) 'Thinking critically about marketing: rearrange into a well-known phrase or saying'. Mimeo, University of Stirling.

Saunders, J. (1994) *The Marketing Initiative: Economic and Social Research Council Studies into British Marketing*. Hemel Hempstead: Prentice-Hall.

Saunders, J. (1995) 'Invited comment on the marketing segmentation content of "A critical review of research in marketing"', *British Journal of Management*, Special Issue, 6: S89–S91.

Sawchuck, K. (1994) 'Semiotics, cybernetics and the ecstasy of marketing communications', in D. Kellner (ed.), *Baudrillard: A Critical Reader*. Oxford: Blackwell. pp. 89–116.

Silverman, D. (1997) 'Towards an aesthetics of research', in D. Silverman (ed.), *Qualitative Research: Theory, Method and Practice*. London: Sage. pp. 239–53.

Van Maanen, J. and Barley, S. (1984) 'Occupational communities: culture and control in organizations', in *Research in Organizational Behavior*, Vol. 6. Greenwich, CT: JAI Press. pp. 287–365.

Vink, N. (1992) 'Historical perspectives in marketing management: explicating experience', *Journal of Marketing Management*, 8 (3): 219–37.

Watson, T. (1994) 'Managing, crafting and researching: words, skill and imagination in shaping management research', *British Journal of Management*, 5 (June): 77–87.

Watson, T. (1997) 'Theorizing managerial work: a pragmatic pluralist approach to interdisciplinary research', *British Journal of Management*, 8: 3–8.

Weil, S. (1963) *Gravity and Grace*. London: Routledge.

Wensley, R. (1990) 'The voice of the consumer? Speculations on the limits to the marketing analogy', *European Journal of Marketing*, 24 (7): 49–60.

Wensley, R. (1995) 'A critical review of research in marketing', *British Journal of Management*, 6: 63–82.

Wensley, R. (1996) 'Another oxymoron on marketing: marketing strategy', in S. Shaw and N. Hood (eds), *Marketing in Evolution: Essays in Honour of Michael J. Baker*. London: Macmillan.

Wensley, R. (1997) 'The meeting of light and dark: the marketing concept in the shadows', in S. Brown, A.-M. Doherty and B. Clarke (eds), *Marketing Illuminations Spectacular*, *Proceedings*, 5–7 September, University of Ulster.

Whittington, R. (1996) 'Strategy as practice', *Long Range Planning*, 29 (5): 731–5.

Whittington, R. and Whipp, R. (1992) 'Marketing ideology and implementation', *European Journal of Marketing*, 26 (1): 52–63.

Whittington, R., McNulty, T. and Whipp, R. (1994) 'Market-driven change in professional services: problems and processes', *Journal of Management Studies*, 31 (6).

Willmott, H. (1993) 'Strength is ignorance; slavery is freedom: managing culture in modern organizations', *Journal of Management Studies*, 30 (4): 515–52.

Wittgenstein, L. (1968) *Philosophical Investigations*, trans. G.E.M. Ansrumbe. Oxford: Blackwell.

Part I

MARKETING PHILOSOPHY

As befits a book, and indeed the original structure of the symposium, the first part focuses on the debate concerning the nature of our understanding of marketing, its epistemology and methodologies of research.

We start by summarizing a paper that Shelby Hunt delivered to the symposium and which has already been subsequently published. In this Shelby develops a theme which has been consistent in his writings since he raised important questions about the future of marketing in the 1976 fortieth anniversary volume of the *Journal of Marketing*, pursuing the twin themes of the importance of a scientific approach to the study of marketing and the inevitable fact, in his view, that such a scientific approach meant challenging what he saw as a strong practitioner viewpoint: 'if marketing is to be restricted to only the profit/micro/normative dimension, as many practitioners would view it, then marketing is not a science and could not become one' (Hunt, 1976: 27).

Shelby Hunt throughout his career as a distinguished contributor to the debates in marketing academe has continued to emphasize these twin concerns: the importance of the scientific method, and the need to define the domain and interest of marketing knowledge more widely than that derived from a purely managerial view of the subject. More recently, Hunt and Goolsby (1988) argued that much of the cause of the managerial emphasis can be traced to the twin pressures of scientification and relevance that the study of marketing, particularly in the USA, was subjected to in the early 1960s. Rightly or wrongly, the response to much of this pressure was to focus attention on what we might now term the operational details of marketing such as the development of marketing mix response models which moved the interest and attention even further away from the broader context.

However, as in previous work, the quality of the rhetoric as much as that of the underlying analysis is clear. By defining, some might say over-defining, the position of his 'opponents' very clearly he can assert strongly that they are wrong. In this process it is noticeable that he resorts to clear and unambiguous assertions about the positions of others rather than using their own words in the context of the problematics that he identifies. Equally, in his espousal of a realistic perspective it is perhaps surprising to find no reference to the works of those such as Bhaskar and Harré who might have interpreted terms such as critical realism in rather a different way, or certainly with a different emphasis.

In response to Shelby Hunt, Stephen Brown confronts the question of the relationship between postmodernism and marketing directly. Stephen has also made a considerable impact in this area, even if over a shorter time than Shelby Hunt, with his numerous writings which challenge some of the central notions of what might be termed conventional marketing. His chapter does two things. First, it challenges some of the central notions raised by Shelby Hunt in a substantial manner, both in terms of his assertions about the nature of others' arguments and also in his partial use of the various positions and concepts that he applies. Secondly, however, we are also witnessing a discourse between two accomplished rhetoricians, so to some extent Stephen attempts to deconstruct the position of his adversary just as Shelby has done, even if in rather less personal and direct terms, with his.

Gibson Burrell, in his commentary, focuses attention on this later aspect. As he rightly points out we are witnessing something like an academic version of a gladiatorial combat. However, given his established position outside the field of marketing, it is not perhaps surprising that he misses one further irony in his commentary. In portraying Shelby Hunt as the defender of the 'establishment', he is avoiding the issue that Shelby too is very committed to 'rethinking'. Not perhaps surprisingly, what is missing is the voice of those who really see no need to challenge the established order: to misquote a cult TV series, for both Shelby Hunt and Stephen Brown the 'real' opponent is 'out there' and strangely silent – but then perhaps they feel there is no need or reason to engage in the debate in the first place. Finally, in the end, as often, we face a further apparent paradox. Stephen Brown, given his underlying position in terms of epistemology, would have little problem with the elision of philosophy and person that we see going on in front of our eyes. Shelby Hunt, however, would clearly see this as a problem of confusing ideas with personalities, yet, in many ways, he himself is a very successful proponent of the related rhetorical skills.

At the original Rethinking Marketing Symposium, Shelby Hunt presented one of the keynote sessions entitled 'Rethinking marketing: our discipline, our practice, our methods', which was subsequently published in full in the *European Journal of Marketing* (Hunt, 1994).

In his paper, Shelby argues that in rethinking marketing we should start with three questions:

> Why has our discipline made so few original contributions to the strategy dialogue? Why have we focused on dysfunctional rather than functional relationships, i.e. on unsuccessful marketing practice, rather than successful practice? Why do qualitative studies lack acceptance in marketing? (1994: 13)

He argues that the key issue underlying the first question is the way in which marketers have themselves defined marketing as an applied discipline. In a particular sense, he claims, this has meant that whilst ideas which are new to marketing may be published in our own journals, ideas which are new elsewhere are excluded because they lack some form of theoretical credibility.

In the case of the second question, he is concerned with marketing's lack of focus on cooperative rather than competitive relationships. He particularly argues that:

> Since marketing's 'job' is to apply the theories of other disciplines to marketing phenomena – according to the 'applied discipline' notion – and since no discipline has developed a general theory of co-operation, is it any wonder that the marketing discipline's 'theories' and empirical studies have failed to keep up with relationship marketing practice? (1994: 17)

Finally, he considers the bias to publication in the major journals for studies based on quantitative methods. He argues that this can be explored by considering what he terms the 'standard argument for qualitative methods'. He claims that:

> The argument can be succinctly summarised in six assertions:
>
> 1 All disciplines have paradigms and, because paradigms are incommensurable, objective choice between paradigms is impossible.
> 2 There is one paradigm which is dominant in marketing.
> 3 The dominant paradigm in marketing is positivism (logical positivism or logical empiricism) which implies the use of quantitative methods, the adoption of realism, the search for causality and the assumption of determinism.
> 4 As a result of the writings of Kuhn, Hanson and Feyerabend, among others, by the 1970s the philosophy of science had abandoned positivism and, therefore, marketing's dominant paradigm is discredited or passé.
> 5 Upon the abandonment of positivism, the philosophy of science embraced relativism, constructionism and subjectivism.
> 6 Therefore, marketing should accept qualitative methods (e.g. naturalistic inquiry, humanistic inquiry, historicism, ethnography, postmodernism, critical theory, semiotics, semiology, deconstructionism, Marxism and feminism) because (a) marketing's dominant paradigm has been discredited and (b) qualitative methods embrace the 'new' philosophy of science, i.e. relativism, constructionism and subjectivism.
>
> The problem with the standard argument for qualitative methods is that, of the five premises [which lead to the sixth], four (1, 2, 3 and 5) are false whilst the remaining one (4) is misleading. As a result the argument degenerates into obfuscation, obscurantism and what is now referred to as 'post-modern episto-babble' [Coyne, 1982]. (1994: 17)

In more detail he argues that

> no interpretation of paradigm 'incommensurability' has ever been put forth which can justify the claim that choice between genuinely rival paradigms, i.e. paradigms which make conflicting claims, cannot be made on objective grounds. (1994: 18)

As a committed positivist himself, he goes on to argue that positivism does not imply quantitative methods, the search for causality, scientific realism or the assumption of deterministic theories, and similarly that 'relativism, constructionism and subjectivism' are minority views in the philosophy of science:

> Relativism does not imply a constructively critical stance toward knowledge claims, nor does it imply acknowledging that the knowledge claims of science are fallible. Relativism implies nihilism – the belief that we can never have genuine knowledge about anything. Relativists, incoherently, know that no one else can ever know anything. Furthermore relativism does not imply a tolerant stance towards outside ideas and other cultures: it implies indifference to the norm of tolerance. Moreover, relativism does not imply ethical sensitivity; it implies ethical impotence. Finally, subjectivism does not caution science to work at minimising bias, it maintains that the human condition makes the very ideas of objectivity to be a chimera. (1994: 20–1)

Finally, Hunt argues for qualitative methods to be seen as a useful complement to quantitative methods in marketing research. Serious consideration should be given to critical pluralism and scientific realism, and he defines the latter as:

- The world exists independently of its being perceived (classical realism).
- The job of science is to develop genuine knowledge about the world, even though such knowledge will never be known with certainty (fallibilistic realism).
- All knowledge claims must be critically evaluated and tested to determine the extent to which they do, or do not, truly represent, correspond, or are in accord with the world (critical realism).
- The long-term success of any scientific theory gives us reason to believe that something like the entities and structure postulated by that theory actually exists. (1994: 24)

References

Coyne, J.C. (1982) 'A brief introduction to epistobabble', *Family Therapy Networker*, 6: 27–8.
Hunt, S.D. (1976) 'The nature and scope of marketing', *Journal of Marketing*, 40 (3): 17–28.
Hunt, S.D. (1994) 'On rethinking marketing: our discipline, our practice, our methods', *European Journal of Marketing*, 28 (3): 13–25.
Hunt, S.D. and Goolsby, J. (1988) 'The rise and fall of the functional approach to marketing: a paradigm displacement perspective', in T. Nevett and R.A. Fullerton (eds), *Historical Perspectives in Marketing*. Lexington, MA: Lexington Books.

2 Postmodernism: The End of Marketing?

Stephen Brown

Postmodernism, according to Fielding, 'is something that gets everywhere but no-one can quite explain what it is' (1992: 21). Variously described as 'a con' (Hattenstone, 1992: 7), 'the kiss of death to any art form, high or low' (Burchill, 1994: 4) and 'the new perspective on life and the human condition that is sweeping across the globe' (Firat and Venkatesh, 1993: 227), postmodernism has generated an enormous amount of academic and lay discussion in recent years. It is regularly profiled in quality newspapers and magazines (*Financial Times*, 1992; *Observer Life*, 1994); it has entered popular parlance as a fashionable euphemism for subversive, ironic or chaotic (Andrews, 1993; Bradshaw, 1993); it has affected almost every arena of cultural and artistic endeavour (music, film, fashion, drama, dance, architecture, literature, television etc.); and it has infiltrated the A to Z of academic disciplines, albeit with varying degrees of success (see Brown, 1995a).

As Table 2.1 indicates, postmodernism has been defined in a host of different ways ranging from the humorous to the incomprehensible. However, a moment's reflection on the term 'postmodernism', or any of the associated family of terms (postmodern, postmodernity, postmodernization, postmodernist etc.), reveals that they are ostensibly meaningless. If 'modern' is that which is current, up-to-date or progressive, and 'post' is that which lies beyond, comes after or exceeds, how is it possible, outside perhaps of the pages of science fiction, to be beyond the present, to be later than the latest, to exceed the extant – to be postmodern? And, accepting for a moment the existence of this incongruous futuristic milieu, the question has to be asked, does the prefix 'post' mean that we have broken with the present – in either a positive (freedom, renewal, innovation) or negative (diminution, decay, entropy) sense – or are we attached by an umbilicus, and, if so, what is the precise nature of the connection?

Faced with these unanswerable questions, many marketers might be tempted to dismiss the whole postmodern project as an unnecessary distraction, a passing intellectual fad. While such sentiments are understandable, they overlook two important facts. First, marketing and postmodernism are already tightly interwoven. On reading the copious postmodern literature, almost irrespective of discipline or source, one is struck not only by the

Table 2.1   *What is postmodernism? Some examples*

Something that seems to entail buildings which have been constructed of Lego from designs commissioned by the Mayor of Toytown and novels about novelists experiencing difficulty writing novels. (Watkins, 1991: 21)

The Toyota of thought, produced and assembled in several different places and then sold everywhere. (Connor, 1989: 19)

Never having to say you're sorry for not having an original idea in your head. (Beaumont, 1993: 43)

Not a gesture of the cut, a permanent refusal, nor (most of all) a division of existence into polarised opposites. The postmodern scene begins and ends with transgression as the 'lightening flash' which illuminates the sky for an instant only to reveal the immensity of the darkness within: absence as the disappearing sign of the limitlessness of the void within and without: Nietzsche's 'throw of the dice' across a spider's web of existence. (Kroker and Cook, 1986: 8–9)

The philosophy of inverted commas. (Scruton, 1994: 504)

An attempt to think the present historically in an age that has forgotten how to think historically in the first place. (Jameson, 1991: viii)

A kind of cartoon-cat version of modernism – the cat keeps running even though he has only air beneath him. (Updike, 1991: 694)

Finding the places of difference within texts and institutions, examining the inscriptions of indecidability, noting the dispersal of significance, identity and centred unity across a plurivalent texture of epistemological and metaphysical knowledge production. (Silverman, 1990: 1)

Postmodernism *isn't*! (Brown, 1995a)

---

sheer prevalence of marketing artefacts and institutions – shopping centres, department stores, advertising campaigns, package designs, new product development and the entire consumption experience – but also by the sheer originality and often dazzling acuity of these 'extra-marketing' marketing analyses. Second, just as postmodernism has often been described as a *crisis of representation*, where the old theoretical, epistemological and ontological certitudes of rationality, truth and progress have been challenged, subverted and replaced with, well, a refusal to act as replacement (Boyne and Rattansi, 1990; Callinicos, 1990), so too many commentators on the current marketing scene contend that our discipline is in the throes of a very serious intellectual crisis (Brady and Davis, 1993; Freeling, 1994; Thomas, 1994). True, people have been declaring that marketing is in crisis from time immemorial (Bartels, 1962; Bell and Emory, 1971; Bennett and Cooper, 1981) and not everyone concurs with the crisis-mongers' diagnosis of marketing's present state of health, but it is undeniable that a great many leading authorities maintain that marketing is facing a 'mid-life crisis', a fundamental crisis of representation.

Given the apparent interpenetration of marketing and postmodernism, this chapter will seek to explore the nature of the relationship between the two. It commences with an overview of the postmodern condition, turns to an analysis of postmodern marketing practices, continues with a discussion of postmodern marketing concepts, culminates in a deconstruction of the celebrated 'realism versus relativism' debate, and concludes with an attempt to answer the simple but all-important question: is postmodernism the end of marketing?

Are you now, or have you ever been, a postmodernist?

Modern times

If, as the terminology implies, postmodernism is connected in some way to modernism, perhaps the best way of comprehending the former is in terms of its differences from the latter. Although the nature and characteristics of modernism have been subject to almost as much debate as postmodernism, if not more, there is a degree of agreement that the modern world emerged from a series of profound political, economic, social and cultural transformations which began with the Age of Discovery in the fifteenth century; saw the creation of the modern nation state in the sixteenth; witnessed the gradual secularization and democratization of Western society in the seventeenth and eighteenth centuries; and climaxed in the Agricultural and Industrial Revolutions of the nineteenth. In fact, it was the excesses of the last of these that spawned the artistic and cultural movement commonly known as 'modernism'. This began with avant-garde developments in mid-nineteenth-century Paris, reached its apogee prior to the First World War, and continued to dominate artistic sensibilities until the late 1950s or early 1960s (Johnson, 1991; Toulmin, 1990; Wagner, 1994).

Alongside the inexorable 'rise of the West', the emergence of the modern world was characterized by a dramatic transformation in scientific and intellectual endeavour. Prefigured by the insights of Galileo, Newton and Kepler in the physical sciences and Bacon, Descartes and Locke in philosophical method, this intellectual revolution came to fruition in the Enlightenment project of the eighteenth century. Like most intellectual movements, the Enlightenment exhibited considerable internal diversity. Nevertheless it embraced a constellation of concepts including: a belief in the primacy of *reason* and rationality as a means of organizing knowledge; *empiricism*, the idea that knowledge of the world is premised on empirical facts which can be apprehended through sense organs; the assumption that *science*, and the experimental method, is the key to isolating truth and expanding human knowledge; *universalism*, the presupposition that reason and science are invariant and apply in all circumstances and that general laws could be derived; *scepticism*, the conviction that no knowledge claims should be accepted at face value but should be subject to detailed, objective scrutiny; and, not least, *secularism*, a belief that the disinterested pursuit of objective knowledge would lead to the extinction of ignorance, religious dogma, superstition and oppressive clericalism, and hence to a better, more tolerant, free and open society (Porter, 1990).

As the foregoing synopsis indicates, modernity is a complex phenomenon, involving a variety of tightly interwoven, often contradictory, processes operating over an extended time scale. But, if it had to be summarized in a single word, that word would probably be *progress*. The modern condition is characterized, above all, by a belief that humanity 'has advanced in the past . . . is now advancing, and will continue to advance through the foreseeable future' (Nisbet, 1980: 4–5). Although the idea of progress is a commonplace today – we naturally expect 'next year's model' to be better than the one being replaced – it remains nonetheless a comparatively recent worldview (Bowler, 1989; Gordon, 1991). Prior to the Enlightenment, the prevailing perspective was that the past was superior to the present, that human achievements could never hope to match those of ancient civilizations and that life was lived against a backdrop of irredeemable decline (Bury, 1987). However, the sixteenth century 'battle of the books' – won by the 'moderns' – coupled with the Enlightenment-inspired belief that rational, objective, 'scientific' methods could be applied to any arena of intellectual inquiry, led eventually to remarkable advances in medicine, engineering, architecture, technology and the natural sciences. Accordingly, the comforts of modern life – washing machines, refrigerators, televisions, telephones, aeroplanes, computers, motor cars, microwave ovens, egg-timers *inter alia* – have been made available to almost every stratum of Western society, thereby relieving us of the existential drudgery endured by our great-grandparents. As Toulmin (1990) emphasizes, compared with the bestiality, squalor and degradation of earlier times, it is our good fortune to be born into the modern world. We are better fed and educated, more affluent and live longer than our ancestors; we are free (within limits, of course) to think and say what we like; and we live in the reasonable expectation that things will continue to improve, diseases will be conquered, technological breakthroughs achieved and, periodic economic crises notwithstanding, our material wellbeing maintained.

Postmodern possibilities

Just as the project of modernity was distinguished by the complex inter-penetration of contrasting artistic, technological, socio-economic and intellectual components, so too the postmodern moment is made up of a multiplicity of highly diverse, often antithetical, elements. Indeed, in our endeavours to comprehend this fascinating yet frustrating phenomenon, perhaps the single most important point to note about 'postmodernism' is that it is a portmanteau or umbrella term, comprising four separate but interdependent strands.

The first and, for most people, probably the most clearly identifiable aspect of the postmodern condition is a very distinctive post-war artistic and cultural movement (in fact, some commentators restrict use of the term 'postmodernism' to this particular arena – hence the confusion that often arises concerning its domain). In essence, postmodernism in the arts comprises a latter-day reaction against the once radical and challenging, but subsequently tamed and canonized, 'modern' movement of the first half of the present century, and a tongue-in-cheek return to premodern precepts of representation. Whether it be fine art, architecture, literature, music, dance, design, drama or whatever, the postmodern project is characterized by the belief that there is no artistic orthodoxy, or single overarching style. All traditions have some merit; there is a smorgasbord of choice; the challenge is to combine elements of existing traditions in an eclectic, hybrid, ironic style; and, not least, the traditional boundary between elite and popular cultural pursuits no longer exists. Just as popular preoccupations have been appropriated by 'high' culture (vernacular architecture, pop art, science fiction etc.), so too serious treatment is now accorded to what were once dismissed as 'low' or degraded cultural forms – film, television, popular music, fashion, football, comic books, hairstyles and, indeed, marketing and advertising (Boyne and Rattansi, 1990; Jencks, 1989).

The second element of the postmodern project, which is often accorded the epithet 'postmodernity', pertains to a series of significant post-war social and economic developments (Bocock and Thompson, 1992; Smart, 1993). Socially, these include the decline of organized religion, the fragmentation of nation states and political blocs, the collapse of traditional party politics, the demise of the nuclear family, and the proliferation of media and communications technologies, which, according to the high priest of postmodernism, Jean Baudrillard (1983), has created a depthless world of simulation where images bear no discernible relationship to external 'reality' and where artifice is even better than the real thing. In economic terms, moreover, recent years have witnessed a post-Fordist revolution in the workplace, where the computer-aided, flexible production of specialized or semi-bespoke products for niche markets has superseded the traditional Fordist regime of the mass production of standardized products for mass markets (Cooke, 1990). This has been accompanied by the emergence of an increasingly information and services driven post-industrial order. In short, Silicon Glen rather than Clyde shipbuilding, science parks rather than steel plants, and mining museums rather than working pits (Rose, 1991).

The third and, for most people, the most convoluted and impenetrable aspect of the postmodern moment derives from the work of several prominent poststructuralist thinkers, principally Jacques Derrida, Roland Barthes, Michel Foucault, Jacques Lacan and Jean-François Lyotard. Although the contributions of these poststructuralists are many and varied, ranging across fields as diverse as linguistics, literary theory, philosophy, history and psychoanalysis, they all exhibit a concern with textuality, narrative, discourse and language. Language, for Derrida (1991; 1992), is neither translucent nor stable, and linguistic meaning is both context-dependent and impossible to tie down. Barthes (1977a; 1977b) maintains that the 'meaning' of literary works depends not on authorial intention but on the idiosyncratic interpretations of the readership. Foucault (1972; 1974) claims that discourses not only determine what can be written, thought and acted upon and what counts as knowledge in any given field, but that they constitute our very being, our sense of ourselves as individual, free-thinking, autonomous human subjects. Lacan (1977) maintains that the unconscious is structured like a language and, as is the case with language, it is never entirely under our control. Lyotard (1984; 1992), likewise, contends that the Western worldview – the modernist search for impartial knowledge, valid and verifiable laws, absolute truths and eventual release from slavery and oppression – is a myth legitimized by a high-level storyline, or metanarrative, such as the pursuit of 'progress', 'emancipation', 'reason' or 'profit'. The postmodern condition, therefore, is one of 'incredulity towards metanarratives', a refusal to accept that there is one particular way of doing things and one way only. No form of knowledge is privileged, no overarching theory obtains and, rather than search for non-existent truths, we should seek to oppose, subvert and destabilize the 'regimes of phrases' of those in authority.

According to Lyotard, conspicuous examples of attempts to subvert or overthrow the existing orthodoxy can be found in the physical sciences, the fourth and final strand of postmodernism. In particular, he cites postmodern scientists' growing concern with such things as 'undecidables, the limits of precise control, conflicts characterised by incomplete information, "fracta", catastrophes, and pragmatic paradoxes' (1984: 60). In other words, an emphasis on the unknown rather than the known, with dissent from, rather than consensus around, the prevailing paradigm. Although Lyotard was not the first to employ the term 'postmodern science' (see Best, 1991; Griffin, 1988) and although some theorists do not consider such phenomena to be part and parcel of the postmodern moment (Connor, 1989), latter-day developments within the physical sciences (chaos theory, fuzzy logic, Gaia hypothesis etc.) and, moreover, the history and philosophy of science (Kuhn's scientific 'revolutions', Feyerabend's methodological anarchism, the copious sociology of scientific knowledge (SSK) literature and so on), undoubtedly parallel the postmodern penchant for discontinuity, instability, adhocracy, subjectivity, indeterminacy and paradox (see Brown, 1995a; 1997).

Postmodern USPs

While it is possible to identify four broad strands within the postmodern project – cultural, socio-economic, linguistic and scientific – it is important to emphasize that these strands are not entirely separate, nor are they directly related to one another. Just as the project of modernity involved several deeply interwoven components, sometimes cancelling out, sometimes working together, so too the postmodern movement is a complex, inchoate phenomenon. Nevertheless, at the risk of gross oversimplification, it can be

contended that postmodernism is characterized by five key features: fragmentation, dedifferentiation, hyper-reality, pastiche and anti-foundationalism.
Fragmentation refers to the seemingly inexorable disintegration of political
stability, social organization, nation states, mass market economics and,
inevitably, the disconnected array of vivid images generated by the increasingly hydra-headed media. *Dedifferentiation* involves the erosion, effacement and elision of established hierarchies – high and low culture, education
and training, politics and showbusiness – and the blurring of what were once
clear-cut boundaries (philosophy and literature, science and religion, male
and female, etc.). *Hyper-reality*, as exemplified by the fantasy worlds of
theme parks, virtual reality and computer games, involves the loss of a sense
of authenticity and the becoming 'real' of what was originally a simulation.
Pastiche consists of a playful, tongue-in-cheek collage or medley of available
styles, an ironic, self-referential mixing of existing codes, be they architec-
tural, artistic, cinematic, literary, musical or whatever. *Anti-foundationalism*,
finally, is postmodernism's characteristically deconstructive urge, its antipathy towards orthodoxy, complacency, the establishment and, not least,
systematic generalizations, most notably the totalizing metanarratives which
form part of the modern movement's discredited search for universal truths
and objective knowledge.

Important though these five key features are, not least for expositional
purposes, the single most distinctive aspect of the postmodern condition is
the all-pervasive air of finality and fatigue. If, as noted earlier, modernity
was characterized by the notion of *progress*, postmodernity is distinguished
by its complete and utter *exhaustion*. Whereas modernism was predicated on
advance, achievement, amelioration, betterment, breakthrough, exuberance,
innovation and inexorable forward movement, postmodernism is suffused
with stasis, debilitation, dissipation, enfeeblement, entropy, stagnation and
cessation. Indeed, almost every commentator emphasizes this particular
aspect of the postmodern project. Barthes (1977a), for example, describes
'the death of the author', Derrida (1991) foresees the 'end of man', Lacan
(1977) kills off Freud's mechanistic model of the unconscious, Foucault
(1972) announces the 'death of the subject', and Vattimo (1991) predicts the
demise of Western philosophy. Jameson (1985), moreover, maintains that
artistic innovation is no longer possible, Lyotard (1984) argues that the same
is true of science (and predicts the demise of metanarratives, for good
measure), and Gilbert Adair (1992: 15) considers postmodernism to be 'the
last gasp of the past'. For Jean Baudrillard (1988; 1989), furthermore, every
possibility in art, life, theory, politics and society has already been tried.
Originality is impossible, history has ended, the future has already happened
and all that remains is to play with the pieces among the anorexic ruins. In
other words, the only available option is to recycle, rearrange, rediscover,
recombine and reuse the forms, styles, genres, approaches, techniques and
methods that already exist, usually in an ironic or irreverent manner. Thus,
although postmodernism is in many ways the terminus, the outer limit, the
dead-end of modernism, it is also characterized by a strange but remarkably

compelling sense of playfulness, of exhilaration in the face of failure, of feeling that there's nothing we can do, so let's have a party.

Just like reality only better: postmodern marketing practices

As marketing, in many respects, reflects developments in the social, economic and cultural spheres generally, it is only to be expected that the characteristic features of postmodernism are apparent – and deeply inscribed – in today's marketing environment. Indeed, if it were not such a blatantly modernist approach to the subject, it would be possible to imagine a matrix with the distinguishing features of postmodernism along one axis and the elements of the marketing mix along the other. Such an exercise, of course, is doomed to inevitable failure, as it is totally contrary to the cavalier, insouciant and genre-busting spirit of postmodernism. Nonetheless, it is undeniable that all of the distinguishing features of postmodernism are discernible on the current marketing scene and discernible, moreover, across every facet of marketing from pricing to promotions.

Thus, for example, the *fragmentation* of markets into smaller and smaller segments, each with its complement of carefully positioned products, is everywhere apparent. Whether it be the market for computers, coffee, cola, cameras, cigarettes, breakfast cereals, ice cream, financial services, sports shoes, package holidays, pet foods, disposable nappies, washing powder, recorded music, mineral water, traction batteries, machine tools or the gamut of health and beauty aids, a bewildering array of product and service offers typically obtains. Ten years ago, there were seven brands of toothpaste on sale in the UK. Today, there are more than 30, many of which provide a number of distinct product variations (tartar control, pump action dispensers and so on). In the USA, there are now 240 Weight Watchers products spread across 78 different categories; the number of lagers on sale in Britain has increased by 66 per cent in the last six years; and such is the prevailing range of credit cards and payment systems that the days of hard cash, personal cheques or, *in extremis*, Access/Barclaycard seem like a dim and distant memory. Indeed, in the new car market it appears that you can now have any colour, engine size, bodywork variant, trim level, sound system, safety features, optional extras and licence plate you like, as long as you're in the black.

This seemingly inexorable process of fragmentation is counterpointed to some extent by a clearly discernible trend towards *dedifferentiation*, the blurring of what were once clear-cut marketing boundaries (infomercials, advertorials, edutainment, retail warehouses, factory outlets, interactive advertising, manufacturer brands and own label, etc.). From a marketing management perspective, perhaps the most important instances of dedifferentiation emanate from the recent and much vaunted rise of strategic alliances, joint ventures, collaborative networks and boundaryless corporations (de Jonquieres, 1993; Lorenz, 1993). As the partnerships between Nestlé and Coca-

Cola, Pepsico and Unilever, Sears and McDonald's, Time Warner and West Inc., and Pearson and the BBC amply illustrate, the traditional barriers between marketing organizations are in the process of erosion. Alongside the blurring of 'horizontal' boundaries, recent years have also been characterized by the effacement of 'vertical' organizational forms. Complete tiers of middle management have been swept away by post-Fordist companies bent on 're-engineering', 'delayering' or 'downsizing', and flat or matrix structures have increasingly replaced the traditional hierarchical arrangements. The inevitable result of this combination of vertical and horizontal restructuring is what has sometimes been described as a 'hollow' or 'virtual' company, the non-existent organization organization – in effect, Baudrillard's world of hyper-reality made manifest in business.

Hyper-reality, however, is not confined to the discovery of the black holes of organization theory; it is apparent across the entire marketing spectrum. The most obvious instantiations are found in the fantasy worlds of theme hotels, theme restaurants and themed shopping centres, but hyper-reality is also discernible in marketing arenas as diverse as personal selling, new product development and sales promotions. Reflect for a moment on the 'pretence' of the typical service encounter, where the salesperson's adherence to a preordained script, rote responses to anticipated enquiries and heroic endeavours to fake sincerity can give the whole experience a not unpleasant but nonetheless unreal, illusory, slightly phantasmagorical quality. How, moreover, can we forget those supreme monuments to the new product development process – fat-free fat, beefless beef, decaffeinated coffee, alcohol-less alcohol, sugar-free sugar and, as the appropriately hyper-real brand name 'I Can't Believe It's Not Butter!' constantly reminds us, butterless butter? Consider, furthermore, the infamous Hoover 'free flights' promotion, where airline tickets to American and European destinations were made available for the price of a £100 vacuum cleaner. This led to a bizarre situation in which the Hoover factory was working round the clock to satisfy the demand, newspapers were swamped with small ads placed by people eager to dispose of unused, second-hand vacuums, carpet retailers were giving away free Hoovers with every purchase, travel agents were accepting vacuum cleaners as a deposit for summer holiday bookings, and, in the middle of a deep recession, some commentators were predicting a complete economic recovery predicated on Hoover's ill-fated sales promotion!

If hyper-reality is the most ubiquitous manifestation of postmodernism on the contemporary marketing scene, *pastiche* is perhaps most deeply engrained within a particular subfield. As the examples in Table 2.2 illustrate, contemporary British advertising is replete with in-jokes, parody commercials and wry self-referentiality, though the palette of advertising allusions is by no means confined to other advertisements. Films, television series, books, architecture, politics, current affairs and almost every item on the agenda of popular culture are grist to the marketing mill and exploited as and when advertisers deem it necessary. Indeed, a veritable industry of advertising

Table 2.2   *Pastiche (parody and self-referentiality) in UK television advertising: some examples*

Category	Content	Examples
Parody		
Direct	One advertisement parodies another	Carling Black Label (lager) spoof of Levi's (jeans) celebrated 'launderette' sequence
		Irn Bru (Scottish soft drink) musical take-off of archetypal (Coke) soda advertisement
		Hotpoint (washing machines) parody of British Airways' 'face' (Britain's favourite washing line)
Indirect	Advert 'appropriates' byline/icon etc. of another	Lemon Fairy (washing-up liquid) exploits AMEX's 'that will do nicely' for penurious couple facing prospect of washing up in expensive restaurant
		Hamlet (cigars) use of Andrex (toilet tissue) Labrador puppy in tale of woe concerning last of toilet roll
		Do It All (DIY superstores) advertised 'the united colours of Do It All' (Benetton)
Self-referentiality		
Direct	Adverts about advertising (set in advertising agency, adverts for forthcoming adverts etc.)	Vauxhall 'every car you'll ever need' campaign features Tom Conti and Nigel Hawthorne as inept advertising executives
		Next 'instalment' of advertising soap operas (Renault 21 family, Gold Blend couple etc.) advertised beforehand
		Nationwide Building Society: advert about making advertisement designed by and starring employees of the organization
Indirect	Retransmition of old adverts that have acquired new meanings in the interim, or stylistic evocation of old adverts	Repeat showings of 'I'm going well, I'm going Shell' series featuring Bing Crosby etc.: once innovative, now quaint
		Hovis's 'as good today as it's ever been' sells nostalgia through an advert which is itself nostalgic (the golden age of UK advertising; early work of famous film director Ridley Scott)
		Update of 'everyone's a fruit and nut case' for Cadbury's

spinoffs now seems to exist in Great Britain. These range from books (*Fly Fishing, Love Over Gold*), records (both classical and rock) and television series (Clive James, Chris Tarrant) to comedy routines (Ben Elton, Jasper Carrott), car stickers (Texas Tom) and video anthologies of long-running campaigns (Hamlet, PG Tips). Few, however, have captured the public's imagination to the extent of Levi's celebrated 1986 'launderette' advertisement. Not only did sales of the jeans increase by 800 per cent, and the backing track 'I Heard It through the Grapevine' reach number one in the popular music charts, but, as a consequence of the actor's 'revelation' that he wore boxer shorts under his 501s, the prevailing fashions in men's underwear were transformed at the drop of a . . . belt buckle.

It is, of course, a very small step from pastiche to *anti-foundationalism*. The latter is evident in today's penchant for parody products (Death brand cigarettes, TNT cider), anti-fashion fashions (grunge, deconstruction), anarchistic or subversive advertising campaigns (Benetton, Sega Megadrive) and even pricing policies such as cigarette manufacturer Philip Morris's seismic decision, of 2 April 1993, to slash the price of Marlboro, its premier product and the world's biggest-selling brand. The after-shocks of Marlboro's 20 per cent price cut have since reverberated throughout the global marketing landscape as the brand leaders in a host of markets – computers, sports shoes, credit cards, champagne, condoms, electrical goods, newspapers, nappies, air travel and many more – have followed suit, thereby risking their carefully nurtured and expensively acquired brand equities (Smith and Lynn, 1993). More significant still than this wilful disregard of marketing's conventional wisdom is the latter-day emergence of the 'green' movement. With its anti-consumption, anti-waste, anti-exploitation outlook, the green movement represents the antithesis of all that marketing stands for, or, rather, is presumed to stand for by the community at large. Notwithstanding the genuine concerns that many marketing organizations express about green issues, and the significant advances which have been made in recent years, it is undeniable that there is something profoundly paradoxical – not to say morally questionable – about vilifying the market, adopting an anti-business ethos and condemning overconsumption, while purveying consumables, being in business and profiting from the anti-market market (Shenk, 1993). As Peattie rightly points out, 'since green thinking involves reducing the very consumption which marketing aims to stimulate . . . this makes the concept of "green marketing" appear to be a contradiction in terms' (1992: 85).

Just as fragmentation, dedifferentiation, hyper-reality, pastiche and anti-foundationalism are clearly discernible on the contemporary marketing scene, so too postmodernism's characteristic air of exhaustion is everywhere apparent. As Barsoux has recently highlighted, 'marketing creativity is impossible . . . there can only be the exhuming and recycling of the old' (1993: 12). This recycling tendency is evident in the revival and relaunch of products whose life-cycles had seemingly run their course. Prominent British examples include Spangles, Vimto, Brylcream, Silkience, Action Man, Pacamac, Parker Duo-fold pen, Gossard Wonderbra, Worthington's White Shield Ale, Russell Hobbs coffee percolators (1952 vintage) and, not least, the tie-in products from reruns of old television series such as 'Thunderbirds', 'Stingray', 'Batman', 'Captain Scarlet' and 'Joe 90'. A similar trend is evident in the USA where, among others, Morton salt, Jell-O, Ovaltine, Kool Aid, Bazooka bubble gum, Skippy peanut butter, Birkenstocks shoes, PF Flyers sneakers and Raggedy Ann/Raggedy Andy dolls have been relaunched with some success (Miller, 1990; 1992).

If, however, established, original and long-dead products are not available for exhumation, nothing could be easier than the creation or appropriation of an entirely imaginary past. As the recent, rapid rise of the 'retro' product convincingly demonstrates, a combination of the latest technological advances with appropriately nostalgic styling can prove enormously popular. The current marketing scene is awash with Art Deco Walkmans and ghetto-blasters, 1950s-style freezers, Box Brownie lookalikes (with motor wind and auto-focus, naturally) and motor cars like the Nissan Figaro and Mazda Miata, which, to quote the promotional blurb, 'not only gives you a glimpse of the 90s . . . it takes you back, as well'. Retro radios, televisions, hi-fis, coffee makers, motor cycles, airlines, restaurants, rock bands, soft drinks, bar snacks, magazines, sports shoes, perfume, jewellery and underwear are now available; retro communities are being constructed (Poundbury in Dorset); retro radio stations (Capital Gold) and television channels (UK Gold) are attracting substantial audiences; retro packaging is regularly utilized (Ovaltine, Best Health seltzers); retro sales brochures are not un-known (Oakdale Batteries); retro promotions and promotional icons are back in fashion (Green Shield Stamps, the Bisto Kids); retro pricing policies are discernible (the present 1970s-style price war in British grocery retailing); retro locations are being occupied by retail organizations (Tesco Metro, Sainsbury Central) and in-store environments created (Cullens, Co-op Pioneer); and, not least, retro advertisements, in grainy black and white or featuring long-dead celebrities (Humphrey Bogart, James Dean, Marilyn Monroe), have become a commonplace (Tedre, 1993). After unsuccessful attempts at diversification, moreover, many companies appear to be resorting to retro marketing strategies. Habitat's back-to-basics retailing strategy, aptly described by the chief executive as 'our future lies in recapturing the past' (Hollinger, 1993: 20), is an excellent case in point, as are Laura Ashley's extraordinary endeavours to re-create its original bucolic image of softness, femininity and quintessential Englishness. However, as the latter organization traded on nostalgia to begin with, its strategy could quite legitimately be described as retro-retro (or neo-retro) retailing (Mulvagh, 1993).

No representation without taxation: postmodern marketing concepts

Entropic marketing

The advent of retro marketing practices clearly parallels postmodernism's characteristic air of *fin de siècle* exhaustion, but the relationship doesn't end there. This feeling of fatigue is equally apparent in the sphere of marketing theory and thought. Despite the enormous advances that 'modern' marketing scholarship has made in the post-war era, contemporary thinking seems suffused with an all-pervasive sense of doubt, directionlessness and despair. The vigorous, thrusting project, the 'marketing revolution', of 40 years ago, which knew no bounds, took no prisoners and swept all before it, has – depending upon which metaphor you prefer – come to a halt, lost its way, seen better days, fallen from grace, run aground/out of steam/into the sand.

As a glance at the journals amply testifies, doubts are increasingly being cast on the continuing veracity of the marketing concept (Brownlie and Saren, 1992). Marketing principles no longer appear relevant to the real world and, if anything, appear to do more harm than good (McKiernan, 1992). Leading figures in our field are marketing's most outspoken critics rather than the propagators of the marketing message (Day, 1992; Wensley, 1994). Reports on the plight of marketing scholarship are periodically produced and their recommendations routinely ignored (American Marketing Association, 1988; Coopers and Lybrand, 1994). Academic research which seeks to extend existing conceptual frameworks is greeted with a resounding 'so what?' or dismissed as 'me-too' and 'minor twist' (Ingene, 1993; Peterson, 1992). The sense of academic cohesion, solidarity and commitment to the marketing cause that once prevailed has been torn asunder by a series of bitter philosophical disputes and declarations of epistemological independence (see Kavanagh, 1994). In these depressing circumstances, it is little wonder that the enthusiasm of marketing's early exponents now strikes us as supremely naive; that the seminal contributions of our discipline's foremost thinkers seem both extraordinarily ambitious and embarrassingly obsolete (for instance, the comprehensive models of consumer behaviour); and that many believe the marketing concept is an anachronism, an aberration, a throwback to a bygone age of mass markets and mass marketing (Hoyt, 1991; McKenna, 1991).

Not everyone, admittedly, would concur with this disconcerting diagnosis of marketing's current state of health. As the recent comments of Bass (1993) and Little et al. (1994) indicate, there is no shortage of marketing optimists, individuals who are happy to expound on the discipline's illustrious lineage and exciting prospects. In the main, however, these people are fully paid up members of marketing's macho-modelling community, those who appear to take enormous pride in wrestling with structural equations and matrix algebra, boast about the size of their hard disks, doubtless tear telephone directories in half or inflate hot water bottles as their party pieces, and take every opportunity to kick sand (or silicon chips at least) in the faces of the seven stone weaklings of qualitative research. Although the unshakeable faith of marketing's *Übermenschen* is deeply touching, it is fair to say that a great many contemporary commentators on the marketing condition maintain that it is in the throes of a serious 'mid-life crisis', a fundamental crisis of representation (Anderson, 1994; Freeling, 1994; McDonald, 1994).

Conceptual construction

In these unsettling circumstances, where the present is uncertain, the future is threatening and cries of marketing apocalypse are all around (Brown et al., 1996), it is perhaps not surprising that many marketing thinkers are returning to the conceptual accomplishments of the past. This retro-theory tendency is nowhere better illustrated than in latter-day discussions of the marketing concept itself. As originally formulated, the marketing concept comprised three elements: an awareness of customer wants, which are considered to be the point of departure for a marketing-led organization; the integration and coordination of all the activities of the firm around this basic customer orientation; and regarding profit rather than sales volume as the measure of success of the organization's marketing activities (see Hollander, 1986). Through time, and thanks to the intellectual endeavours of Levitt, Kotler, Levy, Hunt, etc., the nature and scope of the marketing concept were extended considerably. Summarized in Figure 2.1, this process of development can be described – ironically, of course, since postmodernists would never dream of using a modernist model – in terms of Ansoff's (1958) celebrated and much cited product–market matrix.

The first cell, *penetration*, comprises the early attempts to demonstrate the veracity of the modern marketing concept, to highlight its superiority over the sales and product orientations that once prevailed, and to promote its acceptance throughout the business community (Keith, 1960; Levitt, 1960). The second cell, *market development*, refers to the revolution, initiated by Kotler and Levy (1969), involving the broadening of the marketing concept and its application to all manner of non-business organizations, from charities to high schools, and to arenas as diverse as aesthetic accomplishment and religious experiences. *Product development*, the third cell, pertains to the subsequent modifications of the original marketing concept, which was

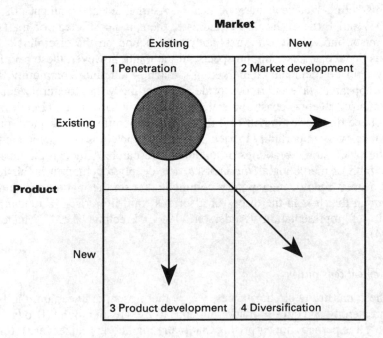

Figure 2.1   *The construction of the modern marketing concept (adapted from Ansoff, 1958)*

expanded to embrace the competitive environment, strategic concerns, technological push and suchlike (Samli et al., 1987). The final cell, *diversification*, alludes to the societal concept of marketing, in so far as this involved a reformulation of both the product/concept itself (the key issue is not consumer needs or profit but societal concerns) and the market/domain to which it pertains – public policy, consumerism, resource exploitation, the deficiencies of the marketing system etc. (Kotler and Zaltman, 1971).

Conceptual deconstruction

In recent years, however, the imperialistic advance of the marketing concept has been halted and, as Figure 2.2 illustrates, thrown into reverse. The first contemporary position, *realization*, inclines to the view that the modern marketing concept is basically sound, but that the problem is one of implementation. In other words, the traditional difficulties of getting the concept accepted by top management, of distinguishing successfully between marketing philosophy and function, trappings and substance, rhetoric and reality, etc., have been superseded by a concern with *making marketing work* through a heightened understanding of organizational politics and interfunctional rivalry. To this end, a programme of internal marketing – marketing the marketing concept within organizations – is often advocated (see, for example, Piercy, 1992; Whittington and Whipp, 1992).

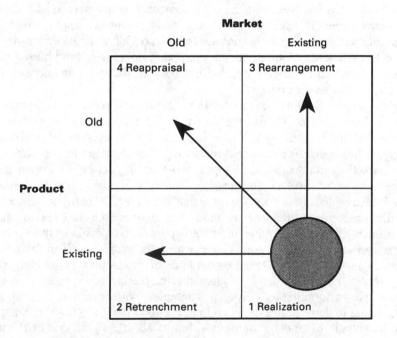

Figure 2.2   *The deconstruction of the modern marketing concept (adapted from Ansoff, 1958)*

The second position, *retrenchment*, also regards the marketing concept as reasonably acceptable in itself, but acknowledges that there are certain circumstances in which it is either inappropriate or of minor rather than major relevance. For some people, it is irrelevant in hi-tech industries where discontinuous innovation is the norm and traditional marketing research can inhibit rather than enhance the process (Workman, 1993). For others, it is unsuitable in basic commodity markets where the opportunities for meaningful differentiation are less clearly marked than is the case elsewhere (Narver and Slater, 1990). For yet others, the concept has shortcomings when applied to certain sectors, such as services, public administration and not-for-profit (Wensley, 1990); in certain countries, most notably in Eastern Europe (Thomas, 1993); for certain companies depending on their specific organizational, competitive and market circumstances (Kohli and Jaworski, 1990); and in certain macro-economic conditions (Foxall, 1984).

Rearrangement, the third position, takes issue not so much with the domain of the discipline as with the very character of the marketing concept itself, and how it needs to be modified to meet today's marketing realities. According to Webster (1988), for example, it has become necessary to 'rediscover' marketing, to scrape away the encrustations of strategic management, which have led to an unhealthy and myopic preoccupation with competitor activity and market share, and replace it with a renewed focus on the customer. To get back, in effect, to the basics of the original marketing concept – customer orientation. Baker (1989), by contrast, contends that too much emphasis has been placed on the consumer, consumerism and societal concerns generally. Marketing, he argues is about exchanges which are *mutually satisfying* for both consumers and providers. In other words, we need to eschew the notion that the marketing concept is the philosopher's stone, an eternal human verity, and get back to the quotidian concerns of practising marketing managers.

Reappraisal, the final and by far the most radical position, comprises an acknowledgement of the simple fact that the marketing concept has not succeeded and is unlikely to prove successful in its present form. Accordingly, it has been suggested that marketing should revert to pre-marketing era marketing; in other words, adopt a neo-sales or post-product orientation. Dickinson et al. (1986), for instance, stress that marketing is basically manipulative and monopoly seeking, that customers in many instances are totally unaware of their needs, and that marketing's task is to shape consumers' wants, determine their perceptions and persuade them of the attractiveness of what the company has on sale. Likewise, Chen et al. have recently made a case for the pre-eminence of production, concluding with the words: 'the conventional wisdom that marketing is expected to play a major role in formulating corporate strategies, with manufacturing simply responding to these strategies, is no longer affordable' (1992: 441). Another, and potentially the most extreme position of all, highlights that marketing-oriented management is a historical artefact which emerged in certain countries under a particular set of socio-economic conditions (Baker, 1989;

Foxall, 1984). Just as the sales and product orientations were appropriate to their own particular historical eras, so too a marketing orientation is a product of its time. For a growing number of commentators, that time has passed and we are facing nothing less than a marketing apocalypse (Brownlie et al., 1994; Lynch, 1994).

In light of the foregoing, it is arguable that the current debate over marketing's precise domain is actually a rerun of the 'broadening' debate of 25 years ago, albeit in reverse. As we have seen, moreover, the exact composition of the marketing concept is also in a state of reconceptualization, though few advocates of the micro-marketing or relationship marketing paradigms seem prepared to acknowledge that they are merely regurgitating certain aspects of the original notion of customer orientation. Relationships, as Baker (1994) and Wensley (1994) have recently pointed out, have always been an important aspect of marketing. Relationship marketing is a sheep in sheep's clothing. Indeed, according to some commentators, marketing ought to abandon its unattainable 'scientific' aspirations and revert to an intuitive, creative, flexible, idiographic, essentially 'artistic' approach. This perspective recognizes that 'each marketing situation should be treated as unique in its own right, drawing upon all the available knowledge that may help in handling the situation' (Gummesson, 1987: 19). It thus appears that marketing's current crisis of representation is actually a re-presentation of the same debates that characterized previous episodes of marketing crisis – art versus science, marketing's domain, the core construct and so on – though the terminology employed is slightly different. Marketing, in fact, seems to be facing a retro-crisis of retro-representation (Brown, 1995b).

Deconstructing Shelby D. Hunt

Postmodern marketing theory is not, of course, confined to re-presenting the marketing concept, or (say) debating the marginal utility of 'new and improved' versions of long-established marketing constructs (for example, does the 'market maven' construct add *anything* of substance to what is already known about the diffusion of innovations?). It also raises the spectre of what proved to be the most profound, prolonged, polemical and personalized debate in the history of marketing thought – realism versus relativism. The confrontation commenced in 1983 when Paul Anderson challenged the fundamental philosophical premises of marketing scholarship. The received view, variously if imprecisely described as 'positivist', 'positivistic' or 'logical empiricist', rests on the assumption that a single, external world exists, that this social reality can be empirically measured by independent observers using objective methods, and that it can be explained and predicted through the identification of universal laws or law-like generalizations. Anderson (1983; 1986; 1989), by contrast, argued that a relativist approach, subsequently termed 'critical relativism', has much more to offer. This maintains that, although an external world may well exist 'out there', it is impossible to access this world independently of human sensations, perceptions and interpretations. Hence, 'reality' is not objective and external to the observer but is socially constructed and given meaning by human actors. What counts as knowledge about this world is *relative* to different times, contexts and research communities.

Needless to say, the relativists' eschewal of the orthodox idea of marketing scholarship – as objectively proven knowledge – and its replacement with the notion of knowledge as societal consensus, provoked a ferocious reaction. The foremost defender of the faith, Shelby Hunt (1984; 1990; 1992; 1994), was particularly scathing about relativism, arguing that it leads inexorably to nihilism, irrationalism, incoherence and irrelevance. 'The discipline of marketing,' he thundered, 'is hardly advanced by adopting a philosophy that sees no difference between astronomy and medical science on the one hand and astrology and palmistry on the other' (1984: 34). Battle was thus joined and, over the next decade or so, marketing's philosophical heavyweights slugged it out on terrain as diverse as 'demarcation', 'truth', 'reification' and 'incommensurability'. The precise assumptions of logical positivists, logical empiricists and falsificationists were clarified; 'scientific realism' (which holds that the world external to human cognition is a real world comprising hard, tangible, measurable and ultimately knowable structures) was advanced as a candidate for marketing's philosophical redemption; and the manifold variants of relativism and realism were explained (Kavanagh, 1994). However, just as Hunt was declaring the battle won by the realists, and urging academic marketers to stick to their empirical lasts, another heavily armed combatant entered the fray – postmodernism.

Although, like most intellectual and philosophical movements, postmodernism comes in many shapes and forms, it is essentially a relativist position. As the realism/relativism arguments are well known, their reiteration herein is unnecessary. Nevertheless, a succinct deconstruction of the debate may prove instructive (see also Thompson, 1993). Deconstruction, as formulated by Jacques Derrida, is a technique for investigating 'texts', which, by means of a careful and detailed reading, seeks to uncover their inconsistencies, contradictions, unrecognized assumptions and implicit conceptual hierarchies (Norris, 1991). Although Derrida was at pains to deny its methodological status, and the procedure is not without its critics, deconstruction has been applied to all manner of phenomena ranging from the literary and philosophical canon to food, fashions, architecture and advertisements. Indeed, as virtually anything can be considered a 'text', almost everything is fodder for deconstructive analyses.

When the 'text' of the realism/relativism debate is examined from a deconstructive perspective, several interesting points emerge. The first of these is that Shelby Hunt, the indefatigable champion of realism, has done more to advance the cause of relativism than any of its advocates! In his self-appointed role as the high priest of marketing scholarship, Hunt's apparent determination to condemn all marketing heretics to the flames of philosophical perdition merely served to focus attention on, and thereby helped legitimize, the relativist position. Conspiracy theorists might even conclude that the relativists engineered the confrontation, because it is only through conflict with the establishment that challenging groups can generate a sense of internal cohesion and shared purpose and succeed in attracting the support of the disenchanted, dispossessed and disenfranchised. Be that as it may, it is quite likely that the marketing mainstream would have continued in its merry hypothetico-deductive way if it were not for the inquisitorial endeavours of the witch-hunter general. Granted, a great many marketing scholars – perhaps the majority – may continue to work within a broadly realist/empiricist/instrumentalist/positivistic framework, but one suspects very few are unaware of the alternative epistemological options that now exist.

The second point concerns Hunt's often-repeated pronouncement that the adoption of relativism threatens the scientific and technological *progress* which characterizes the modern world, the Enlightenment project of the past 400 years. It is undeniable, as we noted earlier, that the project of modernity has provided unimaginable material wellbeing, incalculable knowledge accumulation, astonishing aesthetic accomplishment and incredible techno-logical innovation. Postmodernists, however, emphasize that the material benefits of modernity and its promise of perpetual plenitude have been achieved at a very heavy social, environmental and political price. The mass of society may be better off than before but, as the homeless and destitute daily remind us, the division of wealth is as unequal, arguably more unequal than ever. The rise of the West has been at the expense of the subjugation, exploitation, usurpation and coca-colonization of 'the rest', and has left a legacy of political instability, famine, desertification, ethnic conflict, racial strife and economic dependency. Technological and industrial innovations may have produced the wonders of modern medicine, motorized transport, household appliances, the Sony Walkman and Nintendo Gameboy, but they have also spawned weapons of mass destruction, raised the prospect of genetic engineering and contributed to resource depletion, environmental despoliation and the threat of ecological catastrophe. Postmodernists, in short, recognize that while 'progress' may have been made by certain groups of people (white, male, heterosexual, university professors in the Western world, for instance), the same is not necessarily true for others – coloured, female, homosexual, unemployed, non-Westerners and many more. Indeed, numerous commentators maintain that modernism's inexorable drive for order, control and progress culminated not in its utopian vision of cosmo-polis, a rationally ordered society characterized by emancipation, freedom, equality and political tolerance, but in death camps, the Gulag, Tiananmen Square and Yugoslavia (Burrell, 1994). Moral relativists, as Hunt often points out, may not be in a position to condemn such iniquities, but at least they are absolved from their perpetration.

A third and closely related point involves what may be termed the 'receptacle theory of knowledge'. According to Hunt, the sum total of human knowledge has increased markedly in the 400 years of the modern era. Hence, the bucket of knowledge is gradually filling up, sometimes slowly, sometimes more quickly, and will continue to fill up provided relativistic heresies are prevented from draining our energies, diverting our commitment and siphoning off our achievements. Although this receptacle metaphor is deeply ingrained in the intellectual psyche of the Western world – so much so that it is easy to forget its figurative status – it is perfectly possible to manipulate, subvert or even replace the analogy. It can be argued, for example, that the receptacle of human knowledge is *always* full (there is no shortage of competing explanations about the nature of the world and there never has been), albeit the contents of the container are constantly changing. In other words, we don't know *more* about the world than we did 400 years ago, we know *different* things. Admittedly, the amount of 'scientific' knowledge has certainly increased in the modern era, but this has been achieved by displacing other, 'non-scientific' kinds of knowledge – religious, folklore, narrative traditions etc. While it is often contended that scientific knowledge is 'superior' to non-scientific knowledge – after all, it is objective, rigorous, dispassionate, cumulative and, not least, *true* – the studies of Kuhn (1970), Feyerabend (1975) and the SSK suggest otherwise (Barnes, 1985; Pickering, 1992). These show that Western science is not a unique form of objective knowledge unaffected by context or culture. On the contrary, science is irredeemably social, inherently messy and deeply affected by political, professional and personal interests. Scientists, as Woolgar describes it, 'are not engaged in the passive description of pre-existing facts in the world, but are actually engaged in formulating or constructing the character of that world' (1988: 87). *Contra* the conventional wisdom of scientific accomplishment, there is no dispassionate search for the truth. Scientific 'truths' and 'falsehoods' are social constructs, agreements to agree, which are culture bound, context-dependent and relative rather than absolute.

The fourth point arising from the realism/relativism debate also pertains to the question of 'truth'. On numerous occasions, Hunt states that the relativists' position on truth is that there is no truth. Clearly, this position is self-contradictory in that, if it is true, then it can't be true that there is no truth; and, if it is false, then the hypothesis is confounded in any event. Faced with this philosophical aporia, it is tempting to challenge the truth of Hunt's truth statement on truth: in other words, to argue that it is *not* true that relativists hold true to the belief that there is no truth. On the contrary, relativists maintain that there are many truths, that truths are *relative* to given societies, times, perspectives or paradigms, that there is no such thing as an eternal, unchanging, objective truth (singular). Unfortunately, how-ever, this position also suffers from the self-same problem of self-refutation (how can we be sure that the 'many truths' argument is itself truthful?), and this has prompted the postmodern philosopher Richard Rorty (1980; 1989; 1991) to adopt another stance: namely, that we are wasting our time trying to discover the truth about the world. According to Rorty, it is essential to distinguish the philosophical claim that the world is 'out there' (i.e. external to our senses) from the claim that the truth is out there. Although the external world may well exist independently of our consciousness of it, truth cannot exist independently of the human mind because truth is reliant on language and language is a human construct. Truth, therefore, is made rather than found, a creation rather than a representation of how things really are. It is, admittedly, easy to conclude that our beliefs about the world are true, especially if the world appears to correspond with our descriptions, but we should consider our descriptions to be a succession of increasingly useful metaphors rather than an increased understanding of how things truly are.

Apart from the four major points, a number of minor albeit interesting issues arise from a close, deconstructive reading of the realism/relativism text. These include Hunt's frequent but unsupported assertion that most contemporary philosophers of science are realists by inclination and, as a corollary, that relativism was a passing fad, an anti-foundational aberration of the 1960s counterculture. Yet, none other than Harvey Siegel, a realist philosopher whom Hunt often quotes with approval, has recently stated that 'the doctrine is alive and well, and is the subject of intense philosophical debate . . . The current scene is then one in which interest in relativism remains high' (1992: 430). It is, moreover, somewhat ironic that Hunt should condemn his opponents for using the term 'positivist' in a pejorative sense, rather than in terms of the precise, historically accurate, meaning of the intellectual position, when he does precisely the same with phrases like 'anarchist', 'nihilist' or 'Marxist', which are arguably much more pejorative than the epithet 'positivist' ever was or is.

A final, and perhaps the most intriguing aspect of the whole debate, concerns Hunt's indubitable rhetorical skills. His papers are so brilliantly written and exude an air of such compelling logic that their spellbinding sophistry seems eminently plausible *even after* careful examination indicates otherwise. As Magnus et al. point out about another extraordinary exponent of arresting philosophical arguments, Friedrich Nietzsche, 'their appeal is not diminished by exposure . . . they seem plausible somehow, they continue to recommend themselves to us' (1993: 23). Hunt, of course, would doubtless object to the Nietzschean comparison, not least because Nietzsche is purportedly a prime mover of the nihilistic, anarchistic worldview that Hunt warns us against, and deem the 'rhetorician' charge derogatory. If, however, he were to embrace the relativist position, which openly acknowledges the importance of rhetoric and persuasiveness in having scholarly arguments accepted, he would come to appreciate the 'real' import of his (elevated) place in our discipline's intellectual firmament. It is nothing less than astonishing that the foremost relativist of marketing scholarship – potentially at least – and the person who has done most to disseminate the message of relativism, should continue to position himself as the undefeated champion of realism.

Marketing eschatology: ending ended

If, as the above discussion indicates, postmodernism is deeply inscribed in contemporary marketing practice and parallels the crisis of representation in marketing theory and thought, then the ultimate question must be asked: does postmodernism mean the end of marketing? Must we give up modern marketing as a lost cause? Must we abandon all that has been achieved hitherto? Must we tell our constituents – practitioners, students and the policy-making community at large – that we have nothing new to say to them, that we have all been wasting our time, our very lives? Must we capitulate to the pessimistic postmodern view of the human condition? Is there no hope for the future?

Profound though these questions are, the answer to them all is very simple, albeit less than satisfactory: 'It depends.' Does postmodernism mean the end of marketing? Well, it all depends on what is meant by the words 'end', 'postmodernism' and, not least 'marketing'. The term 'end', for example, can be taken to mean the end, as in finish/terminus/demise, or the end as in destination/objective/goal. Marketing can pertain to function or philosophy, practice or theory, verb, noun or adjective and a host of other things besides. Postmodernism, moreover, is a very broad church embracing all manner of philosophical positions. So much so, that a number of attempts have been made to subdivide its intellectual spectrum. Foster (1985) distinguishes between a 'postmodernism of resistance', devoted to the deconstruction of modernism while defying the inexorable descent into populism, and a 'postmodernism of reaction', which repudiates modernism completely and celebrates the achievements of popular culture. Griffin (1988) contrasts 'deconstructive or eliminative' postmodernism, the nihilistic worldview advanced by Baudrillard in particular, and 'constructive or revisionary' postmodernism, the positive possibilities offered by an amalgam of postmodern science and religion. And, Rosenau (1992) identifies what she terms 'sceptical' and 'affirmative' schools of postmodern thought. Mainly continental European in origin, the sceptics offer a negative, gloomy, despairing assessment of the human condition and see little in the way of comfort for the future. Affirmative postmodernists, by contrast, are predominantly Anglo-American and posit a more hopeful vision of the postmodern age, one where the dogmatic, ideological straitjacket of modernism has been cast off and new forms of political activism, personal development and knowledge gathering obtain.

Although the multitude of interpretive possibilities inscribed in the terms 'end', 'postmodernism' and 'marketing' is appropriately postmodern in itself, and tempting though it is to let the readership decide on their preferred answer to the 'end of marketing' question, it may be worthwhile endeavouring to conclude this chapter by distinguishing between *positive* (affirmative-destination) and *negative* (sceptical-demise) interpretations of the postmodern marketing (practice-theory) condition.

The positive perspective, in effect, involves mapping the characteristics of postmodernism onto contemporary marketing and exploring the very strong parallels between the two. As we have already noted, many of the distinguishing features of the postmodern moment – fragmentation, dedifferentiation, hyper-reality, pastiche and anti-foundationalism – are clearly discernible on the current marketing scene. It is arguable, therefore, that postmodernism provides a perspective on, and a means of conceptualizing, the dramatic changes that are taking place in the marketing arena, whether it be the fragmentation and turbulence of markets and competition, the emergence of strategic alliances and boundaryless corporations, the rise of the retro product and parodic advertising, and, not least, the advent of anarchistic, iconoclastic, anti-marketing marketing practices ranging from shock-horror advertising campaigns to the green marketing 'revolution'.

More fundamentally perhaps, some of the most prominent precepts of postmodernism are readily translatable into marketing terms. Foucault's (1980) concept of power/knowledge is clearly relevant to channel relationships, especially at a time when retailers' scanning systems enable them to provide or withhold precious product performance information from their suppliers. His emphasis on the positive – as opposed to the coercive – effects of power is in tune with the present marketing emphasis on relationships, networks and alliances. Indeed, his late flirtation with individuality-cum-subjectivity, in the shape of 'technologies of the self', is not far removed from today's preoccupation with micro-marketing, one-on-one marketing, database marketing and the like (Foucault, 1990). Lacan's (1977) emphasis on the inexorable slippage of the signified under the signifier is highly relevant to the brand-building process and, in an expositional triumph, Desmond (1993) has demonstrated the parallels between the mirror stage and market orientation, arguing that the latter is a misrecognition, a profound myopia, a fundamental misunderstanding of how the world is believed to be. Lyotard's (1994) latter-day emphasis on the Kantian sublime is also pertinent to analyses of hedonic consumption, which, we are reliably informed (Holbrook and Hirschman, 1982), is often described in terms of the indescribable: 'you had to be there', 'I can't put it into words' etc. In a similar vein, Gummesson's (1991) recent prediction of the end of marketing as a separate function, and its replacement by a decentred form of marketing practice, which is disseminated across the entire organizational archipelago, could just as easily have been made by Jacques Derrida. Even Barthes's (1977a) 'death of the author' thesis, which may seem quite shocking in terms of our conventional (untutored) views of literature and criticism, turns out to be anything but. In elevating the interpretations of the reader over the authority of the author, Barthes was arguably espousing the marketing concept by another name. After all, the revolutionary aspect of the marketing concept was that it considered the needs of the consumer (reader), not those of the producer (author), to be the key to success in business.

This positive interpretation of postmodernism as the end of marketing is all very well and it is likely to endear the movement to many mainstream marketers. Not only does it draw neat parallels between the postmodern moment and extant marketing issues, plus offering ample opportunities for future research endeavour, but it also comprises an exploitable buzzword for individuals bent on pursuing a strategy of academic self-aggrandizement (the author, naturally, is above such grubby careerism). As Featherstone (1991) stresses, the term 'postmodern' is often employed for essentially political purposes, as a weapon in hegemonic and internecine struggles for control of individual subject areas. Indeed, the proponents of most innovative academic constructs indulge in a form of avant-garde strategy, which involves coining a term to legitimize a break within a particular field and promote a new mode of analysis ('relationship marketing' is a contemporary case in point).

Although such an approach may do much to propagate the postmodern paradigm, it also brings with it the dangers of recuperation – dissipation, emasculation and the blunting of postmodernism's iconoclastic cutting edge. By complete contrast, the negative interpretation of postmodernism as the end of marketing comprises nothing less than disciplinary apocalypse (Brown et al., 1996). It regards as unattainable the modernist marketing vision of analysis, planning, implementation and control. It subverts marketing's preoccupation with either/or scenarios (low cost *or* differentiation strategies, premium *or* penetration pricing, restricted *or* extensive distribution etc.). It highlights the failure of manifold marketing generalizations ranging from STP and the four Ps to the strategic matrices of Ansoff, Porter and the Boston Consulting Group. It dismisses, moreover, the various 'stage-type' theories (e.g. growth of the firm, stages of internationalization, the production–sales–marketing eras typology, Maslow's hierarchy of needs) as misconceived manifestations of the Western metaphysic of inexorable human progress. Granted, there is some debate about the status of concepts premised on the notion of cyclical (rather than linear) time, but it is fair to conclude that the negative stance,

> highlights the inherent limitations of many extant marketing models and theories. It asks not only whether exposure to the Boston matrix causes 'cows' to be milked and 'dogs' put to sleep unnecessarily, or whether the inordinate failure rate of new products is due, not to the inadequacies of the products themselves, but to companies' adherence to marketing's misconceptualisation of the NPD process. It also asks the all-important question of whether companies/products/campaigns etc. succumb because they stray from the path of marketing righteousness, as marketers are wont to assume, or because the path itself is heading in the wrong direction. (Brown, 1993: 25)

Clearly, this is an extreme interpretation of the situation, with few crumbs of comfort for the disorientated survivors of postmodernism's disciplinary holocaust. Disconcerting though it appears – and shared as it is by almost every commentator on postmodern marketing theory (Cova, 1993; Elliott, 1993; Firat, 1992; Tornroos and Ranta, 1993) – (this apocalyptic version of postmodernism should not be dismissed out of hand. With its 'anything goes' ethos; its assumption that nothing is excluded; its abandonment of stultifying orthodoxy; its determination to wipe the conceptual slate clean; and its preparedness to let a thousand methodological flowers bloom, the approach can be viewed as liberatory rather than threatening. Although a number of benefits flow from this particular standpoint (see Brown, 1995a), perhaps the most important is the profound process of critical self-examination that it imposes upon the marketing discipline. It draws our attention to the unassailability of the marketing concept, in that successful marketing practices are invariably lauded as exemplars of the concept in action and marketplace disasters are summarily dismissed for failing to adhere to the 'proper' approach. It reminds us that the propagation of unproven or debatable principles, be it the product life-cycle, Boston matrix or stages theory of internationalization, is counterproductive at best and pernicious at worst. After all, part of the reason for (say) the latter-day fragmentation of markets is the *rise of marketing* with the enormous stress it places on segmentation, targeting and positioning. The micro-marketing/database-marketing/maxi-marketing revolution has *spawned*, not simply served, the much prophesied 'markets of one', the prospect of which is causing so much anguish and heart searching among marketing practitioners. Even the popular notion of 'science', the ideal to which marketing scholarship aspires but will never gain admittance, is partly a marketing *creation* thanks to generations of washing powder, cosmetics, shampoo and patent medicine commercials (white coats, spotless labs, all-pervasive air of rigour and objectivity). This version of postmodernism, in other words, reminds us of the reflexive or circular nature of social knowledge, where the very existence of a concept influences and alters the phenomena to which it pertains. As Giddens rightly points out,

> new knowledge (concepts, theories, findings) does not simply render the social world more transparent, but alters its nature, spinning it off in novel directions . . . Concepts . . . are not merely handy devices whereby agents are somehow more clearly able to understand their behaviour than they would do otherwise. They actively constitute what that behaviour is and inform the reasons for which it is undertaken. (1990: 41, 153)

Negative interpretations of postmodernism may not provide us with any answers, but they certainly make us think. They make us think about marketing thinking. They force us to rethink marketing and ask questions about the nature of marketing 'knowledge'. Granted, they may necessitate the elision of many of marketing's intellectual achievements, but it can be contended that, in light of their manifest inadequacies, most of the incumbents of marketing's conceptual hall of fame aren't worth maintaining anyway. Apocalyptic postmodernism, to conclude, tells us that the proponents of marketing orientation have become product oriented. It suggests that if being different is the secret of marketing success, then the marketing concept ought to be abandoned, given its virtual ubiquity. Above all, it implies that the fundamental issue to which we should address ourselves is not marketing myopia but the *myopia of marketing*. Is that not an end in itself?

References

Adair, G. (1992) *The Postmodernist Always Rings Twice*. London: Fourth Estate.
American Marketing Association (1988) AMA Task Force on the Development of Marketing Thought, 'Developing, disseminating and utilizing marketing knowledge', *Journal of Marketing*, 52 (October): 1–25.
Anderson, L.M. (1994) 'Marketing science: where's the beef?', *Business Horizons*, 37 (January–February): 8–16.
Anderson, P.F. (1983) 'Marketing, scientific progress and scientific method', *Journal of Marketing*, 47 (Fall): 18–31.
Anderson, P.F. (1986) 'On method in consumer research: a critical relativist perspective', *Journal of Consumer Research*, 13 (September): 155–73.
Anderson, P.F. (1989) 'On relativism and interpretivism – with a prolegomenon to the "why" question' in E.C. Hirschman (ed.), *Interpretive Consumer Research*. Provo, UT Association for Consumer Research. pp. 10–23.
Andrews, N. (1993) 'Review of "Last Action Hero" ', *Financial Times*, Thursday 29 July: 13.
Ansoff, H.I. (1958) 'Strategies for diversification', *Harvard Business Review*, 35 (5): 113–24.
Baker, M.J. (1989) 'Marketing – a new philosophy of management', *The Quarterly Review of Marketing*, 14 (2): 1–4.
Baker, M.J. (1994) 'Research myopia: recency, relevance, reinvention and renaissance (the 4 R's of marketing?)'. Working Paper 94/2, Department of Marketing, University of Strathclyde, Glasgow.
Barnes, B. (1985) *About Science*. Oxford: Blackwell.
Barsoux, J.-L. (1993) 'When the jokes start to wear thin', *Financial Times*, Thursday 29 July: 12.
Bartels, R. (1962) *The Development of Marketing Thought*. Homewood, IL: Irwin.
Barthes, R. (1977a) 'The death of the author' (1968), in R. Barthes, *Image Music Text*, trans. S. Heath. London: Fontana. pp. 142–8.
Barthes, R. (1977b) 'From work to text' (1971), in R. Barthes, *Image Music Text*, trans. S. Heath. London: Fontana. pp. 155–64.
Bass, F.M. (1993) 'The future of research in marketing: marketing science', *Journal of Marketing Research*, 30 (February): 1–6.
Baudrillard, J. (1983) *Simulations* (1981), trans. P. Foss, P. Patton and P. Beitchman. New York: Semiotext(e).
Baudrillard, J. (1988) 'The year 2000 has already happened', in A. Kroker and M. Kroker (eds), *Body Invaders: Panic Sex in America*. Montreal: New World Perspectives. pp. 35–44.
Baudrillard, J. (1989) 'The anorexic ruins', in D. Kamper and C. Wulf (eds), *Looking Back on the End of the World*, trans. D. Antal. New York: Semiotext(e). pp. 29–45.
Beaumont, P. (1993) 'Postmodernism', *The Observer*, Sunday 9 May: 43.
Bell, M.L. and Emory, C.W. (1971) 'The faltering marketing concept', *Journal of Marketing*, 35 (October): 37–42.
Bennett, R.C. and Cooper, R.G. (1981) 'The misuse of marketing: an American tragedy', *Business Horizons*, 24 (6): 51–61.
Best, S. (1991) 'Chaos and entropy: metaphors in postmodern science and social theory', *Science as Culture*, 11: 188–226.

Bocock, R. and Thompson, K. (eds) (1992) *Social and Cultural Forms of Modernity*. Cambridge: Polity.

Bowler, P.J. (1989) *The Invention of Progress: The Victorians and the Past*. Oxford: Blackwell.

Boyne, R. and Rattansi, A. (1990) 'The theory and politics of postmodernism: by way of an introduction', in R. Boyne and A. Rattansi (eds), *Postmodernism and Society*. Basingstoke: Macmillan. pp. 1–45.

Bradshaw, P. (1993) 'Keywords: POST-', *The Modern Review*, 1 (11): 23.

Brady, J. and Davis, I. (1993) 'Marketing's mid-life crisis', *McKinsey Quarterly*, 2: 17–28.

Brown, S. (1993) 'Postmodern marketing?' *European Journal of Marketing*, 27 (4): 19–34.

Brown, S. (1995a) *Postmodern Marketing*. London: Routledge.

Brown, S. (1995b) 'Life begins at forty?', *Marketing Intelligence and Planning*, 13 (1): 4–12.

Brown, S. (1997) *Postmodern Marketing Two: Telling Tales*. London: ITBP.

Brown, S., Bell, J. and Carson, D. (1996) 'Apocaholics anonymous: looking back on the end of marketing', in S. Brown et al. (eds), *Marketing Apocalypse*. London: Routledge. pp. 1–20.

Brownlie, D. and Saren, M. (1992) 'The four Ps of the marketing concept: prescriptive, polemical, permanent and problematical', *European Journal of Marketing*, 26 (4): 34–47.

Brownlie, D., Saren, M., Whittington, R. and Wensley, R. (1994) 'The new marketing myopia: critical perspectives on theory and research in marketing – introduction', *European Journal of Marketing*, 28 (3): 6–12.

Burchill, J. (1994) 'The terrible spoof', *Sunday Times*, 22 May, 10: 4–5.

Burrell, G. (1994) 'Modernism, postmodernism and organizational analysis 4: the contribution of Jürgen Habermas', *Organization Studies*, 15 (1): 1–19.

Bury, J.B. (1987) *The Idea of Progress: An Inquiry into its Origins and Growth* (1932). New York: Dover.

Callinicos, A. (1990) 'Reactionary postmodernism?', in R. Boyne and A. Rattansi (eds), *Postmodernism and Society*. Basingstoke: Macmillan. pp. 97–118.

Chen, I.J., Calantone, R.J. and Chung, C.-H. (1992) 'The marketing–manufacturing interface and manufacturing flexibility', *Omega*, 20 (4): 431–43.

Connor, S. (1989) *Postmodernist Culture: An Introduction to Theories of the Contemporary*. Oxford: Blackwell.

Cooke, P. (1990) *Back to the Future: Modernity, Postmodernity and Locality*. London: Unwin Hyman.

Coopers and Lybrand (1994) *Marketing at the Crossroads – a Survey on the Role of Marketing*. London: Coopers & Lybrand.

Cova, B. (1993) 'Beyond marketing: from marketing to societing', in D. Brownlie, M. Saren, R. Wensley and R. Whittington (eds), *Rethinking Marketing*. Coventry: Warwick Business School Research Bureau. pp. 12–23.

Day, G.S. (1992) 'Marketing's contribution to the strategy dialogue', *Journal of the Academy of Marketing Science*, 20 (4): 323–9.

de Jonquieres, G. (1993) 'Growing taste for alliances in the food industry', *Financial Times*, Friday 22 January: 15.

Derrida, J. (1991) *A Derrida Reader: Between the Blinds*, ed. P. Kamuf. Hemel Hempstead: Harvester Wheatsheaf.

Derrida, J. (1992) *Acts of Literature*, ed. D. Attridge. London: Routledge.

Desmond, J. (1993) 'Marketing: the split subject', in D. Brownlie, M. Saren, R. Wensley and R. Whittington (eds), *Rethinking Marketing*. Coventry: Warwick Business School Research Bureau. pp. 259–69.

Dickinson, R.A., Herbst, A. and O'Shaughnessy, J. (1986) 'Marketing concept and customer orientation', *European Journal of Marketing*, 20 (10): 18–23.

Elliott, R. (1993) 'Marketing and the meaning of postmodern consumer culture', in Brownlie, D., Saren, M., Wensley, R. and Whittington, R. (eds), *Rethinking Marketing*. Coventry: Warwick Business School Research Bureau. pp. 134–42.

Featherstone, M. (1991) *Consumer Culture and Postmodernism*. London: Sage.

Feyerabend, P. (1975) *Against Method*. London: Verso.

Fielding, H. (1992) 'Teach yourself postmodernism', *The Independent on Sunday*, 15 November: 21.

Financial Times (1992) 'The verbiage of creativity that is . . . mad, bad and dangerous to use', *Financial Times*, Saturday 24 December: vi–vii.

Firat, A.F. (1992) 'Postmodernism and the marketing organization', *Journal of Organizational Change Management*, 5 (1): 79–83.

Firat, A.F. and Venkatesh, A. (1993) 'Postmodernity: the age of marketing', *International Journal of Research in Marketing*, 10 (3): 227–49.

Foster, H. (1985) 'Postmodernism: a preface', in H. Foster (ed.), *Postmodern Culture*. London: Pluto. pp. vii–xiv.

Foucault, M. (1972) *The Order of Things: An Archaeology of the Human Sciences* (1966), trans. A. Sheridan. London: Routledge.

Foucault, M. (1974) *The Archaeology of Knowledge* (1969), trans. A.M. Sheridan Smith. London: Routledge.

Foucault, M. (1980) *Power/Knowledge: Selected Interviews and Other Writings 1972–1977*, ed. C. Gordon. Hemel Hempstead: Harvester Wheatsheaf.

Foucault, M. (1990) *The Care of the Self: The History of Sexuality Volume Three* (1984), trans. R. Hurley. Harmondsworth: Penguin.

Foxall, G.R. (1984) 'Marketing's domain', *European Journal of Marketing*, 18 (1): 25–40.

Freeling, A. (1994) 'Marketing is in crisis – can market research help?', *Journal of the Market Research Society*, 36 (2): 97–104.

Giddens, A. (1990) *The Consequences of Modernity*. Cambridge: Polity.

Gordon, S. (1991) *The History and Philosophy of Social Science*. London: Routledge.

Griffin, D.R. (ed.) (1988) *The Reenchantment of Science: Postmodern Proposals*. Albany, NY: State University of New York Press.

Gummesson, E. (1987) 'The new marketing – developing long-term interactive relationships', *Long Range Planning*, 20 (4): 10–20.

Gummesson, E. (1991) 'Marketing-orientation revisited: the crucial role of the part-time marketer', *European Journal of Marketing*, 25 (2): 60–75.

Hattenstone, S. (1992) 'All mod cons', *The Observer Magazine*, Sunday 23 August: 7.

Holbrook, M.B. and Hirschman, E.C. (1982) 'The experiential aspects of consumption: consumer fantasies, feelings and fun', *Journal of Consumer Research*, 9 (September): 132–40.

Hollander, S.C. (1986) 'The marketing concept: a *déjà vu*', in G. Fisk (ed.), *Marketing Management Technology as a Social Process*. New York: Praeger. pp. 3–29.

Hollinger, P. (1993) 'An attempt at reviving the Habitat habit', *Financial Times*, Monday 18 October: 20.

Hoyt, F.B. (1991) 'We don't do marketing here anymore', *Marketing News*, 25 (1): 4.

Hunt, S.D. (1984) 'Should marketing adopt relativism?' in P.F. Anderson and M.J. Ryan (eds), *Scientific Method in Marketing*. Chicago: American Marketing Association. pp. 30–4.

Hunt, S.D. (1990) 'Truth in marketing theory and research', *Journal of Marketing*, 54 (July): 1–15.

Hunt, S.D. (1992) 'For reason and realism in marketing', *Journal of Marketing*, 56 (April): 89–102.

Hunt, S.D. (1994) 'On rethinking marketing: our discipline, our practice, our methods', *European Journal of Marketing*, 28 (3): 13–25.

Ingene, C.A. (1993) 'Comments at "Meet the Editors" session', Academy of Marketing Science Annual Conference Miami Beach, May.

Jameson, F. (1985) 'Postmodernism and consumer society', in H. Foster (ed.), *Postmodern Culture*. London: Pluto. pp. 111–25.

Jameson, F. (1991) *Postmodernism, or, the Cultural Logic of Late Capitalism*. London: Verso.

Jencks, C. (1989) *What is Postmodernism?* London: Academy.

Johnson, P. (1991) *The Birth of the Modern: World Society 1815–1830*. London: Weidenfeld & Nicolson.

Kavanagh, D. (1994) 'Hunt versus Anderson: round 16', *European Journal of Marketing*, 28 (3): 26–41.

Keith, R.J. (1960) 'The marketing revolution', *Journal of Marketing*, 24 (January): 35–38.

Kohli, A.K. and Jaworski, B.J. (1990) 'Market orientation: the construct, research propositions and managerial implications', *Journal of Marketing*, 54 (April): 1–18.

Kotler, P. and Levy, S.J. (1969) 'Broadening the concept of marketing', *Journal of Marketing*, 33 (January): 10–15.

Kotler, P. and Zaltman, G. (1971) 'Social marketing: an approach to planned social change', *Journal of Marketing*, 35 (July): 3–12.

Kroker, A. and Cook, D. (1986) *The Postmodern Scene: Excremental Culture and Hyper-aesthetics*. Montreal: New World Perspectives.

Kuhn, T.S. (1970) *The Structure of Scientific Revolutions*, 2nd edn (1st edn 1962). Chicago: University of Chicago Press.

Lacan, J. (1977) *Écrits: A Selection* (1966), trans. A. Sheridan. London: Routledge.

Levitt, T. (1960) 'Marketing myopia', *Harvard Business Review*, 38 (July–August): 45–56.

Little, J.D.C., Lodish, L.M., Hauser, J.R. and Urban, G.L. (1994) 'Commentary', in G. Laurent, G.L. Lilien and B. Pras (eds), *Research Traditions in Marketing*. Dordrecht: Kluwer. pp. 44–51.

Lorenz, C. (1993) 'A meeting of minds', *Financial Times*, Monday 25 October: 15.

Lynch, J.E. (1994) 'The end of marketing?', in O. Westall (ed.), *British Academy of Management Annual Conference Proceedings*, Lancaster: Lancaster University. pp. 322–4.

Lyotard, J.-F. (1984) *The Postmodern Condition: A Report on Knowledge* (1979), trans. G. Bennington and B. Massumi. Manchester: Manchester University Press.

Lyotard, J.-F. (1992) *The Postmodern Explained to Children: Correspondence 1982–1985* (1986), trans. D. Barry et al. London: Turnaround.

Lyotard, J.-F. (1994) *Lessons on the Analytic of the Sublime* (1991), trans. E. Rottenberg. Stanford, CA: Stanford University Press.

Magnus, B., Stewart, S. and Mileur, J.-P. (1993) *Nietzsche's Case: Philosophy as/ and Literature*. New York: Routledge.

McDonald, M.H.B. (1994) 'Marketing – a mid-life crisis?', *Marketing Business*, 30 (May): 10–14.

McKenna, R. (1991) 'Marketing is everything', *Harvard Business Review*, 69 (1): 65–79.

McKiernan, P. (1992) *Strategies of Growth: Maturity, Recovery and Internationalization*. London: Routledge.

Miller, C. (1990) 'Nostalgia makes boomers buy', *Marketing News*, 24 (24): 1–2.

Miller, C. (1992) 'P.F. Flyers relaunch targets nostalgic baby boomers', *Marketing News*, 26 (4): 2.

Mulvagh, J. (1993) 'Back to the past at Laura Ashley', *Financial Times*, Saturday 3 April: xii.

Narver, J.C. and Slater, S.F. (1990) 'The effect of a market orientation on business profitability', *Journal of Marketing*, 54 (October): 20–35.

Nisbet, R. (1980) *A History of the Idea of Progress*. New York: Basic Books.

Norris, C. (1991) *Deconstruction: Theory and Practice*. London: Routledge.

Observer Life (1994) 'Post-modernism deconstructed', *Observer Life*, Sunday 12 June: 6.

Peattie, K. (1992) *Green Marketing*. London: Pitman.

Peterson, R.A. (1992) 'Introduction to the special issue', *Journal of the Academy of Marketing Science*, 20 (4): 295–7.

Pickering, A. (ed.) (1992) *Science as Practice and Culture*. Chicago: University of Chicago Press.

Piercy, N. (1992) *Market-Led Strategic Change*. Oxford: Butterworth-Heinemann.

Porter, R. (1990) *The Enlightenment*. Basingstoke: Macmillan.

Rorty, R. (1980) *Philosophy and the Mirror of Nature*. Oxford: Blackwell.

Rorty, R. (1989) *Contingency, Irony, and Solidarity*. Cambridge: Cambridge University Press.

Rorty, R. (1991) *Consequences of Pragmatism (Essays 1972–1980)*. Hemel Hempstead: Harvester Wheatsheaf.

Rose, G. (1991) *The Post-Modern and the Post-Industrial: A Critical Analysis*. Cambridge: Cambridge University Press.

Rosenau, P.M. (1992) *Postmodernism and the Social Sciences*. Princeton, NJ: Princeton University Press.

Samli, A.C., Palda, K. and Barker, A.T. (1987) 'Toward a mature marketing concept', *Sloan Management Review*, 28 (2): 45–51.

Scruton, R. (1994) *Modern Philosophy: An Introduction and Survey*. London: Sinclair-Stevenson.

Shenk, D. (1993) 'Buy a hat, save the earth', *Hemispheres*, May: 25–8.

Siegel, H. (1992) 'Relativism', in J. Dancy and E. Sosa (eds), *A Companion to Epistemology*. Oxford: Blackwell. pp. 428–30.

Silverman, H.J. (1990) 'Introduction – the philosophy of postmodernism', in H.J. Silverman (ed.), *Postmodernism – Philosophy and the Arts*. New York: Routledge. pp. 1–9.

Smart, B. (1993) *Postmodernity*. London: Routledge.

Smith, D. and Lynn, M. (1993) 'Price wars', *Sunday Times*, 26 September, 3: 3.

Tedre, R. (1993) 'Shock of the old', *Observer Life*, Sunday 24 October: 24–5.

Thomas, M.J. (1993) 'Marketing – in chaos or transition?', in D. Brownlie, M. Saren, R. Wensley and R. Whittington (eds), *Rethinking Marketing*. Coventry: Warwick Business School Research Bureau. pp. 114–23.

Thomas, M.J. (1994) 'Do marketing educators have a future?', in J. Bell et al. (eds), *Marketing: Unity in Diversity, Proceedings*, Marketing Education Group Conference, Coleraine. pp. 939–47.

Thompson, C.J. (1993) 'Modern truth and postmodern incredulity: a hermeneutic deconstruction of the metanarrative of "scientific truth" in marketing research', *International Journal of Research in Marketing*, 10 (3): 325–38.

Tornroos, J.-A. and Ranta, T. (1993) 'Marketing as image management – a postmodern reformulation of the marketing concept', in D. Brownlie, M. Saren, R. Wensley and R. Whittington (eds), *Rethinking Marketing*. Coventry: Warwick Business School Research Bureau. pp. 166–75.

Toulmin, S. (1990) *Cosmopolis: The Hidden Agenda of Modernity*. Chicago: University of Chicago Press.

Updike, J. (1991) *Odd Jobs: Essays and Criticism*. Harmondsworth: Penguin.

Vattimo, G. (1991) *The End of Modernity* (1985), trans. J.R. Snyder. Baltimore: Johns Hopkins University Press.

Wagner, P. (1994) *A Sociology of Modernity: Liberty and Discipline.* London: Routledge.

Watkins, A. (1991) 'Mr Heseltine may get his secret wish', *Observer*, Sunday 20 October: 21.

Webster, F.E. (1988) 'The rediscovery of the marketing concept', *Business Horizons*, 31 (3): 29–39.

Wensley, R. (1990) ' "The voice of the consumer?": speculations on the limits to the marketing analogy', *European Journal of Marketing*, 24 (7): 49–60.

Wensley, R. (1994) 'A critical review of research in marketing', paper presented at BAM Conference, Lancaster University, September.

Whittington, R. and Whipp, R. (1992) 'Marketing ideology and implementation', *European Journal of Marketing*, 24 (7): 52–63.

Woolgar, S. (1988) *Science: The Very Idea.* London: Routledge.

Workman, J.P. (1993) 'Marketing's limited role in new product development in one computer systems firm', *Journal of Marketing Research*, 30 (4): 405–21.

3 Commentary

Gibson Burrell

The paper by Shelby Hunt and the chapter by Stephen Brown are purportedly concerned with the philosophy of marketing, but it takes only a moment to see that they are as much about disciplinary politics as they are about underlying philosophy. But since these distinctions themselves are difficult to justify, perhaps we should not be overly concerned that the one masquerades as the other. It is easy to see the two pieces as an exchange, as a debate between two eloquent and committed academics who are keen to offer differing images of the way ahead. The first finds that original contributions in marketing are difficult to detect because any such articles are reviewed by the referees of journals in a negative way. Hunt goes on to tell us that marketing is an 'applied' discipline and is dependent (therefore?) on other disciplines. This being so, marketing academics must rethink their discipline and 'must adopt the university value system'. This has to be done by addressing the research methods currently used and by providing a 'rethought philosophy'. Brown, by seeking to provide an analysis of the 'interpenetration of marketing and postmodernism', might be thought by some to provide exactly this attempt at rethinking the philosophy of marketing and therefore to be firmly aligned with Hunt. If their problematic is the same then surely they are bedfellows? But you know, of course, that close proximity without affection breeds contempt. Let us listen to their talk.

Here is Brown's relatively new voice in the debate:

> at the risk of gross oversimplification, it can be contended that postmodernism is characterized by five key features: fragmentation, dedifferentiation, hyper-reality, pastiche and anti-foundationalism . . . [and] an all-pervasive air of finality and fatigue.

Counterpose this to the voice of the establishment:

> The problem with the standard argument for qualitative methods is that, of the five premisses, four . . . are false whilst the remaining one . . . is misleading. As a result the argument degenerates into obfuscation, obscurantism and what is now referred to as 'post-modern' epistobabble. (Hunt, 1994: 17)

For Brown, epistemology is a way of understanding, critiquing and self-revelation: 'It is . . . characterized by a strange but remarkably compelling sense of playfulness, of exhilaration in the face of failure, of feeling that there's nothing we can do, so let's have a party.' For Hunt, epistemology is a weakness which has to be defended by resort to 'the ideals of truth and objectivity' or by injunctions to seek for reason, evidence, openness and civility. Or somewhat paradoxically, given these values, by a quote from Hintikka which asserts that what is argued by others is 'simply fallacious'. So that's alright then. It is reasonable and civil to assert fallacy wherever one confronts difference.

Notice that Hunt calls for the reader to address *our* discipline, *our* practice, *our* methods. Here is the call to all for the recognition and the pursuit of a common identity. There are no indications that differences of a substantial nature exist, for all are part of the same *Volk*. Commonality not heterogeneity are the orders of the day. But this takes us to politics.

In my own discipline of organization theory, it is possible to recognize a very small number of paradigm *warriors* and paradigm *walsinghams*. This is a crude distinction and it by no means includes anything but a very small fragment of the relevant academic populace. Nevertheless, allow me to pursue the distinction. Both types are vocal, have much of interest to say, are listened to by many and most importantly are playing for high stakes – the conscience of the discipline. A paradigm warrior is characterized by a relatively peripheral institutional position, by an energetic zeal born of youth, by a deep-seated antipathy to the ways in which her or his discipline is organized and controlled, and by a drive to see political change as well as intellectual movement within their discipline.

A paradigm walsingham is someone who takes on the role of Sir Francis Walsingham, spymaster general in Queen Elizabeth I's government. For present purposes, walsinghams are powerful keepers of the monarch's peace and implacable enemies of her opponents. They spend their time in testing the loyalty of the population and identifying those who are likely to harbour resentment and resistance to the prevailing good order. These men and women – and it is much more likely to be the former – are central members of the discipline's ruling orthodoxy. Indeed, this is why the term 'discipline' is used so frequently by those firmly entrenched within the oligarchy. Their self-appointed task is to suppress internal dissension within the state's boundaries and to maintain good law and order, simultaneously allowing the wealthy and powerful to retain their position and privileges. In organization theory, Jeffrey Pfeffer and Lex Donaldson have adopted this role of 'M' with vim and vigour, presumably seeking a metaphorical knighthood in the process.

In these two pieces we address another discipline, marketing, but the similarities are evident. Here the role of the warrior is played by Stephen Brown and that of the walsingham by Shelby Hunt. Both play their parts with gusto. Now it is important in this act of interpreting their play of words to look carefully at the metaphors and terms they use. This after all is all we have. We must perforce read what they say with attention. Spot the following. The walsingham speaks of the high seas, of scuttling and of navigation, of the main stream, of Great Britain's slave trade and of not staying too long in the same place. The seafaring allusion is clear – as is, you will remember, the appeal to a sense of shared community. The imperial trade routes are open for all to witness. For the walsingham who is Hunt, the land of the free left behind by 'our' navigators offers cooperation, commitment, trust, relationships, reason, evidence, openness and civility. Using terms that a British (or more accurately English) audience might understand best, ships are at sea precisely to protect the sceptred isle of marketing and make it a home fit for heroes. Flying from the topgallants are the ideals of truth and objectivity so that they may be held in high regard. The enemies of the realm, both within and without, are continental and on their banners we are shown the suffix ISMS. This band of corsairs marches to the tunes of anarchism, nihilism, relativism, subjectivism, constructionism and scepticism, and their overall strategy is obscurantism. Overdrawn, you may say. But read the piece carefully for its analogies and rhetorical devices.

Now Hunt's enemies, all identified as living in Suffix, happen to be philosophical ISMS with which I would be happy to briefly consort and cavort. I would like to know them better. But getting them in the same ship, never mind the same mess, is exceptionally difficult. Hunt seems unaware that his imperial policies of consigning all those who are not legitimate into the category of *other* hide their internal differences. It is a technique which suggests a lack of knowledge, a lack of understanding and an enthusiastic willingness to downplay the deep and significant differences which exist within those who are not part of the chosen few. The policy of exclusion of the other encourages in the mind of the normal member of the insider community a lack of any pretence of understanding. Walsinghams seek to be powerful enough to define that all those that are not like us are the same as each other. 'They' should be consigned to outer darkness.

Our paradigm warrior Brown, meanwhile, revealingly describes Hunt as 'the foremost defender of the faith', as one of the 'philosophical heavy-weights', and as 'the indefatigable champion of realism'. Notice here the language of fisticuffs and pugilism. The language is very violent, quasi-militaristic and clearly of the threatened. It is the pugnacious language of someone who feels their academic survival to be threatened by bigger and better provisioned battalions.

Compare these twin sets of linguistic artifices, and what is revealed? The walsingham's text is replete with the metaphors of trade and networks and the protection of one's partners. The warrior speaks much more of physical violence, interpenetration and anxiety for one's safety. Perhaps Brown fears condemnation as a marketing heretic 'to the flames of philosophical perdition'. Does this textual difference reflect their relative con*textual* positions at centre and periphery, late maturity and early career, mainstream and non-imperial? When Kuhn saw the intergenerational tensions at work within a 'paradigm' as the key driving force behind academic development, perhaps he foresaw the Brown–Hunt effect in marketing. Or then again perhaps not.

Given the foregoing analysis, when disciplinary walsinghams and warriors meet, face to face, one might expect violent and bloody confrontation between them. And this may well bring out the crowd to see and feel the pleasure of the spectacle. Rarely does this happen however. The typical walsingham is much happier at putting in the knife behind closed doors and typical warriors are often too polite and respectful. Nevertheless, for the vast majority of us for whom the term 'normal science' was developed, textual confrontations such as the one in this part are good fun. We can listen, take sides, continue to trade and not be too bloodied in the process. We can see in the niceties of published rhetoric and discourse that, below the surface, this is serious stuff, for the one apparently attempts to keep the other from appearance in 'marketing's hall of fame' while the second seeks to 'scuttle' the ship of the postmodernists. The somewhat crude warrior/walsingham differentiation is one of which I am fond. It is a role-set which faces every social science discipline. It is a duality in which I am happy to take sides and I suspect this is so for most of this book's readership. But as the years pass, inside and outside, old and new, mature and retired, and so on are dualities whose meanings change before one's rheumy eyes. Today's warrior soon becomes tomorrow's walsingham. But, nevertheless, in a world replete with paradigm *workers*, the warriors and walsinghams give us much to talk about. For the majority of knowledge workers sitting at their university desks who are happy with neither role of prominence, it may be, nevertheless, that we wish to take paper-borne pleasure in disciplinary bread and circuses. Such exchanges as we have before us offer vicarious pleasure. Hunt and Brown, of differing age, stature and nation, are the chosen champions who face each other across the Valley of Elah (1 *Samuel* 17:2) offering us a Foucauldian 'spectacle'. Let us not disappoint them. Let us watch.

The exchange in this book is a good exchange which asks of us, not too onerously, to read and to think. It represents those marginalized at the centre defending vigorously against those put on centre stage by their energetic marginalization. And of such contradictions is the excitement of academic discourse composed. But let us recognize that dialogue is dangerous. Above all, it is a weapon of the powerful. Perhaps silence is enough.

References

Hintikka, J. (1988) 'On the incommensurability of theories', *Philosophy of Science*, 55: 25–38.
Hunt, S.D. (1994) 'On rethinking marketing: our discipline, our practice, our methods', *European Journal of Marketing*, 28 (3): 13–25.

Part II

REDEFINING MARKETS

All three pieces in this part are about links. They express a common reflex against the atomistic individualization of orthodox micro-economics, the foundation for so much in mainstream marketing. But each takes us in different directions: Cova towards a postmodern form of marketing, in which the value of whatever is being marketed lies at least as much in the social linkages which come with it as in the object itself; Araujo towards a stronger recognition of temporality in marketing relationships, the connection of the past with the future in the instant of exchange; and Wensley in his final commentary towards a historical perspective, in which contemporary theoretical concerns are traced back to old but oft neglected traditions of marketing thought.

Cova's challenging thesis is that Anglo-Saxons have got the postmodern wrong. Postmodernity is often presented as the culmination of modernism's gradual freeing of the individual from social bonds. The postmodern consumer becomes a free-floating, unclassifiable, butterfly-like individual, perpetually eluding the orderly segmentations of conventional marketing (see Elliott, Chapter 8 in this volume). Cova presents an alternative, 'Latin', characterization of postmodernity. Here the urge is not to celebrate freedom from social constraints, but to re-establish social embeddedness. The citizen of postmodernity is less interested in the objects of consumption than in the social links and identities that come from them. On the Latin view, the effective marketing of the postmodern era is not to accept and exploit consumers in their contemporary individualization, as Anglo-Saxons might. Rather the future of marketing is in offering a renewed sense of community. Marketing becomes 'societing'.

Araujo underlines the importance of social embeddedness in marketing by deepening conventional notions of exchange. Marketing orthodoxy has inherited the asocialized view of human actors of neo-classical economics. But marketing in practice is typically about establishing repeated exchanges, in other words, enduring social relationships. Araujo introduces the notion of 'relational time', in which past, present and future are connected within any exchange relationship. People remember and anticipate. The orthodox conception of marketing exchanges as successions of discrete events is therefore dangerous. Araujo's stress on temporality and relationships leads him to emphasize instead the importance of 'relationship development investment', a notion that puts value on future exchanges.

With his quotations of Glucksman and Giddens at the start, Wensley's final commentary explicitly recognizes the potential of social theory for a renewed discipline of marketing. He reminds us too that sociologists have been struggling for two decades or more with issues that marketers are only now beginning to take on board. But Wensley's contribution is also to warn that the new marketing theorists should not forget their links with their own disciplinary past. Ardnt, Bagozzi and Ogilvy foreshadowed many of the perspectives emerging today. Past, present and future are linked in marketing theory as well as in marketing practice.

4 From Marketing to Societing: When the Link Is More Important than the Thing

Bernard Cova

A postmodern era

Characterized by a crisis of consumption, 'deconsumption', a consumer who is more and more described as a 'chameleon' or an 'ant', our postmodern era (Lyotard, 1979) seems to be a period of extreme disorder in consumption, and consequently, of unpredictability in consumer behaviour. This is an undoubted fact, even if there is still much debate surrounding the nature and the respective weight of the various explanatory factors. There is the question of how to separate factors resulting from the socio-economic conditions of the day from purely structural factors: economic, sociological and technological explanations are played off against each other. For our part, it appeared relevant to take as a starting point an ethnosociological analysis structuring the passage from modernity to postmodernity around the 'crisis of the social link' (Farrugia, 1993) in order to arrive at a clearer understanding of the present day phenomenon of the so-called 'confusion in consumption' and of its implications for the theory and practice of marketing in postmodernity.

Metamorphosis of the social link

The term 'postmodernity' renders accurately the defining traits of the socio-economic condition that emerged through the affluent countries of Europe and of European descent in the course of the second half of the twentieth century. The term is accurate as it draws attention to continuity and discontinuity as two faces of the intricate relationship between the present socio-economic condition and the formation that it preceded and gestated. It brings into relief the intimate, genetic bond that ties the new, postmodern condition to modernity – the socio-economic formation that emerged in the same part of the world in the course of the eighteenth century, and took its final shape during the nineteenth (Bauman, 1992: 149). Postmodernity may be interpreted as fully developed modernity; as modernity which goes beyond its false consciousness and comes to understand what it actually was doing all along, that is, producing ambivalence and pluralism, and also reconciles itself to the fact that the purposes which were originally set, for example, rational order and individual freedom, will never be reached (1992: 134).

Modernity entered history as a progressive force promising to liberate humankind from ignorance and irrationality – but one can readily wonder whether that promise has been sustained. As long as traditional forms of communal mediations have existed (family, village, religion, etc.), the modern being has constantly tried to liberate him/herself from them in order to make the 'enlightened' project of the free subject come true. In this perspective, the social link was understood, in the strict sense of the word, as something that ties individuals, i.e. that hinders them (Farrugia, 1993). And the contract appeared as a way to escape the condition of the 'bad community', the community that enslaved people. Modernity, in this way, opposed the notion of contract, a voluntary and reversible choice made by each individual to associate rationally with others in a specified and limited framework, to the traditional notion of community, an irreversible obligation imposed on each of its members to share the same fate. In the modern view, the individual was primary, he/she existed first as a pre-social being, and relations were secondary and essentially instrumental. Differentiation, more than communion, guided the action of individuals. In order to uproot him/herself from the communal debris of the Middle Ages, the modern being relied on new forms of mediation which were rational and near universal aggregations of impersonal ties, like the nation state or the social class. Modernity thus opposed the personal intimacy, emotional depth, moral commitment, social cohesion and continuity in time of the traditional relations within a community, to the impersonality, rationality, transparency and universality of modern relations based on a utilitarian approach. To achieve his/her freedom the modern being was supported by the market economy that soon appeared as the strongest force behind the destruction of old communities.

But, in fact, 'nous n'avons jamais été modernes', as stated by Latour (1991), and the new and modern mediations have lasted as much because of their contractual basis as thanks to the shared emotion of their members and their 'natural' instinct to re-create the communal link. Then, what we call 'class consciousness' or 'national consciousness' relied, as well as on their rational justification, on a form of communal enthusiasm made up of shared feelings and passions (Maffesoli, 1993). Certain periods of history and certain regions did however come near to attaining the modern social link. This was apparently the case in eighteenth century England, where, as Disraeli wrote in no uncertain terms in *Sybil*, 'modern society acknowledged no neighbour', and where isolation between individuals in big cities was extreme. The twentieth century, which put into practice the great political and scientific utopias of the nineteenth century, has lived out very intensively the myth of the liberation of the individual. This tension has resulted in

the breaking up and 'delegitimization' of all forms of contractual aggregations inherited from the last two centuries, and from the so-called uni-
formization of behaviour. The individual has never been so free in his/her
private and public choices as today, and never so alone and cut off from the
spirit of community.

Consequently, and according to a first current of sociological research
(Ehrenberg, 1991; Lipovetsky, 1983; 1987; 1990), postmodernity is characterized by *individualism*, the logical conclusion of the modern quest for
liberation from social bonds, whether those of traditional communities or
those of complex modern societies. The postmodern individual, freed from
the restricting limits of communities, is restored to him/herself and able to
become totally autonomous (Elias, 1991). In postmodernity, 'the conquest of
self' has become inescapable and each individual, wherever he/she comes
from, must accomplish the feat of 'becoming someone' by showing his/her
difference (Ehrenberg, 1991). The right to liberty unbounded in theory – but
limited in modernity to the economic, political and intellectual field – is
affecting all aspects of daily life. The idea is gaining ground of a postmodern
condition where the individual, freed of the constraints of collective ideals in
matters concerning education, the family, sex (Lipovetsky, 1990), is operating a process of personalization as a way of managing behaviour, not
through the tyranny of details, but with as few constraints and as many
choices as possible. We have now entered 'the age of the ordinary individual' (Ehrenberg, 1991), that is to say an age when any individual can (and
must) take personal action so as to produce and show his/her own existence,
his/her own difference. Mobility characterizes the action of this 'ordinary
individual' on both the spatial and the social level: as in the case of North
Americans, 'a liberated person is one who is geographically mobile, who
changes sex, clothes, and customs, according to fashion, and not according
to moral conviction, who changes opinion according to models of opinion
and not in accordance with his conscience' (Baudrillard, 1986: 192). The
postmodern individual has thus become a 'nomad of the present' (Melucci,
1989): he/she has no more, or few, durable social links. The fragmentation
of society, and in particular the fragmentation (and the ephemeral nature) of
consumption, are among the most visible consequences of this postmodern
individualism. This fragmentation is made possible and fostered by the
developments of industry and commerce: products and services have progressively freed the individual of all alienating tasks left behind by tradition,
even purchasing itself. From his/her own home, and without the necessity of
a physical social contact (distance purchasing), the postmodern individual
can obtain almost everything he/she desires. All the products and services
offered thus increase the isolation of the postmodern individual while
permitting him/her to be in virtual touch with the whole world (fax, TV,
telephone, CD-ROM, etc.). The process of 'egocentration' (Virilio, 1993:
139), induced by the development and above all the widespread use of
computers in all aspects of human existence, thus characterizes postmodern
daily life.

Postmodernity can therefore be understood as a period of severe social dissolution and extreme individualism. But attempts at social recomposition can also be glimpsed: the individual who has finally managed to liberate him/herself from archaic or modern social links is embarking on a reverse movement to recompose his/her social universe on the basis of an 'emotional' free choice (Melucci, 1991). Less than differentiation, it is dedifferentiation which seems to be guiding individual action. If, as Baudrillard writes,

> liberty is a critical form, liberation on the other hand, is a potentially catastrophic form. The former confronts the subject with his/her own alienation and transcendence. The latter leads to metastases, to chain reactions, to the disconnection of all the elements and finally to the radical expropriation of the subject. Liberation is the effective fulfillment of the metaphor of liberty, and in this sense it is also its end. (1992: 151)

Postmodernity can therefore be said, according to a second sociological current (Bauman, 1992; Maffesoli, 1988; 1990; 1992; 1993), not to crown the triumph of individualism, but the beginning of its end with the emergence of a reverse movement of a desperate search for the social link. In this view, individualism corresponded solely to a short period of transition – 'late modernity' as described by architects – and not to postmodernity.

Certain scholars (Maffesoli, 1988) advocate that the social dynamics characteristic of our postmodern era are made up of a multiplicity of experiences, of representations and of daily-experienced emotions which are very often not properly understood. Whilst such dynamics are, most of the time, explained by individualism, they stress the *tribalism* which is developing more and more. The word 'tribe' refers to the re-emergence of quasi-archaic values: a local sense of identification, religiosity, syncretism, group narcissism, etc., the common denominator of which is the community dimension. These tribes try to revive the community archetype of the village or the district, but they are not communities which are clearly definable in spatial terms; some use all the resources of the latest technical means of communication (microcomputers, minitels, fax) in order to form virtual tribes in which face-to-face encounters or collocation are not compulsory. These tribes are inherently unstable, small-scale, affectual and not fixed by any of the established parameters of modern society; instead they can be maintained through shared emotions, styles of life, new moral beliefs, senses of injustice – and consumption practices. They exist in no other form but the symbolically and ritually manifested commitment of their members. They can rely neither on executive powers able to coerce their constituency into submission to the tribal rules (seldom do they have clearly codified rules to which the submission could be demanded), nor on the strength of neighbourly bonds or intensity of reciprocal exchange. Postmodern tribes are, therefore, constantly in *statu nascendi* rather than *essendi*, brought ever again into being by repetitive symbolic ritual of the members but persisting no longer than these rituals' power of attraction (Bauman, 1992: 157–8). Postmodern society, unlike modern society – conceived as an ensemble of social groups (socio-professional categories, classes, etc.) – looks like a network of societal micro-groups in which individuals share strong emotional links, a common subculture, a vision of life. Hunters, computer maniacs, Somalian immigrants, Vietnam veterans, skinheads, entomologists, residents of a polluted site, and so on, form more or less stable communities which are invisible to the categories of modern sociology. The postmodern communities taken as a whole are referred to by the term 'sociality' which is different from 'social' as it stresses not the mechanical and instrumental function of an individual member of a contractual aggregation, but the symbolic and emotional role of persons within ephemeral tribes. Each postmodern individual belongs to several tribes in each of which he/she might play a different role and wear a specific mask; this means that the modern tools of sociological analysis cannot classify him/her. And the fact of belonging to these tribes has become, for him/her, more important than belonging to a modern social class; this makes every attempt at classification impossible. The 'social status', that is to say the static position of an individual in one of the social classes of modernity, is progressively replaced by the 'societal configuration', that is to say the dynamic and flexible positioning of the individual within and between his/her postmodern tribes.

In fact, late modern individualism has moved to an 'aestheticization of everyday life' (Cova and Svanfeldt, 1993; Featherstone, 1991; Maffesoli, 1990) made up of shared emotions favouring the concatenation of small ephemeral entities.[1] In a sense, 'it can be said that there is aesthetic enjoyment in everyday life, in the collective passions of the tribes, in all ephemeral communions' (Maffesoli, 1992: 269). These opportunities for communion in private life are in opposition to the duplicity behind which individuals hide in public life where there is less and less emotional investment. Emotion and communion lead postmodern persons to the reintegration of rituals and transcendence in everydayness: 'the seeking for a relational meaning which is a joint construction of existence is parallel to the rediscovery of the sacred and of traditions' (Lipovetsky, 1992: 73). There are numerous sociological studies which emphasize the return of rituals, but in a profane and not religious manifestation. Religion has often been given a purely divine meaning, whereas the basic Latin etymology is indeed the linking (*re-ligare*): linking humans with the divine and thus linking humans with each other. It can therefore be said that religion is not on the wane in our postmodern societies, but has changed form: it is less institutional, more improvised, but always present as a factor of social link, a sort of faith without a dogma (Ferrarotti, 1993). This new rituality therefore expresses the creativity of postmodern society and its numerous tribes.

So, there is no consensus as to what postmodernity is. One current of thought declares it to be the accomplishment of the process of individualization (Lipovetsky, 1983; 1987; 1990; 1992), while another claims it is the beginning of a reverse movement of social recomposition on the basis of ephemeral tribes (Maffesoli, 1988; 1990; 1992; 1993). In fact, it even seems to be the case that the four modes of social links presented in Figure 4.1

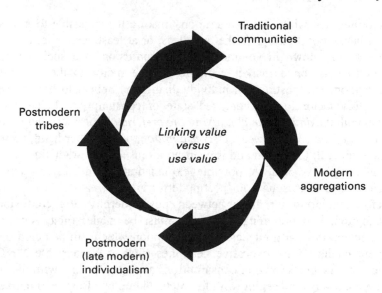

Figure 4.1 *A social link approach (Cova, 1993)*

coexist today: traditional communities, modern aggregations, postmodern (or late modern) individualism, and postmodern tribes. This can explain the coexistence of different forms of consumption: from an individualized consumption to a tribalized consumption with, in between, modern mass consumption and traditional local consumption (founded on reciprocity of a non-economic nature). And these different modes of consumption, like the different modes of social link, can be experienced by the same person in the course of daily life.

Confusion in consumption

A marketing revolution! In the coming years, consumer hunting is going to be a really difficult sport. My target? My segment? My lifestyle? How simple it was when the customer corresponded to categories, when his/her SPC [socio-professional category], his/her sex and his/her age indicated the contents of his/her trolley and the capacity of his/her car. Today, panels [market tests] are going crazy, life-cycles can be counted in months, and the consumer no longer heeds the seasons since the champions of the short circuit offer six a year . . . At the turn of the century, the consumer is giddy.

'Profile of the new consumer', *L'Expansion*, 15 October 1992

The consumer is giddy, he/she does as he/she pleases, upsetting all the modern reference systems which had organized individuals according to categories. Furthermore, he/she is fickle and unreliable, he/she buys black in the morning and white in the afternoon, making it impossible to pin down his/her behaviour. Finally, he/she buys less, or at least spends less (as sales have not gone down in volume), causing confusion in a socio-economic system founded on a market economy whose motor is the increase of consumption. So, 'postmodern individualism' may appear to be a powerful explanatory factor for the confused state of consumption. Indeed, it can explain both the *difficulty in classifying the preferences* of consumers and the *instability of these preferences. Deconsumption*, on the other hand, seems to be more difficult to explain and is even, in a sense, in contradiction with the individualist movement. A possible explanation for deconsumption will therefore have to be sought in 'postmodern tribalism'.

Before exploring the links between postmodernity and confusion in consumption, two preliminary remarks must be made. First, sensational comments on the confused state of consumption which can be heard on the different media with provocative headlines such as 'Impossible Mr Consumer' or 'The breakdown in consumption' are often in tune with the times but are not always in keeping with the facts. Numerous European marketing managers and consultants[2] talk of the relative stability of the majority of consumers, confusion being limited to a fringe, perhaps growing, but still a fringe of all consumers. Some socio-economic studies conducted among readers of the women's press (Cova et al., 1993) show that, at the beginning of the 1990s, the percentage of women who could be called postmodern was about 30 per cent for countries like France or Italy, 25 per cent for the Netherlands, and down to 17 per cent for Germany, and to less than 5 per cent for Portugal. In each country a great difference has been recorded between the increasingly postmodern urban woman and the rural woman, who is sometimes not yet modern but remains traditional.

Secondly, confusion and giddiness are relative. From a modernist mechanistic perspective, the fact that more and more consumers no longer fit into predefined categories, which make their behaviour predictable, is a cause of real confusion. From a postmodernist perspective, it is first possible to think of categories other than those defined by modernity to classify the consumer (lifestyles are a first attempt at this, already overtaken by events). Above all, it may be possible to consider giving up the study and the classifying of the consumer and instead to take an interest in consumption: 'by having limited the study of consumption to the study of the customer, the research has only achieved partial results. In fact, it has obstacled the acquisition of a real understanding of market phenomena, because it has not been able to reflect the complex, multidimensional nature of the process of purchasing, nor its evolution' (Fabris, 1990: 67). Instead of pinning down the consumer, postmodern consumer research has to take an interest in the situations of consumption (Dubois, 1991) and their physical surroundings (Aubert, 1992), in the rituals of consumption (Belk et al., 1989; Wallendorf and Arnould, 1991), in consumption trends (Morace, 1990), and so on, all of which influence the mood and the behaviour of the customer. And this does not make it necessary to hunt down the consumer to fit him/her into segments or even niches.

So, individualism seems to be able to explain, in large part, the present confusion over consumption. The *difficulty in classifying the preferences* of the consumer, that is to say the impossibility of explaining and predicting his/her behaviour according to social indicators, can be explained by the determination to be a person, in the full sense of the word, and not a number in a social class where behaviour is supposed to be identical. The days are gone (the 1960s) when a secretary could cause a scandal in a company because she arrived at the factory in a car associated with another social class. At that time, no words were strong enough to describe her behaviour: 'but who does she think she is?', 'she doesn't know what she's doing!', and other, even crueller, remarks. Sometimes, the scandal could even make the person go back on her choice and buy a car more in keeping with her social status. Today, a minister can arrive at Matignon in a 2CV and an unemployed person can drive a BMW or Mercedes without anyone turning a hair, apart from tax inspectors. The possibility of free choice for the postmodern individual in all aspects of daily life, without limits being imposed by any social constraints, is totally in step with preferences which have nothing to do with class. In fact, for him/her, the essential quality of products and services is the 'zero defect' and their main virtue is to serve and satisfy his/her slightest needs in a personalized fashion. Their use value may be functional (material attributes), symbolic (immaterial attributes) or a mixture of the two; what seems always at stake is the person in his/her independence and his/her distinction compared with others. Objects circulate from producers to consumers who have no *a priori* social link (self-service); if a minimum social link exists, it is at the service of the economic link, and therefore at the service of the independence of the person freed of his/her public, social obligations and who can choose the obligations he/she wishes in the private sphere.

In the same vein, the *instability of the preferences* of the consumer indicates the free choice of the postmodern individual in every sphere of daily life. He/she may purchase the same food item one day at the most basic hard discounter and the next day at Marks and Spencer or even Fauchon. He/she may dress in the morning like the concierge and in the afternoon like a top model. He/she may adopt several different lifestyles in the same day. In fact, for the postmodern person, the leitmotif is: 'it is as I wish and when I wish' according to the mood of the moment. The postmodern person is therefore in perpetual social movement, and he/she is unpredictable even in relation to his/her former behaviour. Some see in this erratic behaviour the very ransom of liberty and of social destructuring: 'the individual is certainly freer, but he/she also pays the ransom for this liberty and for the profusion of brands and products. Without orientation and a compass, he/she yields to the temptation of trying everything as if consumption were a game. Therefore, he/she becomes increasingly unfaithful to products and takes ever greater pleasure in changing the way he/she consumes' (Weil, 1993: 26). He/she is so unpredictable that some think that the individualism of today opens the way for a different representation of the consciousness of the individual (Dennett, 1993): not a single consciousness, but a multiple one, thus breaking with the Cartesian tradition. According to this idea, the conscious self is only a weaving, a momentary coming together of functions, at times linked by a single common thread. The extreme case of multiple personality disorder (MPD: Putnam, 1989), when a person assumes successively different personalities, is evidence of the re-emergence of the multiple consciousness, repressed by modernity and rationality.

One of the important consequences of individualism is that the postmodern individual, who has become his/her own Pygmalion, is on a ceaseless identity quest (Weil, 1993), a quest for the meaning of his/her life. Everyone constructs him/herself and his/her life like a work of art, which leads to an aestheticization of everyday life, and consequently to an aestheticization of consumption (Featherstone, 1991). In the absence of traditional or modern references – a consequence of the decomposition of traditional communities and modern utopias – the individual turns towards objects and services, that is to say the system of consumption, in order to forge an identity. He/she has 'thirst for values' reads another provocative title in the press, and this thirst for values appears to be the consequence of a 'lack of community' (Elliott, 1993: 138). Thus, the system of consumption becomes central to the existence of the individual (Featherstone, 1991), and the products represent veritable social hybrids, quasi-objects and quasi-subjects (Latour, 1991), which are increasingly replacing the other (human) in the process of identity creation. Thus, entire stretches of life, yesterday sheltered from the market sphere, today become commodities that can be exchanged for cash. Consequently, by paying, the postmodern individual can build an identity for him/herself with cultural symbols and references (plays, exhibitions, films, books), humanitarian references (the French doctors, Bosnia, Somalia), but also sporting references (the complete outfit of the Manchester United supporter), and, in fact, all possible references, since, in a postmodern universe where eclecticism and the confusion of values reign, everything can be taken and assembled according to the free choice of the individual.

And this phenomenon is likely to expand with the development of virtual reality where the individual will be able to build for him/herself successive virtual identities ('liquid selves') totally under control, without having to take all the risks involved in the social link. All instruments invented by science and technology, and particularly electronics, are 'anti-link' instruments which are likely to increase the isolation of the individual while paradoxically favouring communication and the circulation of people: virtual shops, working from home, E money, all-in-one computer-fax-telephone and so on. The notion of 'nomad of the present' adopted by numerous technocrats in order to promote a new organization of work ('the virtual company'), and the development of new technical objects ('nomadic objects'), thus hide a vision of the relatively dehumanized man woman: 'an interactive communicational particle, in perpetual feed-back, plugged into the network and visualizing the podium' (Baudrillard, 1992: 149). Taken to the extreme, this means the individual will be able to do without direct contact with others. This is already happening for some computer specialists as shown in the following extract from an interview with David Kusek, CEO of Passport Design, a pioneer in music and personal computers:

> The thing I like about computing is you design your own world on this machine and you have total, 100 per cent control of it, and very few external things can affect what happens to you. I got attracted to that, having played in bands for years and having to deal with people, mostly unreliable and unprofessional people. I really was attracted to the computer environment as something I could control and manipulate myself. I got into it. (*Morph's Outpost*, January 1994)

But, on the other side 'a rebellion against objects' is worrying observers of society: 'what strikes me most is the rebellion! Look at the number of people who let things drop. This acute collective clumsiness is spreading like an epidemic. In everything that drops, there is subversion. In fact, these things are dropped because there is today a relationship with objects of hysterical rejection. Before, there was an idyllic and conjugal relationship with objects – it has become hysterical' (Sarduy, 1994). It is possible to suppose that at the beginning of the last century, a four-person family of average means was surrounded by 150 to 200 elements at most, including crockery and clothes. Today, the same family would have a system of about 2500 to 3000 objects (Branzi, 1988), including electrical household appliances and decorative objects – excepting books and cassettes. Throughout a slow but steady process, it has been possible to witness a true revolution which has replaced by goods and various industrial products the traditional presence of a community made up of neighbourhood, and rows of houses where daily tasks were carried out (the wash-house, washing lines, wells). Wishing to liberate the individual from his/her daily tasks, modernity cut him/her off from his/her environment and isolated him/her in the midst of its productions. Today, as one of the consequences of this revolution, daily acts of clumsiness towards objects are perhaps the signal of a deep crisis of the postmodern individual, who has not totally given up satisfying his/her desire for community in a direct way rather than, in a compensatory way, through the products and services of the consumer society.

And *deconsumption*, at its structural level – and not at its transitory level, a consequence of the rise in unemployment and in anxiety – could be linked to the search for the satisfaction of this desire for community which could take two forms:

- rejection of virtual satisfaction through the purchasing and above all the repeated purchasing of the 'new' which lost all its meaning with the crumbling of the modern myth of progress
- seeking for direct satisfaction through emotion shared with others, not through consuming with them, but through 'being' with them.

Tribalism therefore appears to be much more powerful than individualism as an explanation of the phenomenon of deconsumption. The phenomenon of a loss of landmarks and of meaning in daily life – and particularly at work with the redundancies of today – and of having much more free time (not always through choice), together with the phenomenon of rebellion against objects, reinforces the idea of a postmodern tribalist individual who, via consumption, is looking less for a direct means of giving meaning to life than for a means to form links with others in the context of one or several communities of reference. Then, the system of consumption is not always perceived as first and using the social link, but often as second and in the service of the social link.

The link is more important than the thing.

In other words, the postmodern individual values the social aspects of life at the cost of consumption and the use of goods and services. The only goods and services which are valued are those which, through their *linking value*, permit and facilitate social interaction of the communal type. The consequence for consumption may be important. There could be a decrease in the consumption of products and services which isolate people and an increase in those which bring people together. But, as these last are few in number, individuals would go back to 'vectors of linking' not sold on the market (example: hashish as a vector of communion and of shared emotion), or would turn the existing vectors away from their original utilitarian finality (example: shopping malls as favourite meeting places for urban tribes: Shields, 1992). Ephemeral tribes which need to consolidate and affirm their union are, in fact, on the lookout for everything that could facilitate and symbolize the communion: a site, an emblem, the support of a ritual of integration, or of recognition. Thus, to satisfy their desire for communities, postmodern individuals seek products and services less for their use value than for their linking value (Godbout and Caillé, 1992). The new tribalism which characterizes postmodernity therefore seems to necessitate a redefinition of the value of objects (Figure 4.1), the latter having to serve at the same time the person in his/her individuality and the group togetherness, the 'among several', the 'between two' and so on. They thus play the role of 'cult object' or of 'cult place', meaning the link and the interdependence between people (link and interdependence refused and even denied by modernity). In postmodernity, the object 'does not isolate but is, on the contrary, like the totem for primitive tribes; it serves as a pole of attraction for postmodern tribes' (Maffesoli, 1993: 22).

In the extreme case, if the hypothesis of 'tribalism plus linking value' comes up against that of 'individualism plus use value', there could be a two-speed consumption, as in the model of the egg-timer: a rise in the consumption of basic products (but with no defects) sold in places like hard discounters, combined with a rise in the consumption of cult objects sold in cult places. Between the two, all products and services too burdensome for their use value (functional or symbolic) and with no linking value would see their sales decline progressively. They would be the main victims of the phenomenon of deconsumption. This outline needs to be tempered by a semiotic reflexion about the meaning ascribed to objects (McCracken, 1988): it is not the producer who decrees that his/her product has a linking value, it is the people who are going to use it who will give it this meaning. Moreover as the meanings of objects are no longer fixed and connected with their functions, but are free-floating, each individual may ascribe different meanings to the objects. There is therefore an extreme relativity in the linking value of a product or a service, contrary to its 'universal' use value as it was perceived in modernity.

From marketing to societing

In the marketing conceptualizations applied to postmodernity, the duality individualism/tribalism, brought to light by the ethnosociological analysis of the social link, can be observed. This duality is even expressed geographically as North American and Anglo-Saxon marketing conceptualizations stem from late modern individualism, whereas the sole marketing conceptualizations stemming from postmodern tribalism can be attributed to authors from Mediterranean cultures.

A feature common to the numerous North American and Anglo-Saxon marketing approaches which are trying to adapt to postmodern fragmentation and individualism is the search for the 'proximity of the consumer'. Be it 'one-to-one marketing' (Rapp and Collins, 1990), 'micro-marketing' (Hapoienu, 1990), 'database marketing' (Davies, 1992) or 'relationship marketing' (Christopher et al., 1992) and other panaceas (see Brown, 1993 for a more complete panorama), their principal aim seems to be to build, develop and maintain the relationship with the customer as an individual, rather than to bombard a market made up of an anonymous mass broken up into homogeneous segments. In order to do so, it is generally recommended to give up mass marketing in favour of direct marketing with the help of a database of clients and known prospects. The credo of marketing practice adapted to the 'age of the individual' can therefore be the following: 'a very personal form of marketing that recognizes, acknowledges, appreciates, and serves the interests and needs of selected groups of consumers whose individual identities and marketing profiles are or become known to advertiser' (Rapp and Collins, 1990: 36). Companies like Quaker Oats or American Airlines adopted such an approach in the USA at the end of the 1980s (see Rapp and Collins, 1990 for detailed case studies).

These approaches are justified by the following arguments:

1   If the market can no longer be cut up into homogeneous and stable segments, the only alternative is to pin down the consumer individually (with the help of computerized information systems), with the possibility

of forming, a posteriori, small groups of consumers in order to facilitate marketing action.

2   If the consumer is fickle and unpredictable it is not as important to predict his/her behaviour as to be able to react immediately to his/her new aspirations through the maintenance of a continuous relationship.

3   If the consumer is individualistic, he/she seeks everything that will permit him/her to maintain and develop his/her liberty, that is to say a relationship of trust with a supplier which guarantees the 'zero defect' or 'total quality' of the material aspects of life.

4   If the consumer wishes to differentiate him/herself, he/she asks for personalized products and services which only a continuous, close and interactive relationship can assure.

Taken together, proponents of these approaches do not call themselves post-modern. They are researchers in marketing interested in postmodernity (Badot and Cova, 1992; Brown, 1993) who have reintegrated these approaches in a postmodern perspective.

The work of Firat and Venkatesh (1993), on the other hand, clearly expressed the wish to examine the impacts of postmodernity for marketing practice. Following on from their early works, and starting with the observation (1993: 239) that the market has become central in our societies whereas all other institutions and forms of mediation have lost a large part of their legitimacy (state, class, school, family etc.), they consider that the postmodern individual gives a meaning to his/her life essentially through consumption and that marketing may already be the major postmodern institution ('Postmodernity: the age of marketing'). They derive seven possible consequences of this for the practice of marketing in postmodernity:

1   Thanks to the confusion of values and generalized eclecticism, marketing can today penetrate areas which had so far been closed to it, such as art, culture and ideology: 'the consumer increasingly becomes a consumer of culture, and culture increasingly becomes a marketable commodity' (1993: 245).

2   Because of the fragmentation, the transience and the diversity of styles, marketing is having to constantly renew the meanings and representations ascribed to the product which, itself, has no need to change: 'the image does not represent the product, but the product represent the image' (1993: 244).

3   Because of the rejection by individuals of the dominant values and of everything that is 'normal' (or is in the process of becoming normal), and the desire to do 'one's own thing', marketing is as interested in the diversity of marginal lifestyles as in the dominant model in society.

4   As the postmodern individual prefers simulation to 'reality', he/she can choose to live all his/her consumption activities in a virtual manner (in the sense of virtual images) and favour a marketing system which enables him/her to do shopping without leaving home.

5 As the educational system is still based on modern institutions which are not adapted to the postmodern generation, the marketing system, which plays the role of generating values and meanings, has therefore become the principal vector of education in our societies.
6 Because of the confusion of 'genres' and particularly the blurring of feminine/masculine bipolar categorization, marketing has to change its representation of the 'ideal' consumer (the housewife) both on the level of strategic thinking and on the level of communication and of images: 'both men and women thus become ideal consumers and producers' (1993: 244).
7 Thanks to the globalization of culture, transnational companies are becoming, through their marketing actions, agents of cultural change *par excellence*. Firat and Venkatesh consider that, in postmodernity, 'marketing is the conscious and planned practice of signification and representation' (1993: 246).

Firat and Venkatesh (1993) therefore go further than the previous North American and Anglo-Saxon approaches which were only interested in one aspect of postmodernity: the mechanical aspect of market fragmentation. These approaches seem in fact still too modern for they focus on the functionality of the offer and do not manage to take into account the postmodern movement of aestheticization of everyday life which gives a privileged place to emotions, representations, symbolism and the cultural aspects of the offer (Featherstone, 1991). Elliott (1993: 136), in the same vein as Firat and Venkatesh, considers that the meanings conveyed by objects have, for the postmodern person, as much importance (if not more!) as their instrumental functions. He insists on the fact that the meanings of objects are no longer fixed and linked to their functions, but are free-floating as each individual may ascribe the meanings he/she desires to the objects. Finally, Elliott (1993: 138) makes the hypothesis that, in a more and more individualistic and atomized society, the 'lack of community' has to be compensated by the consumption of signs and symbols which reassures the individual of his/her identity and gives a meaning to his/her life,[3] while giving him/her the illusion of belonging to a virtual community of consumers (Belk and Bryce, 1993: 293). Elliott concludes from this (like Firat and Venkatesh, 1993) that the marketing system plays a primordial role in the construction of the identity of postmodern individuals.

Firat and Venkatesh (1993) and Elliott (1993) thus share the preoccupations of the so-called Latin school of thought in postmodern marketing which aims to make marketing play a societal role. But where Firat and Venkatesh (1993) and Elliott (1993) perceive marketing as a system, making it possible to fill the postmodern vacuum caused by the 'lack of community', the Latin researchers propose a view of marketing as a 'vector of the community link'. This Latin view, sometimes called *societing* (Badot et al.,

1993), sees the marketing as the activity of project and design of innovations destined to facilitate the co-presence and the tribal aggregations of
individuals.

In a more precise way, the representatives of the Latin view (Badot et al.,
1993; Bucci, 1992; Cova and Svanfeldt, 1993; Gobbi et al., 1990; 1993)
also reproach 'one-to-one marketing' and other individualistic marketing
panaceas (Brown, 1993) with not being completely in step with postmodern
times in their desire to be the closest to a known customer, without sharing
any emotion with him/her. They reproach them with confusing proximity
and intimacy, and with basing everything on 'customer service': postmodern
persons do not want to be only the object of an individualized service in
terms of personalization of functions, they also want a personalized link. In
the same way, postmodern persons are looking not only for products and
services which enable them to be freer, but also for products and services
which can link them to others, to a community, to a tribe. In order to grasp
the specificity of the Latin approaches in postmodern marketing, it is
necessary to return to the principle underlying postmodern tribalism: in
products and services, the *use value* (functions and symbols at the service of
the individual as a means of distinction) is being sought as much as the
linking value (link with the other or with others and means of tribal
symbiosis). A product or a service would thus be able to play the societal
role of mediator between individuals. It would be a factor of co-presence,
and of effective co-presence, not of solitude in a lonely crowd! Again, we
can use the postmodern leitmotif: the link is more important than the thing
(e.g. the thing is only the societal support of the link).

According to the Latin view, the marketing problem companies are facing
in postmodernity therefore seems to be that they produce goods and services
which, when placed on the market, become commodities with a certain use
value (even symbolic) for an individual taken in isolation, but are only rarely
objects or places with an aesthetical potential of linking value for a
community of individuals. On the basis of this statement, some propositions
have been put forward by Mediterranean representatives.

The concept of *socio-sensitive innovation* (Gobbi et al., 1990) or *societal
innovation* (Cova and Svanfeldt, 1993) has been put forward to designate the
process through which new significations and new possibilities of emotion
are introduced in the postmodern social system. Societal innovations appear
capable of bringing together emergent socio-cultural trends and enlarged
technological possibilities. They result from the recombination of familiar
material in unconventional ways and they serve as a means by which a
society both encourages and endures change. Societal innovations completely renew the product or the service through the more or less conscious
consideration of a new experience shared by customers: see, for example,
the cases of the Acova radiators and the Découvertes Gallimard collection in
France (Cova and Svanfeldt, 1993) and the cases of the weekly paper *Cuore*
and the boutiques Max and Co. in Italy (Gobbi et al., 1993). These

innovations are supported by socio-cultural trends that, at the same time, they reinforce and sometimes even start up; consequently, some (Badot and Cova, 1992; Bucci, 1992) speak in this case of 'trend marketing' to qualify this postmodern marketing practice. Societal innovations can have a trans-segmented potential (Gobbi et al., 1993) and be adopted by several groups or have limited potential and only affect some tribes. Their success (1993: 210) seems to stem from the spontaneous communion of the individuals they provoke and their resulting role of social support. The conditions of this success were brought to light by Cova and Svanfeldt (1993): Japanese flavoured marketing and management methods blended with the vision of an artist-entrepreneur. Along the same line of thought, Bucci (1992) insists on the conditions behind the emergence and the development of innovations with a strong aesthetic potential: a design director (or art director) capable of inspiring the company to adopt a particular style and rhythm, thus giving the company a true competitive advantage based on emotion.

The concept of ethnomarketing (Badot et al., 1993), or the analysis of postmodern rituals of consumption (see also Belk et al., 1989; Wallendorf and Arnould, 1991), has been developed to bring together the return of rituals in their profane form and the practice of marketing. Ethnomarketing seeks out the link between the practices of consumption and the tribal *imaginaire*, starting with the idea that people do not function in a social vacuum, acting on the sole impulse of advertising impacts. The meaning ascribed to products and services is often related to societal occasions and to social links, and rituals are one of the best collective opportunities to affirm, evoke, assign, or revise these meanings. Consequently, the objective of ethnomarketing is to pin down elements of an intangible nature which are inperceptible taken one by one, but can be discerned in situations taking place in an atmosphere of trust established over a period of time. These situations when repeatedly enacted are in fact rituals created around objects or places in circumstances of both functional and aesthetic use. In modernity, a few privileged moments existed to enact rituals and many rituals have disappeared, thus depriving the product or the service of this aura of mystery and sacredness which used to give it a specific identity by giving it a meaning. With the rejection of materialism and the aestheticization of every-day life which characterize the postmodern condition, the search for rituals and their integration in the design of products and services can play the role of the active memory of a society seeking the sacred. So it is that today 'many businesses owe their livelihoods to their ability to supply ritual artifacts, or items used in the performance of rituals, to consumers' (Solomon, 1992: 529). Ethnomarketing isolates repeated fragments of daily life in order to derive deep significations from them, together with forms of relation between objects or places and people. The ecology of human relations, that is to say the aptitude to define new ritual codes of behaviour between people, particularly through objects and places, has therefore become one of the major themes of postmodern marketing (Badot et al., 1993).

Finally, services marketing provides an ideal context for the concept of linking value to be seen in action. Indeed, service sites design is today still largely oriented towards the functional maximization of space for the satisfaction of an isolated user (Aubert, 1992). In a postmodern perspective, if service sites were to assume the role of social support (Goodwin et al., 1992) they traditionally provided (the wash-house, the town square, the pub), they would be perceived as the favourite places of urban tribes for the enactment of their rituals of integration and recognition. This is already the case when shopping malls are taken over by gangs of teenagers (Shields, 1992). This is the move certain service companies are trying to make: through the creation of 'common places' they try to participate in the (re)construction of social links and make a very favourable impact on customer satisfaction. Hotel chains are now moving in this direction as they realize that postmodern individuals are no longer seeking the 'cocoon-prison' hotel (to borrow an expression used in a RISC survey) where they remain cloistered in their rooms in order to benefit from all the personalized services of the hotel. What they are looking for now is the 'contact hotel' which has an open, friendly atmosphere where new acquaintances can be made, and where they can share their evening meal with the hotel managers (see for example the development of the Campanile chain in France).

Conclusion: the re-embeddedness of marketing

This chapter has investigated the phenomenon of postmodernity as it influences consumption and marketing. First, it explored the consequences of postmodernity at the level of social links. Secondly, it derived an ethno-sociological framework to understand the confusion in consumption. Thirdly, it related this framework to postmodern marketing conceptualizations and especially the so-called 'societing'. The central leitmotif of 'societing' – *the link is more important than the thing* – leads researchers to analyse economic activity not as an independent activity but as one embedded in a societal context which, at the same time, encompasses it and renders it possible. Today, some researchers prefer to speak of socio-economic activity to designate the action of companies. Consequently, we are witnessing the end of the modern phenomenon of the disjunction of spheres of activity (economic, social, religious, political) and the reintegration of each activity within a total societal context. Consumption can therefore be studied as much for its functional and symbolic aspects relative to the individual as for its emotional and aesthetic aspects relative to the link between individuals. And marketing can be defined less as the launching of a product on a market than as the ascribing of a meaning in a society. After having borrowed extensively from economics and psychosociology, marketing seems to need to resort to anthropology and ethnosociology in order to re-embed its approach. Rethinking marketing is rethinking its essence in the socio-economic paradigm.

Notes

1 Aesthetics has to be understood here, not in its restricted modern sense of superficial beauty, but in the full sense of the word as living emotions, feelings, shared passions (Maffesoli, 1990).
2 European Survey conducted in 1993 by the Laboratoire d'Analyses et de Recherches sur la Mutation des Marchés (LARMM), EAP, Paris.
3 Where we speak of meaning here, it is of the meaning individuals give to their social relations, i.e. the societal meaning. And it is clearly of this meaning that people are speaking when they discuss the meaning of their life (Augé, 1994).

References

Aubert, V. (1992) 'Le design d'environnement commercial: un outil de gestion pour les entreprises de service', in *Actes du 2ème Séminaire International de Recherche en Management des Activités de Service*, La Londe Les Maures, Juin. pp. 2–23.
Augé, M. (1994) *Le Sens des autres: actualité de l'anthropologie*. Paris: Fayard.
Badot, O. and Cova, B. (1992) *Le Néo-marketing*. Paris: ESF.
Badot, O., Bucci, A. and Cova, B. (1993) 'Societing: managerial response to European aestheticization', *European Management Journal*, Special Issue EAP 20th Anniversary: 48–56.
Baudrillard, J. (1986) *Amérique*. Paris: Grasset.
Baudrillard, J. (1992) *L'Illusion de la fin, ou la grève des évènements*. Paris: Galilée.
Bauman, Z. (1992) 'A sociological theory of postmodernity', in P. Beilharz, G., Robinson and J. Rundell (eds), *Between Totalitarianism and Postmodernity*. Cambridge, MA: MIT Press. pp. 149–62.
Belk, R.W. and Bryce, W. (1993) 'Christmas shopping scenes: from modern miracle to postmodern mall', *International Journal of Research in Marketing*, 10: 277–96.
Belk, R.W., Wallendorf, M. and Sherry, F. Jr (1989) 'The sacred and the profane in consumer behavior: theodicy on the Odyssey', *Journal of Consumer Research*, 16 (June): 1–38.
Branzi, A. (1988) *Pomeriggi alla media industria*. Milan: Idea Books.
Brown, S. (1993) 'Postmodern marketing?', *European Journal of Marketing*, 27 (4): 19–34.
Bucci, A. (1992) *L'impresa guidata dalle idee: management dell'estetica e della moda*. Milan: Domus Academy.
Christopher, M., Payne, A. and Ballantyne, D. (1992) *Relationship Marketing: Bringing Quality, Customer Service and Marketing Together*. Oxford: Butterworth-Heinemann.
Cova, B. and Svanfeldt, C. (1993) 'Societal innovations and the postmodern aestheticization of everyday life', *International Journal of Research in Marketing*, 10: 297–310.
Cova, B., Rad-Serecht, F. and Weil, M.C. (1993) '*Elle* goes European: the internationalization of *Elle* magazine', in C. Halliburton and R. Hünerberg (eds), *European Marketing: Readings and Cases*. Wokingham: Addison-Wesley. pp. 476–89.
Davies, J.M. (1992) *The Essential Guide to Database Marketing*. London: McGraw-Hill.
Dennett, D.C. (1993) *La Conscience expliquée*. Paris: Odile Jacob.
Dubois, B. (1991) 'Le consommateur caméléon', *Harvard – L'Expansion*, Eté: 7–13.

Ehrenberg, A. (1991) *Le Culte de la performance*. Paris: Calmann-Lévy.

Elias, N. (1991) *La Société des individus*. Paris: Fayard.

Elliott, R. (1993) 'Marketing and the meaning of postmodern culture', in D. Brownlie, M. Saren, R. Wensley and R. Whittington (eds), *Rethinking Marketing. New Perspectives on the Discipline and Profession*. Coventry: Warwick Business School. pp. 134–42.

Fabris, G. (1990) 'Consumer studies: new perspectives', *Marketing and Research Today*, June: 67–73.

Farrugia, F. (1993) *La Crise du lien social: essai de sociologie critique*. Paris: L'Harmattan.

Featherstone, M. (1991) *Consumer Culture and Postmodernism*. London: Sage.

Ferrarotti, F. (1993) *Le Retour du sacré: pour une foi sans dogme*. Paris: Méridiens Klincksieck.

Firat, A.F. and Venkatesh, A. (1993) 'Postmodernity: the age of marketing', *International Journal of Research in Marketing*, 10: 227–49.

Gobbi, L., Morace, F., Brognara, R. and Valente, F. (1990) *I boom: prodotti e società degli anni' 80*. Milan: Lupetti.

Gobbi, L., Morace, F., Brognara, R. and Valente, F. (1993) *I nuovi boom: tendenze e prodotti di successo negli anni della transizione*. Milan: Sperling and Kupfer.

Godbout, J.T. and Caillé, A. (1992) *L'Esprit du don*. Paris: La Découverte.

Goodwin, C., Adelman, M. and Ahuvia, A. (1992) 'Social support through the service interaction', in *Actes du 2ème Séminaire International de Recherche en Management des Activités de Service*, La Londe Les Maures, Juin. pp. 79–90.

Hapoienu, S.L. (1990) 'The rise of micromarketing', *The Journal of Business Strategy*, November/December: 37–42.

Latour, B. (1991) *Nous n'avons jamais été modernes: essai d'anthropologie comparée*. Paris: La Découverte.

Lipovetsky, G. (1983) *L'Ère du vide: essais sur l'individualisme contemporain*. Paris: Gallimard.

Lipovetsky, G. (1987) *L'Empire de l'éphémère: la mode et son destin dans les sociétés modernes*. Paris: Gallimard.

Lipovetsky, G. (1990) 'Virage culturel, persistance du moi', *Le Débat*, May–August: 264–9.

Lipovetsky, G. (1992) *Le Crépuscule du devoir: l'éthique indolore des nouveaux temps démocratiques*. Paris: Gallimard.

Lyotard, J.F. (1979) *La Condition postmoderne*. Paris: Minuit.

Maffesoli, M. (1988) *Le Temps des tribus: le déclin de l'individualisme dans les sociétés de masse*. Paris: Méridiens Klincksieck.

Maffesoli, M. (1990) *Au creux des apparences: pour une éthique de l'esthétique*. Paris: Plon.

Maffesoli, M. (1992) *La Transfiguration du politique: la tribalisation du monde*. Paris: Grasset.

Maffesoli, M. (1993) *La Contemplation du monde: figures du style communautaire*. Paris: Grasset.

McCracken, G. (1988) *Culture and Consumption: New Approaches to the Symbolic Character of Consumer Goods and Activities*. Bloomington, IN: Indiana University Press.

Melucci, A. (1989) *Nomads of the Present*. London: Radius.

Melucci, A. (1991) *Il gioco dell'io: il cambiamento di sé in una società globale*. Milan: Feltrinelli.

Morace, F. (1990) *Controtendenze: una nuova cultura del consumo*. Milan: Domus Academy.

Putnam, F.W. (1989) *Diagnostic and Treatment of Multiple Personality Disorder*. New York: Guilford.

Rapp, S. and Collins, T. (1990) *The Great Marketing Turnaround: the Age of the Individual and How to Profit from It.* Englewood Cliffs, NJ: Prentice-Hall.

Sarduy, S. (1994) 'La rebellion contre les objets', interview with Bernard Cova, *Design Management*, 5: 19–21.

Shields, R. (1992) 'The individual consumption culture and the fate of community', in R. Shields (ed.), *Lifestyle Shopping: the Subject of Consumption.* London: Routledge. pp. 99–113.

Solomon, M.R. (1992) *Consumer Behavior: Buying, Having and Being.* Boston: Allyn & Bacon.

Virilio, P. (1993) *L'Art du moteur.* Paris: Galilée.

Wallendorf, M. and Arnould, E.J. (1991) 'We gather together: consumption rituals of Thanksgiving Day', *Journal of Consumer Research*, 18 (June): 13–31.

Weil, P. (1993) *À quoi rêvent les années 90? Les nouveaux imaginaires. Consommation et communication.* Paris: Seuil.

5   Exchange, Institutions and Time

Luis Araujo

In their book Sheth et al. (1988) identified 12 different schools of marketing thought and might have added to that number. They tacitly acknowledged that the dominant school was that of managerialism. Yet in many ways this school of thought is among the most derivative and impoverished of those described. It springs from micro-economic theory and its success lies not in its conceptual richness or empirical verisimilitude but in its appeal to a constituency, practising and aspiring managers, with the resources to fund its existence and growth. The investment in this school by marketing academics is now so huge it is doubtful that it will be challenged in the foreseeable future.

Occasionally, the supremacy of micro-economics as the core ontology of the managerial school was challenged but with little or no effect on subsequent theorizing. Arndt (1979) attempted to build on the broadening of the concept of 'marketing' to point out the limitations of the traditional concept of 'market'. His main argument was that many competitive markets were being restructured as a result of voluntary and long-term binding agreements between economic actors. Significantly, Arndt (1979: 70) included under the label 'domesticated market' both intra- and interorganizational arrangements, mentioning in the same sentence conglomerates, franchises, joint ventures as well as vertical and lateral integration.

Anderson (1982: 21) puzzled over the question of why marketing, having drifted away from economics because of concerns with greater 'realism', still managed to find itself imprisoned by most of its assumptions. Anderson's main point was that marketing, whilst rejecting most of the methodological and philosophical underpinnings of economics, still managed to retain a large portion of its core ontology. Unlike Arndt, who concentrated on markets, Anderson focused on the lack of an explicit view of the firm in marketing theory.

Nevertheless, while challenging some hidden assumptions both Arndt and Anderson were careful not to rock the foundations of the prevailing orthodoxy. Arndt (1979: 74), for example, calls for a fifth P to be added to the marketing mix for the sake of dealing with administered markets, whilst Anderson (1982: 24) suggests that marketing's role in the constituency-based model of the firm is that of a strong advocate of the marketing concept. The tone of both contributions is one of extension and refinement of key constructs of the managerial school rather than any fundamental redirection.

However there has been, and remains, a concern among marketing academics about the academic respectability and autonomy of the discipline. Over the last decade this concern has manifested itself in a robust debate on the epistemological foundations of research in marketing (see Kavanagh, 1994 for an overview and critique) and sporadic calls for the development of alternative paradigms (Dholakia and Arndt, 1985; Firat et al., 1987). Within the managerial paradigm the concern with academic legitimacy and credibility has resulted in a flight to rigour and quantification, paralleling the path taken by neo-classical economics (see Porter, 1993 and Yonay, 1994 on the triumph of mathematical economics).

Earlier in its history, marketing scholars sought alternative ontologies by which to give the discipline a core of distinctive theory and trace a path that might lead marketing to be recognized as an independent discipline in its own right. Hunt and Goolsby (1988) chronicle the demise of one of these paradigms, the functionalist paradigm, and explain the emergence of the managerial school of thought by reference to the changing nature of the American economy in the 1950s and 1960s and the impact of the two reports on business education commissioned by the Ford and Carnegie Foundations in 1959. In the same vein, Wilson goes as far as stating that the managerially oriented marketing mix approach 'reflected the received theory from the market' (1994: 344).

Recent expressions of dissatisfaction with the managerial paradigm tend to implicitly accept this logic and centre around the demise of the traditional structural contexts for the practice of marketing and the inadequacy of existing frameworks to address new business phenomena (Webster, 1992). Hunt's (1994) critique of current theorizing in marketing questions its status as an applied discipline and blames its self-imposed diet of conjuring up conceptual innovations on an excessive concern with responsibilities towards current practice.

The state of malaise over marketing theory and the need to rethink the discipline's general orientation is now well documented (Brownlie et al., 1994). Proposals for introducing a critical perspective in marketing have been matched by an increasing interest in the history of marketing thought (Cochoy, 1994) and calls for theoretical and methodological pluralism. The rekindled interest in Alderson's work and the concept of exchange is part of this movement as some authors search for integrative 'paradigms' in an effort to redirect marketing theory towards a more systemic approach (Savitt, 1990). For Alderson (1957: 15), marketing is defined as the exchange that takes place between consuming and supplying groups. Alderson is the acknowledged progenitor of this notion and it may have been, ironically, his definitive if cryptic expositions which stifled the development of exchange theory and reduced its influence on the discipline. According to a number of reviewers, his work has been subjected to multiple interpretations and substantial misunderstandings (Barksdale, 1980). Few authors have trod in

Alderson's footsteps and sought to build on the notion of exchange as central to the marketing process (but see Houston, 1994), although the managerial school has paid lip service by incorporating it, detached from its context, into their definitions of marketing. One of the leading exponents and certainly the chief revisionist of the managerial school is Philip Kotler, author of one of the most widely read and reputed marketing textbooks. In its latest edition, Kotler (1997: 11) argues that exchange is the defining concept underlying marketing. Later, the following definition is offered: 'marketing is a social and managerial process by which individuals and groups obtain what they need and want through creating, offering and exchanging products of value with others' (1997: 14).

However, exchange theory has been making a determined comeback in at least one field: that of interorganizational marketing and purchasing. It has done so partly because of the recognition that, in this context at least, it is vital to acknowledge the dyadic nature of market exchanges. Both buyer and seller are important, active parties in the exchange process and may be equally powerful. The concept of exchange also becomes more important where the content and context of exchange is rich and multi-dimensional, and episodes of exchange are embedded into an institutionalized pattern of interorganizational relationships.

In this essay we will contend that the current conceptualization of exchange in marketing is simply too ill defined and hollow to constitute more than a vague foundation for marketing as an academic discipline. The criticisms of the accepted notion of exchange in marketing will be discussed in relation to two interrelated themes: the 'impure' character of economic exchange and the static framework that imprisons conceptions of exchange in marketing.

The first point concerns the fact that economic exchange is often inter-laced with social and political overtones that constitute almost inevitable spillovers of economic exchange. That is not to say that we can't distinguish between economic and other forms of exchange. Indeed the danger is that by promoting a vague and universal definition of exchange, marketing as the 'science of exchange' might be seen to engulf most domains of social, political and economic life (see Walsh, 1994 and Wensley, 1990 for a critique of this notion). Whereas this agenda has consciously been pushed forward by some marketing academics, an expansionist venture founded on such shaky grounds might be ill advised. Economic exchange involves a physical transfer of products, services and money as well as a transfer of property rights (Hodgson, 1988). Economic exchange is embedded in the dense fabric of social relations and is rarely able to rid itself of accessorial baggage such as social and political exchange, kinship and friendship net-works, altruism and gift-giving and a host of other psychological and socio-logical elements (Easton and Araujo, 1992; Friedberg, 1993; Granovetter, 1992).

Those social and political overtones of economic exchange might be seen as minor obstructions or encumbrances but they can also occupy centre stage

if economic actors pursue agendas guided
than the ones envisaged by narrow, util
perspectives on economic action. In other w
complex and varying temporal orientations
exchange episodes may be governed by rul
temporal orientations and mixed motives.

In this essay we rehearse the argument
exchange theory which makes it suitable for
market exchanges, whilst avoiding the probl
tion of exchange. It is a characteristic of
important exchanges are conducted within
stable relationships. This, in turn, implies
tures and such structures must be heavily interconnected. These structures
have, in their turn, been labelled industrial networks and a growing,
complex, diverse and largely European literature in this tradition now exists:
see Johanson and Mattsson (1994) for a recent overview of how research in
this area has evolved in Sweden.

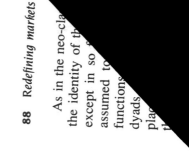

The institutional context of exchange

In traditional marketing theory, transactions are one-time exchanges of value
between two parties that have no prior or subsequent interaction (Webster,
1992). The focus is on voluntary transfer of value from one party to another
with the purpose of enhancing the potency of both parties' assortment
(Houston and Gassenheimer, 1987). Because value may take many different
forms, marketing theory has concentrated on devising comprehensive frameworks for classifying different forms of value and thus understand how
potency is derived from exchange. Few works in marketing theory attempt
to build a more comprehensive view of exchange and distinguish between
different forms of exchange: see Dixon and Wilkinson (1986) for a rare
exception. The relative neglect of the issue of property rights transfer in
economic exchange and the institutional frameworks that support this transfer has, effectively, shunted marketing theory off a comprehensive theory of
markets and exchange. Instead, marketing is regarded as complementary to
economics and, by reducing the level of aggregation, as studying customers
rather than markets (Houston and Gassenheimer, 1987: 15).

The above conclusion is hardly surprising if indeed a one-sided view of
exchange is taken. From an atomized and undersocialized individual as a
market agent, the starting point of neo-classical economics, marketing theory
counter-proposes the atomized and undersocialized dyad as the privileged
unit of analysis. The paths of marketing theory and neo-classical economics
converge again, after the supposedly fundamental distinction between atomized individuals studied at high levels of aggregation, and atomized dyads
studied at low levels of aggregation.

ssical view of markets, marketing theory doesn't regard e parties in exchange as a matter of particular concern – ar as their potency is idiosyncratic – and transactions are be perfectly replaceable across parties with similar utility . In such a world, exchange is effected through atomized sets of abstracted from any social or historical context. An exchange takes e only when actors perceive their holdings to have increased in value hrough the exchange episode. Exchange partners are typically interchangeable given that only their ability to enhance the other party's potency assortment is of interest. In this idealized world, there are no set-up costs involved in establishing an identity in the marketplace since the history of past relations is immaterial and all elements of exchange are contained in sharply defined time frames.

Modern economies, whilst relying on impersonal forms of exchange and complex forms of contracting with third-party enforcement, cannot dispense with other forms of support in the guise of moral, social rules or codes of conduct that are external to the parties involved in the transaction. As North puts it:

> Third party enforcement is never ideal, never perfect and the parties of the exchange still devote immense resources to attempting to clientilise exchange relationships. But neither self-enforcement by parties nor trust can be completely successful. It is not that ideology nor norms do not matter: they do and immense resources are devoted to attempting to promulgate codes of conduct. Equally, however, the returns on opportunism, cheating and shirking rise in complex societies. (1990: 35)

Modern economies are thus characterized by complex patterns of exchange across time and space, deeply embedded in institutional frameworks that support and sustain, albeit imperfectly, those patterns of exchange. Even a simple dyadic exchange is intrinsically woven into an external social and political matrix from which it derives support and which, in turn, contributes to its reproduction and transmutation through the internalization and strategic monitoring of the formal and informal rules involved in the exchange process.

The emergence of market economies, with highly monetized patterns of exchange, does not diminish the need for social solidarity and trust, characteristic of earlier modes of exchange. On the contrary, as Macneil (1986: 592) argues, market economies have acute problems regarding social solidarity. The embeddedness of economic exchange in social structures very often dictates complex legal structures remote from, though essential to, the exchange relations themselves. The solidarity of market exchange is built on – but is not exhausted by – the assumption that property law permits effective present exchanges and that property and contract law permits effective exchanges of obligations. As Mayntz (1993) reminds us, the capacity to act responsibly without being forced to do so and exercise moral self-control is a key characteristic of modern societies and economies. The scope of economic activity and market exchange is encapsulated – to use Etzioni's (1988) expression – in a society's political, legal and social structures but is not totally determined by it. A society's political and social institutions provide a basic structure by which order can emerge and uncertainty can be reduced in exchange, as historical studies of the emergence of market economies (Lie, 1992; 1993) and contemporary, comparative studies of economic systems (see, e.g., Gerlach, 1992; Hamilton, 1994) show.

Giddens (1990) characterizes modernity in similar terms. The separation of time and space in modernity provides the means by which socio-economic activity can be lifted out of the particularities of local contexts and practices. Money, in particular, is singled out by Giddens (1990: 24) as a special case of a disembedding mechanism that reorganizes economic activity across large time–space distances and so lifts exchange out of a particular context. But the use of money as a standardized intermediary in exchange and as a translator of value is dependent on a stabilized and convergent network of actors and institutions that define and sustain the role of money as a universal medium of exchange. Outside these networks, or when these networks do not converge for whatever reason (e.g. lack of trust in the supporting institutional framework), money loses, at least partly, its status as a medium of exchange. In late modernity, trust is displaced from what Giddens (1990: 80) terms 'facework commitments', sustained by and expressed in situations of co-presence, to faceless commitments where trust is placed in abstract systems and institutions. But the emergence of dis-embedding mechanisms in modern societies and economies does not elim-inate the need for facework trust and local rules in economic exchange. It is precisely these informal rules and culturally transmitted norms of behaviour that re-embed economic exchange in specific contexts of action. Economic systems are thus multipolar systems, governed by an impure mixture of different forms of exchange (economic, social, political) that interact and coexist in varied ways. A number of empirical studies have noted that even in commodity and securities markets – close to the idealized notion of perfectly competitive markets – economic activity is embedded in networks of social and political relations that supply rules, norms and relationships that both constitute and govern market processes (Abolafia, 1996; Baker, 1984; Leblebici and Salancik, 1982).

The interdependence between patterns of economic exchange and social structures raises, in contrast to the neo-classical view of exchange taking place between faceless actors, the question of the construction of market actors' identities. Ben-Porath (1980: 6) presents an argument for why there are fixed, non-transferable set-up costs in establishing an actor's identity in the marketplace. First, each actor has some stable traits – for example, honesty, reliability – that interest the other transacting party and affect perceptions of value in exchange. The cost of establishing this mutual view can be regarded as an investment that will facilitate exchange in the future. Secondly, parties to a transaction may have to establish local rules and norms governing their exchange relationships and pertaining to matters such as procedures for settling disputes and conflict resolution mechanisms. The costs of establishing and developing those rules are specific to that relationship and may have to be incurred anew if the parties change. Recourse to third-party enforcement of contractual obligations remains as an option but that too has its costs and is generally avoided (Deakin et al., 1994; Macauly, 1963). Finally, the expectation of continuing exchange and future interactions – 'the shadow of the future' in Axelrod's (1984) felicitous expression – between the two parties has a positive effect on their behaviour. Transacting with individuals and organizations of known identity and reputation generates trust and discourages malfeasance and avoids sole reliance on generalized morality rules or institutional arrangements to guard against broken promises (Granovetter, 1992).

Thus economic exchange in modern societies cannot be reduced to the logic of stable equilibria, as actors pursue self-interest maximization in self-contained and atomized dyads. Even simple transactions involving instantaneous transfer of goods for money depend on a network of linkages connecting the dyad to other economic actors and institutions. Markets are thus not a spontaneous order or a primitive state of nature, but a convergent network of actors and institutions mixing different forms of exchange, and where order is generated by virtue of translation processes and rules that are reproduced across exchanges and over time. Both the stability and the evolution of markets as organized behaviour systems are accomplished outcomes that must be investigated and explained. The failure to research the underlying institutional rules that sustain markets and the multiple logics of exchange that underlie market systems creates a gaping hole in marketing theory.

Recent work in marketing history has looked at early developments of marketing thought and attempted to trace back the origins of the marketing discipline and profession (Fullerton, 1987; 1988a; 1988b; Jones, 1994; Jones and Monieson, 1990a; 1990b). Fullerton concludes that:

> Although marketing in the generic sense of voluntary exchange relationships is timeless, specific variants of marketing thought and practice are historical phenomena – they evolve, and change, and can end. *The advanced marketing of North America and Western Europe – Modern Western Marketing – is a historical phenomenon.* (1988b: 86; added emphasis)

Fullerton's statement is both refreshing and indicative of some of the troubles plaguing vague conceptualizations of exchange in marketing. On the one hand, if we equate marketing with voluntary exchange of any type we will easily find examples of marketing as far back as we care to look (see, for example, Nevett and Nevett, 1994). On the other hand, as Fullerton acknowledges, the practice and theory of marketing are deeply embedded in the development of modern capitalism and its institutionalization as a profession and academic subject taught in business schools. The conditions underlying the formation of markets and the emergence of the modern practice of marketing must thus be the subject of a historical and critical enquiry, aimed at illuminating the conditions underlying their emergence and reproduction. A vague conceptualization of marketing as exchange remains a stumbling block to such an enterprise.

The insensitivity of marketing theory to these issues reflects itself in, for example, an inability to comprehend differences between market systems and to understand that the practice of marketing and the status of marketing professionals are critically dependent on these underlying institutional structures. The fact that, say, marketing is a somewhat peripheral activity in emerging economies in Third World countries or in the advanced Far Eastern business systems reflects a bias towards a universalistic conception of markets and business systems that is unwarranted (Biggart and Hamilton, 1992). Very little is known about how marketing practice and the institutionalization of marketing as a managerial function vary between different contexts and countries, which is rather startling given the purportedly practice-oriented nature of the dominant managerial paradigm (Brownlie et al., 1994).

The implications for marketing theory of a clearer conceptualization of exchange and the understanding of how economic exchange combines with other forms of exchange to produce particular organized behaviour systems are fairly profound. First, by abandoning a vague intention of becoming a 'science of exchange', marketing theory can start to concentrate on what distinguishes economic exchange from other forms of exchange and how these different forms of exchange coexist and interact in economic systems. Secondly, by questioning and researching the rules underlying the formation and workings of different economic systems, marketing can start asking fundamental questions about its own status as a managerial practice and ideology (for a similar argument see Morgan, 1992). The fact that marketing practice is rooted in some fundamental assumptions regarding the workings of economic systems should not blind us to the fact that those assumptions may not apply everywhere and, in any case, are themselves the product of a socially constructed order that needs to be researched and explained.

The temporal nature of exchange

The purpose of this section is to demonstrate that the omission of a notion of time and temporality in marketing theory's view of exchange is also damaging to its aspirations of ever becoming a 'science of exchange'. In particular, we will argue that the move from the study of exchange to exchange relationships in institutional contexts already presupposes a notion of temporality and history. Furthermore, we will attempt to show that a plurality of times rather than one form of time (i.e. standardized clock time) is relevant to the understanding of exchange relationships.

In discussing the primal roots of contract, Macneil (1974) considers that an awareness of time, a perception of the continuum of past, present and future, is crucial to understanding exchange. The notion of relational exchange emerges from the concept that all or most elements of exchange cannot be situated in the present, but are instead projected into the future. In a pure transaction, the goal of both parties is to bring everything from the past and everything in the future to the immediate present – thereby creating a compressed and well-bounded time frame, a sharp-in, sharp-out scenario (Macneil, 1980). But in exchange relations, the parties tend to merge past, present and future in a continuum, taking into account experiential learning in relation to past interactions with the same party and experience from other interactions with whom the focal party has conducted or is conducting relationships. Likewise, the present is often projected into the future through anticipatory action and planning as parties attempt to structure and control their own paths of evolution.

The 'shadow of the future' (Axelrod, 1984) does not simply involve considerations of how trust and cooperation emerge in exchange relationships embedded in networks of social relations. Projection of the future into the present leads parties to look at exchange relationships as more than zero-sum games where self-seeking opportunism in the division of spoils must be guarded against. It provides a clear-cut economic rationale for stable relationships for actors with more than a short-term view of the world. It offers a positive contrast to the negative, atemporal approach implied by neo-classical economics and the transaction cost approach.

Elchardus (1990: 247) presents an insightful distinction between temporal and atemporal or time-negating forms of exchange. A temporal mode of exchange is characterized by a memory of some sort with a capacity to influence the identity of the actors involved, and is able to assimilate the effects of time by redefining itself and the identities of the actors concerned. In addition, it is able to maintain an open future and to leave open the possibility of bracketing or eliminating the effects of memory and the works of time. By contrast an atemporal mode of exchange is constructed on a deliberate attempt at negating the effects of time and memory. The expectation is that the exchange will return to a 'zero state' in which none of the parties is indebted to the other. The notion that one should be able to enter transactions irrespective of past relations and leave without leaving traces for the future is, of course, the hallmark of the theory and practice of discrete, classical contracting (1990: 240).

As Elchardus (1990) points out, the two forms of exchange are heavily interdependent in modern socio-economic systems. The notion that the atemporal mode of exchange is self-regulating and self-reproducing, as implied in neo-classical and marketing theory approaches to exchange, simply neglects the social and political conditions of exchange, as we have argued. Atemporal modes of exchange can be seen as a solution for the 'creation of a world in which action can have foreseeable consequences, while acting will not lead to a locked in position and a closing of the future' (1990: 247). But atemporal exchanges, rather than being self-regulating and self-reproducing, take place in contexts created and reproduced by temporal exchanges. The expansion of market exchanges has been accompanied by a growth in the regulative powers of the state and other collective actors such as corporate hierarchies and different forms of associations (Campbell et al., 1991; Hollingsworth et al., 1994). The lack of a notion of temporality in marketing theory's approach to exchange is thus linked to the neglect of the institutional matrices in which exchange occurs. Even when time is taken into consideration in the context of exchange (Houston and Gassenheimer, 1987; Kaufman and Lane, 1994) it is regarded as a generalized medium of exchange, another resource to be accounted for and traded. Furthermore, if there are variations in how time is accounted for and used, for example as a result of different working patterns or stages in the life-cycle of consumers, it can be usefully employed as another segmentation variable and managerial tool to create competitive advantage (Kaufman and Lane, 1994: 98).

Houston and Gassenheimer (1987: 10) assert that if we limit ourselves to the study of single exchange episodes we ignore much of what is at the heart of marketing. Marketing, they argue, is about building long-term relationships. Relationships, in turn, are regarded as consisting of an established set of expectations about the behaviour of the parties involved. These expectations are assumed either to be built on the moral strictures that each of the parties faces or to be the product of earlier exchange episodes. Expectations, as we argued, are formed at the intersection of general, culturally transmitted formal and informal rules and local rules which re-embed the exchange episode in a specific context of action. Thus the very notion of expectation implies temporality: the horizons of past experience and potential futures are momentarily fused in the intentions and actions of the present.

The standardization and commodification of time in modern economies that Houston and Gassenheimer (1987) and Kaufman and Lane (1994) take for granted is not an independent variable, external to socio-economic processes. As Thompson (1967) and Zerubavel (1981) point out, the notion of time allocation and budgeting, an economy of time, where time is placed on a par with money as a disembedding and universal medium of exchange, is inextricably linked to the rise of modern capitalism. Clock time as unilinear, objective, homogeneous and infinitely divisible time, detached from the phenomenological experience of individuals, is fundamentally implicated in contemporary forms of socio-economic organization (Adam, 1995; Giddens, 1987).

No modern organization or economy can exist outside the realm of standardized clock time. Giddens (1987) regards the timetable as the key chronological device of modern organizations. All timetables, rather than simply describing events and activities and their scheduling, are regarded as essentially time–space coordinating devices. They constitute the medium of coordination of activities dispersed in time and space within and across organizations (1987: 160). Ezzamel and Robson (1995) examine the way in which accounting practices are implicated in the synchronization, sequencing and rate of organizational activities. In particular accounting practices can be instrumental in providing a calculative framework for the allocation of time as a scarce resource and for the scheduling of activities in a particular temporal order.

The commodification and standardization of time have become so all-embracing as to cast doubt on the possibility of the existence of other forms of time (Adam, 1995). But the emergence of clock, universal time doesn't eliminate local forms of time reckoning embedded in the particularities of local contexts and practices. Not all activities, at either intra- or inter-organizational level, need to be aligned or coordinated in terms of clock time or rigid timetables. A plurality of time–space divisions may coexist within the same organization, based for example on task differentiation, or the different cyclical nature of the activities involved (Giddens, 1987). Ezzamel and Robson (1995: 159) underline that some of these cyclical and recursive organizational practices relate to the routines of the state and other institutions (e.g. quarterly financial reports for institutional investors) and escape the discretionary logic of organizational members and the nature of the activities the organization is engaged in.

In the remainder of this chapter we will concentrate on how a plurality of times may impinge upon the logic of interorganizational exchange and how the calculative practices involved in regarding exchange relationships may shape an organization's perceptions of the value of these relationships. Following Halinen and Törnroos (1995) we take the concept of relational time as being particularly relevant to the study of interorganizational exchange.

Relational time has a number of important properties in relation to interorganizational exchange. First, relational time connects past, present and future in an exchange relationship. Interorganizational relationships can be said to exist when exchange episodes form a seamless web, where past events constrain and partly shape the future. The processes that drive the links between small events and the long-run patterns of adaptation between two organizations constitute both the medium and the outcome of what we conceive as the 'relationship'.

These processes have been described in detail by the interaction model to interorganizational exchange patterns (Håkansson, 1982). The conceptualization is of how short-term exchange episodes (which may involve both economic and non-economic forms of exchange) coalesce around patterns that interlock the two parties into an institutionalized relationship. The fact that the relationship becomes institutionalized means effectively that the two organizations are bonded through links that transcend the specific context in which they were forged. The relationship itself becomes an organization, in Giddens's (1987: 153) sense of a social system which has been able to 'bracket time–space' via the reflexive monitoring of its own reproduction and the articulation of its discursive history.

Secondly, relational time is connected to the spatial and cultural order surrounding the relationship. Organizations involved in exchange relationships need to synchronize their activities in time–space. Consider, for example, the case of two organizations involved in a just-in-time delivery system. Deliveries from the supplier need to be finely synchronized with the production schedules of the customer and the two organizations' time schedules become closely intertwined. The common time schedules constitute an important bond between the two organizations (Mattsson, 1985). And as Ezzamel and Robson (1995: 154) point out, delays in delivery may often translate into financial penalties for the party responsible.

At a different level, the cultural order surrounding two organizations has an important bearing on how they relate to each other. Organizations permeated by a cultural order which favours the development of long-term exchange relationships and shuns a logic of utility maximization in every exchange episode may find it hard to deal with organizations subscribing to a short-term, bargain-driving worldview. These different time orientations may stem from idiosyncratic managerial goals and aspirations or from externally imposed chronological codes: consider, for example, the case of a privately owned firm in contrast to a publicly owned corporation, whose managerial team is partly judged on the strength of quarterly or half-yearly results.

Thirdly, relational time is intrinsically related to the problems of agency and structure in socio-economic systems. In this sense, time is not simply standardized, commodified and homogeneous clock time which imposes deadlines, working and leisure time, financial years and planning cycles. Time is also actively constructed and constitutes a way of ordering sets of events, a point of reference for understanding, anticipating and attempting to control other sets of events (Clark, 1990). Temporality is in the events and through the ways they are strung together to form 'histories'; individuals actively pursue the construction and reconstruction of their own lives and career paths, their organization's trajectory of evolution and the relationships it develops. Because these 'histories' are constructed by reflexive selves in interaction with other reflexive selves, they express and create consensus and contribute to the formation of what Sabel (1993) termed deliberate or studied trust.

The way interorganizational relationships are also shaped and cemented by complex forms of social exchange, and involve extensive interpersonal contact patterns often extending beyond the confines of 'working time' (Cunningham and Turnbull, 1982), illustrates how a plurality of time forms is drawn on by individuals to structure their own lives and careers both as organizational employees and as members of society. Interorganizational relationships are primarily marked by events or episodes and some of these episodes can have a lasting impact on how the relationship is perceived and managed on both sides. Mutuality in relationship can only be demonstrated over a period of time, in concrete interaction episodes. Ford et al. (1986: 34) refer to the example of customers of the European pulp and paper industry who in the 1970s still remembered and used in argument how different suppliers had behaved towards them during the scarcity period of the Korean War.

Lastly, organizations may employ a variety of chronological codes in ordering their own activities and in exchange relationships with others. Clark

(1990: 154–5) employs a dichotomy of lean and robust repertoires of chronological codes to exemplify different approaches to the construction of time.
Lean repertoires are homogeneous and emphasize collective punctuality,
formal hours, speed of work, and time as a scarce resource. The future is
regarded as a controllable extension of the present and there are few alternative
chronological codes in managerial cognitive models and language games
to deal with discontinuous change, surprises and unexpected opportunities.
Robust repertoires, by contrast, emphasize heterogeneity of chronological
codes and flexibility. As Clark puts it:

> Robust repertoires are typified by temporal elaboration (cf. conflation) especially
> in the examination of editing of the mutual interpenetration of the past, present
> and future. The future will be prised open by referring to diverse examples in the
> repertoire. Also, the limits of experience will be extended by systematically using
> scenario writing conjointly with the consideration of analytically structured narra-
> tive about past events. These anticipations of the future will involve consideration
> of the contingencies, surprises, hidden consequences and opportunities posed by
> alternatives. (1990: 155)

The concept of lean and robust repertoires is, we suggest, crucial in understanding the way organizations structure their approach to exchange relationships. Lean repertoires internalize the notion of atemporal exchanges
embodied in classical contracting (Elchardus, 1990; Macneil, 1980). The
emphasis on cyclical activities, predictable routines and situating the present
in the future places a premium on protection against surprises, minimizing
risks through the formalization of all aspects of organizational activity and
the reliance on contracts to structure interorganizational exchanges. By
contrast, robust repertoires, by privileging flexibility and taking for granted
the open-ended and uncertain nature of interorganizational exchange, are
open to other forms of structuring interorganizational exchange relationships. The build-up of trust through repeated interactions, an ability to forget
and forgive past mistakes, the existence of informal conflict resolution
mechanisms within a relationship rather than breaking it off or resorting to
the courts, viewing exchange relationships as investments, stand in stark
contrast to the view of exchange relationships presented above.

Thus, the concept of relational time is one way of making the theoretical
leap from discrete, atemporal exchange episodes to exchange relationships
embedded in spatial and temporally delimited institutional contexts. As we
have seen, time does not stand outside exchange relationships but instead
expresses the very nature of what those relationships are. However, the
picture would not be complete if we didn't make a reference to the way
exchange relationships are structured through adaptations that involve
investments in material and human resources and the way time is also
embedded in these investments. Following Johanson and Mattsson (1985)
and Ford et al. (1996) we define investments as processes through which
resources are committed in order to create, build or acquire other resources
which can be used in the future. Ford et al. (1996) warn of the impossibility

of evaluating relationships from a conventional financial perspective. Apart from the problems of reorienting management accounting systems to track down information on relationships, the problems of matching cash inflows and outflows is insurmountable. As they put it:

> Moreover, the incremental benefits and costs to be evaluated also relate to the effect a change in a relationship has on the whole network of relations, and one must seek to isolate these incremental flows from the firm's total flows. Thus it soon becomes apparent that the direct estimation of the financial value of a relationship is impossible. (1996: 151)

Thus somewhat paradoxically, exchange relationships can be seen to both coexist and transcend the calculative processes embodied in normal accounting practices. On the one hand, investment processes in exchange relationships take effect over a period of time, are path-dependent – i.e. the sequence of steps involved in the process of resource commitment and accumulation matters – and create intangible resources whose ownership is distributed and uncertain. Whereas management accounting theory seems to be able to cope with intangible assets whose ownership can be determined (e.g. patents, brand names), the treatment of intangible assets of dubious or uncertain ownership is beyond its frame of reference (Easton and Araujo, 1996). On the other hand, exchange relationships are the very infrastructure through which economic activity is exercised and given meaning (Snehota, 1990). Ford et al. (1986) argue that resources are in themselves passive and fragmented. It is an organization's exchange activities that lead to an activation and integration of these resources. All an organization's decisions on the allocation of, control over, and changes in the resource base occur owing to current or anticipated interaction with others. It is these interactions which define the organization and confer on it an identity, by forcing it to deploy its capabilities and use its resources.

→ The following discussion will attempt to flesh out the meaning of the term 'investment' in interorganizational exchange, bearing in mind the problems associated with stretching the use of the term 'investment' beyond that which is used in conventional accounting theory. For a differently framed discussion on the functions of business relationships but using a similarly nested, multi-level approach to the nature of investments in exchange relationships see Håkansson and Johanson (1993) and Ford et al. (1996). The first kind of investment may be described as minimal investment and is implied by the transaction costs concept of asset specificity and the allied notion of transaction-specific investment. Of the three dimensions used to characterize transactions – frequency, uncertainty and asset specificity – the last has had the highest impact in terms of discriminating between alternative governance structures (Williamson, 1991: 79–80). Asset specificity refers simply to the ease with which an asset can be redeployed to alternative uses and by alternative users without incurring significant loss of value. In practice it is difficult to conceive of many categories of resources – at least in industrial markets – that are so versatile that their value remains constant across a broad range of uses and users. These types of resources are thus non-tradable to a significant degree. From our perspective, minimal investment corresponds to a unilateral investment on an asset or resources that are committed to a limited range of business opportunities. It is simply that investment required to do business. The return to either party is the possibility of exchanges continuing into the future but not its guarantee. It is the ante required to enter and remain in the game. The investment, having been made, is now sunk to a limited range of business opportunities. Both parties can behave opportunistically if they wish.

The second kind of investment may be described as relationship specific. In this case the form of investment is likely to be varied but will be concerned with adaptations of product and production processes, delivery procedures, quality systems, social codes and, perhaps most important of all, trust creation and maintenance activities. The returns to relationship-specific investment will be in the form of increased efficiency, doing the same things but better. Stability in relationships allows both partners to anticipate the future by planning in advance production schedules, deliveries, joint promotion or development activities. The returns can appear anywhere in the organization but can be traced back to the relationship. Stability offers a background of order and predictability against which the future can be brought forward and thus partially controlled.

Asanuma (1989: 21–5) coins the similar term 'relation-specific skill' to characterize the multi-dimensional process of learning and capability development underlying the patterns of interaction and exchange between a supplier and a customer. Asanuma ascribes two basic, interrelated layers to this skill. At a superficial level, the skill consists in the sedimented experience of repeated interactions with the same firm. At a deeper level, the skill consists in the development of basic technological capabilities arising from the problem solving activities involved in responding to customer demands.

The third form of investment is relationship development investment. This allows both parties to invest in the development, as opposed to the utilization, of new and existing resources, of which some may be highly relationship specific (e.g. dedicated machines, skills) and others may be intangible and jointly owned (e.g. image, reputation). The crucial distinction is that the relationship, as a resource, is being used to create other resources: product adaptations, new ways of doing things, access to third parties. The returns have now more to do with effectiveness, having extended the scope, content and process of the relationship. They are more difficult to 'measure' but are also likely to be more valuable.

In both of these cases, related secondary investment decisions may be taken as a result of the opportunities presented by the primary investment in one or more such relationships. They represent the optional benefits attached to the primary, substantive investment decision benefits. As mentioned above, relationship-specific investments generate a variety of resources with varying degrees of specificity. Some of these resources – for example, technological capabilities embodied in human-specific, problem solving skills – may be general purpose and transferable to a broad range of new or existing relationships. The argument here is that relationship-specific investments are crucial in helping organizations to develop general-purpose capabilities and to learn new skills. It is interaction with others and commitment of resources to specific relationships that contribute to organizational growth and learning. This view contrasts with the static view of organizations and resources implied by the transaction cost approach, which sees any transaction-specific investment as having repercussions only at the level of economizing rather than strategizing, to borrow Williamson's (1991) terminology.

On a more general level, stability and the prospect of a continuing relationship reduce uncertainty and lower the threshold risk for new investment of any kind. These secondary investments may or may not be relationship specific and may or may not impact upon the relationships which indirectly promote their conception. The returns are the normal returns to any internal organizational investment. Finally there are the returns generated by the totality of the investments that firms make in the relationships that they enter into. To understand the nature of such investments and returns we have to move from a dyadic perspective to consider a network view of all the relationships a focal firm is involved in. Johanson and Mattsson (1985) use the terms 'marketing' and 'market investments' to refer to the long-term and cumulative nature of the commitment of resources to the build-up of respectively dyadic relationships and network positions. These sets of intangible resources generate a position for the individual firm in the context of the network of other exchange relationships that define its strategic identity. A firm's network position is thus a set of partially controlled, intangible resources that have arisen as a result of the investment nature of the firm's activities. The creation of these intangible resources is the consequence of the alignment and coordination of investments in complementary and co-specialized resources by the focal firm and its exchange partners. Thus the consequences of these investment processes are also interdependent and the timing of investment decisions is crucial.

These notions add up to a picture of firms occupying positions and performing roles in a network of relationships, social and historical entities, located in space and time. Positions in networks create both opportunities and constraints. There are opportunities to access resources controlled by partners (e.g. skills, capital, raw materials) and opportunities to develop new resources through mobilization of complementary resources or interaction of different types of resources (e.g. as when customer knowledge of uses and applications of supplier technology results in the development of new products or production processes). Constraints exist because of the lock-in effect of relationships which results in switching costs if firms have to break existing relationships and create new ones.

Conclusions

This chapter has had as its central concern the connection of a neglected stream of theory in marketing, namely exchange theory, to the new and burgeoning field of interorganizational exchange relationships. At the simplest level, we wanted to demonstrate that current views of exchange in marketing theory suffer from an atomistic bias, compatible with the methodological individualism reigning in neo-classical economics, and from a temporally reductionist perspective. In the former case we argued that all exchanges, individual or organizational, in modern societies are embedded in an institutional matrix which represents an important source of continuity in the operation of markets as organized behaviour systems. As regards the second major criticism of exchange theory, we advanced an argument regarding the need to consider exchange relationships and not simply exchange episodes, based upon temporal and investment arguments. If we conceive durable exchange relationships in organizational markets as being relatively common and understandable via the institutional and investment logic outlined above, then structure and connectedness in industrial systems can be described by the metaphor of a network.

Research on industrial and interorganizational markets has led to the refinement of the concept of exchange and to the conception of markets as networks of connected actors, resources and activities (Axelsson and Easton, 1992; Grabher, 1993; Håkansson and Snehota, 1995). Rather than describe the industrial networks approach, this chapter has been concerned with some of the conceptual foundations of this approach and its conceptual break from current views of exchange prevailing in marketing theory. In this sense, the industrial networks approach attempts to radicalize its opposition to the basic tenets of neo-classical economics that still hold a stifling grip on conceptual developments in mainstream marketing theory. Even though some recent examples of broader-based and critical approaches to exchange have appeared in mainstream marketing theory (see, for example, Gundlach and Murphy, 1993), the need to couch these approaches in terms of usefulness to current managerial practice hampers their development and impact outside the discipline.

The roots and intellectual antecedents of the industrial networks approach have thus more in common with strands of institutional economics and sociological theory, relational contracting approaches in legal theory and innovation studies than with marketing theory of the managerial school variant. It is fundamentally concerned with how different types of economic actors transform, consume, create and use economic resources in industrial systems but views these actors as constituted in interaction with others, their identity being inseparable from the network of exchanges in which they are involved. As we have attempted to show in this chapter, a conceptualizing of exchange relationships outside the strictures of *Homo economicus* implies accounting for the ways economic exchange is itself infused and penetrated by other forms of exchange. Similarly, introducing a temporal perspective into exchange brings into question the sole reliance on clock, universal time as a container of socio-economic life and calls for a conceptualization of the plurality of times implicated in exchange relationships. Furthermore, the notion of economic value created through exchange relationships stands in stark contrast to the calculative and disciplining practices of accounting (Miller, 1994).

In short, a focus on exchange relationships brings to light the ways in which economic exchange is constituted as a practice and a separate sphere of life in contemporary Western societies. It is within this universe that marketing practices and ideology are constituted and legitimized. But rather than to take this universe for granted or to assume its totalizing effect on socio-economic life, a focus on exchange relationships helps to highlight the constructed, provisional and incomplete grip on economic life held by the disciplining effects of practices embodied in institutions such as contract law and accounting. The challenge to marketing theory is thus to resist carrying on with the running repairs on the dominant managerial approach, and to start examining the implications of how an elaboration of exchange theory might help to illuminate the constitution of marketing practice and theory. A heightened sense of history and a genealogy of marketing practices within specific socio-economic contexts might be a useful first step in removing the shackles of the dominant managerial paradigm and fostering the critical perspectives on marketing that this volume is helping to cultivate.

Note

An earlier version of this chapter was presented at the Rethinking Marketing Symposium held at the University of Warwick, 1–2 July 1993. A revised version of that paper was published in the *European Journal of Marketing*, 28 (3): 72–84, 1994. Both of these publications were co-authored with Geoff Easton. His comments and encouragement are gratefully acknowledged. All errors and omissions remain the sole responsibility of the present author.

References

Abolafia, M.Y. (1996) *Making Markets: Opportunism and Restraint in Wall Street.* Cambridge, MA: Harvard University Press.

Adam, B. (1995) *Timewatch: The Social Analysis of Time.* Cambridge: Polity.

Alderson, W. (1957) *Marketing Behavior and Executive Action: A Functionalist Approach to Marketing.* Homewood, IL: Irwin.

Anderson, P.F. (1982) 'Marketing, strategic planning and the theory of the firm', *Journal of Marketing*, 46 (1): 15–26.

Arndt, J. (1979) 'Towards a concept of domesticated markets', *Journal of Marketing*, 43 (4): 69–75.

Asanuma, B. (1989) 'Manufacturer–supplier relationships in Japan and the concept of relation-specific skill', *Journal of the Japanese and International Economies*, 3 (1): 1–30.

Axelrod, R. (1984) *The Evolution of Cooperation.* New York: Basic Books.

Axelsson, B. and Easton, G. (eds) (1992) *Industrial Networks: A New View of Reality*. London: Routledge.

Baker, W. (1984) 'The social structure of a national securities market', *American Journal of Sociology*, 89 (4): 775–811.

Barksdale, H.C. (1980) 'Wroe Alderson's contribution to marketing theory', in P.M. Lamb and C.W. Dunne (eds), *Theoretical Developments in Marketing*. Chicago: American Marketing Association.

Ben-Porath, Y. (1980) 'The F-connection: families, friends and firms in the organization of exchange', *Population and Development Studies*, 6 (1): 1–30.

Biggart, N.W. and Hamilton, G.G. (1992) 'On the limits of a firm-based theory to explain business networks: the Western bias of neoclassical economics', in N. Nohria and R.G. Eccles (eds), *Networks and Organizations: Structure, Form and Action*. Cambridge, MA: Harvard Business School Press.

Brownlie, D., Saren, M., Whittington, R. and Wensley, R. (1994) 'The new marketing myopia: critical perspectives on theory and research in marketing – introduction', *European Journal of Marketing*, 28 (3): 6–10.

Campbell, J.L., Hollingsworth, J.R. and Lindberg, L.N. (eds) (1991) *Governance of the American Economy*. New York: Cambridge University Press.

Clark, P. (1990) 'Chronological codes and organizational analysis', in J. Hassard and D. Pym (eds), *The Theory and Philosophy of Organizations: Critical Issues and New Perspectives*. London: Routledge.

Cochoy, F. (1994) 'The Emerging tradition of historical research in marketing: history of marketing and marketing of history', in G. Laurent, G.L. Lilien and B. Pras (eds), *Research Traditions in Marketing*. Boston: Kluwer.

Cunningham, M.T. and Turnbull, P. (1982) 'Interorganizational personal contact patterns', in H. Håkansson (ed.), *International Marketing and Purchasing of Industrial Goods*. Chichester: Wiley.

Deakin, S., Lane, C. and Wilkinson, F. (1994) 'Trust or law – towards an integrated theory of contractual relations between firms', *Journal of Law and Society*, 21 (3): 329–49.

Dholakia, N. and Arndt, J. (eds) (1985) *Changing the Course of Marketing: Alternative Paradigms for Widening Market Theory*. Research in Marketing Series, Supplement 2 (series editor J.N. Sheth). Greenwich, CT: JAI Press.

Dixon, D.F. and Wilkinson, I.F. (1986) 'Toward a theory of channel structure', in L.P. Bucklin and J.M. Carman (eds), *Distribution Channels and Institutions*. Vol. 8 of Research in Marketing Series (series editor J.N. Sheth). Greenwich, CT: JAI Press.

Easton, G. and Araujo, L. (1992) 'Non-economic exchange in industrial networks', in B. Axelsson and G. Easton (eds), *Industrial Networks: A New View of Reality*. London: Routledge.

Easton, G. and Araujo, L. (1996) 'Characterizing resources as an organizational competence: an industrial networks approach', in R. Sanchez, A. Heene and H. Thomas (eds), *Dynamics of Competence Based Competition: Theory and Practice in the New Strategic Management*. New York: Pergamon Press.

Elchardus, M. (1990) 'The temporalities of exchange: the case of self-organization for societal governance', in B. Marin (ed.), *Generalized Political Exchange: Antagonistic Cooperation and Integrated Policy Circuits*. Frankfurt: Campus.

Etzioni, A. (1988) *The Moral Dimension*. New York: Free Press.

Ezzamel, M. and Robson, K. (1995) 'Accounting in time: organizational time-reckoning and accounting practice', *Critical Perspectives on Accounting*, 6 (1): 149–70.

Firat, A.F., Dholakia, N. and Bagozzi, R.P. (eds) (1987) *Philosophical and Radical Thought in Marketing*. Lexington, MA: Lexington.

Ford, D., Johanson, J. and Håkansson, H. (1986) 'How do companies interact?', *Industrial Marketing and Purchasing*, 1 (1): 25–41.

Ford, D., McDowell, R. and Tomkins, C. (1996) 'Relationship strategy, investments, and decision making', in D. Iacobucci (ed.), *Networks in Marketing*. Beverly Hills, CA: Sage.

Friedberg, E. (1993) *Le Pouvoir et la règle: dynamiques de l'action organisée*. Paris: Seuil.

Fullerton, R.A. (1987) 'The poverty of ahistorical analysis: present weakness and future cure for US marketing thought', in A.F. Firat, N. Dholakia and R.P. Bagozzi (eds), *Philosophical and Radical Thought in Marketing*. Lexington, MA: Lexington Books.

Fullerton, R.A. (1988a) 'How modern is modern marketing? Marketing's evolution and the myth of the production era', *Journal of Marketing*, 52 (1): 108–25.

Fullerton, R.A. (1988b) 'Modern Western marketing as a historical phenomenon: theory and illustration', in T. Nevett and R.A. Fullerton (eds), *Historical Perspectives in Marketing: Essays in Honor of Stanley C. Hollander*. Lexington, MA: Lexington Books.

Gerlach, M.L. (1992) *Alliance Capitalism: The Social Organization of Japanese Business*. Berkeley, CA: University of California Press.

Giddens, A. (1987) *Social Theory and Modern Sociology*. Cambridge: Polity.

Giddens, A. (1990) *The Consequences of Modernity*. Cambridge: Polity.

Grabher, G. (ed.) (1993) *The Embedded Firm: On the Socioeconomics of Industrial Networks*. London: Routledge.

Granovetter, M. (1992) 'Problems of explanation in economic sociology', in N. Nohria and R.G. Eccles (eds), *Networks and Organizations: Structure, Form and Action*. Cambridge, MA: Harvard Business School Press.

Gundlach, G.T. and Murphy, P.E. (1993) 'Ethical and legal foundations of relational marketing exchanges', *Journal of Marketing*, 57 (4): 35–46.

Håkansson, H. (ed.) (1982) *International Marketing and Purchasing of Industrial Goods*. Chichester: Wiley.

Håkansson, H. and Johanson, J. (1993) 'Industrial functions of business relationships', in D. Sharma (ed.), *Industrial Networks*. Vol. 5 of Advances in International Marketing (series editor S.T. Cavusgil). Greenwich, CT: JAI Press.

Håkansson, H. and Snehota, I. (1995) *Developing Relationships in Business Networks*. London: Routledge.

Halinen, A. and Törnroos, J.-A. (1995) 'The meaning of time in the study of industrial buyer–supplier relationships', in K. Möller and D.T. Wilson (eds), *Business Marketing: An Interaction and Network Perspective*. Boston, MA: Kluwer.

Hamilton, G.G. (1994) 'Civilizations and the organization of economies', in N.J. Smelser and R. Swedberg (eds), *The Handbook of Economic Sociology*. Princeton, NJ and New York: Princeton University Press and Russell Sage Foundation.

Hodgson, G.M. (1988) *Economics and Institutions*. Cambridge: Polity.

Hollingsworth, J.R., Schmitter, P.C. and Streeck, W. (eds) (1994) *Governing Capitalist Economies: Performance and Control of Economic Sectors*. New York: Oxford University Press.

Houston, F.S. (ed.) (1994) *Marketing Exchange, Relationships, Transactions and Their Media*. Westport, CT: Quorum.

Houston, F.S. and Gassenheimer, J.B. (1987) 'Marketing and exchange', *Journal of Marketing*, 51 (4): 3–18.

Hunt, S.D. (1994) 'On rethinking marketing: our discipline, our practice, our methods', *European Journal of Marketing*, 28 (3): 13–25.

Hunt, S.D. and Goolsby, J. (1988) 'The rise and fall of the functional approach to marketing: a paradigm displacement perspective', in T. Nevett and R.A. Fullerton (eds), *Historical Perspectives in Marketing: Essays in Honor of Stanley C. Hollander*. Lexington, MA: Lexington Books.

Johanson, J. and Mattsson, L.-G. (1985) 'Market investments and marketing investments in industrial networks', *International Journal of Research in Marketing*, 3 (2): 185–95.
Johanson, J. and Mattsson, L.-G. (1994) 'The markets-as-networks tradition in Sweden', in G. Laurent, G.L. Lilien and B. Pras (eds), *Research Traditions in Marketing*. Boston: Kluwer.
Jones, D.G.B. (1994) 'Biography and the history of marketing thought: Henry Charles Taylor and Edward David Jones', in R.A. Fullerton (ed.), *Explorations in the History of Marketing*. Research in Marketing Series, Supplement 6 (series editor J.N. Sheth). Greenwich, CT: JAI Press.
Jones, D.G.B. and Monieson, D.D. (1990a) 'Early development of the philosophy of marketing thought', *Journal of Marketing*, 54 (1): 102–13.
Jones, D.G.B. and Monieson, D.D. (1990b) 'Historical research in marketing: retrospect and prospect', *Journal of the Academy of Marketing Science*, 18 (4): 269–78.
Kaufman, C.F. and Lane, P.M. (1994) 'Time, potency and exchange: making the most of the time resource', in F.S. Houston (ed.), *Marketing Exchange, Relationships, Transactions and Their Media*. Westport, CT: Quorum.
Kavanagh, D. (1994) 'Hunt versus Anderson: round 16', *European Journal of Marketing*, 28 (3): 26–41.
Kotler, P. (1997) *Marketing Management: Analysis, Planning, Implementation and Control*, 9th edn. Upper Saddle River, NJ: Prentice-Hall.
Leblebici, H. and Salancik, G.R. (1982) 'Stability in interorganizational exchanges: rule-making processes in the Chicago Board of Trade', *Administrative Science Quarterly*, 27 (2): 227–42.
Lie, J. (1992) 'The concept of mode of exchange', *American Sociological Review*, 57(4): 508–23.
Lie, J. (1993) 'Visualizing the invisible hand – the social origins of market society in England, 1550–1750', *Politics and Society*, 21 (3): 275–305.
Macauly, S. (1963) 'Non-contractual relations in business: a preliminary study', *American Sociological Review*, 28 (1): 55–67.
Macneil, I.R. (1974) 'The Many futures of contracts', *Southern California Law Review*, 47 (3): 691–816.
Macneil, I.R. (1980) *The New Social Contract: An Inquiry into Modern Contractual Relations*. New Haven, CT: Yale University Press.
Macneil, I.R. (1986) 'Exchange revisited: individual utility and social solidarity', *Ethics*, 96 (3): 567–93.
Mattsson, L.-G. (1985) 'Application of a network approach to marketing: defending and changing market positions', in N. Dholakia and J. Arndt (eds), *Changing the Course of Marketing: Alternative Paradigms for Widening Market Theory*. Research in Marketing Series, Supplement 2 (series editor J.N. Sheth). Greenwich, CT: JAI Press.
Mayntz, R. (1993) 'Modernization and the logic of interorganizational networks', in J. Child, M. Crozier, R. Mayntz et al. (eds), *Societal Change between Market and Organization*. Aldershot: Avebury.
Miller, P. (1994) 'Accounting and objectivity: the invention of calculating selves and calculable spaces', in A. Megill (ed.), *Rethinking Objectivity*. Durham, NC and London: Duke University Press.
Morgan, G. (1992) 'Marketing discourse and practice: towards a critical analysis', in M. Alvesson and H. Wilmott (eds), *Critical Management Studies*. London: Sage.
Nevett, T.R. and Nevett, L. (1994) 'The origins of marketing: evidence from classical and early Hellenistic Greece (500–300 BC)', in R.A. Fullerton (ed.), *Explorations in the History of Marketing*. Research in Marketing Series, Supplement 6 (series editor J.N. Sheth). Greenwich, CT: JAI Press.

North, D.C. (1990) *Institutions, Institutional Change and Economic Performance.* Cambridge: Cambridge University Press.

Porter, T.M. (1993) 'Interpreting the triumph of mathematical economics', in N. de Marchi (ed.), *Non-Natural Social Sciences: Reflecting on the Enterprise of More Heat than Light.* History of Political Economy, Annual Supplement to Vol. 25. Durham, NC and London: Duke University Press.

Sabel, C.F. (1993) 'Studied trust: building new forms of cooperation in a volatile economy', in D. Foray and C. Freeman (eds), *Technology and the Wealth of Nations: the Dynamics of Constructed Advantage.* London: Pinter.

Savitt, R. (1990) 'Pre-Aldersonian antecedents to macromarketing: insights from the textual literature', *Journal of the Academy of Marketing Science,* 18 (4): 293–301.

Sheth, J.N., Gardner, D.M. and Garrett, D.E. (1988) *Marketing Theory: Evolution and Evaluation.* New York: Wiley.

Snehota, I. (1990) 'Notes on a theory of business enterprise'. Doctoral dissertation, Department of Business Administration, University of Uppsala, Uppsala, Sweden.

Thompson, E.P. (1967) 'Work, time-discipline and industrial capitalism', *Past and Present,* 38: 56–97.

Walsh, K. (1994) 'Marketing and public sector management', *European Journal of Marketing,* 28 (3): 63–71.

Webster, F.W. (1992) 'The changing role of marketing in the corporation', *Journal of Marketing,* 56 (1): 1–17.

Wensley, R. (1990) ' "The voice of the consumer?" Speculations on the limits to the marketing analogy', *European Journal of Marketing,* 24 (7): 49–60.

Williamson, O.E. (1991) 'Strategizing, economizing, and economic organization', *Strategic Management Journal,* Special Issue, 12 (Winter): 75–94.

Wilson, D.T. (1994) 'Commentary on J. Johanson and L.-G. Mattsson's "The Markets-as-Networks Tradition in Sweden" ', in G. Laurent, G.L. Lilien and B. Pras (eds), *Research Traditions in Marketing.* Boston: Kluwer.

Yonay, Y.P. (1994) 'When black boxes clash: competing ideas of what science is in economics, 1924–39', *Social Studies of Science,* 24 (1): 39–80.

Zerubavel, E. (1981) *Hidden Rhythms: Schedules and Calendars in Social Life.* Chicago: Chicago University Press.

6 Commentary

Robin Wensley

A function is explained by its role in the system of which it is part, that is according to the ends which determine its course. When explanation relies on the time factor, causality is restricted to linearity and temporality, and this ignores the possibility of variations in the time scales of different phenomena, and that the relationship between cause and effect may be more complex than sequence. In other words historical explanation is inadequate in itself: analysis of social institutions in terms of their genesis is necessarily partial in ignoring the synchronic dimension. Society is a structure which can be understood in terms of the inter-relation of its parts and a process which can be understood in terms of its past. Exclusive concentration on the process aspect neglects that the meaning of each part is visible synchronically in the present. There is a third type of explanation, in terms of individual motivation, showing how the personality structure is articulated to and reinforces the social structure. These three types of explanation are not separate; individual motivation is determined by socialization which is rooted in the social structure, and in turn maintains it; social structure depends ultimately on the activity of individuals which has a historical aspect, and social change must be on the basis of a given social structure.

(Glucksman, 1974: 150–1)

Most forms of social theory have failed to take seriously enough not only the temporality of social conduct but also its spatial attributes. At first sight nothing seems more banal and uninstructive than to assert that social activity occurs in time and space. But neither time nor space have been incorporated into the centre of social theory, rather, they are ordinarily treated as 'environments' in which social conduct is enacted.

(Giddens, 1979: 201)

Both of the chapters in this part can be seen as very direct responses to the critique that marketing phenomena tend most often to be discussed in a way which ignores the relativities and subjectivities of the time–space context in which they are embedded. Judging by the quotations above it could also be argued that marketing was still only slowly coming to terms with central issues in the sociology of 20 years ago!

Both Cova and Araujo focus attention on the degree to which the basic underlying assumption of much of what might be termed the marketing analysis of market behaviour has remained within the bounds of what can nowadays be termed traditional economic analysis: the world of individual preference functions and spatially and serially independent transactions.

Araujo mainly focuses attention on one type of embeddedness, particularly the extent to which single actions or transactions are embedded in time. He is particularly concerned to trace the historical development of the marketing approach and, in his view, its failure to discard the inherent assumptions of micro-economic analysis. He sees the dominant trend in marketing as having been a shift to managerialism which, despite various rhetorical claims at various times, did not really challenge the transactions-oriented view of the relationship between buyer and seller. He recognizes that some of the key influencers in this development were Wroe Alderson, with his focus on the functional view of marketing, and Philip Kotler, with his seminal textbook(s).[1]

Araujo recognizes that he is not alone in this concern. Bagozzi (1975), for instance, previously attempted to shift the central focus towards an exchange rather than a transactions perspective,[2] and indeed Alderson himself, despite being seen as a prime mover in the functionalist approach, also advocated much more attention to the exchange perspective. However Aruajo's observation is that those who have tried to wrest the central marketing focus away from an individual transactions perspective have remained at best 'footnotes' in the overall development of the field. What might have happened without the early loss of perhaps one of the most effective contributors to this debate on both sides of the Atlantic – Johan Ardnt – is inevitably now just a matter of speculation.

Araujo argues that a central focus on exchange requires both a 'conceptualization of the plurality of times' and a 'notion of economic value . . . in stark contrast to the calculative and disciplining practices of accounting'.[3]

Cova considers how postmodernity supports the notion that in various ways in the process of consumption the links are more important than the thing: or in other terms the object is less important than its embeddedness in social relations and meaning. In covering this area, Cova gives a detailed analysis and review of a field which has acquired the label 'interpretive consumer research' but also emphasizes two particularly important aspects: first, that use value or functionality can remain a central issue; and secondly, that the meaning or the links are to be seen as defined and interpreted by the individual themselves, not by the producer.[4]

This leads him to a number of interesting speculations. One is that a process of 'deconsumption' might result in

> a rise in the consumption of basic products (but with no defects) sold in places like hard discounters combined with a rise in the consumption of cult objects sold in cult places.[5]

A second is that the development of so-called 'one-to-one marketing' is not really, despite its claims, to be seen as a thorough response to the changing nature of the customer. As Cova puts it:

> [they are] confusing proximity and intimacy, and . . . basing everything on 'customer service' . . . postmodern persons are looking not only for products and services which enable them to be freer, but also for products and services which can link them to others, to a community, to a tribe.

Both these chapters raise very significant issues about the nature of marketing as it is commonly researched, taught and codified in our textbooks. Both the authors are clear that in talking about a redefinition of marketing they are also in a sense suggesting that the central focus of study needs to be shifted: in Araujo's case to the nature of 'exchange' and in Cova's to the nature of 'consumption'. Both contributors also recognize that either of these shifts requires that the managerialist orientation of much of current marketing would be challenged directly. Yet as other contributors to this volume elsewhere observe, the praxis of marketing is closely linked in certain domains at least with the legitimacy of marketing itself. Whether we can redefine marketing in the ways that are suggested and yet still retain it as a somewhat coherent domain of study and body of knowledge is itself likely to prove an interesting question!

Notes

1   It is interesting that despite previous work such as Hunt and Goolsby (1988), to which Araujo refers, the historical development of marketing thought remains obscure, or more correctly the extant narratives are very partial. In particular, the relationship between the functionalist, socio-economic perspective that underlies much of Alderson's work and the managerial view which dominates that of Philip Kotler is not well explained.

2   Reflecting, however, Araujo's concern that the espousal of the exchange perspective by a number of marketing writers has remained conflated with notions of marketing management, it is interesting to note the word 'control' in Bagozzi's own summary of his proposal: 'Thus, social marketing is really a subset of the generic concept of marketing in that it deals with the creation and resolution of exchanges in social relationships. Marketers can make contributions to other areas that contain social exchanges by providing theories and techniques for understanding and control of such transactions' (1975: 39).

3   Although neither is strictly in the marketing area, Titmuss (1970) remains worthy of close reading for both his evidence and his comments on the limitations of the market transactions view in health policy, whilst more recently Davies (1995) provides an excellent survey of the issues in terms of the impact of 'the plurality of times'.

4   Cova illustrates this point partly by reference to issues of significance and meaning in ownership of particular car marques. Of course, one of the key issues in marketing management is how the producers respond to the emergence of such meanings. It was reputed that when Lexus in America discovered that the actual purchasers of its product were significantly higher up the socio-economic and aspirational scale than its original target market it merely decided to

reposition its advertising and promotion. On the other hand, the dilemma was rather more difficult for BMW when it emerged that its marque had become the new status symbol amongst the drug dealing fraternity (popularly represented as B(lack) M(ans) W(heels)): like Volvo before them, they chose to ignore this new 'market segment' (or indeed 'tribe' to use Cova's terminology).

5   Of course, there are strong echoes of the much earlier debate in advertising, initiated in particular by David Ogilvy (1963), about the choice between promoting products in terms of specific functional attributes, or more generally the U(nique) S(elling) P(roposition) approach, and his proposal that the approach should be based much more specifically on the inherent image of the product concerned.

References

Bagozzi, Richard P. (1975) 'Marketing as exchange', *Journal of Marketing*, 39 (4): 32–9.

Davies, Paul (1995) *About Time: Einstein's Unfinished Revolution*.

Giddens, Anthony (1979) *Central Problems in Social Theory: Action, Structure and Contradiction in Social Analysis*. London: Macmillan.

Glucksman, Miriam (1974) *Structuralist Analysis in Contemporary Social Thought*. London: Routledge & Kegan Paul.

Hunt, S.D. and Goolsby, J. (1988) 'The rise and fall of the functional approach to marketing: a paradigm displacement perspective', in T. Nevett and R.A. Fullerton (eds), *Historical Perspectives in Marketing: Essays in Honour of Stanley C. Hollander*. Lexington, MA: Lexington Books.

Ogilvy, David (1963) *Confessions of an Advertising Man*. London: Longmans.

Titmuss, Richard (1963) *The Gift Relationship: From Human Blood to Social Policy*, London: Allen & Unwin.

Part III

REFRAMING CONSUMERS

As Morris Holbrook observes in his commentary, framing affects outcome. Perhaps then, 'Reframing Consumers' is the wrong heading for this part. Neither the authors, nor the editors, nor the commentator are aiming to substitute one 'framework' of consumers for another. On the contrary, all in their different ways are arguing for a 'loosening up' of the frame itself or, as Holbrook suggests (see 'Rocky at play' in Chapter 9), a three-dimensional, pluralistic vision of the consumer, as opposed to the one-dimensional, rational, information processor that is (non-)pictured in marketing textbooks.

The consumer is supposed to be the central focus of marketing, but our understanding of how consumers behave and what they consume is incomplete. Explanations of consumption can be regarded as having developed historically (a fashionable perspective to adopt) through a linear (unfashionable) progression (very unfashionable) of stages (unmentionable) in terms of: (1) consumption of labour (Smith, Marx), (2) use or utility (Jevons, Marshall), (3) exchange value (Edgeworth) and (4) consumption of culture and meaning (Bourdieu, Baudrillard, Debord).

Elliott's chapter reviews and develops this latest perspective in terms of the postmodern consumer culture. In doing so he covers a lot of ground – and shifts some of it! ('Still a useful review of well-travelled terrain': is Holbrook damning with faint praise?) Not only can consumption be viewed as culture and signs, but in this 'semiotic democracy' (Fiske) consumers can resignify meanings and through this their self-identity. Through the process of 'DIY consumption' (Elliott) consumers can dynamically engage with society and culture. (Indeed it might be argued that this is the most powerful engagement that people now have with society!) As Elliott notes, none of this will be surprising to students of anthropology or Jungian or Lacanian psychology.

One is tempted to draw (*mutatis mutandis*) parallels here with the (very fashionable) relationship marketing literature, but the implications for marketing research of this move to an existential cultural view of the consumer are even more far-reaching methodologically. Like Knights and Odih, Elliott argues for a variety of ethnographic and phenomenological research methods in studying the consumer and consumption. Additionally, he explains how the interpretivist approaches of social representations and discourse analysis, both integrated into 'ethnosemiotics' (Fiske, 1990), can be usefully employed to gain insights into the consumer phenomenon, which – as Holbrook re-emphasizes – can only be partially understood or explained through language.

There are two further elements which should be encompassed within our reframing of the consumer. Knights and Odih question the traditional assumptions about time and gender in the consumer behaviour literature. Time as an ontological construct that is linear, external and divisible has been the dominant 'objective' conceptualization of most consumer research. They argue that even 'subjective' psychological, perceptual models still prioritize linear time. Their study of the consumption of financial services, in which time is central to their production, consumption and value, leads Knights and Odih to uncover significant gender differences in consumption attitudes and behaviour. These go well beyond the different 'woman's target segment' aspects. They postulate an alternative sort of time, which they describe as 'feminine' time, which in contrast to the 'masculine', linear view is socially constructed involving a simultaneous overlapping of multiple events. The reasons why women conceive time differently include their distinctive social situations, their domestic, work and leisure connections and pressures.

As Holbrook states, Knights and Odih extract some important conclusions from work. Time and gender differences in consumers have been, at best, 'tightly framed' by traditional marketing research and, arguably, these methodologies are incapable of taking them into account at all. He therefore argues for a rethink based on more phenomenological, symbolic and socially constructed viewpoints.

Holbrook goes on however to suggest that Knights and Odih 'take a wrong turn' in distinguishing between objective, subjective and social conceptions of time and argues *against* their 'failure to preserve the objective–subjective distinction in the context of social time'. While agreeing that men and women perceive temporalities differently, he nevertheless argues that 'whether we like it or not, a linear and sequential time frame appears to be the essence of finance'. Most unfashionable!

Taken together, the chapters in this part of the book present a strong case for a broader framework within which to construct our, at present rather limited, understanding of the consumer and consumption. They also indicate that significant advances and a broader perspective will be required in the research methodologies applied by marketing academics if we are to know better what to put in the frame, and what to leave out.

Reference

Fiske, J. (1990) 'Ethnosemiotics: some personal and theoretical reflections', *Cultural Studies*, 4 (1): 85–100.

7 Symbolic Meaning and Postmodern Consumer Culture

Richard Elliott

Contemporary social theory has begun to focus on consumption as playing a central role in the way in which the social world is constructed (Campbell, 1991) and developments in poststructural anthropology have led to a renewed interest in the relationship between society and material culture (Miller, 1987). These trends can be subsumed into the development of postmodern theories of consumer culture which focus on aspects of cultural practice in the construction of consumer society rather than just on consumption itself (Featherstone, 1991). The implications for the marketing of consumer goods and services under conditions of postmodernity are that many assumptions about the consumer, consumption and marketing research methodology require fundamental reassessment because 'The postmodern predicament is indeed one of crisis, a crisis of our truths, our values, our most cherished beliefs' (Lawson, 1985).

Central to postmodern theory is the proposition that consumers no longer consume products for their material utilities but consume the symbolic meaning of those products as portrayed in their images: products in fact become commodity signs (Baudrillard, 1981). 'The real consumer becomes a consumer of illusions' (Debord, 1977) and 'the ad-dict buys images not things' (Taylor and Saarinen, 1994). This semiotic perspective of products as symbols raises difficult questions about the location of cultural meaning. The term 'symbol' itself can relate to the product that carries meaning or to the meaning it carries, and the interpretation of meaning is a complex product of what is contained in the representation and what the individual brings to the representation (LeVine, 1984). Symbolism can be analysed semiotically by examination of the system of signs and what they signify; however, it has been realized that this leads to an infinite regress as one sign leads to another without there ever being anything 'real' outside the system. All meaning is socially constructed and there is no essential external reference point, so ultimately 'There is nothing outside the text' (Derrida, 1977). To complicate matters further, symbolic interpretation is essentially non-rational improvisation that does not obey the codes of language but operates at the unconscious level (Sperber, 1975). A Jungian analysis goes even further and suggests that the full significance of a symbol cannot be grasped in purely intellectual terms: if it becomes fully definable in rational terms it is no longer a true symbol (Storr, 1973).

The functions of the symbolic meanings of products operate in two directions: outward in constructing the social world, *social symbolism*; and inward towards constructing our self-identity, *self-symbolism*. Consumption of the symbolic meaning of products is a social process that helps make visible and stable the basic categories of a culture which are under constant change, and consumption choices 'become a vital source of the culture of the moment' (Douglas and Isherwood, 1978). The meanings of consumer goods are grounded in their social context and the demand for goods derives more from their role in cultural practices than from the satisfaction of simple human needs (Appadurai, 1986). Consumer goods then are more than just objects of economic exchange, 'they are goods to think with, goods to speak with' (Fiske, 1989). Consumption as a cultural practice is one way of participating in social life and may be an important element in cementing social relationships (Osterberg, 1988), whilst the whole system of consumption is an unconscious expression of the existing social structure through a seductive process which pushes the purchasing impulse until it reaches the 'limits of economic potential' (Baudrillard, 1988). It is within this social context that the individual uses consumer goods and the consumption process as the materials with which to construct and maintain an identity, form relationships and frame psychological events (Lunt and Livingstone, 1992).

Consumer goods are used to maintain hierarchical distinctions of social status through distinctions in taste, where the operation of consumer choice through the selection of a particular constellation of goods both 'classifies and classifies the classifier' (Bourdieu, 1984). What is important is not the material possessions themselves or the demonstration of wealth by their display, but the accumulation of 'symbolic capital' through the informational use of goods to demonstrate knowledge of the appropriate taste code. The consumer is engaged in a search for knowledge about new consumer goods and how they should be used to demonstrate taste and thus construct identity. As the availability of symbolic goods increases so demand grows for cultural intermediaries such as the marketing industry who 'have the capacity to ransack various traditions and cultures in order to produce new symbolic goods' and to develop meaning interpretations for their use (Featherstone, 1991). Ewen (1988) has suggested that the use and consumption of *style* have become a central feature of everyday life where the freedom to desire achieves its power through the association between objects and action and 'this systematic association is a continuous function of advertising'. In this sense then, marketing is a social practice located at the centre of the construction of symbolic capital and thus involved in the development of the meaning of consumer culture.

However, the creation of meaning is not deterministic and unidirectional, in that consumers do not passively accept marketing communications but may actively renegotiate the meaning subjectively and construct their own interpretations (Elliott et al., 1993). Owing to 'the relative autonomy of the symbolic' (Bourdieu, 1984) the reader of a symbolic discourse is able to 'poach' its content and resignify meanings in unintended directions (de Certeau, 1984). From this poststructuralist perspective limited freedom is allowed to the individual through consumption choices. 'For most members of contemporary society individual freedom, if available at all, comes in the form of consumer freedom' through which the individual must take responsibility to invent and consciously create a self-identity (Bauman, 1988). Through the 'new existentialism' (Laermans, 1993) consumers can exercise the freedom to create new meanings for goods through their own idiosyncratic performance of everyday life (de Certeau, 1984). This freedom can be used for collective and individual resistance against the imposed meanings of the dominant cultural categories, particularly through the choice of style and the use of *bricolage* tactics (Hebdige, 1979). A sustained argument for the active exercise of freedom through consumption is developed by Willis (1990) who characterizes the consumption choices of the young as the behaviour of 'practical existentialists'. The young are seen as exercising choice through consumption-related symbolic creativity which operates via the concept of 'grounded aesthetics', a process which builds higher-level symbolic meaning structures from the mundane concrete experiences of everyday life. Advertisements can be seen as cultural products in their own right, and young people consume them independently of the product being marketed (Nava, 1991) and have a creative symbolic relationship with them. Individuals use advertising images as personal and social resources, and these are invested with specific meanings anchored in daily life, via the process of grounded aesthetics, which are then used to construct or maintain personal and social identities. Each small act of existential consumption allows the individual to play a part in constructing both their subjectivity and their social reality (Elliott and Ritson, 1995). More prosaically, it is clear from recent developments in active audience theory that any particular text can have a wide range of possible meanings (polysemy) contingent upon the consumer's identity, gender, and cultural background (Morley, 1992; Radway, 1987). Although Fiske (1987) goes so far as to claim that television delegates the production of meanings and pleasures to its viewers in a 'semiotic democracy', there is evidence that the audience exerts at least some control over the meanings they construct from texts and that this meaning is nested in the social action of everyday life (Livingstone, 1990).

Gender differences in the reading of symbolic meaning may further complicate matters as there may be a basic difference in the language code (Tannen, 1990) and there is evidence that the symbolic meaning of brands can be very different between genders (Elliott, 1994). This can be related to one of the key manifestations of postmodernity: *fragmentation*, where there is the separation of products from their original function, of the signifier from the signified, and of the product from the need (Firat, 1992). The symbolic meaning of products is no longer fixed but is 'free-floating', and each individual may ascribe different and inconsistent cultural meanings to a product depending on the extent to which they share the collective imagination and thus escape from 'the regime of truth' (Foucault, 1977). At the heart of social symbolism then is differentiation, and it is here that there arise both problems and opportunities for marketing theory. The consumer's relentless search for difference in order to construct and sustain social order may entail the possibility of a positive-sum market. Rather than a zero-sum game of the distribution of material goods with winners and losers, at the symbolic level the market may be a positive-sum win/win game (Ogilvy, 1990). As each good may have a different meaning for each consumer, then perceptions and emotions may be unique and not reducible by conventional market segmentation techniques.

The self-symbolic role of material goods is long established in anthropology and the individual's attachment to objects may be a culturally universal function which symbolizes security, expresses the self-concept and signifies connection to society (Wallendorf and Arnould, 1988). Consumer goods are not only used to construct our self-identity but are also used by others to make inferences about us that guide their behaviour towards us (Dittmar, 1992). But now in postmodernity we are able to use consumer products to become any of our 'possible selves' (Markus and Nurius, 1986) in which we utilize consumer goods to construct pastiches of others we have been exposed to via the media or more directly. 'In cyberspace, I can change myself as easily as I change my clothes' (Taylor and Saarinen, 1994). This postmodern fragmentation of the experience of self has been termed the condition of 'multiphrenia' by Gergen (1991), who points out that the new opportunities for exercise of choice are almost unlimited and so bring with them a 'vertigo of the valued' where the expansion of 'wants' reduces our choice to 'want not', a multiplicity of competing values and beliefs which make 'the very idea of rational choice become meaningless'. The mass media, and advertising in particular, are responsible for an 'expansion of inadequacy' which is encouraged by a barrage of new criteria for self-evaluation. Cushman (1990) argues that we are in an era of the 'empty self' in which alienation and loss of community can be solved by the 'lifestyle' solution in which the consumer constructs a 'self' by purchasing and 'ingesting' products featured in advertising. This desperate search for meaning in a disintegrating social order is part of what Lyotard (1984) calls the 'postmodern condition' and again means that marketing practice plays a significant role in cultural life, particularly through the symbolic gratification promised by advertising which manages to recode a commodity as a desirable psycho-ideological sign (Wernick, 1991).

The operation of advertising at the unconscious level is driven by the search for an imaginary self which motivates the individual with desire for coherence and meaning (Lacan, 1977). Advertising feeds the desire to achieve the unobtainable unity of the self with destabilized meanings (Featherstone, 1991), images which separate commodities from their original use and offer the possibility to reconstruct the self by purchasing the symbolic meaning of goods (Bauman, 1991). For as Williamson (1978) points out, 'The conscious chosen meaning in most people's lives comes from what they consume', and this is linked with the attachment to bodily desire of symbolic meaning (Lacan, 1977). Central to Lacanian theory is the mirror phase, where the child recognizes itself in a mirror and assumes an image through a transformation from the imaginary to the symbolic. The symbolic for Lacan is linked with absence, in that symbols represent a world of people and things that are not there. The 'real' can only be approached through the symbolic medium of language, yet language itself contains the contradictions and fragmentations of gender, power and meaning (Kristeva, 1980). The symbolic focus of much promotional activity in postmodernity is *desire*, and for Lacan desire exists in the gap between language and the unconscious. 'Desire does not desire satisfaction. To the contrary desire desires desire. The reason images are so desirable is that they never satisfy' (Taylor and Saarinen, 1994). Postmodern consumption is inextricably linked with aspects of sexuality, both conscious and unconscious, as it promises the satisfaction of previously taboo desires through imagery and representations (Mort, 1988). These desires are constructed through the symbolic linkage between consumption and the human body (Kellner, 1992), and operate in large part through the consumption imagery with which we are surrounded and which makes mundane consumer actions, such as looking in shop windows, highly significant in our psychic lives (Bocock, 1993).

The symbolic interactionist perspective suggests that although consumers employ product symbolism to define social reality, the meaning of a product can also be consumed for private meaning driven by internal, emotional cues (Solomon, 1983). This use of products may, in part, be due to a dislocation of a systematic relationship between need and action. Rather than consumption being an instrumental action to satisfy a specific need, some aspects of consumption may be a reaction to a generalized lack of need satisfaction and the use of compensatory consumption as an inadequate attempt to achieve satisfaction (Gronmo, 1988). In some cases, consumption may also function as a means for people to escape from aversive self-awareness by focusing attention on the immediate present. Awareness of personal shortcomings in relation to the self can create negative emotional states such as anxiety or depression (Higgins, 1987) and in order to escape from these feelings the individual may use cognitive narrowing to focus on concrete, low-level thinking (Baumeister, 1990). One aspect of cognitive narrowing is the deconstruction of events by stripping them of their high-level symbolic meaning constructs, leaving mere stimuli; for example, alcohol use may narrow attention to immediate, pleasant experiences, and unpleasant thoughts about identity and long-term implications are blotted out of awareness (Steele and Josephs, 1990). Consumption, and especially the shopping experience, may also produce this form of cognitive narrowing and focus attention on immediate pleasure, where the experience itself takes over and becomes deconstructed from the high-level symbolic meanings of the goods: 'the act of consumption itself, celebrated by these new bright environments, is the real buzz. It doesn't matter what you buy, only that you buy' (Gardner and

Sheppard, 1989). This reliance on vivid, immediate, affect-charged experience or simulations is another aspect of the postmodern condition (Baudrillard, 1983; Jameson, 1984) and the shopping centre is a major source of these experiences where consumers can fantasize in 'modern, self-illusory hedonism' which operates through emotional and sensory stimulation, enhanced by the separation of consumption from cash via the credit card (Campbell, 1987).

In the Lacanian perspective there is a stress on the individual subject as being fragmented and incoherent, and this leads to the framing of the consumer as simultaneously both rational and irrational, able to both consume and reject what is being consumed, to desire and yet consume without satisfaction (Nava, 1991). 'Identity becomes infinitely plastic in a play of images that knows no end. Consistency is no longer a virtue but becomes a vice; integration is limitation' (Taylor and Saarinen, 1994). The consumption of meaning, even the meaning of supposedly unambiguous television soap operas, is always ambivalent and contradictory (Ang, 1985). These non-rational, emotional aspects of consumption are paralleled by the recent development in social cognition of the theory of *motivated choice* which emphasizes the role of emotion in decision processes (Forgas, 1992; Kunda, 1990). Motivated choice is where judgement is driven by an emotional desire to arrive at a particular conclusion, where biased information search and reasoning processes are used 'to arrive at those conclusions they want to arrive at' (Kunda, 1990). Emotions have also been proposed as a separate and primary system to the influence of cognition by Zajonc (1984; Murphy and Zajonc, 1993) and incorporated into a choice model including normative commitments by Etzioni (1992). From these perspectives, cool, rational, information-processing choice is at least uncommon, and may in fact be very rare, even when high involvement is present (Kunda, 1990). Consumer choice processes have usually been studied using positivist methods which have typically involved experimental procedures using simulated product decisions and students as subjects. Although some researchers have used these same experimental methods and student subjects in order to study emotional aspects of consumer choice (Gardner and Hill, 1988; Mittal, 1988), it has been recognized by others that the very nature of emotion requires interpretive research methods in order to capture the essential richness of the subject matter (Holbrook, 1990). This requirement for an interpretive research approach has been emphasized by the social constructionist theory of emotions (Averill, 1980; Harré, 1986) which views emotions not as natural responses elicited by natural features in a situation, but as socio-cultural constructions which serve a situated social function, so that the meaning of an emotion is located within the socio-cultural system in which it is culturally appropriate. The process of the social construction of emotions by interaction between the self and social structures has been studied using such techniques as 'memory work' (Kippax et al., 1988). But despite their situational contingency, emotions may be law-like in their effect upon us. The 'law of apparent reality' states that once events are subjectively perceived to be real, often through imagination and fantasy, then the emotional responses overwhelm objective evidence; and the 'law of closure' proposes that emotions are blind to reason and that they 'know no probabilities . . . they do not weigh likelihoods' (Frijda, 1988). In this sense then, preferences really do direct inferences and emotion does dominate cognition (Zajonc, 1980). However, the most important emotional element of consumer choice may not be to choose that which is most pleasing, but to reject that which is most distasteful. Bourdieu (1984) suggests of tastes that 'when they have to be justified, they are asserted purely negatively, by the refusal of other tastes'. We may define ourselves not by what we like, but by what we dislike, and it is strong negative emotional reactions to the consumption practices of others that may structure our social categories.

The very nature of artefactual symbolism is that it is a much less controlled form of communication than language and much more likely to evoke variable responses (Miller, 1987). This poses difficult problems for marketing research as it may well be that language is not an appropriate medium for evoking the non-lineal organization of everyday cognition (Bloch, 1992), as 'language disguises thought' and may make it impossible to infer the underlying nature of cognition (Wittgenstein, 1971). One of the effects of modernist social research has been to seek univocal definitions of terms, and thus to lose a recognition of the cultural and social functions that ambiguity serves in the promotion of community (Levine, 1985). We need to develop methodologies for investigating the meaning of consumer goods which elude the artificial limitations of positivist approaches that assume homogeneity of meaning within market segments, and recognize that the consumer may find it difficult to reduce the consumption experience to simple verbal labels (Hirschman and Holbrook, 1992). This is particularly relevant in relation to consumption imagery carried by electronic media where 'You sorta listen with your eyes' (Hodge and Tripp, 1986).

The meaning of these postmodern perspectives on consumption and consumers poses a fundamental challenge to marketing research methodology. The operation of the symbolic is non-rational, emotional, largely unconscious, open to multiple interpretations; meaning is in constant flux, and is of both the internal cognitive and of the external social world. Because individuals interact with consumption objects and may always reinterpret the signification of any signifier, the behaviour of the consumer in the marketplace tends to be stochastic (Rawwas and Barnes, 1989). The positivist practice of 'scientific' marketing research cannot cope with such a constructed reality and is likely to produce superficial knowledge rather than meaningful understanding. Fundamental to the postmodern view is that the eventual triumph of science is an illusion or myth (Habermas, 1983). Postmodernism not only encourages tolerance of incompatible alternatives (Lyotard, 1984) and refuses to accept that any one perspective has superiority, but rather encourages the juxtaposition of opposites and contradictions (Foster, 1983). The paradoxical nature of postmodern culture which impacts on the consumer through fragmentation and ambiguity must also impact upon consumer researchers in that we, too, must learn to cope with paradox. This entails the development of mixed methodologies to generate multiple perspectives on socially constructed reality.

An interpretive research paradigm appropriate for studying the subjective experience and constructed reality of symbolic meaning is that of phenomenology (Thompson et al., 1989) which seeks to describe experience as it is lived in the life-world of the individual. The focus here is on the contextualized experience of consumption as it emerges in recurring experiential patterns. Phenomenological approaches offer a way forward to understanding the consumption experience from the consumer's perspective, which capture the richness of the individual's emotional responses yet offer opportunities for identifying structures with which to organize data through a Gestalt portrayal (Thompson et al., 1990).

A research approach which may retain more of the socially shared meanings of consumer goods is the concept of *social representations*, which are not mental creations that have social effects but rather are social creations, constructed via mental processes that acquire reality, and are proposed as 'the psychology of postmodern society' (Moscovici, 1990). Social representations are composed of two mental entities, concepts and images, and the iconic aspect usually dominates the abstract in the construction of a figurative nucleus (Moscovici, 1984). This pictorial aspect means that they are not required to obey the laws of logic, such as the rule of non-contradiction, and thus social representations can exist which cannot accord with reality (McKinlay and Potter, 1987). This is particularly important in relation to the meaning of advertising, for in the electronic culture of the simulacrum 'the word is never simply a word but is always an image. The audio-visual trace of the word involves an inescapable materiality that can only be thought if it is figured' (Taylor and Saarinen, 1994). Recognition of the possibility for images to operate in ways that challenge verbal language has led to a call for the adoption of poststructuralist approaches to the study of advertising visuals (Scott, 1992). The theory of social representations holds out the prospect of eluding the limitations of linguistic meaning structures and engaging with the complexity of a constructed world of both reality and illusion.

Variability in meaning is the focus of *discourse analysis* (Parker, 1992; Potter and Wetherall, 1987), a recent theoretical development in social psychology which attempts to incorporate aspects of semiotics and poststructuralism. This perspective draws on linguistic philosophy and pragmatics for an emphasis on the performative social action aspects of language, and on ethnomethodology for a focus on how people use language in everyday situations to make sense of their world. Poststructuralism provides the idea that language embodies the 'sediment' of social practices and thus cannot be a neutral medium of description (Eagleton, 1983). The fundamental assumptions of discourse analysis are that people use language to construct accounts of the social world, this active process of construction being demonstrated in language variation. Discourse does not necessarily reflect underlying attitudes or dispositions, but the focus is on the discourse itself and the functions to which it is put (Potter and Wetherall, 1987). Methodologically, discourse analysis is concerned with naturally occurring speech and its social rather than linguistic organization. Analytically, discourse analysis is concerned with *interpretive repertoires*, recurrently used systems of meaning which are constructed from a restricted range of terms, and with variability in accounts which may reveal the situated and functional character of different versions (Edwards and Potter, 1992). Wetherall (1986) maintains that although many of the interpretive repertoires identified in discourse may seem mundane and obvious, it is precisely their commonplace role in the structure of everyday thought that may help in capturing the richness and subtlety of everyday concepts.

These three research approaches – phenomenology, social representations and discourse analysis – can be integrated through the concept of *ethnosemiotics*, a term originally coined by Fiske (1990) to describe a critical approach to ethnography. Ethnography includes participant observation methods and is essentially the most fundamental form of social research, which in recent years has emerged as consisting of a variety of flexible approaches to data collection which all share the explicit recognition that the researcher and the research act itself are part and parcel of the social world under investigation (Hammersley and Atkinson, 1983). Postmodern ethnography (Tyler, 1986) has developed the early interpretive assertion that ethnographic accounts could be seen as 'fiction' (Geertz, 1973) by highlighting the constructed nature of accounts and rejecting any claim that they represent the social world, instead maintaining that they merely evoke images of the discontinuities, paradoxes and inconsistencies of social action and culture (Atkinson and Hammersley, 1994). Ethnographic information can be collected in a variety of forms, such as observational data, audio and video recordings, non-directive and directive interview data, and documentary data. It is the very richness of the data forms that makes ethnography such a suitable method for exploring the complexities of consumer culture. Ethnosemiotics as framed by Fiske (1990) adds two important elements to ethnography. The first is a semiotic concern with what is absent from the text as being as important as what is present, and draws attention to the incoherent and paradoxical nature of much human behaviour. The second is the avoidance of the psychological reductionism apparent in much ethnography and a concern with explicating the linkage between individual action and meaning and the ideological hegemony within which subjectivity is constrained. Additionally, it is proposed here that ethnosemiotics should be extended to adopt a critical stance and involve a concern with the well-being of the subject. This critical element constructs research in the context of the empowerment of individuals and thus becomes a transformative endeavour (Kinchloe and McLaren, 1994). This suggests that consumer research for the consumer's sake needs to start from the substantive domain of consumer-related issues, rather than be largely concerned with the conceptual domain of theory testing (Olander, 1993).

The methodology of ethnosemiotics allows for the mixing of data collection approaches, such as Mort's (1988) use of impressionistic forms of looking and listening, together with personal phenomenological narratives and more formal interview techniques. Once captured, data can be analysed using the concept of social representations to identify shared imagery, and consumer discourse analysed for variability in meaning and functional purpose. It is only through utilizing multiple perspectives that we can hope to develop our understanding of postmodern consumption, whose major characteristic is the paradoxical juxtaposition of opposites (van Raaij, 1993). The emotion-laden experiences of the consumer: irrational, incoherent and driven by unconscious desire; constrained by the market economy yet obtaining limited freedom through existential consumption and symbolic creativity; able to build a DIY self through consumption yet suffering an expansion of inadequacy through advertising; these pose an enormous challenge to consumer research. We need to strive for 'conscious pluralism' in research practice, designed to generate as many different meanings as possible (Morgan, 1983). This postmodern perspective on methodology has a striking similarity with the views of Feyerabend (1975) who conceived of knowledge as 'an ever increasing ocean of mutually incompatible (and perhaps incommensurable) alternatives'. This requires a willingness to undertake research that does not assume any one answer to explaining consumer behaviour, no one single solution, but approaches consumer culture expecting to find multiple meanings and a rich construction of reality and illusion beyond the merely rational.

References

Ang, I. (1985) *Watching Dallas: Soap Opera and the Melodramatic Imagination.* London: Methuen.

Appadurai, A. (1986) *The Social Life of Things: Commodities in Cultural Perspective.* Cambridge: Cambridge University Press.

Atkinson, P. and Hammersley, M. (1994) 'Ethnography and participant Observation', in N. Denzin and Y. Lincoln (eds), *Handbook of Qualitative Research.* London: Sage.

Averill, J. (1980) 'A constructivist view of emotion', in R. Plutchik and H. Kellerman (eds), *Emotion Theory, Research and Experience.* New York: Academic Press.

Baudrillard, J. (1981) *For a Critique of the Political Economy of the Sign.* St Louis, MO: Telos.

Baudrillard, J. (1983) *In the Shadow of the Silent Majorities.* New York: Semiotext(e).

Baudrillard, J. (1988) 'Consumer society', in M. Poster (ed.), *Jean Baudrillard: Selected Writings.* Cambridge: Polity.

Bauman, Z. (1988) *Freedom.* Milton Keynes: Open University Press.

Bauman, Z. (1991) *Modernity and Ambivalence.* Ithaca, NY: Cornell University Press.

Baumeister, R. (1990) 'Anxiety and deconstruction: on escaping the self', in J. Olson and M. Zanna (eds), *Self Inference Processes: The Ontario Symposium,* Vol. 6. Hillsdale, NJ: Erlbaum.

Bloch, M. (1992) 'What goes without saying: the conceptualization of Zafimaniry society', in Adam Kuper (ed.), *Conceptualizing Society.* London: Routledge.

Bocock, R. (1993) *Consumption.* London: Routledge.

Bourdieu, P. (1984) *Distinction: A Social Critique of the Judgement of Taste,* trans. R. Nice. London: Routledge & Kegan Paul.

Campbell, C. (1987) *The Romantic Ethic and the Spirit of Modern Consumerism.* Oxford: Blackwell.

Campbell, C. (1991) 'Consumption: the new wave of research in the humanities and social sciences', in F.W. Rudmin (ed.), *To Have Possessions: A Handbook on Ownership and Property, Journal of Social Behavior and Personality,* Special Issue, 6: 57–74.

Cushman, P. (1990) 'Why the self is empty: toward a historically situated psychology', *American Psychologist,* 45 (5): 599–611.

Debord, G. (1977) *Society of the Spectacle.* Detroit: Black & Red.

de Certeau, M. (1984) *The Practice of Everyday Life.* Berkeley, CA: University of California Press.

Derrida, J. (1977) *Of Grammatology,* trans. G. Spivak. Baltimore: Johns Hopkins University Press.

Dittmar, H. (1992) *The Social Psychology of Material Possessions: To Have Is To Be.* Hemel Hempstead: Harvester Wheatsheaf.

Douglas, M. and Isherwood, B. (1978) *The World of Goods: Towards an Anthropology of Consumption.* London: Allen Lane.

Eagleton, T. (1983) *Literary Theory: An Introduction.* Oxford: Blackwell.

Edwards, D. and Potter, J. (1992) *Discursive Psychology.* London: Sage.

Elliott, R. (1994) 'Exploring the symbolic meaning of brands', *British Journal of Management,* Special Issue, 5: S13–S19.

Elliott, R. and Ritson, M. (1995) 'Practicing existential consumption: the lived meaning of sexuality in advertising', *Advances in Consumer Research,* 22.

Elliott, R., Eccles, S. and Hodgson, M. (1993) 'Re-coding gender representations: women, cleaning products, and advertising's "New Man" ', *International Journal of Research in Marketing,* 10: 1–14.

Etzioni, A. (1992) 'Normative-affective factors: towards a new decision-making model', in M. Zey (ed.), *Decision Making: Alternatives to Rational Choice Models.* Newbury Park, CA: Sage.

Ewen, S. (1988) *All Consuming Images: The Politics of Style in Contemporary Culture.* New York: Basic Books.

Featherstone, M. (1991) *Consumer Culture and Postmodernism.* London: Sage.

Feyerabend, P. (1975) *Against Method: Outline of an Anarchistic Theory of Knowledge.* London: Verso.

Firat, A.F. (1992) 'Fragmentations in the postmodern', *Advances in Consumer Research,* 19: 203–5.

Fiske, J. (1987) *Television Culture.* London: Routledge.

Fiske, J. (1989) *Reading the Popular.* Boston: Unwin Hyman.

Fiske, J. (1990) 'Ethnosemiotics: some personal and theoretical reflections', *Cultural Studies,* 4 (1): 85–100.

Forgas, J.P. (1992) 'Affect in social judgements and decisions: a multiprocess model', *Advances in Experimental Social Psychology,* 25: 227–78.

Foster, H. (1983) 'Postmodernism: a preface', in Hal Foster (ed.), *The Anti-Aesthetic: Essays on Postmodern Culture.* Port Townsend, WA: Bay Press.

Foucault, M. (1977) *Discipline and Punish.* Harmondsworth: Penguin.

Frijda, N.H. (1988) 'The laws of emotion', *American Psychologist*, 43 (5): 349–58.

Gardner, C. and Sheppard, J. (1989) *Consuming Passion: The Rise of Retail Culture*. London: Unwin Hyman.

Gardner, M.P. and Hill, R.P. (1988) 'Consumers' mood states: antecedents and consequences of experiential versus informational strategies for brand choice', *Psychology and Marketing*, 5 (2): 169–82.

Geertz, C. (1973) *The Interpretation of Cultures: Selected Essays*. New York: Basic Books.

Gergen, K. (1991) *The Saturated Self: Dilemmas of Identity in Contemporary Life*. New York: Basic Books.

Gronmo, S. (1988) 'Compensatory consumer behaviour: elements of a critical sociology of consumption', in Per Otnes (ed.), *The Sociology of Consumption*. Oslo: Solum Forlag.

Habermas, J. (1983) 'Modernity: an incomplete project', in H. Foster (ed.), *The Anti-Aesthetic: Essays on Postmodern Culture*. Port Townsend, WA: Bay Press.

Hammersley, M. and Atkinson, P. (1983) *Ethnography: Principles in Practice*. London: Routledge.

Harré, R. (ed.) (1986) *The Social Construction of Emotions*. Oxford: Basil Blackwell.

Hebdige, D. (1979) *Subculture: The Meaning of Style*. London: Methuen.

Higgins, T. (1987) 'Self-discrepancy: a theory relating self to affect', *Psychological Review*, 94: 319–40.

Hirschman, E. and Holbrook, M. (1992) *Postmodern Consumer Research: The Study of Consumption as Text*. Newbury Park, CA: Sage.

Hodge, R. and Tripp, D. (1986) *Children and Television: A Semiotic Analysis*. Cambridge: Polity.

Holbrook, M.B. (1990) 'The role of lyricism in research on consumer emotions: skylark, have you anything to say to me?', *Advances in Consumer Research*, 17: 1–18.

Jameson, F. (1984) 'Postmodernism and the consumer society', in H. Foster (ed.), *The Anti-Aesthetic: Essays on Postmodern Culture*. Port Townsend, WA: Bay Press.

Kellner, D. (1992) 'Popular culture and the construction of postmodern identities', in S. Lash and J. Friedman (eds), *Modernity and Identity*. Oxford: Blackwell.

Kinchloe, J. and McLaren, P. (1994) 'Rethinking critical theory and qualitative research', in N. Denzin and Y. Lincoln (eds), *Handbook of Qualitative Research*. London: Sage.

Kippax, S., Crawford, J., Benton, P., Gault, U. and Noesjirwan, J. (1988) 'Constructing emotions: weaving meaning from memories', *British Journal of Social Psychology*, 27: 19–33.

Kristeva, J. (1980) *Desire in Language: A Semiotic Approach to Literature and Art*. Oxford: Blackwell.

Kunda, Z. (1990) 'The case for motivated reasoning', *Psychological Bulletin*, 108: 480–98.

Lacan, J. (1977) *Ecrits: A Selection*. London: Tavistock.

Laermans, R. (1993) 'Bringing the consumer back in', *Theory, Culture & Society*, 10: 153–61.

Lawson, H. (1985) *Reflexitivity: Problems of Modern European Thought*. London: Anchor.

Levine, D. (1985) *The Flight from Ambiguity: Essays in Social and Cultural Theory*. Chicago: University of Chicago Press.

LeVine, R. (1984) 'Properties of culture: an ethnographic view', in R. Schweder and R. LeVine (eds), *Culture Theory: Essays on Mind, Self, and Emotion*. Cambridge: Cambridge University Press.

Livingstone, S. (1990) *Making Sense of Television: The Psychology of Audience Interpretation*. Oxford: Pergamon.

Lunt, P. and Livingstone, S. (1992) *Mass Consumption and Personal Identity: Everyday Economic Experience*. Buckingham: Open University Press.

Lyotard, J. (1984) *The Postmodern Condition: A Report on Knowledge*. Manchester: Manchester University Press.

Markus, H. and Nurius, P. (1986) 'Possible selves', *American Psychologist*, 41: 954–69.

McKinlay, A. and Potter, J. (1987) 'Social representations: a conceptual critique', *Journal for the Theory of Social Behaviour*, 17 (4): 471–87.

Miller, D. (1987) *Material Culture and Mass Consumption*. Oxford: Blackwell.

Mittal, B. (1988) 'The role of affective choice mode in the consumer purchase of expressive products', *Journal of Economic Psychology*, 9: 499–524.

Morgan, G. (1983) *Beyond Method: Strategies for Social Research*. Beverly Hills, CA: Sage.

Morley, D. (1992) *Television, Audiences and Cultural Studies*. London: Routledge.

Mort, F. (1988) 'Boy's own? Masculinity, style and popular culture', in R. Chapman and J. Rutherford (eds), *Male Order*. London: Lawrence & Wishart.

Moscovici, S. (1984) 'The phenomenon of social representations', in R. Farr and S. Moscovici (eds), *Social Representations*. Cambridge: Cambridge University Press.

Moscovici, S. (1990) 'The generalized self and mass society', in H. Himmelweit and G. Gaskell (eds), *Societal Psychology*. London: Sage.

Murphy, S.T. and Zajonc, R.B. (1993) 'Affect, cognition, and awareness: affective priming with optimal and suboptimal stimulus exposures', *Journal of Personality and Social Psychology*, 64 (5): 723–39.

Nava, M. (1991) 'Consumerism reconsidered: buying and power', *Cultural Studies*, 5 (2): 157–73.

Ogilvy, J. (1990) 'This postmodern business', *Marketing and Research Today*, February: 4–21.

Olander, F. (1993) 'Consumer psychology for the consumer's sake?', *Journal of Economic Psychology*, 14: 565–76.

Osterberg, D. (1988) 'Two notes on consumption', in P. Otnes (ed.), *The Sociology of Consumption*. Oslo: Solum Forlag.

Parker, I. (1992) *Discourse Dynamics: Critical Analysis for Social and Individual Psychology*. London: Routledge.

Potter, J. and Wetherall, M. (1987) *Discourse and Social Psychology: Beyond Attitudes and Behaviour*. London: Sage.

Radway, L. (1987) *Reading the Romance*. London: Verso.

Rawwas, M. and Barnes, J. (1989) 'A theoretical model of modern consumption symbolism: a merger of functionalism and hedonistic theories', *Advances in Consumer Research*, 16: 231–7.

Scott, L. (1992) 'Playing with pictures: postmodernism, poststructuralism, and advertising visuals', *Advances in Consumer Research*, 19: 596–612.

Solomon, M. (1983) 'The role of products as social stimuli: a symbolic interactionism perspective', *Journal of Consumer Research*, 10: 319–29.

Sperber, D. (1975) *Rethinking Symbolism*, trans. A. Morton. Cambridge: Cambridge University Press.

Steele, C. and Josephs, R. (1990) 'Alcoholic myopia: its prized and dangerous effects', *American Psychologist*, 45: 921–33.

Storr, A. (1973) *Jung*. London: Fontana.

Tannen, D. (1990) *You Just Don't Understand: Men and Women in Conversation*. London: Virago Press.

Taylor, M. and Saarinen, E. (1994) *Imagologies: Media Philosophy*. London: Routledge.

Thompson, C., Locander, W. and Pollio, H. (1989) 'Putting consumer experience back into consumer research: the philosophy and method of existential phenomenology', *Journal of Consumer Research*, 17: 133–47.

Thompson, C., Locander, W. and Pollio, H. (1990) 'The lived meaning of free choice: an existential-phenomenological description of everyday consumer experiences of contemporary married women', *Journal of Consumer Research*, 17: 346–61.

Tyler, S. (1986) 'Post-modern ethnography: from document of the occult to occult document', in J. Cliffford and G. Marcus (eds), *Writing Culture: The Poetics and Politics of Ethnography*. Berkeley, CA: University of California Press.

van Raaij, F. (1993) 'Postmodern consumption', *Journal of Economic Psychology*, 14: 541–63.

Wallendorf, M. and Arnould, E.J. (1988) ' "My favourite things": a cross-cultural inquiry into object attachment, possessiveness, and social linkage', *Journal of Consumer Research*, 14: 531–47.

Wernick, A. (1991) *Promotional Culture: Advertising, Ideology and Symbolic Expression*. London: Sage.

Wetherall, M. (1986) 'Linguistic repertoires and literary criticism: new directions for a social psychology of gender', in S. Wilkinson (ed.), *Feminist Social Psychology: Developing Theory and Practice*. Milton Keynes: Open University Press.

Williamson, J. (1978) *Decoding Advertisements: Ideology and Meaning in Advertising*. London: Marion Boyars.

Willis, P. (1990) *Common Culture: Symbolic Work at Play in the Everyday Cultures of the Young*. Milton Keynes: Open University Press.

Wittgenstein, L. (1971) *Tractatus Logico-Philosophicus*, 2nd edn. London: Routledge & Kegan Paul.

Zajonc, R.B. (1980) 'Feeling and thinking: preferences need no inferences', *American Psychologist*, 35: 151–75.

Zajonc, R.B. (1984) 'On the primacy of affect', *American Psychologist*, 39: 117–24.

8 It's a Matter of Time: The Significance of the Women's Market in Consumption

David Knights and Pamela Odih

After generations of stability and steady growth, economic deregulation and political reregulation has stimulated the financial services sector to break from its complacent past. Banks, building societies and insurance companies have therefore begun to diversify, compete strategically and adopt the modern management methods and techniques of their manufacturing peers. Amongst these, marketing management techniques such as product differentiation and market segmentation have taken a high profile, particularly in the fee earning sphere of insurance-related products and sales within bancassurance operations (Knights et al., 1994). Alongside these changes, a number of companies have identified women as a market segment that has remained relatively unexplored (Odih, 1998). Given the dramatic post-war increase in the participation rate of women in the labour market to a point almost matching that of men (Keegan, 1994), it is not surprising that, though belatedly, financial services have become aware of the potential of this market. While efforts have been made, only a minority of companies have identified a specific and differentiated means of developing the market for financial products among women. Strategies have remained largely informed by traditional product and service distribution methods where the target is predominantly male 'heads' of households.

This chapter draws upon theoretically informed empirical research of gender issues as they might have a bearing on the consumption of financial services by women. More specifically, our focus is upon conceptions of 'time', 'masculinity' and 'femininity', and how their differences may affect the consumption of financial services products. If, as we suggest, 'feminine' conceptions of time are less linear and sequential than those associated with 'masculine' dominated horizons, then our thesis has considerable implications for the redirection of marketing in financial services, where women are becoming an important target segment. It may also have importance for marketing in general but that is not the focus of this chapter.

The chapter is organized into two main sections with a concluding section that examines the implications of the analysis for marketing research. The first section contains a discussion of our analytical framework. It commences with a critical review of previous marketing approaches to the significance of time in consumer behaviour. Broadly, marketing research into time may be seen as dominated by three approaches: the objective, the subjective and the social. In this review we argue that, to varying degrees, these approaches serve to reinforce the hegemonic status of linear conceptions of time. In an attempt to deconstruct this hegemony, we seek to reveal how linear time is grounded in class, religious and gender power–knowledge relations. In addressing the social construction of linear time through these relations, we draw attention to the inextricable link between dominant conceptions of time, power and knowledge. The role of masculinity in the discursive formation of linear time, coupled with a recognition of its ultimate grounding in Western androcentric and homophobic discourse, encourage us to attribute to linear time the insignia 'masculine time'. Our central argument is that the discursively constituted constructions of linear time are predominantly aligned with the equally discursively constituted constructions of 'masculinity'. Based in part on our empirical findings, we contrast the masculinity of linear time with what may be seen as a conception of time that reflects and reproduces feminine practices. We argue that feminine concepts of time as contextual, continuous, processual and contingent are incompatible with and difficult to understand using linear notions of time. Our intention is not to elevate a 'feminine time' over and above linear time, or to provide a polemic in favour of its deployment. Rather we simply wish to draw attention to this alternative understanding of temporality, and to explore some of its implications.

The second section commences with a critical examination of existing financial services corporate strategies attempting to capture the 'women's market'. Although aware of certain gender distinctions, we argue that the over-reliance on psychodynamic constructs of behaviour often results in strategies that obscure the gender dimensions of time. In particular the strategies remain oblivious of the incongruence between feminine times and what we argue is the embedded linear temporality of long-term contractual products. The most crucial dimension of this incongruence relates to the linear basis of financial contributions (i.e. premiums) around which contractual products are structured. An assumption underlying this structure is that consumers have continuous and stable earnings through which to service financial commitments over the individual adult's working life span. Moreover, there are financial penalties against disruptions to, or discontinuities in, these contributions. Such commitments are incompatible with the employment histories of many women and increasingly men in today's conditions of unemployment. Both the employment opportunities for women and often their 'choices', which reflect their embeddedness in relational conceptions of time (i.e. where it is tied to the obligations to, or demands of, significant others such as children and spouses), result in lifetime working experiences characterized by job interruptions, low pay and part-time employment.

In so far as financial services companies continue to subscribe to a linear model of time, reproduced through marketing discourses and embedded within their temporally oriented products, their attempts to capture the 'women's market' will continue to be constrained. In the concluding section of this chapter we draw out the implications of our analysis for marketing strategies of financial services and indicate the importance of further research in this field.

Time and consumer research: a critical review

Encouraged in part by several influential articles (e.g. Gross, 1987; Hirschman, 1987; Jacoby et al., 1976), the concept of time has increasingly become an important construct in consumer research. The realization of the full potential of this construct is, however, restricted by the predominance of a linear and absolutist perspective. 'Time' is presumed to exist as a linear object, outside the individual. It is perceived as a quantity, an abstract singular unit, homogeneous, though divisible into discrete elements. Linear time is frequently deployed without reference to content and context. As the duration between events, time is unaffected by the transformations it charts (Adam, 1993: 166). Linear time and the positivist methods of investigation which it embraces rarely take account of the polymorphous rhythms of social life, let alone comprehend them. Yet 'time' is bound up precisely with meanings that are constituted through social interaction, on both the behavioural and the symbolic plane (Nowotny, 1992). Nonetheless, linearity is evident within the three implicit notions of time predominant in consumer research: the objective, the subjective and the social temporal models.

Within the objective temporal model, 'time' is conceptualized as unproblematically existing external to the individual, in fixed immutable units (Becker, 1965). These units in turn yield an implicit utility to the consumer. This implicit utility facilitates the transformation of time into other entities such as money or products (Becker and Michael, 1973; Berry, 1979). Time is therefore assumed to constitute a controllable scarce resource (Becker, 1965). The 'clockwork precision' of this objective notion of time has encouraged its application to a wide variety of buying instances and issues. For example, Howard and Sheth (1969) included 'time pressure' in their multivariable decision-making models. They define 'time pressure' as 'the inverse of the amount of time the buyer has available to perform the behaviour required of purchasing and consumption. With this behaviour including the information seeking which precedes the purchasing act' (1969: 419).

In studies of household consumption, economic models treat the household as a 'productive unit' attempting to maximize utility through a combination of monetary resources, goods, services and time (e.g. Becker and Michael, 1973; Etgar, 1978; Hornik, 1984a; Liebermann and Silber, 1983;

Schary, 1971). These studies not only take for granted time as an absolute object with linear dimensions, but also subscribe to a calculative rational conception of human behaviour. There are clear parallels between assumptions of linear time and those of rational calculative action. These have been the subject of some critical scrutiny in recent times (e.g. Gibbs, 1993; Hirschman, 1987; Venkatesan and Anderson, 1980). For example, Hirschman (1987) questions the validity of rationalist ideas empowering the human mind with pre-existing tendencies, which enable the categorization and structuring of external stimuli. She identifies several anomalies embedded within the economic models of time, the most significant of which relate to the notion of time existing as a tradable unit of exchange (i.e. an expendable resource). Through the use of scenarios, she illustrates the inadequacy of this notion, as it fails to recognize that situational factors greatly affect the so-called exchange value of time. Similarly Gibbs has stated that 'situational and individual differences determine the phenomenological, personal experience of time and the value placed upon it, dependent upon the transaction not independent of it' (1993: 9). Although we agree with these critiques of human rationality and linear time, as we shall discuss later, they fail to provide a detailed examination of how time is constituted through power and knowledge relations.

Subjective notions of time, in contrast to objective external approaches, focus on the cognitive, perceptual apparatus by which individuals comprehend time (Hirschman, 1987). This approach to 'time', popularly embodied in psychological temporal models, has been used within consumer research to ascertain subjective perceptions of duration (e.g. Holman, 1981; Hornik, 1984b), time allocation (e.g. Hendrix, 1980; Wilson and Holman, 1980), time-inconsistent buying preferences (e.g. Hoch and Loewenstein, 1991) and individual positioning in relation to past, present and future (e.g. Daz, 1991; Holman, 1981; Morello, 1988). The subjective, person-centred, conceptual orientation which binds these studies is presented as a significant departure from objective rationalistic approaches to 'time' (e.g. economic temporal models). However these subjective temporal models, as with their objective counterparts, also prioritize linear time. They draw upon a linear conception of time to evaluate subjective temporal perceptions (Hirschman, 1987). This is best exemplified by the psychophysical research traditions, whereby time is envisaged as an 'external flow of physical units', and used to evaluate individual subjective temporal perceptions (1987: 67).

In its unquestioning prioritization of abstract linear time, the subjective model does not recognize that activities and actions take place in and serve to constitute our social temporal environment. This shortcoming is partially rectified within the third predominant approach to time in consumer research – which is more reflective of our position – i.e. the notion of social time. Social notions of time describe the category of time as being rooted in social activities, and thus socially constituted by virtue of the 'rhythms of social life' (Durkheim, 1912: 17). Social time exists within the wider realm of symbolic time, a cultural phenomenon constituted by individuals and groups in the social relations that shape their lives.

The concept of social time has featured within consumer research, in one of two capacities. In the first it represents an all-embracing analytical construct wherein all forms of time are assumed to be products of social construction. This usage is exemplified by studies highlighting the relativity of time perception to a given socio-cultural context (e.g. Graham, 1981; Gronomo, 1989; Nicosia and Meyer, 1976). Through establishing time as a multifaceted notion constituted by the social system in which it is experienced, these researchers present their work as engaging with absolutist notions of time (Gibbs, 1993: 11). In the second usage, social time features as part of an eclectic fusion of phenomenology, psychological time and social psychological time, in experiential temporal models (e.g. Bergadaa, 1992; Gjesme, 1981; Hirschman, 1987; Hirschman and Holbrook, 1992; Wright and Weitz, 1977) and the 'relativity' temporal model of Gibbs (1993). Within the experiential and relativity models of time, temporal realities are presented as determining and also forming part of self-identity. More specifically, the 'relativity' model of Gibbs (1993) draws our attention towards the omnipresent nature of time: 'the total time environment' and the 'dynamic interaction of a changing self over extended periods of time' (1993: 20). The relativity and experiential models of time represent a radical departure from our modern formulation of time and consciousness which has been inherited largely from the eighteenth century. These models focus on the phenomenological 'event' where, in contrast to previous studies, subjective and objective conceptions of time are indistinguishable. Phenomenological time anticipates the always embedded subjectivity in social (and temporal) processes. The subject is no longer discrete or separate from events that constitute it through time and space and their limitations (Ermarth, 1992).

Although social conceptions of time are less mechanistic and technically rational than previous approaches, they appear to remain bound to an unproblematic understanding of time as essentially linear. By failing to engage theoretically with the social mechanisms which serve to constitute linear time, social models are equally unable to recognize the inextricable link between linear time, power and knowledge. Consequently, they are unable to appreciate the social processes through which alternative conceptions of time (e.g. feminine time) are subjugated or obscured by the dominance of linear time. Despite problematizing asocial conceptions of time, these approaches continue to reinforce the hegemony of linear time, and thereby inadvertently contribute to marginalizing their own discourse. In order to avoid these problems we believe it is necessary to embark upon a deconstruction of linear time. While some authors (e.g. Nowotny, 1975; 1988; Thompson, 1967; Thrift, 1981; 1990; Young, 1988) have shown how linear (e.g. clock) time was closely associated with the industrial and regulatory demands of capitalist workplaces, our focus is upon equally pervasive gendered constructions of time.

Gendered time, masculinity, femininity and the constituted female

> Traditionally, we conceive of time as being an equally distributed
> resource where each individual receives his/her allotted share. Even in
> working life we start from the premise of individual time. But if we take
> a look at how women use their time it's obvious that it is rather a question
> of 'collective' time which others, for example their families, have a right
> to lay a claim to.

> (Gunnarsson and Ressner, 1985: 109–10)

Whilst conducting our empirical research,[1] it became increasingly apparent
that specific gender differences existed in terms of 'male' and 'female'
relations to and perceptions of linear time. These findings were supported by
existing feminist research, which has suggested that men and women tend to
use time differently owing to their distinct life situations (e.g. Davies, 1990;
Forman and Sowton, 1989; Gunnarsson and Ressner, 1985; Kahn, 1989;
O'Brien, 1989; Wadel, 1979). Common to these literatures is the assertion
that, when discussing the everyday lives of women, we cannot focus solely
on individual time. This is because 'women's time' is relational; it exists in
relation to the time demands of significant others (e.g. family members).
That is to say, women are thought to live within a set of relations that are
demanding on their time in ways that are often not the case for men. This is
captured by the phrase 'a woman's time is never her own'. Issues of time
ownership have been articulated by Helga Hernes, who has stated that 'time
disposal is partly determined by the individual, partly by social and legal
coercion and partly through negotiation with others' (1987: 104). Social and
legal coercion as well as negotiation with others are, however, related to
issues of power. Women's subordinate position in the public sphere, as well
as their ascribed domestic role in the private sphere, significantly inhibits
their power to decide over their own time, and that of others (Davies, 1990).
This situation is further accentuated by the historically specific power of
discourses of femininity, for example the discourse of *motherhood and self-
sacrifice*, which in turn serve to constitute the meanings we attribute to
femininity and feminine roles.

The routinized circularity and repetitiveness of domestic labour encapsulated by the phrase 'a woman's work is never done' exemplify the
incompatibility of women's work with linear conceptions of time. Rarely in
the domestic sphere can time be conceived to exist in finite, quantitatively
discrete units that are readily demarcated between, for example, work and
leisure or personal time (Adam, 1993: 172). For 'women's time' is 'continuous': the temporal density (i.e. times embedded within time, as reported
by Lewis and Weigart, 1990) and complexity of feminine roles displace
any sense of 'time out' (Davies, 1990). The unparalleled significance of
'continuity' in 'feminine time' warrants its further elaboration. To achieve
this we draw upon the work of Davies (1990), Lewis and Weigart (1990),
Maines and Hardesty (1987) and Miller et al. (1975). In attempting to
ascertain subjective perceptions of temporal distance, Lewis and Weigart

(1990) develop the idea of 'temporal embeddedness'. The concept of 'temporal embeddedness' recognizes that human life and the social actions which constitute it are a complex overlap of actions and meanings at various stages of enactment (1990: 92). Each action, in turn, is embedded within a perceived or prescribed duration. In contrast, the predominant notion of linearity in human action assumes that events transpire in a sequential, chronological and discrete manner such that there is a linear progression of separate events whereby the beginning of one event signals the end of a previous event. Temporal embeddedness runs directly counter to such linearity since it involves the simultaneous overlapping of multiple events. Along with Davies (1990), Maines and Hardesty (1987) and Schuller (1988), we argue that the everyday lives of many women are characterized by simultaneous actions, each embedded within overlapping temporalities.

Increasing rates of formal employment by women has meant that they are faced with the task of managing the most demanding temporal constraints of economic labour during precisely the same periods of their life-cycle as domestic pressures (i.e. family care) are at their greatest (see, for example, Chambers, 1986; Deem, 1988; Le Feuvre, 1993; Seymour, 1992; Woodward and Green, 1988). At the same time, and encouraged through the experience of subordination in paid work, women are socialized into prioritizing their domestic commitments over formal employment (Davies, 1990: 231). As Chambers (1986) argues, women's perceptions of time have been developed within a domestic ideology in which time not spent in paid employment is used for unpaid domestic duties. Consequently 'time out' or free time is often impossible, or translated into other 'self-sacrificing activities'. It is quite obvious that the perpetuation and maintenance of this gendered conception of time is inextricably linked to power, as time out is quite simply a question of one's own time. Historically, men have been able to demand time out – time for themselves in the pub, sporting activities and other forms of 'unproductive' leisure. This is facilitated and legitimized by discourses which serve to constitute the meanings attributed to men and masculinity in terms of an ideology of the male 'breadwinner'. Through a seemingly impenetrable domestic division of labour, men are comparatively free from the daily routines of childcare and running a home. In contrast:

> women's lives appear to be characterised by a meshing of activities making up the complicated patterns of the cat's cradle. Whereas the steel cable [a metaphorical representation of male temporal structuring] can be cut at points and laid out end to end, making its continuum possible, cutting the thread in the cat's cradle destroys the whole design and renders it unusable. Time out is impossible. (Davies, 1990: 256)

This incongruence between 'feminine time' and linear time is further enhanced by the existence of a feminine care-oriented, processual time (Balbo,

1987; Cunnison, 1986; Davies and Esseveld, 1989; 1990; 1992; Prokop, 1981). Prokop (1981) has suggested that in 'need-oriented' communication (care) work, the clock is of limited importance; rather it is the task at hand that is definitive. Cunnison has suggested that 'the imperative of response to human need plays an important part in care work' (1986: 189). Davies (1990) has argued that this need-oriented response requires a more flexible relation to time. She describes this relation as 'process time', in that 'the task itself defines the amount of time to be consumed, rather than a time limit or temporal demarcation being placed on the task' (1990: 37). Within our empirical research, we also observed a task-oriented time associated with certain domestic activities (e.g. childcare, nurturing sick relatives, and creative activities such as preparing a special meal). These activities are with difficulty contained within clock time. Rather they are embedded in a temporality that is specific to the activity, and in turn dictates its length.

Within this section we have attempted to illustrate the incompatibility of feminine time with a linear perspective which separates work from leisure, the public from the private, and task from clock-based orientations to time. We have described feminine time as relational, continuous, processual and cyclical. It is not the abstract and decontextualized notion of time that is readily measured, commodified and controlled. Mediated through significant others, feminine time is shared rather than personal, and relational rather than linear (Adam, 1993: 172). Our identification of a feminine time, diametrically opposed to linear time, serves to further undermine absolutist notions of linear time. However, our work is of further significance in identifying the incongruence of feminine time with the inherent temporality of financial services contractual products. The remainder of this chapter is devoted to a discussion of this incongruence and the relevance of our analytical framework to its understanding.

Gendered time and financial services consumption

With minor exceptions, traditional selling practices within the financial services industry have been deeply rooted in gendered perceptions about male 'breadwinners' as their target market. Consequently one half of the population – women – are neglected as direct, rather than indirect, potential customers. Apparently encouraged by a recognition of increasing patterns of female economic activity, the industry has become highly sensitive to this 'untapped' market. Accordingly, numerous financial services companies have focused attention on the potential of marketing specifically to women (e.g. National and Provincial Building Society, Royal Bank of Scotland, Halifax Building Society, Bradford and Bingley Building Society and National Westminster Bank). Typical of the activity in the area is a Halifax Building Society study, conducted by Andrew Irving Associates, which argues that an 'increasing understanding of women's needs enables product

offerings, customer services and promotional activities to be tailored appropriately . . . to make them more convenient, appealing and relevant to the
female market' (1992: 4).

Relational time and the linear structuring of contractual products

The inextricable link between relational time and financial services consumption becomes evident when we examine feminine time and its consequences for formal employment. The organization of the workplace, as of
the home, reflects and reinforces a hierarchy of time control; the time of subordinates is largely controlled by superiors whereas senior people have
'gatekeepers' to protect them from the pressures of others' time demands.
Since women are disproportionately represented in the subordinate ranks of
organizations, their time is more regulated by others than by themselves. The
combination of this subordination and the pressure of domestic responsibilities
which women readily assume frequently results in broken or part-time
patterns of employment. But even when working full-time, women are dis-
advantaged in the career stakes because of their family commitments,
whereas men may manage excessive time demands at work through this
labour being serviced domestically by a woman.

Financial services products, especially those involving long-term contractual commitments, are frequently incompatible with the relational context
of women's time and subsequent working patterns. Part of our empirical
research involved an examination of the financial contribution structures of
selected contractual products (namely insurance, investments and personal
pensions). These commitment structures were tested against a set of pre-
determined 'employment scenarios' that reflected dominant national patterns
of female employment. The findings demonstrated that these employment scenarios were incompatible with the consumption of many financial
services products where a linear/chronological structuring imposes regular
contractual financial contributions, any interruption of which is severely
penalized. This incongruence may be more fully grasped in the following
brief discussion of the results obtained from one employment scenario
(namely, 'part-time work') for its influence on the ability to sustain financial
commitments to personal pensions. As an introduction to this discussion, we
have provided in Table 8.1 a review of recent pension consumption statistics
by sex.[2]

Part-time work and financial contributions to personal pension schemes

As has been well documented (see de Neubourg, 1985; *Labour Research*,
1991; Layard et al., 1978), part-time employment is predominantly the experience of women in the labour market and it is very closely associated with low
pay. Consequently the contribution of part-time women employees to pension schemes is low or non-existent, with the resulting implications that
retired women are either wholly dependent upon the retirement income of

Table 8.1 *Pension schemes by sex, 1991 (per cent)*

	Any pension	PPP	Non-contributory	Contributory	Any AVCS
Penetration[1]	58	17	8	34	7
Distribution by sex					
Male	64	70	61	61	68
Female	36	30	39	39	32

Base: all adults (18+) in employment (22.0 million).
[1] Percentage of adults (18+) in employment holding such pensions.
PPP: Personal Pensions Plans.
AVCS: Additional Voluntary Contribution Schemes.
Source: NOP/FRS *The Financial Consumer 1995*

their partners and/or subjected to a poverty line existence in later life. While this is a social problem extending well beyond our subject matter here, the structure and arrangement of financial service products exacerbate rather than ameliorate the inequities. This is because part-time employees do not normally qualify for admission to final salary pension schemes and, there-fore, are restricted to money purchase personal pensions where the retirement benefits are directly tied to the contributions. Rarely, in these circumstances, can they contribute sufficient to secure a pension that would take them beyond the poverty line. Furthermore, it is illegal to contribute to a pension out of savings when out of work – a situation that is quite common for part-time workers who are often in temporary employment. Moreover the structure of charges (i.e. fixed fees) for many personal pension schemes is such that they will always have a disproportionate effect on low earners' benefits since fixed fees or minimum charges will have a larger effect on low premiums than on high ones. Davies and Ward, in their review of Britain's pension structure, concluded that 'women on lower levels of income need a higher replacement ratio in order to keep their incomes in retirement above poverty level' (1992: 20). The present system of personal pensions tends to provide the opposite, with a higher replacement ratio being provided for people on higher incomes.

The broad conclusion that can be drawn from these findings is that for the majority of women, with their long periods of low earnings and interrupted career patterns, any pension strategy that depends on a link with earnings during their paid working lives will produce a low income in retirement. Moreover a strategy which depends on making contributions from dis-posable earnings during those working lives and then relying on investment returns to deliver the benefits, as with personal pensions, adds an additional layer of uncertainty to an already uncertain future (Davies and Ward, 1992). If, however, products were developed to accommodate women's (and increasingly men's) fluctuating and diverse relationship to the labour market, it would threaten the profit base of financial services companies. Part of the problem is the system of paying high front-end-loaded commissions to sales persons which lengthens the period before profit is achieved out of the policy charges on contracts. But as this system of commission is the subject of criticism by the regulators, it may be restructured, thus removing one of the several obstacles to changing contractual products in directions that would be more appropriate to women.

Marketing research implications of gendered time

In general, marketing research either ignores time completely or, as discussed previously, ascribes time the status of an object with linear dimensions. Within this chapter, we have discussed several of the resultant effects of a linear approach to time, one of the most significant of which is its ability to obscure alternative discourses of temporality. Our identification of gendered time represents a dramatic discursive shift away from this predominant approach to time, and this has certain implications for marketing research. First, the relational conceptions of time associated with femininity may begin to expand as changes in the labour market (e.g. the expansion of jobs for women, part-time and self-employment), feminist politics and environmentalism have their effect upon populations. A serious weakness of marketing research, as it stands at present, is its failure to recognize the dynamic polymorphic nature of time. A second marketing implication is that gendered time draws our attention to the significance of future perceptions in consumption (most especially contractual product consumption), and the existence of variations in these perceptions. Finally, alternative discourses of social time encourage a recognition of product as well as consumer temporality, and the consumption consequences of a disharmony between these two temporalities. Each of these marketing research implications will now be discussed in turn.

Paradigmatic shift: towards a more socially contingent approach to consumer behaviour research

The study of consumer behaviour by marketing research currently embraces a perspective of time as linear, to the exclusion of other less quantifiable times. This is unsurprising if we reflect once again on the characteristics ascribed to time when viewed through the lens of linearity. Time is presumed to exist as an object, external to the individual. It is perceived as a quantity, an abstract singular unit, homogeneous although divisible into discrete elements. This perspective on time reflects and reinforces the dominant positivist approaches of consumer behaviour. It enables the study of consumer behaviour to swim with the tide of a growing interest in temporality whilst still retaining its positivist foundations.

Although there are a variety of frameworks for understanding what constitutes marketing knowledge, a central feature is its unproblematic allegiance to positivist methods within an empiricist epistemology.[3] This allegiance can in part be understood by marketing's seemingly insatiable urge to achieve parity with 'higher-order' scientific disciplines. To achieve this, marketing phenomena within the social world must be amenable to causal analysis involving their reduction to a set of quantifiable variables similar to those of the natural sciences. The social world is assumed to exist independently of the observer, although made knowable only through sense perception of social actions and events. It can be thought of as a stable, predictable structure composed of a network of determinate relationships between constituent parts. Reality is to be found in the concrete behaviour and relationships between these parts (Morgan and Smircich, 1980: 485). In the same way that knowledge and control of the 'natural' world have been made possible through scientific methods and engineering technologies, so it is thought that society can be measured and controlled once the 'correct' techniques of analysis are devised and developed.

Within the study of consumer behaviour this analogy between the material and the social world most commonly takes the form of behaviourism (Skinner, 1953). Just as natural phenomena are seen to reside in chains of cause and effect which the scientist unravels, so consumer behaviour is seen to be best explained through resort to stimulus–response models that refuse to acknowledge the interpretive and constructive aspects of human conduct. An associated, alternative 'psychodynamic' paradigm relies upon a model of consumer behaviour drawn from cognitive psychology which depicts individuals as possessing rational motives, cognitive designs and information-processing mental capacities. The emphasis of this paradigm on observable behaviour and quantification fits comfortably within the overall positivist framework of consumer behaviour. It also provides the 'theoretical' foundation for the highly influential information-processing models of Bettman (1979), Engel et al. (1968) and Howard and Sheth (1969). These models assume that consumers transform environmental information from a jumble of sensory data to a neat, coherent set of concepts that is stored in a 'systematic memory structure' and then brought into consciousness when processed according to a linear logical sequence of thought (Hirschman, 1992: 48).

Over recent decades a series of marketing literatures have questioned the reliance of consumer research on this psychodynamic paradigm (e.g. Anderson, 1989; Arndt, 1985; Foxall, 1986; 1987; 1990; Graham, 1981; Olshavsky and Granbois, 1979). Despite these criticisms the paradigm continues to dominate consumer behaviour literature, research and course textbooks. It may be argued that a factor contributing to the continued resilience of the paradigm is the failure of critics to do more than substitute one positivist framework for another when objecting to psychodynamic research. While appearing to displace the unobservable mental processes of psychodynamics, for example, radical behaviourism (Foxall, 1986; 1990) relies implicitly upon the 'mind' as a repository of sensory experiences, recollection of which can be readily brought to memory for purposes of classifying stimuli as positive (pleasurable) or negative (painful). This memory, in turn, is dependent upon a linear conception of time wherein stimulus–response experiences can be stored sequentially in a history bank, as it were, to provide subjects with instantaneous guides to behaviour.

In contrast, we perceive time as existing within the wider realm of symbolic and cultural processes constituted by individuals and groups in the social relations that shape their lives. By focusing on a phenomenological approach where a separation between subjects and objects is not so taken for granted, our discourse of time anticipates subjectivity as already embedded and in the process of reconstitution through time 'events'. This position is in complete opposition to classical or humanistic understandings of the subject, subjectivity and the self. For there subjectivity is understood as freedom against constraint or, 'that creative autonomy or personal space not yet captured by political economy' (Knights, 1990: 319), the Cartesian *cogito* of linear time. Following Foucault (1982), by contrast, human beings may be seen as constituted as subjects through a multiplicity and diverse range of often contradictory discourses. This multiplicity of determinations opens up the space for reversals, resistances and changes in subjectivity over time. Subjectivity is therefore historically and culturally contingent, discontinuous, potentially fractured and multiple. It is not stable, continuous and consistent as and between distinct linear time frames as reflected in positivist studies of consumer behaviour.

This conception of self and subjectivity as almost arbitrary interventions in the flow and flux of social experience through time has significant implications for marketing in general and the distribution of financial services in particular. More precisely, the long-term contractual products of the insurance and pensions industry, which at present are perceived as a major source of profit in financial services, require that providers sustain an enduring relationship throughout the lifetime of the consumer. It is therefore necessary that providers recognize the consumption effects of changes in the consumer's framework as, through time, there are transformations in self and subjectivity. Assumptions, held by product providers, of a static rather than a changing self may lead to a mismatch between the strategic behaviour of providers and the changing perceptual realities of the consumers. Possible strategies towards reconciling this potential temporal disharmony involve regular communication between providers and their clients, adjusting pricing strategies to match changes in product relevance and 'need', and the introduction of products whose temporalities attempt to match those of the provider's 'target groups'. Finally, it is important for companies to recognize that the conception of self which embarked on purchasing a long-term business product may not remain consistent throughout this experience and may differ dramatically by the end of the contract.

Conclusion

Within this chapter, we have refrained from treating time exclusively in a linear, quantitative fashion, suggesting instead its construction and reconstruction through social interaction and cultural norms. Consequently we have argued that subjective dimensions of temporality are shaped by characteristics of the social and cultural situation and thus are open to wide variations. This was exemplified through the identification of a significant disparity between the discursively constituted nature of feminine non-linear and masculine linear conceptions of time. Our research also suggests that where a disparity exists between the temporal construction of the product and the time orientations of the consumer, this may have adverse consumption consequences (e.g. a rejection of, or inability to relate to the significance of the product to the consumer's everyday life). This partly explains the disparity in consumption rates between the sexes of long-term contractual financial service's products such as pensions and life insurance. It is necessary that product providers recognize the existence of variations in the time perceptions of their potential clients. Especially significant is the situation where the product requires the consumer to draw upon temporal horizons outside the immediacy of everyday life, as is the case with 'security' and long-term contractual products. Many product providers have been oblivious to alternative time orientations partly because of their distribution systems, where personal selling and financial advice have mediated the relationship between producer and consumer. Consequently marketing strategies and sales training have been comparatively gender blind and, we would argue, for this reason limited in their ability to extend their market beyond the more conventional security parameters of masculine time horizons.

Our discourse of social time recognizes that, just as in the case of natural objects, time is not simply an environment or set of dimensions in which the elapsing of an event can be recorded and given boundaries. Rather, time is constitutive of social events and forms of activity; it is embedded in the very social reality it is deemed to structure and frame. This understanding of time embeddedness has several implications for marketing, only a few of which we have alluded to in this chapter. We have focused primarily on long-term business products in financial services.

Within consumer research, there exists limited recognition of product temporality and the consumption significance of a given product temporality. Even where it is recognized (e.g. Gibbs, 1993), product temporality is often approached as given (i.e. ascribed an ontological existence outside human construction or interpretation). In contrast, we have focused on the constitution of contractual products through dominant marketing discourses, and the resultant instilling of these products with a linear temporality. Our approach to social time and time embeddedness facilitated the recognition of a hitherto unrecognized temporal disharmony between the linear temporality of contractual products and feminine times. The likelihood of temporal disharmony between product and subjective consumer temporalities is, however, not restricted to feminine subjectivity. Through failing to recognize that temporality exists as both a characteristic of the consumer and an attribute of the good or service being consumed, current marketing strategies inevitably encourage instances of temporal disharmony in consumption. For example, one consumer may perceive the duration of the maturity of an investment product to pass quickly and thus be encouraged to purchase or retain this product. Another consumer may perceive the embedded temporality of this same product as protracted, as far beyond their everyday temporal horizons. Their concern for a more immediate gratification may result in a rejection of the product or, if it is purchased through 'high-pressure' selling, early encashment. The high rate of surrenders in life insurance products could be partly explained as relating to temporal disharmonies between products and consumers. It is therefore crucial for the marketing of life insurance to recognize that time is a subjective attribute of both the consumer and the product. Dominant discourses which come into play in the construction of products and their distribution may also serve to instil a conception of time into products which may or may not be compatible with the time horizons of consumers. Above all, it is of importance to marketing researchers and practitioners to realize the unparalleled significance of time in consumption. We conclude that an understanding of time must be included in any investigation of consumer behaviour and market/sales strategy.

Notes

An earlier version of this chapter was published with the title 'It's about time: the significance of gendered time for financial services consumption', *Time and Society*, 1995, 4 (2): 205–31. We thank Janet Kavanagh and Annette Ashton-Redlin (Financial Services for Women; National and Provincial Building Society), for providing support for this research.

1   The empirical research involved conducting 60 in-depth thematically 'structured interviews', with both men and women, within a wide range of life-stages and socio-economic groupings. These interviews were taped and transcribed. Ethnograph (a software package designed to analyse data deriving from qualitative research) was used to 'arrange' the data. A derivative of grounded theory was used to analyse the data emanating from the interviews. A more in-depth discussion of the research procedure is provided within Odih (1995).

2   If the volume of contributions to pensions were taken into account, the sex comparisons would be much more skewed than these statistics, but this is not surprising given the arguments we have presented so far.

3   There is not space to discuss these philosophy of social science issues in any detail here. Suffice it to say that an empiricist epistemology is one subscribing to a belief that knowledge can only be derived from sensory experience, and positivism is a method of acquiring knowledge of the social world that refuses to accept ontological discontinuity between human and natural phenomena.

References

Adam, B. (1993) 'Within and beyond the time economy of employment relations: conceptual issues pertinent to research on time and work', *Social Science Information*, 32 (2): 163–84.

Anderson, P.F. (1989) 'On relativism and interpretivism with a prolegomenon to the why question', in E.C. Hirschman (ed.), *Interpretive Consumer Research*. Provo, UT: Association for Consumer Research.

Andrew Irving Associates (1992) *Women's Research Report*. Andrew Irving Marketing Association.

Arndt, J. (1985) 'The tyranny of paradigms: the case for paradigmatic pluralism in marketing', in N. Dholakia and J. Arndt (eds), *Changing the Course of Marketing: Alternative Paradigms for Widening Marketing Theory*. Greenwich, CT: JAI Press.

Balbo, L. (1987) 'Crazy quilts: rethinking the welfare state debate from a woman's point of view', in S. Sasson (ed.), *Women and the State*. London: Hutchinson.

Becker, G. (1965) 'A theory of the allocation of time', *Economic Journal*, 75 (September): 493–517.

Becker, G. and Michael, R. (1973) 'On the new theory of consumer behaviour', *Swedish Journal of Economics*, 75 (September): 493–517.

Bergadaa, M. (1992) 'The role of time in the action of the consumer', *Journal of Consumer Research*, 17 (December): 289–302.

Berry, L. (1979) 'The time buying consumer', *Journal of Retailing*, 55 (Winter): 58–69.

Bettman, J. (1979) *An Information Processing Theory of Consumer Choice*. Reading, MA: Addison-Wesley.

Chambers, D. (1986) 'The constraints of work and domestic schedules on women's leisure studies', *Leisure Studies*, 15: 309–25.

Cunnison, S. (1986) 'Gender, consent and exploitation among sheltered housing wardens', in K. Purcell et al. (eds), *The Changing Experience of Employment*. Basingstoke: Macmillan.

Davies, B. and Ward, S. (1992) *Women and Personal Pensions*. Equal Opportunities Commission, London: HMSO.

Davies, K. (1990) *Women and Time: Weaving the Strands of Everyday Life*. Aldershot: Avebury.

Davies, K. (1992) 'Gender and the life course: what do you mean by time?', in G. Bjeren and L. Elgrist-Saltman (eds), *The Life-Line Approach to the Study of Social Change and Gender*. Aldershot: Avebury.

Davies, K. and Esseveld, J. (1989) 'Factory women, redundancy and the search for work: towards a reconceptualization of employment and unemployment', *Sociological Review*, May: 219–52.

Daz, T.K. (1991) 'Time: the hidden dimension in strategic planning', *Journal of Long Range Planning*, 24 (3): 49–57.

Deem, R. (1988) 'Feminism and leisure studies: opening up new directories', in E. Wimbush and M. Talbot (eds), *Relative Freedoms: Women and Leisure*. Milton Keynes: Open University Press. pp. 5–17.

de Neubourg, C. (1985) 'Part-time work: an international quantitative comparison', *International Labour Review*, 124 (5).

Durkheim, E. (1912) *Les Formes elementaires de la vie religieuse*. Paris: Alcan.

Engel, J., Kollat, D. and Blackwell, R. (1968) *Consumer Behavior*. New York: Holt, Rinehart & Winston.

Ermarth, E. (1992) *Sequel to History: Postmodernism and the Crisis of Representational Time*. Princeton, NJ: Princeton University Press.

Etgar, M. (1978) 'The household as a production unit', in J. Sheth (ed.), *Research in Marketing*, Vol. 1. Greenwich, CT: JAI Press. pp. 79–98.

Forman, F. and Sowton, C. (1989) *Taking Our Time: Feminist Perspectives on Temporality*. Oxford: Pergamon.

Foucault, M. (1982) 'The subject and power', in H.L. Dreyfus and P. Rabinow (eds), *Michel Foucault: Beyond Structuralism and Hermeneutics*. Chicago: University of Chicago Press.

Foxall, G. (1986) 'The role of radical behaviourism in the explanation of consumer choice', *Advances in Consumer Choice*, 13: 187–91.

Foxall, G. (1987) 'Consumer choice in behaviourism and consumer research: theoretical promise and empirical process', *International Journal of Research Marketing*, 4: 111–29.

Foxall, G. (1990) *Consumer Psychology in Behavioural Perspective*. London: Routledge.

Gibbs, P. (1992) 'Consumer buying strategies in financial services'. Bournemouth Working Paper Series, Bournemouth University.

Gibbs, P. (1993) 'Time as a dimension of consumption in financial services'. Bournemouth Working Paper Series, Bournemouth University.

Gjesme, T. (1981) 'Some factors influencing perceived goal distance in time: a preliminary check', *Perceptual Motor Skills*, 53 (August): 175–82.

Graham, R. (1981) 'The role of perception of time in consumer research', *Journal of Consumer Research*, 7: 335–42.

Gronomo, S. (1989) 'Concepts of time: some implications for consumer research', *Advances in Consumer Research*, 16: 339–45.

Gross, B. (1987) 'Time scarcity: interdisciplinary perspectives and implications for consumer behaviour research', *Research in Consumer Behaviour*, 2: 1–54.

Gunnarsson, E. and Ressner, U. (1985) *Frontimmers gara Kuinner pa Kontor och Verstadsgolu*. Stockholm: Prisma.

Hendrix, P. (1980) 'Subjective elements in the examination of time expenditure', in W. Wilkie (ed.), *Advances in Consumer Research*, Vol. 6. Ann Arbor, MI: Association for Consumer Research. pp. 38–44.

Hernes, H. (1987) *Welfare State and Women Power*. Oslo: Norwegian University Press.

Hirschman, E. (1987) 'Theoretical perspectives of time use: implications for consumer behaviour research', *Research in Consumer Behaviour*, 2: 55–81.

Hirschman, E. and Holbrook, M. (1992) *Postmodernism Consumer Research: The Study of Consumption as Text*. London: Sage.

Hoch, S. and Loewenstein, G. (1991) 'Time-inconsistent preferences and consumer self-control', *Journal of Consumer Research*, 17 (March): 492–507.

Holman, R. (1981) 'The imagination of the future: a hidden concept in the study of consumer decision making', in K.B. Monroe (ed.), *Advances in Consumer Research*, Vol. 8. Ann Arbor, MI: Association for Consumer Research. pp. 187–91.

Hornik, J. (1984a) 'Household production approach to consumer shopping time behaviour', in E.C. Hirschman and M.B. Holbrook (eds), *Advances in Consumer Research*, Vol. 12. Provo, UT: Association for Consumer Research. pp. 200–3.

Hornik, J. (1984b) 'Subjective vs objective time measures: a note on the perception of time in consumer behaviour', *Journal of Consumer Research*, 11 (June): 615–18.

Howard, J. and Sheth, J. (1969) *The Theory of Buyer Behavior*. New York: Wiley.

Jacoby, J., Szybillo, G. and Berning, C. (1976) 'Time and consumer behaviour: an interdisciplinary overview', *Journal of Consumer Research*, 2: 320–39.

Kahn, R.P. (1989) 'Women and time in childbirth and during lactation', in F. Forman and C. Sowton (eds), *Taking Our Time: Feminist Perspectives on Temporality*. Oxford: Pergamon.

Keegan, V. (1994) 'Girls on top in jobs market', *The Guardian*, 9 April: 25.

Knights, D., Sturdy, A. and Morgan, G. (1994) 'The consumer rules? An examination of the rhetoric and "reality" of marketing in financial services', *European Journal of Marketing*, 33 (3).

Labour Research (1991) 'The widening of the pay divide', *Labour Research*, 80 (1).

Layard, R. et al. (1978) 'The causes of poverty'. Background Paper no. 5, Royal Commission on the Distribution of Income and Wealth, London: HMSO.

Le Feuvre, N. (1993) 'Leisure, work and gender: a sociological study of women's time in France', paper presented at the Association for the Social Study of Time 10th Annual Conference, Dartington, Devon, 16–18 July.

Lewis, D. and Weigart, A. (1990) 'The structures and meanings of social-time', in J. Hassard (ed.), *The Sociology of Time*. London: Macmillan.

Liebermann, Y. and Silber, J. (1983) 'Household economics and market segmentation', *European Journal of Marketing*, 17 (2): 13–25.

Maines, D. and Hardesty, M. (1987) 'Temporality and gender: young adults' career and family plans', *Social Forces*, 66 (1): pp. 103–20.

Miller, D.E., Hintz, R.A. and Couch, C.J. (1975) 'The elements and structure of openings', in C.J. Couch and R.A. Hintz Jr (eds), *Constructing Social Life*.

Morello, G. (1988) 'Business requirements and future expectations in comparative bank services: the issue of time perceptions', paper presented at the Research for Financial Services Seminar, ESOMAR, Milan. pp. 235–45.

Morgan, G. and Smircich, L. (1980) 'The case for qualitative research', *Academy of Management Review*, 5 (4): 491–500.

Niscosia, F. and Meyer, R. (1976) 'Towards a sociology of consumption', *Journal of Consumer Research*, 3 (September): 65–75.

Nowotny, H. (1975) 'Time structuring and time measurement: on the interrelation between time keepers and social time', in J.T. Fraser and N. Lawrence (eds), *The Study of Time 2*. Berlin, Heidelberg: Springer.

Nowotny, H. (1988) 'From the future to the extended present', in G. Kirsch, P. Nijkamp and K. Zimmerman (eds), *The Formation of Time Preferences in Multidisciplinary Perspectives*.

Nowotny, H. (1992) 'Time and social theory: towards a social theory of time', *Time and Society*, 1 (3): 421–55.

O'Brien, M. (1989) 'Periods', in F. Forman and C. Sowton (eds), *Taking Our Time: Feminist Perspectives on Temporality*. Oxford: Pergamon.

Odih, P. (1995) 'Gendered time and financial services consumption'. PhD thesis, Manchester School of Management, UMIST, Manchester.

Olshavsky, R. and Granbois, D. (1979) 'Consumer decision making – fact or fiction', *Journal of Consumer Research*, 6: 93–100.

Prokop, V. (1981) *Kuinnors Livssaammanhang, Bergeransad Strategier och Oma Hliga Onskninger*. Stockholm: Raben and Sjagren.

Schary, P. (1971) 'Consumption and the problem of time', *Journal of Marketing*, 35 (April): 50–5.

Schuller, T. (1988) 'After employment: unemployment time and gender', paper presented at ESRC Workshop on Employment and Unemployment, England, May.

Seymour, J. (1992) ' "No time to call our own": women's time as a household resource'. *Women's Studies International Forum*, 15 (2): 187–92.

Skinner, B.F. (1953) *Science and Human Behavior*. New York: MacMillan.

Thompson, E.P. (1967) 'Time, work-discipline and industrial capitalism', *Past and Present*, 38: 56–97.

Thrift, N. (1981) 'Owners time and own time: the making of capitalist consciousness, 1300–1800', in *Space and Time in Geography*.

Thrift, N. (1990) 'The making of a capitalist time consciousness', in J. Hassard (ed.), *The Sociology of Time*. London: Macmillan.

Venkatesan, J. and Anderson, B. (1980) 'Time budgets and consumer services', in H.R. Bloch, G.D. Block, V.A. Utah and A.M. Zeithmal (eds), *Services Marketing in a Changing Environment*. pp. 52–5.

Wadel, C. (1979) 'The hidden work of everyday life', in *The Social Anthropology of Work*. London: Academic Press.

Wilson, D. and Holman, R. (1980) 'Economic theories of time in consumer behaviour', in C.W. Lamb and P.M. Dunne (eds), *Theoretical Developments in Marketing: Advances in Consumer Research*. Chicago: American Marketing Association. pp. 265–8.

Woodward, D. and Green, E. (1988) *Not Tonight Dear: The Social Control of Women's Leisure*. Milton Keynes: Open University Press.

Wright, P. and Weitz, B. (1977) 'Time horizon effects on product evaluation strategies', *Journal of Marketing Research*, 14 (November): 429–43.

Young, M. (1988) *The Metronomic Society: Natural Rhythms and Human Time Tables*. London: Thames & Hudson.

9 Commentary

Morris B. Holbrook

As we approach the millennium, with the inevitable backward glances that accompany the anticipation of such a historical punctuation mark, many scholars have turned their thoughts to the task of re-examining past events in their intellectual disciplines and speculating on what the next century will witness in a variety of academic specialities – marketing included. Hence, the topic of the present volume – rethinking marketing – seems both timely and propaedeutic toward bringing this field of inquiry gracefully into the twenty-first century.

Recently, our colleagues in Northern Ireland have addressed a similar theme under the heading of *Marketing Eschatology* (Brown et al., 1995) or *Marketing Apocalypse* (Brown et al., 1996). These volumes collect the thoughts of some scholars who met in Belfast during the autumn of 1995 to contemplate the possible end of marketing and to seek plausible prognostications for its future. This conference included some of the same participants who have contributed to the present volume – Stephen Brown, Douglas Brownlie, Morris Holbrook, Michael Thomas, and Robin Wensley.

But whereas the tone of the Ulster conference was rather wild and woolly, that of the work at hand is more tame and temperate. I do not mean this characterization as a criticism. A sober look at where we have been and where we are going should provide important insights that will help move us toward an intellectually enriched future. Nonetheless, sobriety entails costs as well as benefits. Not least among the former is the predicament that if we approach our work with a sufficiently stern demeanour, our readers will likely follow suit. Thus, the two chapters conjoined in this part couch their presentations in a tone that demands to be taken . . . *seriously*. And the editors have lumped these two pieces under a part title that also requires our careful scrutiny – namely, 'Reframing Consumers'.

Thanks to the work of Kahneman, Tversky, and others working in the area of behavioural decision theory, we all know that how a problem is framed (say, in terms of losses versus gains) greatly affects the sorts of conclusions that we reach. Common sense also teaches us that how a work of art is framed (say, a gilded enclosure for a Dutch masterpiece) shapes our appreciation of its aesthetic value. Does it therefore follow that 'reframing consumers' can inspire us to see them in some new and fruitful way? That the postmodern ethos will suggest such a new 'frame'? Or that the eschatological moment

which we slouch, like that rough beast envisioned by W.B. Yeats,
ehow reveal the consumer to be a creature more wondrous than
we have heretofore imagined? I certainly hope so. But on the
of the two chapters presented here, I decidedly fear not.

In his previous writings, Richard Elliott has portrayed himself as an
'interpretivist' (1996: 141) while simultaneously espousing the tastes of 'an
old positivist' (1996: 140) by proclaiming his nearly indignant impatience
with a self-obsessed essayist who has depicted the consumption experience
by means of similes based on 'cats . . . birds . . . dogs . . . and jazz
musicians' (1996: 140). As Elliott puts it succinctly in what I take to be his
studied emulation of Damon Runyon: 'But enough with the cats already!'
(1996: 141).

Here, Elliott (1996) has let the proverbial cat out of the bag. Indeed, this
aphorism has much to teach us about marketing thought in general and about
reframing consumers in particular. It comes from a time when farmers used
to take their pigs to market in sacks; when little piglets were far more
valuable than the much despised cats that cluttered up the barnyards; and
when a vendor of pork might be caught in the act of deceptive marketing if
a potential customer found that he had weighted down his sack of pigs by
stuffing a worthless feline or two into their midst. In other words, letting the
cat out of the bag refers metaphorically to the hermeneutics of suspicion; to
finding some significance hidden below the surface; to the uncovering of
latent meanings in a text. And Elliott has demystified his own text by
warning us in the past of his deeply divided sensibilities as a marketing
thinker.

Thus, in his current chapter, Elliott brings the temperament of a born neo-
positivist to bear on the ethos of postmodernity and thereby demonstrates, if
anything, that never the twain shall meet. He begins by providing a learned
and valuable account of how hyper-reality has intruded upon the consumer's
consciousness, how the symbolic meanings of consumption have eclipsed
the substance that lurks below the surface, and how the images of consumer
products communicate at levels far beyond their utilitarian functions. (So
far, so good.) Further, Elliott helpfully links such phenomena to the social
construction of reality, to the status implications of distinctions in taste, and
to potentially resistant readings of consumption as a text – with the
fragmented tendency of such active reader responses to differ among
consumers (say, between genders or ethnic groups) and with the postmodern
move toward defining one's 'self' in terms of the images or experiences that
one consumes (say, clothing fashions or MTV) – all leading to a 'desperate
search for meaning in a disintegrating social order' that Elliott follows
Lyotard in regarding as symptomatic of the postmodern condition. (Again,
well expressed and insightful as a review of the emerging episteme.) Beyond
these considerations, Elliott points to the emotional and hedonic components
of consumption (found, for example, in the shopping experience), the likely
role of non-rational 'motivated' choices (in which we make 'decisions' to do

what feels good), and the need for interpretive research methods to invest-igate such phenomena (by means of various post-positivistic approaches). (Still a useful review of well-travelled terrain.)

Then Elliott adumbrates a vision that I find quite promising for further development. Specifically, he suggests that owing to all the currents of change already mentioned, language may be an inappropriate medium for investigat-ing the meanings of consumer products – in other words, that in some cases verbal methods may have less to offer than new approaches relying more heavily on visual imagery. This suggests that our understanding of symbolic consumption will benefit from 'the development of mixed methodologies to generate multiple perspectives on socially constructed reality'. I could not agree more wholeheartedly with the pluralistic thrust of this latter argument or with the further implication that a move toward adopting a more diverse set of methods will encourage work drawing on phenomenology, on social representations via visual materials, and on discourse analysis – but, more importantly, on an *integration* of these various approaches via what Elliott (following Fiske, 1990) calls *ethnosemiotics*. In short, Elliott concludes by calling for a 'conscious pluralism' based on 'the mixing of approaches' through 'utilizing multiple perspectives'. (To which I reply, as I have in my past writings, 'Amen!')

Yet somehow, in his relentless logical progress toward this righteous conclusion, Elliott has sacrificed another crucial component of the post-modern ethos – namely, its sense of playfulness, its mood of self-parody, its pervasive feeling of fun. In short, Elliott has more or less self-deconstructed his own work by presenting a call for more visual awareness couched in the form of a verbal treatise. Where, we find ourselves wondering, are the pictures to illustrate the points he makes with such logocentric rigour? How, if at all, do the sounds and sights of his chapter echo and reflect their sense and sensibility?

Elsewhere, I have laboured at length to suggest that the sort of integrative methodological pluralism advocated by Elliott might be illustrated by means of an analogy drawn from the visual phenomenon of *stereopsis* (Holbrook, 1996). Briefly, stereoscopy depends on the simultaneous presentation of two pictures that represent the different perspectives of the left and right eyes, that therefore involve a parallax shift or binocular disparity in which objects occupy different relative positions in the left and right views, and that are fused by the brain into one three-dimensional stereographic visual image that – when compared with a flat two-dimensional representation – conveys an enhanced sense of vividness, clarity, realism, and depth. Thus, in essence, the 3-D experience depends on the integration or fusion of disparate material from different viewpoints. And such an integrative fusion produces insights experienced as the vivid and clear enhancement of detail and depth.

As such, stereopsis provides a striking metaphor for the sort of expanded vision that Elliott purports to advocate. But readers patient enough to consult my title as shown in the references will have noticed that I couch my argu-ments for the implications of stereopsis in the form of playful references to

Figure 9.1   *Rocky at play. To view this stereo pair, hold the page close to the face. Look straight ahead and through the left and right pictures with the left and right eyes, respectively. Pull the page slowly away from the face, continuing to look straight ahead, until the two pictures float together and fuse into one clear three-dimensional image*

cats – including our own fabulous feline Rocky Raccoon, who was gracious enough to pose for the illustrative stereographs presented in my paper and whose resplendent image benefits enormously from the vividness, clarity, realism, and depth conveyed by the 3-D experience (Figure 9.1).

So, in the end, I must respectfully disagree with Richard Elliott. I must continue to maintain that we have still had nowhere near enough cats and to insist, as an antidote to the reliance on verbalization evinced by Elliott, that we will not have had 'enough . . . cats already' until authors like himself begin to put their visually arresting pictorial material – let us call it their 'money' – where their mouth is.

Having thus challenged Elliott on the grounds of what strikes me as his excessively logocentric account of postmodern consumption symbolism, I must now invoke the postmodern embrace of paradox and self-contradiction in a playful and self-parodic spirit by questioning the contribution of Knights and Odih for exactly the opposite reasons. Here, by 'questioning', I do not mean that I doubt the value of their contribution, but rather that I wish to interrogate the nature of their approach by suggesting why I find it rather puzzling and perhaps, in some ways, problematic. Specifically, reversing the criteria that I applied to the piece by Elliott (which, after all, is the postmodernist's prerogative), I wish to suggest that some of the arguments advanced by Knights and Odih simply do not make sense – at least not to me – verbally and logically or otherwise.

I realize, of course, that a critique based on 'not making sense' is a hold-over from the pre-postmodernist perspective that may be more appropriate to our modern 'framing' than to the proposed postmodern '*re*framing' of the consumer. Nevertheless, I just can't help myself. Unable to shed the thought-confining intellectual shackles of my traditional training and incapable of shaking my inveterate habit of looking for logical consistency, I simply find the direction in which these authors push their view of gendered time to be somewhat . . . peculiar.

Knights and Odih begin their chapter on safe and secure ground by offering a commendable review of the ways in which 'masculine' conceptions of time as 'linear and sequential' differ from 'feminine' apperceptions of temporality as 'contextual, continuous, processual, and contingent'. As the authors point out, an 'objective' notion of time views it as a scarce resource that can be allocated among various competing uses in a manner that maximizes overall utility. By contrast, a 'subjective' view treats time as a psychophysical phenomenon in which perceived duration does not necessarily reflect the externally verifiable length of events. Further, 'social' time depends on the nature of activities rooted in the rhythms of communal existence; such socially constructed time is relativistic and experiential; potentially, it differs from one group of consumers to another, as in the case of men versus women. For example, unlike men, women regard time as depending on their relations with others, as governed by the collective concerns of the family, as 'never their own', and as circular because governed by the routinized and repetitive nature of household chores in which 'a woman's work is never done'. Also, this domesticated conception of time reflects power relations between the genders manifested in the subordination of women to men and evident in the ways in which women move in or out of the workforce from full- to part-time jobs, seldom enjoying the sorts of leisure diversions available to their male counterparts.

The authors go on to argue persuasively that the socially constructed feminine sense of temporality is inherently incongruent with the view of time implicit in the services offered by most financial institutions. For example, designed as they often are on the principle of making contractual payments according to some sort of fixed temporal schedule, many financial services are intrinsically ill suited to reflecting the relational-continuous-processual-cyclical conception of time typical of women. Compound interest does not permit alternative methods of calculation in accord with the female consciousness.

From all this, Knights and Odih extract some important conclusions. The first, which commands our agreement, is that traditional marketing research has enshrined an essentially positivistic conceptualization of time as quantifiably linear and as an informational input into decision-making aimed toward the optimal allocation of resources. Clearly, this excessively rational-istic perspective requires rethinking in the work that lies ahead, preferably in the direction of acknowledging the more phenomenological, symbolic, and socially constructed viewpoints advocated by these authors.

But second and more problematically, Knights and Odih also advocate 'the introduction of products whose temporalities attempt to match those of the providers' "target groups" . . . It is necessary that product providers recognize the existence of variations in the time perceptions of their potential clients.' Surely, in the case of financial services, one must ask, 'What does this mean?' My reluctant response is: 'Not much.'

In my view, the arguments presented by Knights and Odih take a wrong turn when these authors distinguish among only three conceptions of time: objective, subjective, and social. By subsequently lumping both gender differences and financial services under the third heading, they make it easy for themselves to argue that the two ought to be brought into better alignment. However, this conclusion rests on what I believe is a serious logical confusion – namely, a failure to preserve the objective–subjective distinction in the context of social time. Specifically, a more complete typology would recognize distinctions among four as opposed to only three conceptions of time: self-objective, self-subjective, social-objective, and social-subjective. The first two remain consistent with those discussed by Knights and Odih. The latter two reflect a contrast that they ignore, but that emerges as the basis for a critique of their conclusion concerning the design of financial services.

By collapsing the quadripartite typology just mentioned into a tripartite classification, Knights and Odih gloss over a crucial distinction between 'gendered time' as subjective-social and 'financial services' as objective-social in nature. While agreeing completely that – by virtue of their immersion in subjective-social time – men and women perceive temporalities differently, we must also recognize that financial services are almost universally grounded on one particular objective-social conception of time. That is, they involve socially agreed contractual commitments to pay or receive quantitatively measurable amounts of money at objectively specified moments in time according to an intersubjectively consensual calendar of events. Entwined as they are in this logocentric, positivistic, linear, sequential framework, such financial services do not appear to lend themselves to 'reframing' in a manner comparable to the way in which we can 'reframe' the consumer to reflect the subjective-social gender differences identified so persuasively by Knights and Odih. Rather, whether we like it or not, a linear and sequential time frame appears to be the essence of finance.

In other words, though this admission may signal some lack of imagination on my part, I do not envision ways to 'reframe' the objective-social time implicit in financial services to accommodate the alternative subjective-social times resulting from gender differences. Here, realistically, we must ask what sort of implications such gender differences might carry for the design of financial offerings. For example, could we persuade banks to offer household loans in which the female head of a family pays interest when she feels that an appropriate length of time has elapsed? I don't think so. Could we convince insurance companies on the merits of providing life insurance with a premium schedule that fluctuates depending on whether the policy holder is engaged in full or part-time employment? Probably not. Could a new type of bond issue be designed to reach maturity when the investor is in the relevant contextual mood? No way.

At bottom, the problem is that financial services are fundamentally enmeshed in an objective-social rather than a subjective-social conception of time. In this, they are inherently masculine – that is, linear and sequential, not to mention hegemonically paternalistic – in nature. From the feminist perspective espoused by Knights and Odih, that is the trouble with men in general and with their intrinsically male-oriented financial services in particular. Unfortunately, financiers always respect the time value of money and always want to charge interest accordingly. Maybe those ancient philosophers and medieval theologians were onto something when they looked the matter squarely in the face and declared usury to be immoral.

Note

The author gratefully acknowledges the support of the Columbia Business School's Faculty Research Fund.

References

Brown, Stephen, Bell, Jim and Carson, David (eds) (1995) *Marketing Eschatology*, Proceedings of the Marketing Eschatology Retreat, St Clement's, University of Ulster, Belfast, Northern Ireland.

Brown, Stephen, Bell, Jim and Carson, David (eds) (1996) *Marketing Apocalypse*, London: Routledge.

Elliott, Richard (1996) 'Book review: *Postmodern Marketing*', *Irish Marketing Review 1966*, 140–1.

Fiske, John (1990) 'Ethnosemiotics: some personal and theoretical reflections', *Cultural Studies*, 4 (1): 85–100.

Holbrook, Morris B. (1996) 'On eschatology, onanist scatology, or honest catology? Cats swinging, scat singing, and cat slinging as riffs, rifts, and writs in a catalytic catechism for the cataclysm', in S. Brown, J. Bell and D. Carson (eds), *Marketing Apocalypse*. London: Routledge.

Part IV

MARKETING ETHICS

Both chapters in this part identify one essential feature of the debate on marketing ethics – i.e. that it cannot be distinguished from its roots in commerce and the existing capitalist enterprise. As Grafton Small puts it: 'the moral underpinning of consumption amongst industrialized peoples is as much a product of commerce as it is a constituent of everyday exchange'. He goes on to take the example of the editorial of *Fast Lane*, a motoring magazine, in order to illustrate the close interdependence of goods, rights, law, social structure, power and the underlying ethics of trading behaviour in the dominant cultural milieu. Indeed, he goes further to reveal the role of 'seduction' and 'repression' in the consumption process, particularly regarding the case of the ethics of excessive speed. Furthermore, Grafton Small has highlighted the general possibility that speed is *the* ethic of consumer culture.

As Aldous Huxley predicted, speed is the defining characteristic of the twentieth century. The elements of production, exchange, information flows, distribution, retailing and consuming which constitute the 'traditional' view of the economic system all require faster and faster performance in order for the system to survive. After all, as Heidegger (1977) noted, the word for all of this frantic activity is 'busy-ness'. *Fast Lane*, fast food, fast track, quick fit, quick save, one stop. 'Speed' itself has become the moral imperative. Growth, accumulation and faster production and consumption are critical requirements of the economic system according to both neo-classical economics and the Marxian analysis of capitalist dynamics, and even more so in the *Fast Lane* vision of a world of hyperconsumption which Grafton Small paints.

Hetrick and Lozada's chapter presents an ethical critique of marketing from critical theory (anti-marketing) and postmodernist (anti-theory) standpoints. Under both modes of analysis the normative ethics that underpin the production/consumption (or hyperconsumption) process are seen to be constructed and imposed by the hegemonic elite who control the socio-economic (or media-sign) system. Each of the two methods of critique is quite different, however, in its analysis of the form, means and nature of the process of ethical construction.

The seminal attitude survey towards business ethics reported by Baumhart in the *Harvard Business Review* in 1961 catalogued the salient problems that business managers wanted to eliminate: gifts, gratuities, bribes, call girls, price discrimination, unfair pricing, dishonest advertising, unfair competitive practices, cheating customers, unfair credit practices, overselling, price collusion and prejudice in hiring. There have been many subsequent studies of managers' ethical attitudes and behaviour, including notably Chonko and Hunt's (1985) empirical examination of marketing management in particular, in which they concluded that top management's actions are more important than the mere existence of corporate or industry codes of ethics.

As the reader can see from the above discussion, compared with this traditional view of ethical issues in marketing, both chapters in this part take a completely different approach, which itself represents a dramatic shift in perspective and field – i.e. from producer ethics to consumer ethics, from personal behavioural ethics to socio-cultural ethics, and from the ethics of operations and practice to the ethics of theory and systems.

References

Baumhart, R.C. (1961) 'How ethical are businessmen?', *Harvard Business Review*, 39 (July–August): 6–19.

Chonko, L.B. and Hunt, S.D. (1985) 'Ethics and marketing management: an empirical examination', *Journal of Business Research*, 13 (August): 339–59.

Heidegger, M. (1977) *The Question Concerning Technology*. New York: Harper & Row.

10 Morality and the Marketplace: An Everyday Story of Consumer Ethics

Robert Grafton Small

> If we got to be saved, we would form programs that would not hurt people, 'cause we would be constantly aware of needs. We would take monies and put them in the right place instead of thinking how to kill somebody. Instead of making more warheads, nuclear heads, and fast-flying planes that don't work, we need to be making houses, we need food. We have no reason not to. God made enough on earth for everyone to eat, for everyone to live. But someone is grabbing it all up.
>
> (Terkel, 1992: 62)

Given recent events in Eastern Europe and the resultant triumphalism typified by Fukuyama (1992), any subsequent disquiet over business ethics or the morality of the marketplace would seem, at first, to be more than a little paradoxical, if not actively misplaced or mischievous. However, as Wernick (1991: 42) has found and others (Grafton-Small and Linstead, 1989: 215–16) have argued, in general rather than specific terms, the moral underpinning of consumption amongst industrialized peoples is as much a product of commerce as it is a constituent of everyday exchange. Moreover, Terkel (1992) clearly demonstrates how even those on the margins of market-based society possess an understanding of both ethical and social structures which far outweighs any involvement they might have with either order through direct trade or experience. This is immediately significant for two reasons, the lesser being that consumption must be seen as a symbolic process, not just a form of applied economics. More importantly, and for similar reasons, markets are themselves cultural artefacts, hence bound by the codes of exchange and the expressions of power (Grafton-Small, 1987: 70) which they make possible.

It follows, then, that despite appearances to the contrary, the current concern over business ethics is not so much a response to unforeseen or unprecedented problems but more a matter of dealing with conflicts and contradictions long implicit in the communal sense-making of everyday commerce and only now beginning to emerge. Consider, for instance, a response (Bennett, 1992) given by the editor of *Fast Lane*, a motoring magazine, to questions about excessive speed and driving in Britain. 'There is an enormous amount of basic prudism [*sic*] about the thing,' expostulates

Andrew English, who supplies his readers with tips on how to evade the new speed-trap cameras, and runs advertisements for radar-beaters.

> Speed is *fun*! It genuinely *is*, and that's not a word that occurs. We're moving into this wonderful society where we all live in a Milton Keynes shopping arcade, with Benetton and so on, and we all give up smoking, and we all know that sex will give you Aids, and it gets to the point where there's this wonderful, homogenised world where everyone is a responsible citizen – it's sadly an extremely boring place to live.

Not for everyone exactly, as excessive speed is a principal cause, in the UK, of the fatal manoeuvres which each year account for 3,500 of us prematurely. Nevertheless, this accidental ethnography does allow a number of notable inferences about the moral and ethical assumptions implicit in our common commitment to motor traffic. That there is such a freight to daily exchange has long been established (Eco, 1979: 21) though the wider repercussions have not often figured in any summary consideration of commercially sponsored goods and services. However, given the cited emphasis on English as editor of just such a product, and bearing in mind the necessary intervention of another, Bennett's newspaper, as his medium, it seems reasonable to assume he is speaking not only on his own behalf but also to, and for, those of us he considers to be his readers and his target audience. The question then is a matter of how we might plausibly understand what he seems to be saying in our name provided, of course, the account is engaging (Giddens, 1977: 41), if not wholly persuasive, and recognizing, too, our complicity as consumers in ceding English possession of 'the power to speak' (Clastres, 1977: 127). We should remember, even so, that any attempt at exegesis can never be exhaustive, for whilst the editor's address will bear a number of interpretations, not least because it is knowingly partial in every sense of the word, none of these reworkings will be absolute either, each of them being a product of the reader's specific skill, culture and background, so prone to continual reformulation.

Caveats notwithstanding, English's opinions on speed and fast driving are both moral and moralizing across a whole range of ethical issues. First and most important is his unquestioning acceptance of motor cars in themselves, thus restricting the debate to one of how they should be used rather than whether or not cars, particularly those with high performance, are a tolerable end nowadays for scarce resources. Indeed, his explicit hedonism would seem to suggest environmental concerns of this kind are just another facet of the responsible citizenship he finds so constraining. In a society such as our own, founded on a 'cultural design of persons and goods' (Sahlins, 1976: 166–7), with an additional implicit obligation on its members to recognize the propriety of any resultant community (Giddens, 1982: 46–7), English and his co-believers threaten more than the law; they expose a fundamental aspect of the economy, the coercive nature of trade and consumption.

These forms of interaction have, according to Giddens (1977: 104), three essential elements: they produce meaning within a social order, they constitute a moral code and they demonstrate the operation of relations of power. Douglas and Isherwood (1980: 72–3) agree, advancing the idea of goods as marking devices in those societies which manufacture articles and have legal structures based on the concepts and rights of possession, ownership, bequeathment and so on. Cults apart, and irrespective of the specific culture under consideration, whether it be ours or not, industrialized or otherwise, the emergent social structure is unlikely to cohere around its own immorality or to promote the perpetual overthrow of any dominant code of ethics.

From such a basis, and with Britain's entire current economy in mind, including, presumably, the business of *Fast Lane*, Bauman (1992: 111–12) has uncovered shifts in the cultural milieu which not only suggest a degree of moral relativism in our own trading behaviour but which also help to explain the ethical underlay of English's apparently contrary remarks. In broad terms, Bauman believes that instead of engaging the rest of society in the role of producers, as was historically the case, capital tends to engage them in the role of consumers. Thus recent UK 'depressions', manifested in massive and stable unemployment, are not latter-day editions of the 1930s, the sufferings of the new poor being unmatched by the tribulations of their richer contemporaries. These two nations do nevertheless coexist because of the interplay between 'seduction' and 'repression' as means of reproducing social control and integration.

In brief, 'seduction' is grounded in life-skills which cannot be employed effectively without commercial mediation, and 'repression' acknowledges a growing penetration of the 'private' sphere by normative regulations pushed to the extreme, hence a loss of individual power and autonomy in an increasingly comprehensive market-centred world. Against such a background, the ethics of excessive speed are surely more in question than ever, the editor of *Fast Lane* having given his answer almost entirely in terms of what certain drivers want – the archetypal recognition of an unmet demand – and why they should evade the constraints of a culture oppressive with dullness. What's more, this exercise in practical morality is only possible as a result of the continuing interaction between English and his ilk, who have surely been seduced, and our present legal system, including those it has already coerced, either directly or else through its commercial surrogates like Benetton and Milton Keynes, ironically designed for motorists – 'safe' motorists, that is.

Equally, as practised consumers, we understand that these exchanges and the various complicit markets for cars, accessories, magazines and even opinions are entirely well-suited and interdependent means of carrying on the debate. We also appreciate, for similar reasons, that whilst they may have no legitimate use now, technically improper devices such as radar-beaters are nonetheless accepted as ways of testing popular tolerance of manifest law and order. If the machines sell sufficiently, there is, we deduce, a less than whole-hearted communal support for the regulation in question. By the same token, the tone of Bennett's interview, hence the representation of English and his opinions, is only to be expected, given the paper which published it, the *Guardian*, recognizably a bastion of that very 'wonderful, homogenised world' so disliked by the editor of *Fast Lane*. Even so, both publications have loyal readers to be catered to, and how better than with a mutually beneficial trade in commercially acceptable stereotypes?

There is a third population concerned in these affairs, yet remarkably, given their obvious physical presence, they are defined by exclusion; for if our commonsensical restructurings of society and the law are a matter of power in the marketplace, the destitute must be unequal partners in any agreement, be it straight coercion or ever so seductive. Whilst this issue is considered elsewhere in terms of everyday exchange (Grafton Small, 1993), the ethical undertow is significant. In effect, those of us who can continue as consumers do so knowing the propriety of our culture makes such a 'design of persons and goods' unavoidable. The same is true for the wider, much heralded environmental costs of the motor industry in general and all its attendant capital investments in roads, services and jobs. When, as is currently the case, the UK economy is not performing entirely as we might wish it, even the government is concerned to revitalize trade by increasing sales of, hence our commitment to, these selfsame goods and services. The moral imperatives of our social structure and its maintenance mean such a course is not only predictable, given our history, but unquestionable.

These resolutions of apparently conflicting interests are utterly character-istic of societies like our own which depend on industrial artefacts as diverse as the Jaguar XJ220 and Salter's Duck (Grafton-Small and Linstead, 1990) to temper our relationships with each other and with the actual world as we commonly see it. The following case in point (Grafton-Small, 1985) clearly demonstrates this vital phenomenon (Eco, 1979: 21) and, significantly, the wider application of Campanis's (1970: 322) dictum whereby managers are paid not to develop new moral codes but to make the existing slippery ones work. In addition, the story suggests that neither the 'creation and movement of goods' nor the ordinary behaviour of lay and professional people is completely free from ethical uncertainty.

Late one night, on a motorway in the south of England, a Luton-bodied Transit van suffered a puncture in one of the rear wheels. The driver, who was travelling in the outside lane, decided not to risk the drive to the hard shoulder but pulled onto the central reservation instead. Here he began to examine the four rear wheels with the hope of swopping the damaged one for the spare tyre. He had just removed the latter from the van when a Mercedes Benz saloon came round the corner at enormous speed and buried itself in the back of the vehicle. The police and the fire brigade were called and so, in time, was the doctor on night duty at a nearby hospital.

The driver of the Mercedes was dead and the police needed a death certificate before they could have the body cut out of the wreck. The doctor arrived and was told that the Mercedes must have been travelling at more than 110 mph (175 kph) as the Transit had been pushed 50 yards (45 metres) up the road by the impact. The van had been hidden by the darkness and the corner, which the Mercedes driver, himself an ex-policeman, had cut, obviously believing the road to be clear. The 18 inch (45 cm) skid marks showed how little time there had been for braking. The nature of the collision can be guessed at from the doctor's recollection that he pronounced the Mercedes driver dead after putting his hand through a hole in the chest cavity and feeling the motionless heart itself.

As he wrote the death certificate, the doctor noticed that two policemen had retrieved the driver's thermos flask and open sandwich box from the front seat of the Mercedes. 'Christ!', said one, 'I'd have done myself in if my missus put broken glass in my sarnies!' A cadet stumbled into the darkness, as did the doctor who had to be on duty for the rest of the night. In passing the crumpled Mercedes, he noticed the registration plates and thought 'last year's model, eh? I wonder . . .'. He walked back to the wreck and looked through the hole that had once been the front seat passenger door. A huge gash in the dashboard showed where the Blaupunkt stereo cassette player and radio once were. The fire crew had finally appraised the situation.

Three interrelated professional kinship groups were present at the scene of the accident: the police, the fire brigade and a representative doctor. Each of these practitioners works within a strict and widely enforced code of behaviour whilst recognizing the others as a necessary part of the emergency services. As such, they are responsible for protecting the public from the sort of unpleasantness which comes with incidents like the destruction of the Mercedes. An important and remarkable part of this cleansing is the indulgence by each group in some form of defilement which nevertheless leaves them as protectors of the public good.

The police took a sandwich filled with potentially lethal windscreen shards from the dead man's last meal and used it as a means of initiating one of their cadets into the gruesome matter of road traffic accidents. The doctor violated the corpse itself by an unnecessary handling of the once vital organs, an act which the fire brigade matched, in symbolic terms, by looting the radio cassette player from the dead man's car. These denials of the deceased's previous existence can also be seen in the deliberate way in which everyone was made aware of his prematurely abandoned career in the police force: he used to be like us but now he's gone – excluded from the kinship group and then from life itself.

Obviously, the common-sense understandings of those involved were such that they could use vehicles for speed and endurance, headlights to defy darkness, tyres to enable controlled motion, and thermos flasks for the retention of heat without questioning their availability. That these industrial artefacts are an essential but entirely unspoken part of everyday perceptions of reality can be demonstrated by reference to the doctor's appearance at the ritual disposal of the dead. The police summoned him in the knowledge that he was not eight miles (11 km) away but a mere 10 or 15 minutes drive from the scene of the accident. Equally, whilst we as laypeople may share in these assumptions about the use of mass-produced items, our common exclusion from the various work groups at the crash means we are unlikely to feel their same ease with the practical mortality we have generally decided is appropriate for the task in hand (Grafton-Small and Linstead, 1986).

Similarly, important ethical difficulties arise from the designs of persons and goods which owe their form to unconventional notions of trade and the marketplace. For instance, Henry (1979: 102), in a study of 'pilferage' and theft from organizations, finds circumstances that can be taken to indicate the use of produce to define both legitimate society and behaviour as well as the contrary. Briefly, the manufacture of goods at a specified rate, price and quantity represents a major part of any system of mass consumption and those who trade their labour do so for the means to continue as consumers, albeit meagrely. Consequently, each item of production which is made to managerial requirements is an underwriting of the given order and an indication of employees' complicity in their own belittlement. Henry (1979: 98) argues that the 'hidden economy' is not hierarchical like the legitimate market-based culture but stratified, so 'pilferage' is restricted by social grouping, as recognized equals trade with each other.

This is, above all, an exchange of gifts signifying friendship and not the search for profit, so existing patterns of community and kinship are accepted and built upon. Such a reading of unofficial trade is reinforced by the view, amongst 'pilferers', that a certain amount of extra items or value from work is 'fair' or part of the wage bargain, an unwritten but assumed form of 'perks'. Whilst this might represent a less than ideal form of behaviour, 'pilferage' also seems to be outside the normal understandings of deviancy maintained at a Merseyside crisp factory, well known for its range of products. Conversation with one of the managers (Grafton-Small, 1985) showed that certain flavours suffered disproportionately from 'pilferage', senior executives being of the opinion that the relevant shifts must be 'completely bent'. It was later decided, as sales returns of new brands came in from all over the country, that the shop floor had conducted a little 'in-house' market research and everyone wanted the same flavours. The shifts concerned with their manufacture were simply catering for as many as possible. Some of the warehousemen were also being less than rigorous.

Some weeks later, when working on a short contract frying potatoes for a rival company whose plant had burned down, a friend from this same factory declared that the crisps in question weren't worth stealing. So they were left alone. This may be taken as an unwillingness to give away something of no value. It might also be a matter of an outside contract getting special supervisory attention. Deservedly, as deviant groups form, amongst other things, an escape mechanism for those who only appear to acknowledge social norms by transgressing them. Thus majority opinions are shown to be so as contrary understandings are made explicit and minority tastes are presented in a way which allows a recognition of dissenters. The important point is that socially constructed and tolerated deviancy mirrors society at large and criminal theft from organizations is, like legitimate trade, for profit to support its own hierarchies (Hobbs, 1989).

'Pilferage' may be argued as contrary to this order in that those who transgress group understandings of 'fairness' for reasons of profit are heavily sanctioned for having brought their social system into disrepute. The punishment involved is generally one of exposure to the legitimate trading hierarchies, leading to either dismissal or prosecution. The criminal 'pilferer' has not only offended the morality of his immediate social circle but also embarrassed the host organization.

The managers of the latter are demonstrably reluctant to clamp down on 'pilfering' within their businesses for as long as it is a self-regulating practice. That there is 'pilferage' at every level of commercial hierarchies, with concomitant notions of 'fairness' or appropriate worth, may go some way to explaining the anger raised by attempts to reduce 'pilferage' to below these limits. Those under investigation are being slighted in that such an evaluation states fairly clearly their inability to manage friendships, make personal judgements or justify trust. There are, too, the imbalances of power (Clegg, 1975: 46; Perrow, 1970: 59) through which, for managers, 'pilferage' may be codified as tax deductible perquisites and so legitimate in a way which serves to underwrite the continuing 'pilferage' by their subordinates. This is not to deny that managers also indulge in more traditional forms of 'pilferage'. As Davis (1973: 172) dryly observes, the negotiation of legitimacy would appear to form an important part of any means of distributing products.

We all recognize as much from our habitual dealings with each other, and with the world in general, just as we appreciate the interplays of goods and morality which not only enable our everyday lives but also emerge reinforced from our complete immersion in consumption as a means of maintaining our entire social fabric. So it is that the previous UK government can seem to have condoned the sale of arms and weapons technology to Iraq, amongst many, all to the massive benefit of British industry, meaning ourselves, yet came to grief solely when these munitions were used in actual terms rather than as metaphors of well-regulated commercial order. This may indeed be the darker side of the wealth and the possibilities created by industrialized life in market-based societies though, as the increasingly regionalized UK economy demonstrates, there are others. It is worth remembering, then, that we as consumers can neither escape the ambiguities of our own culture nor take any active part in it without exercising forms of power and moral judgement over each other, forms which surely demand we each be responsible for the ethics of our communal exchange.

References

Bauman, Z. (1992) *Intimations of Postmodernity*. London: Routledge.
Bennett, C. (1992). 'Live fast, kill young', *Guardian Weekend*, 14 November.
Campanis, P. (1970) 'Normalness in management', in J.D. Douglas (ed.), *Deviance and Respectability: The Social Construction of Moral Meaning*. New York: Basic Books. pp. 291–325.

Clastres, P. (1977) *Society against the State: The Leader as Servant and the Human Uses of Power among the Indians of the Americas*. Oxford: Basil Blackwell/Mole Editions.

Clegg, S. (1975) *Power, Rule and Domination*. London: Routledge & Kegan Paul.

Davis, J. (1973) 'Forms and norms: the economy of social relations', *Man*, 8: 159–76.

Douglas, M. and Isherwood, B. (1980) *The World of Goods: Towards an Anthropology of Consumption*. Harmondsworth: Penguin.

Eco, U. (1979) *A Theory of Semiotics*. Bloomington IN: Midland Books/Indiana University Press.

Fukuyama, F. (1992) *The End of History and the Last Man*. London: Hamish Hamilton.

Giddens, A. (1977) *New Rules of Sociological Method*. London: Hutchinson.

Giddens, A. (1982) *Central Problems in Social Theory*. London: Macmillan.

Grafton-Small, R. (1985) 'Marketing managers: the evocation and structure of socially negotiated meaning'. PhD thesis, Sheffield City Polytechnic (now Sheffield Hallam University).

Grafton-Small, R. (1987) 'Marketing, or the anthropology of consumption', *European Journal of Marketing*, 21 (9): 66–71.

Grafton Small, R. (1993) 'Consumption and significance: the shape of things to come', *Scandinavian Journal of Management*, 9 (2): 88–99.

Grafton-Small, R. and Linstead, S.A. (1986) 'The everyday professional: skill in the symbolic management of occupational kinship', in A. Strati (ed.), *The Symbolics of Skill*. Trento: University of Trento. pp. 53–67.

Grafton-Small, R. and Linstead, S.A. (1989) 'Advertisements and artefacts: everyday understanding and the creative consumer', *International Journal of Advertising*, 8 (3): 205–18.

Grafton-Small, R. and Linstead, S.A. (1990) 'Symbols of innovation: the ultimate Jaguar and the next wave', paper presented at the 7th International Conference on Organizational Symbolism and Corporate Culture, Saarbrücken, June.

Henry, S. (1979) *The Hidden Economy*. Oxford: Martin Robertson.

Hobbs, D. (1989) *Doing the Business*. Oxford: Oxford University Press.

Perrow, C. (1970) 'Departmental power', in M.N. Zald (ed.), *Power in Organizations*. Nashville, TN: Vanderbilt University Press.

Sahlins, M. (1976) *Culture and Political Reason*. Chicago: University of Chicago Press.

Terkel, S. (1992) *Race*. London: Sinclair-Stevenson.

Wernick, A. (1991) *Promotional Culture: Advertising, Ideology and Symbolic Expression*. London: Sage.

11   Theory, Ethical Critique, and the Experience of Marketing

William P. Hetrick and Hector R. Lozada

The purpose of the present chapter is to propose alternative perspectives from which to examine ethics and marketing phenomena. The use of critical theory (Frankfurt Circle version) and/or other radical social theories (e.g. of the new French variety) provide us with such conceptual options. This (re)formulation is necessary because the discipline of marketing, at least in the American context, is constrained by a hyper-functionalist world-view in its somewhat meagre efforts to confront the challenge of corporate social responsibility and ethical behaviour. An implicit objective of this piece is to suggest ways in which marketing academicians, and those outside the university setting, can empower themselves relative to the strong managerial bias and the vast marketing/promotional stimuli to which they constantly bear witness. The multi-dimensional cultural milieu, which includes some reference to aesthetic criteria, has been relatively ignored in the discussion of ethical decision-making in business enterprise. This chapter attempts to partially amend this broad, but highly crucial over-sight.

Current versions of corporate rationality (e.g. profit maximization or efficiency) have deterred us from developing a constructive 'criticalness' toward marketing, and hence have limited the scope of discourse concerning ethics in marketing endeavours. A paradigmatic shift (or shifts), however, will facilitate discursive activity that allows different interpretations of marketing in general, and ethics in marketing specifically. The 'movement' from traditional marketing theory to either *anti-marketing theory* (critical theory) or *marketing anti-theory* (postmodernism) allows us to supersede the strong and perverse adherence to the basic tenets of positivist and logical empiricist thought. The proposed outcome of this change will be a more enlightened and progressive position toward the marketing organization's major stakeholders (e.g. labour, consumer constituencies, the environment etc.). It is neither desirable nor sufficient, however, to only target managers in marketing organizations and academicians with these theoretical diversions. A new-found responsibility of other non-elite peoples (notably consumers themselves) to engage in ethics-oriented discussions could become quite pronounced in our approach.

Critical theory revisited

Although some of the recent work on ethics in marketing (e.g. Ferrell et al., 1989; Robin and Reidenbach, 1987; Williams and Murphy, 1990) has been exceptional, it is suggested here that fundamental ethical concerns that involve marketing directly have been overlooked. A much broader and basic position, which must include a critique of capitalism, should be assumed when establishing the criteria for an 'ethical dilemma' (Ferrell and Gresham, 1985) or a 'perceived ethical problem' (Hunt and Vitell, 1986). One should avoid the mistake that Ryan rightly warns us of when he suggests that 'very often political criticism deals with capitalist ideology and social policy without disturbing their conceptual infrastructure' (1982: 117).

It is believed that the metatheoretical assumptions of the logical empiricist orientation (from which most traditional academic marketing activities are situated) are inappropriate for a study of ethics because of the emphasis on consensus, and the tendency to perpetuate the current social arrangement. A movement, therefore, is proposed from the logical empiricist perspective to a version of critical social theory in an attempt to capture the overall essence of a different philosophical project, and its notion of critique. This onto-epistemological shift allows us to contrast a *traditional theory* and a *critical theory*. A traditional theory reproduces the current social order while a critical theory is subversive to it (Horkheimer, 1972). The questions that now become glaring are: is a subversion even possible, and if so, what form will the subversion take? In other words, how will any subversion or resistance be conceived and constructed in the very late twentieth century, and who will assume the role of detractor? These are questions that we will return to shortly.

For marketing academicians, the use of Johan Arndt's (1985) conflict paradigms provides us with some highly acceptable alternatives. For example, Arndt's 'victimized consumer' and 'alienated man' metaphors, which are generated from his liberating paradigm (where anti-marketing theory would be located), are not represented within traditional conceptualizations of marketing ethics. Consumer society, or the 'high-intensity market setting' (Leiss, 1988), can exhibit oppressive human features including the adverse human effects of conspicuous consumption, and the lost subjectivity that results from panic consumption. Marketing and advertising (as inherently biased processes) perpetuate the emphasis on *exchange value* which the original Frankfurt Circle thought was one of the main problems under capitalist conditions. By substituting exchange value for use value, thereby imposing a fetishistic posture, the capitalist production and consumption apparatus has destroyed any notion of a free and genuine commodity exchange which stresses the intrinsic value of use.

Relatedly, the process of reification should be a central focus for a critical marketing ethics. It must be demonstrated how this mystification (i.e. how the relationship among human subjects is replaced by a contrived and artificial relationship among commodities) blocks the critical consciousness of individuals subjected to the capitalist mode of production (in both the labour process and consumption sphere). Although it goes unrecognized in Hirschman's (1987) article 'People as products', the commodity form has indeed invaded even emotional interactions if a significant number of Americans really perceive dating and romance as mere economic transactions and marketing exchanges. Situating this crass form of behaviour within an ethical analysis of marketing and advertising would be in the spirit of critical theory. The commodity as a 'mysterious thing' should be a central focus of a critique of capitalist society in general, and the Marxian and Lukacsian notions of reification specifically. Incorporating the ideas from *Capital* (Volume 1) and *History and Class Consciousness* would help traditional marketers in this regard as well as assisting them in discovering a crucial link between consumer research and Marx, Lukacs, and the Frankfurt Circle.

The contributions of the Frankfurt Circle (e.g. Marcuse, Adorno, and Horkheimer) to marketing and consumer behaviour theory result in a broad and general critique of late capitalism. For current purposes, the following areas of specific critique are of particular importance: ideology, the culture industry, and aesthetics. For example, the ideological effects of Horkheimer and Adorno's (1986) 'culture industry' become highly relevant for critical researchers analysing the underpinnings of the consumption sphere. The *Dialectic of Enlightenment*, and in particular the section on mass deception, could be a crucial beginning for a formulation of critical marketing ethics. The effects of the culture industry cut deep into the psyche of the American consumer. A consciousness, proletarian or otherwise, is stifled in part because of the culture industry, or to use Kracauerian terminology, the 'distraction factories'.

> The deception is not that the culture industry supplies amusement but that it ruins the fun by allowing business considerations to involve it in the ideological cliches of a culture in the process of self-liquidation. Ethics and taste cut short unrestrained amusement as naive – naivete is thought to be as bad as intellectualism – and even restrict technical possibilities. The culture industry is corrupt; not because it is a sinful Babylon but because it is a cathedral dedicated to elevated pleasure. (Horkheimer and Adorno, 1986: 142–3)

In addition, Horkheimer and Adorno's proposed relationship between the culture industry and advertising is quite revealing:

> Advertising and the culture industry merge technically as well as economically. In both cases the same thing can be seen in innumerable places, and the mechanical repetition of the same culture product has come to be the same as that of the propaganda slogan. In both cases the insistent demand for effectiveness makes technology into psychotechnology, into a procedure for manipulating men. In both cases the standards are striking yet familiar, the easy yet catchy, the skillful yet simple; the object is to overpower the customer, who is conceived as absent-minded or resistant. (1986: 163)

Perhaps more importantly, *Dialectic of Enlightenment* may be considered critical theory's conceptual nexus to postmodernism which seems to be so vital to a contemporary social analysis. This linkage could be viewed as part of the evolution to postmodernism, or as postmodernism's point of departure.[1]

Arndt's 'political economy' metaphor which emanates from the socio-political paradigm ('radical marketing theory') provides insight into the Marxian notions of control and domination. It is now possible, for example, to draw from Marcuse's (1964) and Habermas's (1970) work on technology and its link to the domination of nature (and, of course, (wo)man). This would provide a basis for the critique of the plethora of environmental problems perpetrated by capitalist logic, and could supplement immensely the current conceptualizations of so-called 'green marketing'.

An analysis of the Fordist production model is also possible within the socio-political paradigm. As an industrial era, Murray (1988: 8) characterizes Fordism as follows:

1   standardized work tasks and standardized consumer products
2   mechanized, mass production and special-purpose machinery
3   scientific management principles (Taylorism)
4   factory assembly lines.

Harvey summarizes a conception of Ford's industrial orientation as follows:

> What was special about Ford (and what ultimately separates Fordism from Taylorism), was his vision, his explicit recognition that mass production meant mass consumption, a new system of the reproduction of labour power, a new politics of labour control and management, a new aesthetics and psychology, in short, a new kind of rationalized, modernist, and populist democratic society. (1989: 126)

Fordism, therefore, should be regarded as more than a system of efficient methodologies to facilitate mass production. It has to be viewed as an all-encompassing lifestyle which includes the monolithic dimensions of mass consumption and the culture industry.[2] Except for Benton (1987), members of the marketing discipline are either unwilling or unable to conceptually link their analysis of consumption with that of work and the labour process. It is, of course, impossible to distinguish between a 'worker' and a 'consumer'. They are one and the same. It must be recognized that societal members can be exploited in the production realm and/or within the sphere of consumption.

In summary, an agenda based on critical theory requires substantially different ethical criteria. We first should seek to transcend the confinements of the empirical-analytic sciences, and then work toward deploying the emancipatory qualities of the critically oriented sciences (see Habermas, 1971). Operating from the conflict paradigms permits us to theorize about disparities between potentiality and actuality, or between essence and appearance. What constitutes an ethical problem or dilemma will, of course, dramatically change given this paradigmatic transition. Societal members must understand 'the true nature of their existence' (Fay, 1987: 68) before we demand that attempts be made at transformations of alienating social practices. Integrating a critical approach with ethics and marketing better facilitates Fay's notion of rational self-clarity, and hence this is something that we should strive for in our research activities.

To cite the many problems of late capitalism, however, is in and of itself somewhat vacuous if that is the sole objective. If a critical theory is subversive to the status quo, how then can we facilitate the subversion? We advocate that, in addition to academicians, other consumers must also become constructive critics of corporate tactics and strategies, and that they should provide strong input (e.g. through non-response and resistance) to marketing organizations concerning the latter's ethical behaviour and practices. Specifically, we believe that the stranglehold of the culture industry, and its ideologies, can be broken if the 'left-aesthetic tradition' can be fostered within consumer groups as well as within the marketing research community.

> The aesthetic offers the middle class a superbly versatile model of their political aspirations, exemplifying new forms of autonomy and self-determination, transforming the relations between law and desire, morality and knowledge, recasting the links between individual and totality, and revising social relations on the basis of custom, affection and sympathy. (Eagleton, 1990: 28)

It is argued here that the adverse consequences of consumer capitalism, or the ethical problems or dilemmas thereof (e.g. fetishism, reification, and alienation), can be conceptually captured, explored, and hopefully negated under the left-aesthetic tradition.[3] For Marcuse (1978), Marxist aesthetics treats art as ideology: as ideology, art opposes the current society.

Eagleton (1990: 366) identifies the *cognitive*, the *ethico-political*, and the *libidinal-aesthetic* as the three great areas of concern for philosophy that were addressed before the rise of capitalism. Modernity, which in part is characterized by dissociation and specialization, is the moment when the three spheres of knowledge, politics, and desire become uncoupled. Eagleton believes that the 'aesthetic offers to reverse this division of labour, to bring these three alienated regions back into touch with one another' (1990: 368):[4]

> Art was not sharply separated from the ethico-political, but was one of its primary media; and it was not easily distinguishable from the cognitive either, because it could be seen as a form of knowledge, conducted within certain normative ethical frameworks. It had cognitive functions and ethico-political effects. (1990: 366)

Eagleton further suggests that the aesthetic is 'thought to retain a charge of irreducible particularity, providing us with a kind of paradigm of what a non-alienated mode of cognition might look like'. In addition, the left-aesthetic tradition, at least through the nineteenth century, constructs 'art as critique of alienation, as an exemplary realization of creative powers, as the ideal reconciliation of subject and object, universal and particular, freedom and necessity, theory and practice, individual and society' (1990: 369).[5]

What is the relationship, however, between art and aesthetics, ethics, and late capitalist society? Drawing upon Horkheimer and Adorno's assertion of the culture industry's monolithic character, Huyssen provides us with somewhat of a bleak interpretation:

> The siren song of the commodity has displaced the *promesse de bonheur* once held by bourgeois art, and consumer Odysseus blissfully plunges into the sea of commodities, hoping to find gratification but finding none. More than the museum or the academy even, department store and supermarket have become the cemeteries of culture. (1986: 21)

If one attempts to use art as ethical or ideology critique, the real concern becomes the extent to which art forms have genuine critical potential. Art as we see and perceive it today may simply be the result of the absorbing, coopting, and/or commodifying tendencies inherent in the logic(s) of consumer capitalism.

> Unlike neoconservatives who attribute all the cultural crises of late capitalism to the nearly diabolical strength of avant-garde intellectuals, we must recognize how the commodification of popular culture and the exploitation of nature are consequences of an economic logic of the same capitalism which the neoconservatives are anxious to defend. (Berman, 1989: 50)

It should be remembered, however, that the commodification of 'high' culture, as well as popular culture, is also of crucial interest and importance, and that there has always been a substantial difference between mass culture and modern commercial mass culture. In addition, Huyssen suggests that 'the culture of modernity has been characterized by a volatile relationship between high art and mass culture' (1986: vii). Perhaps some of the works of Andy Warhol can guide us through these complexities.[6]

Warhol 'elevates' simple and mundane consumer products, or perhaps just the packaging thereof, to the status of art.[7] Warhol may be merely trying to represent certain components of mass culture, or he may be attempting to display mass culture's ultimate failure because of its increasingly commercial character. It is believed that we can use Warhol's soup cans, soda pop bottles, and soap pad boxes to portray or represent the relationship that Huyssen expresses in the following passage:

> Just as art works become commodities and are enjoyed as such, the commodity itself in consumer society has become image, representation, spectacle. Use value has been replaced by packaging and advertising. The commodification of art ends up in the aesthetization of the commodity. (1986: 21)

In addition, Warhol may be forcing us to address the collapse of high culture. Are we to celebrate this collapse? Is it a collapse, or an implosion?

An implosion would be high art's absorption or cooption of the objects of low art.[8] Of course the reverse might be true, in that, once passed off as art, low-involvement consumer products with years of strong brand recognition can achieve something that is beyond mere kitsch. People may now be ready to celebrate their years of loyal purchase behaviour by viewing Brillo pad boxes in a corner of a museum showroom.

One could read Warhol as making a mockery of high culture or high art by showing that even a Campbell's soup can will be gazed upon, reviewed and evaluated by respectable art critics. (His art was, of course, displayed in very prominent places such as the Whitney Museum of American Art in New York City and the Los Angeles County Museum of Modern Art.) If this is so, a problem arises in that only those acquainted with the overall agenda of high art, if we can assume that there is indeed such a project, will be able to understand and appreciate the parody of so-called Pop Art. We agree with Huyssen, however, when he suggests that the 'boundaries between high art and mass culture have become increasingly blurred, and we should begin to see that process as one of opportunity rather than lamenting loss of quality and failure of nerve' (1986: ix). On the other hand, one should not dismiss Thacker's assertion that 'the present task facing the aesthetic is to disengage itself from commodified values' (1993: 19).

Marketing anti-theory: the contributions of postmodernism

With the advent of the 'postmodern scene' (Kroker and Cook, 1988), the dilemmas of the human condition will become greatly magnified. It seems that the primacy of consumption over production is characteristic of post-modern society (Jameson, 1984). This, of course, could situate consumer behaviourists as major arbiters of critical discourse. Unfortunately, the study of marketing ethics as it now stands is incapable of analysing 'postmodern-ism' as either a style or a periodizing concept because, in part, we have failed to recognize the possibility that the Frankfurt Circle may indeed be one of the theoretical precursors of postmodernism. Arndt's *conflict* dimen-sion is basically derived from Kantian, Hegelian, and Marxian roots. Post-modernism from a social theoretical perspective is attempting to break from some of these very notions. For example, Baudrillard's (1983) concept of the 'hyper-reality' of simulations moves us away from a traditional critique of political economy, and more toward a critique of images, commodity signs, and media spectacles. Marx's analysis of commodity fetishism is being replaced with Baudrillard's (1981) fetishism of the sign. As the character of society and its subsequent critique changes, so too will the conception of ethics.

The marketing manager within the postmodern era assumes a substantially different role than did the modern predecessor. The traditional version of the manager–consumer relationship, in other words, has to be deconstructed. The following quote by Michel Foucault is most poignant:

He is seen, but he does not see; he is the object of information, never a subject in communication. (1979: 200)

Members of the consuming publics and other non-elites have been excluded by modern marketing discourse, and have been relegated to mere objects of analysis and control. Modern discourse concerning consumer behaviour has always given ontological priority to the Same (e.g. male/white/heterosexual/professional-managerial/affluent). Because of this ability to frame and manipulate discursive formations, certain power/knowledge relationships have developed that asymmetrically benefit society's traditional elites (e.g. those that control production, and those that have the most buying power: Firat, 1987). One can draw a parallel between Foucault's power/knowledge and some initial contentions on 'power/ethics'.[9]

Foucault's discussion on 'another power, another knowledge' (1979: 226) is certainly plausible given the managerial biases and subsequent empirical 'findings' of functionalist versions of marketing theory. Within philosophy there has always been a strong relationship between aesthetics and ethics, that is, between what is *beautiful* and what is *good* (see Thacker, 1993). If we invoke the Foucauldian notion of power, a new and relevant conceptualization of 'power/aesthetics/ethics' becomes evident. Those that can exercise power can also determine or construct (perhaps unilaterally in the case of domination) what is beautiful and attractive, and what is good and what ought to be done.[10]

Relatedly, postmodernism places an emphasis on the examination and precedence of the Other.

The space of the Same is characterized by light; it is the space of discourse. The elements that characterize the space of the Other – the realm of darkness for Foucault – are those that have been excluded by discourse (and the Same); these are the figures of madness, sexuality, desire and death. (Lash, 1990: 81–2)

Marginalized groups (i.e. individuals representing the Other) such as women, people of colour, and those exhibiting a different sexual orientation now assume new roles in the movement toward struggle, communicatively or otherwise. Lash talks of a 'vertical space' (where the likes of Nietzsche, Bataille, de Sade, and Foucault wrote) that was

established at the limit where light met darkness; a space that opened up that limit. This is the space of non-discursive 'literature', where language takes on an opacity, and 'ontological weight'. It is in this *pli*, this fold that the postmodern is constituted. (1990: 82)

The postmodern marketing theoretician, conceptualized from a very ideal perspective and operating from any one of Rosenau's (1992) affirmative positions, is actively engaged with figures from the Other, and encourages them to speak and to move in this space of non-discursive activity. Hence, the discourse of the Same can be criticized and transcended. Foucault rightly warns us, however, that 'we must not imagine a world of discourse divided between accepted discourse and excluded discourse, or between the dominant discourse and the dominated one; but as a multiplicity of discursive elements that can come into play in various strategies' (1978: 100).

In addition to the aforementioned marginalized groups, Laclau and Mouffe (1985) speak of other diverse struggles (as differentiated from class struggles) that would also fall under the broad characterization of 'new social movements'. These would include urban, regional, ecological, anti-authoritarian, and anti-institutional resistances.

> What interests us about these new social movements, then, is not the idea of arbitrarily grouping them into a category opposed to that of class, but the novel role they play in articulating that rapid diffusion of social conflictuality to more and more numerous relations which is characteristic today of advanced industrial societies. (1985: 159–60)

It seems that what was once traditionally thought of as the excluded, the marginal, the repressed, the silenced, the disqualified, or the insignificant (see Rosenau, 1992) can now be construed as potential pockets of resistance. What is intriguing about this 'romance of the marginal' (Connor, 1989) is that the desire for legitimation is achieved by members of the Other not through inclusion, but through opposition. Drawing from Pecheux, Connor (1989) suggests that this opposition is achieved through 'disidentification' as differentiated from identification and counteridentification. Connor, in turn, provides us with a highly relevant example that clarifies these orientations:

> One might instance an industrial conflict in which a workforce would identify with the conventions of labour relations if they accepted no pay rise in the interests of increased productivity, would counteridentify if they struck for higher wages and then negotiated a settlement, and would disidentify if they demanded that the factory be turned into a cultural centre, in the interests of overcoming the ideological separation of work and leisure. (1989: 237)

Disidentification, then, would be a central focus in an attempt to construct a counterhegemonic relationship within the work organization. This would, of course, have consequences in the consumption realm. Disidentification would destroy the appeal of MTV, hyper-real sports events, and imagistic political campaigns.

It is possible within the postmodernist discourse to examine the implications of the so-called post-Fordist agenda. As opposed to Fordism, it is suggested here that post-Fordism (or neo-Fordism, ultra-Fordism, flexible accumulation etc.) can generally be conceived as exhibiting the following features:

1   flexible specialization and market nicheing
2   microelectronics and information technology using general purpose machinery
3   'just-in-time' methods, the 'team concept', and 'organizational culture'
4   flexible production systems (e.g. short, small-batch production runs).

Flexible regimes of accumulation should be conceived of not only as a new system of production, but also as a way of life that exhibits dramatic differences from that of the Fordist agenda. Smart suggests that

> the effects of the transition to flexible accumulation extend beyond the realm of commodity production. Volatility and ephemerality are not confined to the circuits of production and consumption alone but extend to personal values, relationships, life-styles, attachments, and other 'received ways of doing and being'. (1992: 56)

Likewise, Harvey contends that the accelerated turnover time in production must be matched with an equally accelerated turnover time in consumption.

> Flexible accumulation has been accompanied on the consumption side, therefore, by a much greater attention to quick-changing fashions and the mobilization of all the artifices of need inducement and cultural transformation that this implies. The relatively stable aesthetic of Fordist modernism has given way to all the ferment, instability, and fleeting qualities of a postmodernist aesthetic that celebrates difference, ephemerality, spectacle, fashion, and the commodification of cultural forms. (1989: 156)

In addition, Harvey suggests that the production of events, which have an almost immediate turnover time, has taken precedence over the production of goods. It is suggested here that Horkheimer and Adorno's contentions on the effects of the culture industry still make conceptual sense under postmodern conditions, particularly with regard to the production and consumption of spectacles.

Although life for the labourer (and the consumer) under the Fordist era was certainly in need of vast improvement, Gorz (1989) paints an equally bleak picture of the current situation with his analysis of the new, dual nature of the contemporary workforce. Indeed we are now faced with a situation throughout the world

> in which there is, on the one hand, a privileged stratum of permanent workers attached to the enterprise in which they work and, on the other, a growing mass of casual labourers, temporary workers, the unemployed and 'odd jobbers'. (1989: 65)

As far as flexibility goes, both Gorz and Harvey contend that the stable *core* of labourers must be functionally flexible, and the *peripheral* workforce must be numerically flexible. Parent firms can achieve this flexibility by maintaining their highly skilled, stable core while simultaneously exploiting a vast number of workers through subcontracting arrangements with satellite companies. Please note that those individuals comprising the core are also the ones that benefit most from all that late capitalism has to offer in the way of consumption. Those on the periphery, of course, are at best only able to achieve glimpses of the 'happiness' and 'joys' of consumer culture.

Societal members are constituted as subjects from a variety of positions. Although taking no ontological precedence, work is still a viable point of resistance that should not be neglected or overlooked by leftist politics. We must avoid allowing the labour process to be any more marginalized or peripheralized than it already has become (see Lash, 1991). It seems that the inclusion of production-related concerns (as well as those associated strictly with consumption) in social movements would only enhance the strength of such endeavours. We, of course, seek to avoid what Kauffman et al. call a 'postmodern politics of fragmentation', and advocate some conception of a 'progressive renewal, in which the new social movements in coalition with New and Old Lefts and older social movements chart a path toward a plural and radical democracy' (1991: 54–5).

'Maybe the target nowadays is not to discover what we are, but to refuse what we are' (Foucault, 1982: 220). One way to view how the traditional marketing community conceives of 'what we are' is to consider Urban and Star's (1991) decision to use Jasper Johns's *Target with Four Faces* (1955) for the cover of their advanced marketing strategy text. What exactly are Urban and Star trying to do through the use of this cover design, if anything?[11] At the very least, it is quite revealing and a bit disconcerting. One could argue that it is merely a stylistic play (or ploy), or that Urban and Star did not realize the insidious character of their cover design.[12] Levin provides us with an excellent description of *Target* in the following:

> its theme is precisely the inner centre of the target, the bull's eye, and the latter's violent relation to the outer boundaries, the sensuous mouths and nostrils of the eyeless faces poised behind the target, unable to 'see' outward. Few objects comment so brutally on the rationalization of interior spaces. (1987: 47–8)

We believe that, in spite of themselves, Urban and Star have provided us with one fair representation of how corporate executives, marketing researchers and consumer behaviourists view the consumer masses (i.e. as eyeless, mute objects). The individual really has no identity or subjectivity independent of her role as of a consumer. Identity can only be achieved by being part of a marketer-controlled target group. In consumer society, individuals are given 'hope' by being constituted as a subject through the use of target classification. We are unable to see beyond the categorization scheme that has been imposed upon us, and therefore, we are incapable of conceiving of an existence outside late capitalism. The formation of aggregates, which marketing as a discipline absolutely requires, takes priority over individuality.

Conclusion without closure

There is at times considerable conceptual overlap between the Frankfurt Circle, and those espousing postmodern or poststructuralist orientations. Levin (1991), for example, contends that the Marxian concept of reification, which is central to the neo-Marxist position, is very similar to Baudrillard's notion of simulation. Agger (1991) advocates a synthesis of critical theory, poststructuralism, and postmodernism. Agger contends that while critical theory is a much needed critique of positivist science and advanced capitalist culture, 'poststructuralism completes the Frankfurt critique of science by showing that we can read all sorts of nondiscursive texts as rhetoric' (1991: 120), and that the postmodernism of Michel Foucault 'offers valuable insights to students of social control' (1991: 123).

We firmly believe that those engaged in the study of ethics and marketing, as well as those strictly engaged in consumer research, must be able to grapple with such postmodern/post-Marxist phenomena as Kroker and Cook's 'media-scape', Laclau and Mouffe's renewed emphasis on hegemonic processes, Foucault's panoptic mechanisms, Derrida's deconstructive moments, and Baudrillard's 'hyper-reality'. It is perhaps essential that marketing academicians must first be well acquainted with the basic premises of critical theory before such a 'theoretical jump' can be successfully attempted. Unfortunately, the basic premises of functionalist thought have distracted us in this regard, and may have cost us dearly in any integrative endeavour, or in a transition to a postmodern interpretation if one is warranted for marketing ethics. Important phenomena such as the culture industry and aesthetics should not go unnoticed regardless of what version of social theory is employed.

Notes

1 The distractions or 'spectacles' (Debord, 1977) have become even larger, more prolific, and ultimately all-consuming in a postmodern version of consumer culture (e.g. the American public's reliance on 'infotainment' sources, MTV, and the dangerously omnipresent sports broadcasting industry).
2 A parallel can be drawn between the tenets of Fordism and the 'production' that takes place within the culture industry (e.g. most Hollywood films).
3 Eagleton, however, rightly cautions us about the double-edged character of the aesthetic. It can be conceived of as an emancipatory force (e.g. 'a community of subjects now linked by sensuous impulse'), or as an evocation of the Horkheimerian notion of internalized repression, 'inserting social power more deeply into the very bodies of those it subjugates, and so operating as a supremely effective mode of political hegemony' (1990: 28).
4 However, this dedifferentiation is a position not sought by all. Habermas, for instance, views (and ultimately celebrates) cultural modernity as 'the separation of the substantive reason expressed in religion and metaphysics into three autonomous spheres. They are: science, morality and art. These came to be differentiated because the unified, world conceptions of religion and metaphysics fell apart' (1981: 8). Bernstein argues that, for Habermas, 'the possibility of dedifferentiation, of the lapsing or fusing of these autonomous forms of discourse, can only be conceived of as a regression, a re-enchantment of the world, as a re-fusing of nature and culture in such a manner that knowledge and power would again become coeval' (1989: 49).
5 There is a real possibility of a 'right turn' in the aestheticization of politics. At the very worst, a right-aesthetic could lead to a neo-Nazification of art (and ultimately of life in general). The annoyingly conservative American commentator Pat Buchanan has made the assertion that the left has been 'seizing all the commanding heights of American art and culture' (cited in Fox, 1989). As

a result of this type of thinking, we witnessed the National Endowment for the Arts come under constant fire during the Reagan/Bush years. Military marching bands and the waving of American flags were passed off as both the beautiful and the good. The references to God, the Bible, and country were prolific. Anything that challenged these base forms of religiosity and patriotism were deemed immoral, blasphemous, and politically dangerous (e.g. the works of Mapplethorpe and Serrano, and flag burning as protest).

6   Although we use some of Warhol's works for the purposes of our anti-marketing theory, we agree with Herwitz (1993) when he suggests that Warhol is very difficult to interpret, but that his ambivalence and nihilism may make him postmodern. Alternatively, it could be that Warhol's expressions of low culture represent the 'left postmodernist position that claims to discover emancipatory yearnings in the products of the culture industry' (Berman, 1989: 75). Regardless, we disagree with Marcuse when he argues that the 'exhibition of a soup can communicates nothing about the life of the worker who produced it, nor of that of the consumer' (1978: 51).

7   One should not, of course, dismiss the power of everyday consumer products. In the British film *How to Get Ahead in Advertising*, an executive suffers an emotional breakdown because of his inability to mount an advertising campaign for a pimple cream! For a review essay of this important and subversive film, please refer to Hetrick and Durchin (1992). In other works of related interest for our current purposes, Warhol also deals with celebrity figures, some relatively harmless (e.g. Marilyn Monroe), and some notorious and dangerous (e.g. Chairman Mao Zedong). One could only imagine the (re)production of silk-screens of Michael Jackson and Jeffrey Dahmer if Warhol were still alive today.

8   Horkheimer and Adorno reveal the danger of an implosive posture by advocating that the 'fusion of culture and entertainment that is taking place today leads not only to a depravation of culture, but inevitably to an intellectualization of amusement' (1986: 143). The academic fascination with the pop star Madonna (e.g. Paglia, 1992) seems to be a strong case in point for the 'intellectualization of amusement'.

9   Many thanks go to Mike Saren and the other editors for suggesting that we explore these types of relationships.

10 We must be alive, however, to the potential danger(s) of the postmodernist discourses as described by Bronner in the following: 'Semiotics, deconstruction, and various forms of poststructuralism have supplanted Marcuse's aesthetic theory and his attempt to bring words like beauty, softness, and sensuality into the political vocabulary' (1988: 108).

11 This may be indicative of the marketing discipline's ability to coopt things (e.g. theory or art) that should otherwise be very critical of marketing processes. See, for example, Murray and Ozanne's (1991) attempt to use critical theory in a consumer research context, and the rebuttal by Hetrick and Lozada (forthcoming).

12 Ironically, this same Johns work was used by Allan Megill (1985) on the cover of his *Prophets of Extremity*. A detailed analysis of Nietzsche (the will not to will), Heidegger, Foucault (the carceral society), and Derrida may seem humorously inconsistent with discussions of target markets and consumer segmentation. But then again, perhaps not!

References

Agger, Ben (1991) 'Critical theory, poststructuralism, postmodernism: their sociological relevance', *Annual Review of Sociology*, 17: 105–31.

Arndt, Johan (1985) 'On making marketing science more scientific: role of orientations, paradigms, metaphors, and puzzle solving', *Journal of Marketing*, 49 (Summer): 11–23.

Baudrillard, Jean (1981) *For a Critique of the Political Economy of the Sign*. St Louis, MO: Telos.

Baudrillard, Jean (1983) *Simulations*. New York: Semiotext(e).

Benton, Raymond (1987) 'Work, consumption, and the joyless consumer', in A.F. Firat, N. Dholakia and R.P. Bagozzi (eds), *Philosophical and Radical Thought in Marketing*. Lexington, MA: Lexington Books. pp. 235–50.

Berman, Russell (1989) *Modern Culture and Critical Theory*. Madison, WI: University of Wisconsin Press.

Bernstein, Jay (1989) 'Art against Enlightenment: Adorno's critique of Habermas', in Andrew Benjamin (ed.), *The Problems of Modernity*. London: Routledge. pp. 49–66.

Bronner, Stephen Eric (1988) 'Between art and utopia: reconsidering the aesthetic theory', in R. Pippin, A. Feenberg and C. Webel (eds), *Marcuse*. South Hadley, MA: Bergin & Garvey. pp. 107–40.

Connor, Steven (1989) *Postmodernist Culture*. Oxford: Basil Blackwell.

Debord, Guy (1977) *Society of the Spectacle* (1967). Detroit, MI: Black & Red.

Eagleton, Terry (1990) *The Ideology of the Aesthetic*. London: Basil Blackwell.

Fay, Brian (1987) *Critical Social Science*. Ithaca, NY: Cornell University Press.

Ferrell, O.C. and Gresham, L.G. (1985) 'A contingency framework for understanding ethical decision making in marketing', *Journal of Marketing*, 49 (Summer): 87–96.

Ferrell, O.C., Gresham, L.G. and Fraedrich, J. (1989) 'A synthesis of ethical decision models for marketing', *Journal of Macromarketing*, 9 (Fall): 55–64.

Firat, A. Fuat (1987) 'The social construction of consumption patterns: understanding macro consumption phenomena', in A.F. Firat, N. Dholakia and R.P. Bagozzi (eds), *Philosophical and Radical Thought in Marketing*. Lexington, MA: Lexington Books. pp. 251–67.

Foucault, Michel (1978) *The History of Sexuality*, Vol. 1. New York: Random House.

Foucault, Michel (1979) *Discipline and Punish* (1975). New York: Vintage.

Foucault, Michel (1982) 'The subject and power', in Hubert Dreyfus and Paul Rabinow (eds), *Michel Foucault*, 2nd edn. Chicago, IL: University of Chicago Press. pp. 208–26.

Fox, Nicols (1989) 'NEA under siege', *New Art Examiner*, Summer: 18–23.

Gorz, André (1989) *Critique of Economic Reason*. London: Verso.

Habermas, Jürgen (1970) 'Technology and science as "Ideology"' (1968), in *Toward a Rational Society*. Boston, MA: Beacon.

Habermas, Jürgen (1971) *Knowledge and Human Interests*. Boston, MA: Beacon.

Habermas, Jürgen (1981) 'Modernity versus postmodernity', *New German Critique*, 22 (Winter): 3–14.

Harvey, David (1989) *The Condition of Postmodernity*. Oxford: Basil Blackwell.

Herwitz, Daniel (1993) *Making Theory/Constructing Art*. Chicago, IL: University of Chicago Press.

Hetrick, William and Durchin, Jesyca (1992) 'Advertising and (post) modernity: the case of *How to Get Ahead in Advertising*', *Rethinking Marxism*, 5(3): 132–40.

Hirschman, Elizabeth (1987) 'People as products: analysis of a complex marketing exchange', *Journal of Marketing*, 51 (January): 98–108.

Horkheimer, Max (1972) 'Traditional and critical theory' (1937), in *Critical Theory: Selected Essays*. New York: Herder & Herder.

Horkheimer, Max and Adorno, Theodor (1986) *Dialectic of Enlightenment* (1944). New York: Continuum.

Hunt, Shelby and Vitell, Scott (1986) 'A general theory of marketing ethics', *Journal of Macromarketing*, 6 (Spring): 5–16.

Huyssen, Andreas (1986) *After the Great Divide*. Bloomington, IN: Indiana University Press.

Jameson, Fredric (1984) 'Postmodernism, or the cultural logic of late capitalism', *New Left Review*, 146: 53–92.

Kauffman, L.A., Robinson, B. and Rosenthal, M. (1991) 'Post-Fordism: flexible politics in the age of just-in-time production', *Socialist Review*, 21 (1): 53–6.

Kroker, Arthur and Cook, David (1988) *The Postmodern Scene*, 2nd edn. London: Macmillan.

Laclau, Ernesto and Mouffe, Chantal (1985) *Hegemony and Socialist Strategy*. London: Verso.

Lash, Scott (1990) *Sociology of Postmodernism*. London: Routledge.

Lash, Scott (1991) 'Disintegrating firms', *Socialist Review*, 21 (3–4): 99–110.

Leiss, William (1988) *The Limits to Satisfaction* (1976). Montreal: McGill–Queen's University Press.

Levin, Charles (1987) 'Art and the sociological ego: value from a psychoanalytic point of view', in John Fekete (ed.), *Life After Postmodernism*. New York: St Martin's Press. pp. 22–63.

Levin, Charles (1991) 'Baudrillard, critical theory and psychoanalysis', in Arthur and Marilouise Kroker (eds), *Ideology and Power*. New York: St Martin's Press. pp. 170–87.

Lukacs, Georg (1971) *History and Class Consciousness*. Cambridge, MA: MIT Press.

Marcuse, Herbert (1964) *One-Dimensional Man*. Boston, MA: Beacon.

Marcuse, Herbert (1978) *The Aesthetic Dimension*. Boston: Beacon.

Marx, Karl (1977) *Capital*, Vol. 1. New York: Vintage.

Megill, Allan (1985) *Prophets of Extremity*. Los Angeles, CA: University of California Press.

Murray, Jeff and Ozanne, Julie (1991) 'The critical imagination: emancipatory interests in consumer research', *Journal of Consumer Research*, 18 (September): 129–44.

Murray, Robin (1988) 'Life after Henry (Ford)', *Marxism Today*, 32 (10): 8–13.

Paglia, Camille (1992) *Sex, Art, and American Culture*. New York: Vintage.

Robin, Donald and Reidenbach, R. Eric (1987) 'Social responsibility, ethics, and marketing strategy: closing the gap between concept and application', *Journal of Marketing*, 51 (January): 44–58.

Rosenau, Pauline Marie (1992) *Post-Modernism and the Social Sciences*. Princeton, NJ: Princeton University Press.

Ryan, Michael (1982) *Marxism and Deconstruction*. Baltimore, MD: Johns Hopkins University Press.

Smart, Barry (1992) *Modern Conditions, Postmodern Controversies*. London: Routledge.

Thacker, Andrew (1993) 'Foucault's aesthetics of existence', *Radical Philosophy*, 63 (Spring): 13–21.

Urban, Glen and Star, Steven (1991) *Advanced Marketing Strategy*. Englewood Cliffs, NJ: Prentice-Hall.

Williams, O.F. and Murphy, P. (1990) 'The ethics of virtue: a moral theory for marketing', *Journal of Macromarketing*, 10 (Spring): 19–29.

12 Commentary

Peter Binns

The global context of marketing ethics

Over the last 15 years there has been a massive increase in the attention given to ethical issues in business, and this has been accompanied by an awareness of a growing need for an intellectual framework within which these issues can be discussed.

Of course, there have always been frameworks within which critical evaluations of contemporary business life have taken place – most notably from Marxist, Christian, and traditionalist perspectives – but, by and large, these older perspectives looked at business from the outside and sought to influence or oppose it by the use of agencies and mechanisms of a non-business nature: for example, the regulatory mechanisms of the state or the extension of the not-for-profit sector.

In these circumstances the critique of business tended to be an external critique, and the moral or prescriptive consequences drawn from it tended to be framed primarily in the language of religion or politics, rather than in the language of morals and ethics. More recently, however, the material grounds upon which these perspectives were based have been seriously – possibly fatally – undermined. The modern business organization has, apparently, swept all before it. The state sector has been privatized, market-tested, opened to competitive tendering, or shut down; the ability of the state to influence capital, finance and currency markets has been all but written off. The modern business corporation, it has been argued, has broken through its political container, and now, like a metastasizing cancer, is growing unconstrained in the body politic. Similarly, as the shopping mall replaces the church as the arena of Sunday recreation, so too, it has been argued, has the ideological integument within which business used to fit been submerged beneath a flood of materialism and consumerism.

A consequence that has – largely implicitly – been drawn from this line of thinking is that if business is to be influenced to become benign, and therefore in alignment with the personal, social and ecological needs of the current age, it will be necessary to find arenas of debate that are internal to and intrinsic in business life and decision-making. The growth of business ethics marks the recognition of this conclusion. What in earlier times was framed in political, social, religious or spiritual terms, now becomes re-framed within the language of business.

Two key features frequently accompany this approach:

1 The subject or agent, who has to decide what to do in any given context, is seen as having power by virtue of their capacity as purchaser or seller of a commodity. Any critical review of business activity, therefore, has to be undertaken from 'inside the beast' rather than from outside it.

2 This newly found internality of viewpoint is combined with a corresponding extension of the boundary within which the actions of business organizations are seen as the direct responsibility of the businesses themselves. Thus what might in the past have been considered as just part of the business environment – to be dealt with by an appropriate outside agency such as the state – tends now to be seen as more of a question of individual companies getting their own houses in order.

This tendency has been marked in a number of ways in recent debates:

• an increasing engagement with the wider stakeholder community, not just in mission and vision statements, but also in explicit corporate strategies
• a rising concern with issues of governance (as witnessed in the UK by the Cadbury and Greenbury Reports)
• the expansion of such bodies as 'ethical' investment funds; of companies such as the Cooperative Bank and the Body Shop which target the 'ethical consumer'; of other companies such as B&Q which claim that all their processes are environmentally and socially sustainable; and so on.

It is within the context of these two counterposed but coupled features – the shrinking of the ethical agent to a purely internal status within business life, and the increasing globalization required of this agent's vision – that contemporary debates have largely been reconstructed.

The external and the internal critique of market-based society

Chapter 12 by Hetrick and Lozada attempts to resist this changing terrain of ethical debate. It aims to propose alternative perspectives to the 'hyper-functionalist worldview' and managerial bias that it sees as constraining contemporary debates concerning marketing. In particular, it makes a case for the use of critical theory and postmodernist philosophy to broaden the terms of the discussion. It also argues that these two approaches are or can be mutually self-supporting, and it is implied that together they constitute the basis for a powerful alternative to the 'logical empiricist orientation'.

Whether it is appropriate to classify all the views critically referred to under this latter single heading, I shall not discuss further. However, Hetrick and Lozada do not make it clear in what ways the approaches of critical theory and postmodernism are, or can be, mutually self-supporting in creating the alternative that these authors are seeking. This is important, because there are grounds for doubting whether this can actually be achieved.

Critical theory, after all, has, fairly accurately, been referred to as a continuation of the Enlightenment project; Habermas (1978) in particular adopts a rationalist approach in which autonomous agents are seen as able to legislate for the common good. Many postmodern theorists, on the other hand, distance themselves from the notion of autonomous agency altogether; thus for Lacan (1977) the self is 'decentred', while for Derrida (1978) there is only an endless 'play' of language which fails to reveal any 'transcendental signified' or agency underneath this linguistic surface. While both critical theory and postmodernism might make critical remarks about contemporary market societies, this does not mean that they could be mutually self-supporting; indeed their opposed ontologies would suggest rather the opposite.

A similar point could be made with regard to the political or social strategies advocated by varieties of postmodernism and critical theory. Thus for Habermas the excesses of market societies are to be overcome positively by the democratic consensus of rational agents, while for Foucault, by contrast, in so far as there is a single viewpoint, it is that this society is to be challenged by essentially negative forms of resistance on the part of marginalized groupings.

It is therefore difficult to see how a consistent and mutually self-supporting alternative to positivistic conceptions of market society is to be created along the lines suggested: there would appear to be no common ontological base and no common strategies for change from among the approaches cited. At the very least Hetrick and Lozada have yet to show how this might be achieved.

On the other hand, Chapter 11 by Grafton Small, influenced by Giddens and others, approaches the question internally, from the experience of the contemporary marketplace to a critique of the exchange process as a whole.

With regard to the diagnosis of the problems, however, both chapters arrive at broadly similar conclusions. In summary these are that the market form is inherently alienating; Hetrick and Lozada refer to the way it undermines an 'intrinsic value of use', and Grafton Small refers to this phenomenon in the twin form of 'seduction' and 'repression'. The underlying picture is of the market form expanding, and, as it does so, penetrating, distorting and undermining the social relationships between people.

Grafton Small refers to the 'darker side of the wealth and the possibilities created by industrialized life in market-based societies', and concludes that 'we as consumers can neither escape the ambiguities of our own culture nor take any active part in it without exercising forms of power and moral judgement over each other, forms which surely demand we each be responsible for the ethics of our communal exchange'. The approach here is to encourage an increasing awareness of the global and systemic aspects of our current market-based societies as a counterweight to the atomization we experience as purely individual consumers.

This recalls the two features referred to above – the shrinkage of the agent to the status of autonomous consumer, coupled with the requirement of an increasingly globalized awareness of how individual actions fit into the wider whole.

Markets, hierarchies and networks

The view that we are increasingly living in a market-based society must be qualified to an extent. It is true, certainly, that looked at purely from the point of view of the end point of social production, more arenas are now mediated through market mechanisms. This is due to the fact that markets have invaded arenas whose previous forms of regulation have primarily been based on hierarchical structures and mechanisms of command and control. But the overall picture is both more complex and more contradictory than that.

It is more complex, because in addition to hierarchies and markets there is also a third element that has been increasingly recognized in recent literature – networks (Hirschman, 1970; Misztal, 1996; Thompson et al., 1991). This is significant, because at issue in the contributions of Grafton-Small and of Hetrick and Lozada in this volume (and in those of other authors too) is the openness of our societal mechanisms to ethical influence. An expansion of the market at the expense of forms of hierarchy would, considered purely on its own, reduce this openness, since the former is autonomously regulated by principles of profit maximization which are impervious to ethical concerns.

But once this tendency for markets to expand at the expense of hierarchies is put into a wider context that includes the changing role of networks, the ethical consequences to be drawn are by no means so simple or uncontradictory.

What then of the shifting boundary between markets and networks? The notion of a network, in this context, is more elusive. While its everyday sense suggests informality, mutuality and unboundedness, recent literature has tended to underdefine it, or, more usually, to define it in purely negative terms as that which is neither a hierarchy nor a market. Leaving such problems on one side, there would clearly be an issue to address if it could be shown that markets had one-sidedly invaded the erstwhile terrain of networks. For what is at issue here is the plasticity of business decision-making to ethical concerns, and, in the common-sense view of the matter, markets are only concerned with the non-ethical properties of products, and therefore are not open to ethical concerns; while networks, being informal, free-ranging and based on a grounding of mutuality between agencies, are open to ethical concerns.

Here, however, the evidence is more mixed. Some important areas of social life have been increasingly mediated through market mechanisms (the expansion in married women's employment is one indicator of this). But a number of recent authors have also argued that at the level of corporate vision and strategy, companies now need to be – and increasingly are – primarily concerned with the fulfilment of 'higher' goals than those of price, profit and market share.[1] This is not because success in the marketplace is unimportant, but rather because such success is seen by these authors as better achieved as a by-product of a more appropriate alternative aim than it is as a result of directly aiming for such success.

The implication of this point of view is that successful companies increasingly act in a more 'networky' and less 'markety' manner, and therefore in ways that are increasingly open to ethical concern and influence. This is particularly true in three major areas: long-term strategic alliances and partnerships; human resource and organizational development; and the relationship with customers.

The last is particularly interesting from our present point of view, and it reveals an important contrast between the concept of the market as it has been traditionally conceived of by neo-classical economists and the concept of marketing as a process or an activity. According to some recent authors, one key factor in successful marketing is a continuing cycle of reciprocal relationships and information flows between the company and its customers (cf. Nooteboom, 1992), as opposed to the more arm's-length assumptions of the classic economic theory of the market.

At issue here is the question of marketing versus the market. This is not just a question of psychology versus economics, but rather that of an ethical shift from a purely instrumentalist approach to one based on Kantian principles of respect for the autonomy and agency of individuals.[2] It would suggest that marketing needs to be thought of as itself much more 'networky' and less 'markety' than the common root of both words might otherwise imply. And it would also suggest not so much a change in the extent to which businesses can be moved towards ethical behaviour, but rather a change in the ways in which they can be so moved. Typically, the economic theory of the market assumes autonomy and separation for the individual agencies that compose it, and therefore success will depend on the skill with which resources are unilaterally directed, controlled and commanded. On the other hand when success depends more on building a fruitful mutual relationship, the skills of facilitating, influencing and coalition-building are more likely to be significant. This is, to be sure, a messier world for some theoreticians who would like to build a discipline of marketing ethics on clear logical foundations and for whom a more casuistic approach would be seen as less rigorous (Binns, 1994), but by no means so for the practitioner who can move beyond narrower instrumentalist thinking and can develop the combination of skills and vision needed to operate well in this environment (Torbert, 1991).

182   *Marketing ethics*

Notes

Further copies of this commentary, as well as papers on related issues, are available from the Bath Consultancy Group, 24 Gay Street, Bath BA1 2PD.

1   This view has been promoted in recent popular business literature (Drummond and Carmichael, 1989; Handy, 1990; Peters, 1989; Schonberger, 1990) as well as elsewhere (Binney, 1992; Carlisle and Parker, 1989; Kuhn and Shriver, 1991; Torbert, 1991).
2   As Nooteboom has put it: 'In human affairs in general and marketing in particular, one-sided influence is bad from an ethical perspective . . . the point of the present article is that one-sided influence is also bad marketing' (1992: 115).

References

Binney, G. (1992) *Making Quality Work: Lessons from Europe's Leading Companies.* London: Economist Intelligence Unit.
Binns, P. (1994) 'Ethical business: thinking thoughts and facilitating processes', *Business Ethics: A European Review*, 3 (3): 174–9.
Carlisle, J. and Parker, R. (1989) *Beyond Negotiation: Redeeming Customer–Supplier Relationships.* Chichester: Wiley.
Derrida, J. (1978) *Writing and Differance.* London: Routledge.
Drummond, J. and Carmichael, S. (1989) *Good Business.* London: Business Books.
Habermas, J. (1978) *Knowledge and Human Interests.* London: Heinemann.
Handy, C. (1990) *The Age of Unreason.* London: Arrow.
Hirschman, A. (1970) *Exit, Voice and Loyalty.* Cambridge, MA: Harvard University Press.
Kuhn, J. and Shriver, D. (1991) *Beyond Success: Corporations and their Critics in the 1990s.* Oxford: Oxford University Press.
Lacan, J. (1977) *Ecrits: A Selection.* London: Tavistock.
Misztal, B. (1996) *Trust in Modern Societies.* London: Polity.
Nooteboom, B. (1992) 'Marketing, reciprocity and ethics', *Business Ethics: A European Review*, 1 (2): 110–16.
Peters, T. (1989) *Thriving on Chaos.* London: Pan.
Schonberger, R. (1990) *Building a Chain of Customers.* London: Business Books.
Thompson, G., Frances, J., Levacic, R. and Mitchell, J. (1991) *Markets, Hierarchies and Networks.* London: Sage.
Torbert, W.R. (1991) *The Power of Balance: Transforming Self, Society and Scientific Enquiry.* New York: Sage.

13   Commentary

Stephen Fineman

'Marketing . . . needs to be understood and practised, not justified', say Beardshaw and Palfreman (1990: 268) confidently in their introductory text-book on management. They continue with similar surety: 'there's absolutely no point in producing something that nobody wants or in producing something everybody wants and then not telling anybody!'

Marketing is thus presented as an ethically neutral system or management tool serving an unequivocal market 'good' – identifying and satisfying customer requirements. Save the odd 'dilemma' or two (e.g. with cigarettes, sex, pornography, guns, lies) marketing swings into action aboard its 'four Ps' – products, place, promotion and price – to serve our 'needs'. And doing this 'profitably' by creating 'wants' is regarded as part of the package – with few ethical strings attached.

The authors of the chapters in this part burrow far and deep beneath the marketing edifice to shake it quite fundamentally. Marketing is revealed as profoundly value laden and, if we are to take the critiques seriously, morally twisted. It shapes and subordinates 'the consumer' in anything but an innocent and friendly way, where the main moral imperative is the sale. This point is nicely captured by Gabriel and Lang in their exploration of the 'unmanageable' consumer:

> Business is rational, its customers unpredictable. The marketing task, therefore, is to plot the predictability of the unpredictable, and to lay down the rules of how to handle what might seem random . . . To the marketer, there are just pre- and post-purchase satisfaction and dissatisfaction ratings. The entire model can be seen as elitist. (1995: 124)

In serving the sale, the present writers tell us, marketing both reflects and defines a market economy where commodities and consumption symbolize what is 'good'. Such a metatheory slips over other meanings of consumption – such as 'to destroy' and 'to waste'. It reinforces a culture of ephemerality and moments where the act of purchase and exchange becomes an end in itself, remote from the intrinsic usefulness of the commodity or its relation-ship to others' interests or concerns – like privacy, pollution, or resource scarcity.

As the authors warm up, their critiques begin to strip marketing of any final vestiges of innocence. Like other deployments of critical social theory, marketing soon gets unhinged from its imperial position in contributing to the apparent good life and falls into the widening cracks of a capitalist society. In a world where objects both define and mediate who we are and what we do, ethical codes are derived to support local, expedient moralities which stress self-interest and personal gain. Marketing's 'democratic' machineries often overpower 'minority' interests and marginal groups, excluding some to the consistent privilege of others. Some customers are decidedly more interesting than others. Marketing professionals are themselves likely beneficiaries of this unequal contest.

The authors take up the deconstructive project with vigour and skill. If nothing else (and it is a big nothing else) it is hard to leave their writings without a sense that marketing ethics are not all that they appear, and that ethics *per se* are tightly written into the power, structure, knowledge and consumption relations that we blithely take for granted – and perpetuate.

Grafton Small ends on that point – leaving us shaken and perhaps a little stirred. Hetrick and Lozada move on to sketch out a sort of poststructuralist 'resolution' which aims to enfranchise the silent and oppressed and help us contemplate our market-engineered identities and souls. This emancipatory quest probably owes more to writers such as Derrida and Foucault than 'true' postmodernists (such as Lyotard and Baudrillard) whose ultra-relativism gives us no clear reason why any particular social arrangement may be worth striving for – what Gregory Elliott terms postmodernism's 'crippling performative contradictions' (1993: 4). If everything is relative, what is the point of doing anything?

Hetrick and Lozada have a vision of emancipation through resistance: the ethical practices of marketing organizations and corporations are to be stalled (and redefined?) by the non-compliance of traditional stakeholders – especially consumers and academics. Furthermore, doubters may find solace and inspiration in critical art that parodies our consumerist obsessions. I find no quarrel with such aims although, beyond intellectual exhortation, I detect no suggested theory of action which convinces me how such a shift can really occur. How is the Foucauldian ideal of the play of non-privileged discourses to be attained and maintained? What is the social glue that holds the new 'marketing' order(s) together? How will it work?

There is tension here between a reformist posture ('making marketing more ethical') and a transformatory one that does away with marketing as we know it altogether because its foundations are morally bankrupt. For the former, we may observe the fate of reformist consumer voices or organizations such as 'ethical consumers', 'green consumers' and *Which?* These turn out to be far from representative of the majority of consumers and they are easily incorporated into dominant marketing ideologies. There is no need to substantially change the rules or 'working' moralities. If such groups become too threatening they are simply shut out (Fineman, 1996). In the *realpolitik* of resistance and contested ethical orders, those representing the establishment have much to defend, and can do so with force. By definition, reformist politics do not aim to up-end the existing social order, so none of the consumer groups are questioning the very premise of the market economy, or the right of marketing to exist.

The extreme anti-marketing position transforms existing marketing ethics and the marketing industry into something else, although quite what is not clear from the present chapters. Each chapter flirts (in different ways) at the fringes of reformation and transformation. Being an *aware* 'victim' does not in itself change structures – but it is a start. As the writers point out, marketing has its roots in existing capitalist enterprise, so both are tarred with the same ethical brush. If one goes, then so does the other? If this be the case then it is worth, perhaps, pondering on recent world events which seem to suggest that capitalism is the least imperfect of the economic systems.

This part of the book successfully shifts received marketing theory into an exciting and controversial domain. Marketing's implicit value and ethical premises are picked out and picked over – using critical theory as tools. Such inquiry exposes marketing as perpetuating something that has a bitter as well as a sweet effect on our social order, so the examination must continue. We might not know quite where we will end up, but that is no reason not to start the journey.

References

Beardshaw, J. and Palfreman, D. (1990) *The Organization in its Environment*. London: Pitman.

Elliott, G. (1993) 'The cards of confusion', *Radical Philosophy*, 64: 3–12.

Fineman, S. (1996) 'Emotional subtexts in corporate greening', *Organization Studies*. 17 (3): 479–500.

Gabriel, Y. and Lang, T. (1995) *The Unmanageable Consumer*. London: Sage.

Part V

THE MARKETING PROFESSION

The next two chapters address an uncomfortable paradox: the failure of marketing to market itself. The marketing literature worries continually about the low status of marketing both as an academic discipline and as a professional practice. In the academy, the marketing discipline is seen as parasitic and dated (Brown, 1995; Hunt, 1994); in the field, marketers seem for ever to be losing out to rival professional groups, especially finance (Doyle, 1990; Doyle, 1995). Willmott's chapter links the weaknesses of the academic discipline directly to its failures in the field. Eriksson takes a concrete case of repeated defeats to marketing within a particular organizational setting to draw conclusions for the development of marketing as a discipline.

For Willmott, the low status and influence of marketing as a profession are almost perverse. As consumption has become the defining activity of postmodernity, marketing should have an unequalled advantage in its special understanding of consumers and its direct access to the market. The problem Willmott seeks to explain, therefore, is how a function so central to contemporary capitalism could be so poorly recognized. According to Willmott, marketing's failure is due to its reliance on two strategies which are not only individually flawed in themselves, but damagingly contradictory when combined.

For Willmott, marketing's first error is to promote a 'depth strategy' of academic research which relies on an exaggerated and counterproductive 'scientism' (cf. Brown, 1995; Hunt, 1994). Scientist epistemologies and methodologies have bound research to the production of relatively trivial and contingent types of knowledge dedicated to the crude manipulation of human response. The second error lies in marketing's 'strategy of breadth'. Behind Kotler's (1972) 'generic concept of marketing' is the imperialistic claim that marketing should govern all kinds of exchange, internal as well as external. This is a bridge too far. The broader marketing becomes, the less exclusive is its expertise. Marketing thrusts itself into domains for which it is ill equipped and which are already well occupied by rival professional groups. As 'breadth' takes them beyond their true expertise, 'depth' betrays professional marketers into a naively manipulative scientism utterly disabling in the subtle, human realities of organizational politics and competition.

Eriksson's account of marketing's development within a leading Finnish chocolate manufacturer reveals exactly this organizational ineptitude on the part of professional marketers. Over 30 years, marketers in this company repeatedly tried to extend their influence beyond their narrow functional responsibilities. They directly challenged the engineering function in its domain, at the same time as claiming the overarching responsibilities of general management. Too young, too mobile and over-reliant on the naive universalism of Anglo-American marketing theory, these marketers lacked both sensitivity to organizational context and in-depth knowledge of their products. The result was defeat in the marketplace and rebuff by the engineers. Like Willmott, Eriksson attributes failure to overconfidence in marketing's generalizability and an inadequate appreciation of organizational realities.

Though Willmott's approach is theoretical, while Ericksson is empirical, both authors come to broadly similar diagnoses of marketing's problem. The marketing profession suffers from overselling. It has been too imperialistic in its claims to generality and too confident in the superiority of its scientism. The conclusion is seemingly as paradoxical as the original problem. For the marketing profession to progress, it must abandon manipulative self-aggrandizement for the development of a more modest, self-critical and sociable discipline.

References

Brown, S. (1995) *Postmodern Marketing*. Routledge: London.

Doyle, P. (1990) 'Britain's left- and right-handed companies', *MBA Review*, 2 (1): 5–8.

Doyle, P. (1995) 'Marketing in the new millennium', *European Journal of Marketing*, 29 (13): 23–41.

Hunt, S. (1994) 'On rethinking marketing: our discipline, our practice, our methods', *European Journal of Marketing*, 28 (3): 13–25.

Kotler, P. (1972) 'A generic concept of marketing', *Journal of Marketing*, 36 (2): 46–55.

14 The Process of Interprofessional Competition: A Case of Expertise and Politics

Päivi Eriksson

The main objective of this chapter is to demonstrate by means of an empirical case study how the process of interprofessional competition within a single organization is an interplay between, first, the development of professional expertise and, second, the constitution of political capability by which the professional groups can relate their expertise to the organization in question – its history and traditions in particular. Given this concern, I will try to show how the organizational and business context (cf. Pettigrew, 1985; Pettigrew and Whipp, 1991) is relevant in describing and analysing the process of interprofessional competition. Complementing the emerging trend in marketing research – particularly in industrial marketing – which focuses on the external context, this chapter deals extensively with the internal context of an organization (cf. Alajoutsijärvi and Eriksson, 1998).

The academic community has recently pointed at the position and status of marketing specialists within organizations. Marketing has, for example, lost in the competition for senior management positions, which are still more often occupied by other specialists (e.g. Armstrong, 1987a; Lilja and Tainio, 1996). In search for the reasons for this, scholars have looked in various directions. Recent discussions have pointed at the problems of developing marketing as a 'profession', particularly when contrasted with other management groups such as accountancy, personnel and engineering (Morgan, 1992; Whittington and Whipp, 1992; Willmott, Chapter 16 in this volume).

The development of organizational professions can be conceptualized as a process of interprofessional competition, which relies on the metaphor of a 'struggle'. In this process professional groups use different types of 'strategies' in the development and use of their knowledge base and discursive resources. The objective of these strategies is to gain more power in the labour market and in organizational decision-making (Torstendahl, 1990b: 2). Marketing literature has typically advocated strategies such as those described and analysed by Willmott (Chapter 16 in this volume): 'breadth' (strengthening the solidity of marketing knowledge in terms of conventions of science) and 'depth' (extension of the organizational scope of marketing).

However, on the basis of prior research we still know very little about the actual 'strategies for gaining influence' that have been used by marketing people. In particular, we lack knowledge about the strategies pursued by marketing people in different companies, businesses and countries and during different periods of time: what are the origins of the strategies, how are the strategies produced and implemented, how successful are they?

Thomas (1994) has problematized the potential relevance of Anglo-Saxon marketing models in other national and economic contexts. He points out that understanding the environment – both the organizational and the economic environment, as far as I can judge – and the actors in that environment should become a paramount task for marketing people in the light of the discussions on the role of marketing (cf. McKenna, 1988). Indeed, marketing research – particularly industrial marketing (e.g. Halinen and Törnroos, 1998) – has started to pay attention to the external context (cf. Pettigrew and Whipp, 1991: 26) of organizations. This chapter emphasizes that, in addition to the recent attention given to the external context, a sensitivity to the internal context should also be of increasing interest to marketing scholars.

The relationship between a profession and a specific organization has been explored in sociological studies of professional work (Svensson, 1990). There has also been discussion about the need to analyse the development of professions in various national contexts (Torstendahl, 1990a). However, neither the relationship of the marketing profession with specific organizations nor the development of marketing as a profession in different national contexts have been the subject of research within marketing.

The aim of this chapter is to provide an empirical analysis of the process of interprofessional competition between marketing specialists and engineers in one Finnish confectionery company over a period of 40 years. The case study presented in this chapter will show that the success of any 'strategy' for increased organizational influence applied by professional groups is dependent not only on the content of the strategy, but also on how it is introduced and framed by the professionals within specific organizations and businesses. Implementation requires social and political capability, the essence of which is the ability to understand the historical situation of the company and the power relations within the management. This understanding is required to be able to decide how to act: which issues and projects to develop and in which direction (cf. Hosking and Morley, 1991).

In our case company marketing and engineers competed with each other, first, by developing their expertise and by trying to introduce and keep up business problems that could be solved by their own expertise; and second, by trying to expand their expertise into new areas of managerial work. Marketing specialists failed in their attempts to make clear the relevance of textbook-based marketing knowledge and to convince other managers of 'what marketing is good for'. Marketing also failed in its attempts to invade production management's domain of expertise. Engineers, in turn, systematically developed their expertise in cost-efficient production and in the adoption of new production technology, and utilized the close relationships between the owners and the old craft-skilled production management. Engineering won a dominating position over marketing at one stage of the development, but that period ended in financial and organizational crisis. Neither group had success in widening their expertise to become dominating in the field of general management; in this field they were not able to find lasting solutions to the emerging problems of the business on their own.

Expertise and politics in professional competition

Knowledge and skill play an important role in discussions of any professional group, as well as in discussions of interprofessional competition. Expertise of an individual or a group of people is based on the combination of theoretical or formal knowledge and practical or technical skills (Freidson, 1986: 210–17; Svensson, 1990; see also Whitley, 1992). Developing professional expertise through various institutional arrangements and through experience is one avenue for an organizational group towards increased power in organizational decision-making (e.g. Armstrong, 1986; 1987a).

There are two main ways for a professional group to develop and constitute its expertise. First, education and training supply knowledge about theoretical perspectives: concepts, classifications and models. It is also able to produce a certain status and credibility. Second, experience generates practical skills and working methods applicable in specific work situations. Experience is based on learning-by-doing in prior jobs, finished projects and common examples. In a study on the work of architects and psychologists, Svensson (1990: 62) found that experience may throw into question rational theoretical knowledge by emphasizing trial and error, intuition and muddling through. The relationship between formal knowledge and experience is, however, not straightforward; education may also be more practically or scientifically oriented (e.g. Whitley, 1992).

The literature has described strategies in which the claim for either exclusive expertise or the generalizability of expertise is used by management specialists for increased organizational influence (e.g. Armstrong, 1986; 1987a). As an example of the first strategy, marketing has advocated the exclusivity of marketing's expertise on customers and their needs. For example, in Webster's words: 'Marketing as a distinct management function will be responsible for being expert on the customer and keeping the rest of the network organization informed about the customer' (1992: 14). Other strategies, often used simultaneously, strive towards increased influence through generalizability and a wider scope of marketing expertise within organizations and management (cf. Willmott, Chapter 16 in this volume). Marketing has, for example, invaded the field of work of strategic management and claimed that 'customers are the focal point of strategy' (Biggadike, 1981: 621), and further that 'The business will be defined by its customers, not its products or factories or offices' (Webster, 1992: 14).

Making a certain type of expertise relevant in managerial decision-making requires not only the formulation of strategies for professional power, but also an organization- and business-specific understanding, i.e. political capability to implement these strategies. It has been pointed out that the importance of a certain type of professional expertise is often justified by proposing a problem which is best solved by the expertise of a certain professional group (e.g. Torstendahl, 1990a). Armstrong talks about indentifying 'a key problem confronting capital' (1986: 26); here I consider that many business problems can be introduced or reframed as confronting the survival or profitability of the company and thereby they can be used by the professional groups for gaining increased organizational influence (see Knights and Morgan, 1991).

The relevance of a group's expertise for solving a certain business problem can be expressed to others either in words – in formal and informal conversation, statements, speeches and stories – or in other acts by creating and performing certain tasks, activities and projects. This case study is based on the assumption that both discursive and non-discursive events have the ability to produce consequences.

According to prior research, there are also several means by which a professional group can make its expertise relevant to a specific organization: by knowing how the organization functions, why it functions in a certain way, and more specifically, which people one must develop good contacts with, for example, to form alliances in order to achieve common goals (Svensson, 1990: 66). Furthermore, variation in the capability for company and organization-specific 'professional action' produces non-determinate paths in the development of interprofessional competition at the organizational level.

Engineers and marketing specialists in Finnish companies

Both engineers and marketing specialists have been described as examples of professions that failed: they have been found to have lacked the ability to develop a strong professional apparatus and to increase their influence in organizational decision-making in British industry (e.g. Armstrong, 1987b; Smith, 1991). However, in some other European countries engineers have developed privileged positions within company management (Armstrong, 1987a). This has been the case in Finland (Hajba, 1982; Lilja and Tainio, 1996).

There is a broad consensus of opinion about the importance of a production and engineering orientation in Finnish firms (Halttunen, 1981; Tainio et al., 1985). Studies of Finnish management suggest that production special-ists with technical training and experience have traditionally been well inte-grated into Finnish senior management (Laaksonen, 1962: 111). Amongst the other groups with a business training (marketing, accounting, finance and personnel), none was able on its own to challenge the position of engineers and production specialists in senior management (Hajba, 1982: 58–9).

According to Tainio et al. (1985: 77–8) technical and practical superiority afforded engineers a powerful position in Finnish industry until the 1970s. The main problem for the survival of companies was to increase their production capacity in line with market growth, and engineers could offer efficient technical and production-based solutions. The role of sales and marketing was to deliver the goods to the right place at the right time. From the late 1960s through to the 1980s, companies started to face ever fiercer competition, which created an increased demand at first for marketing expertise, and later for general management expertise. In spite of this develop-ment, engineers continued to dominate the senior management of Finnish companies, at least until the 1980s (Hajba, 1982: 59; Lilja and Tainio, 1996).

The professional development of engineers and marketing specialists cannot be characterized by a fair-play situation in Finland. There has been university-level training for sales and marketing experts from the 1950s, but for specialized engineers since the late nineteenth century. The training of engineers has traditionally been largely influenced by the specific needs of each branch of technology supplying engineers with a 'sense of experience' of certain industrial fields. As far as marketing people are concerned, their training has not been as closely tied up with the traditions of certain business branches, and therefore their theoretical knowledge has taken shape through general and universal (mostly Anglo-American) textbook recipes.

Finland can be described as a 'forest-sector society' (Lilja et al., 1992; Lilja and Tainio, 1996) with a management elite strongly rooted in the forest-sector companies. Finland can possibly be described also as 'an engineering society'. The dominance of the forest industry, led by a large number of engineers with a broad science-based training, has certainly had some influence on the general status of the engineering profession in Finland. Forest industry management and the engineers have adopted a firm belief in technological modernism backed by the whole technical education system (Lilja et al., 1992: 137). This means that the training of engineers is strongly geared towards a search for the most advanced technological solutions. Marketing education has been more focused on consumer goods industries and retailing than industrial marketing (cf. Vironmäki, 1997). Therefore, marketing has had closer links to the more peripheral areas of the Finnish business elite, such as food and retailing, for example (cf. Eriksson et al., 1996).

Engineers have also been more successful than marketing in professional regulation and in the creation of exclusive knowledge. Empirical studies show that production management's training is usually technical and that it is more homogeneous than the training of marketing management. Production specialists have also had a university-level training more often than marketing specialists (Ahlstedt, 1978: 95–8).

Marketing specialists have, though, also gained influential positions in some companies. An empirical study reported considerable variation in how important and powerful the marketing department was thought to be within Finnish food processing companies (Eriksson, 1989). Considerable differences were also found in the use of marketing expertise at the senior management level in Finland (Hajba, 1982: 59). Obviously, the issue is complicated by historical company- and business-specific factors. Therefore, in addition to the differences in professional groups' development and the successfulness of their strategies at the level of society at large, we may expect to find variation in the ways in which professional expertise can be incorporated into the management of individual organizations by professionals.

Studies have suggested that senior management is an important organizational factor in fostering a market orientation (Webster, 1988). In addition, senior managers have been found to favour strategies that they best understand in terms of their own professional expertise (Armstrong, 1986: 27). There is a specific historical feature of top management in Finnish companies which is relevant to our case study on a family-owned company. Ownership of some medium and even large Finnish companies has been, and in a few companies still is, in the hands of a small group of members of the founding family (Hajba, 1982: 11). These owners sometimes belong to the top management of the company (1982: 59). In these cases, the owner-managers' professional backgrounds, experiences and goals, and the political capability of the competing professional groups to relate to the owners, play a particular role in gaining influence.

Interprofessional competition between marketing and engineering: Fazer Confectionery 1950–90

Before moving on to our case, a brief note is in order on the research material. This study is based on a series of retrospective depth interviews with marketing people, engineers and other management in the case company. A wide range of documentary data (annual reports, company news-letters, memos of meetings, written speeches, marketing and production plans, etc.) was also used. The case material is extracted from research reported in Eriksson (1991). Although this chapter draws on a single case study, it is also informed by an industrial analysis of the Finnish confectionery industry and considerable research into secondary sources by the author (see, e.g., Eriksson et al., 1996; Eriksson and Räsänen, 1998).

First, the following case analysis will show the difference between the abilities of marketing people and engineers to develop their expertise and to understand and appreciate company traditions and the nature of the business. Second, it will analyse the differences in the abilities of marketing and

Table 14.1   *Strategies used by the professional groups for increasing their organizational influence in Fazer Confectionery, 1950–90*

Strategies used for increased influence	Business problem and areas of expertise development:	
	Engineers	Marketing
Exclusiveness of expertise	*Problem of production inefficiency* Cost-efficient production (1960–78) Adoption of new production technology (1978–83)	*Problem of heterogeneous consumers* Segmentation, differentiation (1965–75) Image, variety by branding (1976–90)
Generalizability of expertise in other areas of functional or general management	Cost-efficient mass production strategy (1975–83)	*Problem of profitability* Sharing of capacity Industry rationalization (1970–75)

engineering to introduce and keep up business problems which could best be solved by their respective professional knowledge and skills, and in their political capabilities to convince the owners of the relevance of their professional expertise. Furthermore, the case analysis demonstrates how marketing people failed in trying to widen their expertise into the field of work of production management, and how both marketing and engineering experts failed in trying to generalize their expertise to become the dominant knowledge base of general management.

Table 14.1 summarizes the strategies used by marketing people and engineers in the process of interprofessional competition from 1950 to 1990. After 1985, both groups started to orientate towards increased cooperation. Marketing and engineering have implemented strategies of exclusiveness and generalizability of expertise for increasing their influence in the case company. Engineers successfully kept up the same business problem for 40 years. Marketing, instead, focused first on the problem of heterogeneous consumers and later, when trying to invade the domain of the engineers, focused more on the problem of profitability. The following sections will analyse these strategies, their implementation and their successfulness in more detail.

Emergence of differentiated professional groups 1950–65

Fazer Confectionery is a division of a major family-owned corporation which was founded in 1919. The company has been the domestic market leader of luxury branded confectionery from the very outset. The high quality and fine taste of the brands won worldwide acclaim and formed a solid basis for the owners' business idea (Eriksson and Räsänen, 1998). From early on, experts in craft production secured a high status in the company, with the founder taking the lead. Thereafter, three generations of owner-managers have been engaged as product and production specialists with expertise in product development and production technology.

Until the late 1950s the management of the company was rather homogeneous and committed to the company traditions and the owners' high-quality philosophy rather than to any professional ideology. All this was to change. During the early 1960s the company was faced with slowly declining profits and a decreasing market share. The Sales Director established a marketing department in 1965 and launched a structural change that was well ahead of its time in Finland: two graduates in marketing were appointed as product managers. Production was reorganized at about the same time. Thereafter, an increasing number of engineers were hired to work with the old craft-skilled masters, particularly within the production function.

Development of marketing organization and marketing expertise

When the marketing department was established, the sales organization was subordinated to the Marketing Director who was the former Sales Director. The people in sales were experienced men with little education, but they possessed other relevant qualifications required by the owners: they were all army officers and they spoke Swedish, the native language of the owners, fluently. Product managers, who in the early 1970s worked under two marketing managers, were mostly young, well-educated men. They had a sound theoretical knowledge of textbook marketing techniques, but little experience in either marketing work or the Finnish confectionery business and very little interest in sales. Therefore, marketing and sales were actually two different functions within the marketing department.

The newly appointed product managers saw an opportunity to climb the career ladder to the position of marketing manager and Marketing Director. However, the post of Marketing Director was firmly in the hands of the former Sales Director until the early 1970s. During the late 1960s ambitious marketing specialists stayed with the company for no more than a few years: they were coming and going much faster than engineers and other production specialists. Therefore, the development of marketing expertise was by no means a smooth process. Young product managers, and some marketing managers in the 1970s, did not usually work within the company long enough to gain much experience of the company traditions and the confectionery business. What is more, the person who left also took with him valuable knowledge of the market and the customers, while his replacement 'had his own theories and wanted to do everything differently'.

In the late 1960s and early 1970s marketing people concentrated on developing skills relevant to product development activities. Marketing emphasized the match between market opportunity and new product development. Segmentation and differentiation were considered important tasks. Controversially, expertise on market research was more or less absent.

In the mid 1970s marketing had to confess that the introduction of new products for heterogeneous consumers was no longer the way to success in the business; what mattered now was the ability to develop 'core brands' and brand loyalty over time. This, in turn, required the development of continuity and consistency in marketing activities during the late 1970s and the 1980s. Expertise was then focused more systematically on promoting Fazer's good image and developing the traditional 'Russian recipe' brands, which had formed the core of the company's product mix for almost a century.

Development of production organization and engineering expertise

Production specialists in the 1950s were experienced and craft-skilled masters who had often learned the occupation through the family. These men often made a lifelong career in one company. In the case company, masters were gradually transferred to the product development department during the late 1960s and 1970s, whereafter technicians and engineers started to occupy production management. The production organization was changed several times after the mid 1960s. At first it was decentralized as the number of departments subordinated to the Production Director was increased from two to seven between 1967 and 1979. However, in the early 1980s the production organization was heavily centralized in the hands of the strong Technical Director.

Production engineers started to build up their expertise in cost accounting and numerical sales planning, which were closely related to their production efficiency objective. Engineers at Fazer Confectionery have consistently advocated a change towards more capital-intensive production processes in a situation of more or less continuous labour shortage. During the late 1960s and early 1970s the company moved towards mechanized production processes, and in the late 1970s to automated production. Engineers and other production specialists developed their expertise, first on cost-efficient production processes, for example by means of eliminating dead and waste time, and later on the adoption of new production technology. They also generated new expertise in areas relevant to their own and the owners' objectives: quality control, technical product development, maintenance and process design.

Engineers succeed in relating their expertise to the company traditions and the owners

Donner (1991: 93–4) describes the close relationship between the owners and the masters in production before the 1960s. High quality was their common objective and a solid basis for the Fazer spirit. He also refers to the masters' early desire to improve the efficiency of production, a desire that was later adopted by other production specialists as well. The development of new cost accounting techniques was a good example of how production management introduced the problem of low production efficiency into the company. New cost accounting techniques made it possible for the Production Director to make calculations on the profit margins of individual product groups for the first time in 1960.

Thereafter, the Production Director raised the issue of excess costs in confectionery production: the problem of production inefficiency, he said, was caused by the extensive and frequently renewed product mix. During 1960–75 production engineers were able to rationalize the product mix slowly but continuously as the company shifted from handmade production to mechanized production. The relevance of expertise in cost-efficient production methods was justified in a speech by the Production Director by referring to the owners' high-quality priority: 'In this situation of intensive competition we must be able to produce high-quality products in a cost-effective manner and ensure that we retain our ability to deliver on time.'

There had been a change in top management in 1965 when the second-generation owner-CEO handed over his post to his engineer son who (according to one manager in production) 'was at the time primarily interested in leading the production processes'. The third-generation owner-CEO described the development of the company in the early 1970s as follows: 'The company has been rationalized with a heavy hand. An increasing part of the work is now done by machines. With the onset of price control, the company has had to cut back on its production costs at an accelerating rate' (Luotonen, 1973: 17).

The process of buying a poorly performing Swedish confectionery company in 1975 was another example of production management's ability to convince and persuade the owners. The machinery in the Swedish company was technologically outdated: the engineers claimed that if Fazer Confectionery did not modernize its production machinery, it would itself soon be taken over by some larger firm. This argument really hit home with the owners who have always fought for the independence of the company (e.g. Donner, 1991).

Marketing people fail in relating their expertise to the company and the owners

From the very outset, marketing had difficulties in 'finding its place in the organization' and in 'speaking the right language'. First, marketing management attempted to dress up its concerns in general slogans like 'The customer is king'. The owners did not see what was new about this: they considered themselves the best experts in customer needs and preferences. Marketing tried to introduce problems for which it could develop effective solutions on the basis of modern textbook marketing techniques. This, however, proved to be difficult: marketing people had little practical experience of the business they were dealing with, and even less of the deep-rooted company traditions and culture. An instructive example was the difference in the cultural background of marketing management on the one hand, and the owners and the old production management (masters) on the other. Many of the marketing managers came from Finnish families in a company that had a very solid Finnish–Swedish background.

In the late 1960s, marketing made a bold move and challenged the owners' policy of giving priority to high quality. They declared that in order to maintain the company's market share it was necessary to offer low-quality, low-price brands for the new child and teenager segments in the chocolate confectionery market. The company's main competitor had already implemented this type of change in its own product strategy. However, the suggestion and the product specimens met with an unfavourable reception in the owner-led 'taste panel'. The attempt to introduce brands that were not up to Fazer's quality standards, and particularly in the chocolate business which was the 'heart and core' of the company, seriously decreased the credibility of marketing in the eyes of the owners.

By the 1970s, marketing had turned its prior concern from the end-user to the distribution channel and to profitability problems. Instead of developing its own domain of expertise, marketing tried to contest the expertise of the engineers in production profitability issues. Marketing had given its product managers 'profit centre' responsibility for their products, but without formal authority for control in production processes. This caused increasing conflicts between marketing people and production people on issues such as 'how to divide production capacity between the brands'. The engineers felt threatened by the product managers' attempts to invade their field of work. Product managers became 'internal entrepreneurs' who competed with each other by lobbying around in production (Näsi, 1978). Marketing also tried to gain access to sales statistics, which traditionally were in the hands of the production people.

The owners of the company had developed a solid 'product orientation'. The taste and reputation of the company's products was very important to them. It has been said of the owners that just as some people have an 'ear for music', they had 'a tongue for chocolate taste' (Karsi, 1991: 39). Marketing, however, headed along very different lines in its orientation in the early 1970s. This was of little help in trying to convince the owners of the relevance of marketing expertise for the development of the company. Marketing policy in the early 1970s was formulated in a speech by the Marketing Director as follows:

> In fact we are not selling products but opportunities to earn money . . . From a purely commercial point of view the most important quality of our company's products is not their taste – whether they taste of this herb or that – but how they generate a return on investment.

As marketing people had relatively little experience of the Finnish confectionery business, their professional identity was based on universal marketing theories. The marketing people wanted to be more 'experts in marketing' than 'experts in confectionery marketing'.

In the early 1970s, marketing tried to extend its expertise into the domain of business management. The Marketing Director promoted the idea of industry rationalization to decrease overcapacity in the business – an idea that had previously been abandoned by the owners. However, as a result of heavy persuasion by the competitors through the Marketing Director, a rationalization agreement was signed between the three largest competitors. The agreement was not very favourable for Fazer Confectionery.

Another change initiated by the Marketing Director was even less successful. Marketing management wanted to maintain variety in the product mix at a low cost. The proposed solution was to include low-quality items produced by foreign companies into the product mix. According to the owners, this seriously damaged the image of the company. The Marketing Director had to leave.

The victory of engineering over marketing: professional dominance leads to organizational crisis in the mid-1980s

According to an internal survey in 1978, the professional managers reported that the owners had withdrawn from operative management but that the division of labour between marketing, production and product development was increasingly unclear. The former Marketing Director had been promoted to Managing Director. However, he was unable to take the perspective of business management and tried to manage by marketing principles focusing, for example, on the development of product families.

A major reorganization and changes in management in 1975 had already afforded increased formal power to production management as the owner-managers responded to their concerns over production inefficiency, and also to their concern on the increasing influence of marketing. According to production 'marketing had far more power than it deserved on the basis of its knowledge and experience of the business'. A new Production Director had been appointed from another division of the company – a division that had successfully carried out a production automation and rationalization project. The Production Director, in turn, hand-selected his new partner: an experienced engineer from outside the company who was known to be highly committed to production efficiency and rationalization problems. Asked to identify the major concerns of production management at that moment, the new Production Director answered: 'Profitability, rationalization, raw material losses and delivery on time. All these factors have immediate economic precision; at the same time they ensure that we maintain our high quality standards' (Fasuri, 1975: 8).

In the early 1980s, engineering ideology emphasizing the importance of modern production processes had taken a strong hold on the company. Engineers and production specialists made an effort to move into the area of general management: they wanted to formulate a new business strategy for the company. The owners' past experience strengthened confidence in the possibility of solving business problems through the expertise of the engineers.

Therefore, in spite of the sudden and unexpected death of the Production Director in 1977, the rest of production management was able to push through a radical production automation and rationalization initiative, which was based on a cost-effective mass production strategy. This type of strategy was based more on popular 'success stories' than the production management's experience within the Finnish confectionery business.

The engineers' initiative ran counter to the owners' luxury product strategy, and the first plan suggesting a totally new automated factory alongside the old one was rejected. However, after a few months of persuasion using extensive calculations on expected improvements in productivity and business profits, a plan for renewing the machinery in the old factory was accepted. With hindsight, top management admits that the project was extremely poorly planned and the calculations very over-optimistic. Therefore, the project eventually led to a serious profitability crisis, motivation problems in production, a massive reorganization, and a return to the owners' high-quality strategy complemented by a market differentiation strategy.

Marketing makes an effort to combine experience and new ideas

During 1977–9, a renewed marketing management, now equipped with more practical experience within the industry, made serious efforts to develop marketing expertise and to express its relevance to the company under the leadership of the Managing Director with a marketing background. Marketing concentrated more systematically than before on the core problem of consumer preferences, image and brand-building, which, after the withdrawal of many members of the owner family from operational management, now provided marketing with exclusive knowledge. Marketing management introduced a system of short- and long-term planning with analyses of competitors, consumers and the markets.

That marketing also had the willingness to incorporate new practices into the company was clearly reflected in the slogan 'lean on research rather than past experience, show an openness to new products and product groups'. Marketing had made several attempts to break the tradition of homogeneity in production, based first on the owners' high-quality priority and later on production's low-cost priority. Marketing attempted to incorporate new ideas about differentiation which did not require complicated production processes, such as product families and variety by package types, pricing, quality and image advertising. However, implementation of these ideas was prevented by the powerful engineers during 1979–83.

Marketing had to wait for the failure of production management's pure mass production strategy before it could push through its own ideas. It was only with the financial crisis of 1982–4 that the owners started to question the generalizability of production management's expertise. This crisis of the mass production strategy provided the starting point for increased marketing influence and implementation in the company after the mid 1980s. However, the increasing influence of marketing did not imply its dominance over production or the owners; on the contrary, it implied increased integration and cooperation between these groups.

Summary and conclusions

It has been argued in this chapter that in order to understand the outcomes of interprofessional competition between marketing and other organizational specialisms, we need to analyse the process in its proper organizational and business context. It was suggested that the failure of marketing in increasing its influence in managerial decision-making in one family-owned Finnish confectionery company was due to the long-standing reluctance and inability of marketing people to produce a high level of expertise that the other actors of the organization would consider relevant in terms of future success.

Some scholars have voiced suspicions about the applicability of Anglo-Saxon marketing models to other economic and social contexts (e.g. Gummesson, 1993; Thomas, 1994). The same can of course be said of all other universal business models in all contexts. The usefulness of universal marketing models as the core of the professional knowledge basis can equally be questioned. The case study presented here clearly lends support to such doubts and highlights the importance of continuing the discussion.

In their attempt to increase their organizational influence, marketing people at Fazer Confectionery used strategies that were based on both exclusiveness and generalizability of marketing expertise. The strategy of exclusiveness was at first based more on 'talk', i.e. introducing the academic discourse into the organization, than on more concrete 'action'. The owners were offended by the claims that marketing was the best expert on customers: the owners had been in the business for more than 50 years and they thought they knew all there was to know about the customers. Later, when the owners had withdrawn from operative management, and marketing had gained more experience of the confectionery business and the company traditions, it was easier for marketing to convince others that it had some relevant and exclusive expertise.

The strategy based on widening and generalizing marketing expertise, first into the domain of production management and later into the field of general management, was not successful. The invasion of the domain of engineers and other production specialists caused increasing competition and conflicts between marketing and production. Difficulties were also encountered in the attempt to widen marketing expertise into the field of general management; marketing methods and techniques were not enough for managing the whole business. The engineers responded quickly and took the lead of business management away from marketing with the help of the owners. However, the engineers also failed to generalize their expertise based on 'productivist ideology' (Armstrong, 1987b: 430) as the dominant and sufficient knowledge basis for general management at Fazer Confectionery.

There has been discussion for and against the possibility of extending the scope of marketing and of generalizing marketing's expertise within the organization (e.g. Eriksson and Räsänen, 1998; Webster, 1992; Willmott, Chapter 16 in this volume). The case of Fazer Confectionery drew attention to several problems concerning, first, the generalizability of marketing's expertise, and secondly, the consequences of extending the expertise of any professional specialism. The empirical evidence clearly shows that the attempts by marketing and engineering to extend their professional expertise did not have positive organizational consequences. This was the case particularly when engineering expertise totally dominated other views of business. Even though in this case it was engineering expertise which was generalized to gain predominance with negative results, it should make marketing very suspicious of the usefulness of advocating the pre-eminence of marketing within the organization.

An important point that needs to be made on the basis of the case analysis is that increasing the influence of one professional group should not require repressing and dominating other actors nor other discourses, which has been the spirit of much of the marketing literature and often the strategy pursued by marketing people within organizations. A better way to increase the influence of marketing could be to learn how to interact and cooperate with other management specialists, i.e. how to establish and maintain an ongoing dialogue between various management discourses.

The arguments presented in this chapter suggest that research in marketing should be geared towards more organizationally based processual case studies in order to understand what the role of marketing really is within different types of organizations, and how and why the position and status of marketing changes over time. In addition, marketing research should pay more attention to the various national and business contexts instead of focusing on the development of universal marketing models. Finally, future research could question the common presumption of unified groups of marketing and engineering experts with similar strategies and world views. As the changing strategies of the marketing people in this case have shown, the reality is more complex. A prime Finnish example of the complexity of organizational professions is provided by the marketing experts with an engineering education, which is typical of many forest-sector and high-tech companies.

Note

I am grateful to Kari Lilja, Keijo Räsänen and Richard Whittington for helpful comments on earlier versions of this chapter. I acknowledge financial support from the Academy of Finland in undertaking the research on which this chapter is based.

References

Ahlstedt, Leo (1978) 'Erikoistuminen ja liikkuvuus liikkeenjohtajan urakehitysteki-jöinä'. Series A:25, Helsinki School of Economics.

Alajoutsijävi, Kimmo and Eriksson, Päivi (1998) 'In search of buyer–seller inter-action: context and narratives as keys for a more complete understanding', *Journal of International Selling and Sales Management*. 4 (2): 89–107.

Armstrong, Peter (1986) 'Management control strategies and inter-professional competition: the cases of accountancy and personnel management', in D. Knights and H. Willmott (eds), *Managing the Labour Process*. Cambridge: Gower.

Armstrong, Peter (1987a) 'The rise of accounting controls in British capitalist enterprises', *Accounting, Organizations and Society*, 12 (5): 415–36.

Armstrong, Peter (1987b) 'Engineers, management and trust', *Work, Employment and Society*, 1 (4): 412–40.

Biggadike, R.E. (1981) 'The contributions of marketing to strategic management', *Academy of Management Review*, 6 (4): 621–32.

Donner, Jörn (1991) *Fazer 100*. Otava: Helsinki and Keuruu.

Eriksson, Päivi (1989) 'Conflicts among the basic subunits of the firm'. Studies B-91, Helsinki School of Economics and Business Administration, Helsinki.

Eriksson, Päivi (1991) 'Managerial processes behind long-term product mix changes'. Series A:74, Helsinki School of Economics and Business Administration, Helsinki.

Eriksson, Päivi and Räsänen, Keijo (1998) 'The bitter and the sweet: evolving constellations of product mix management in a confectionery company', *European Journal of Marketing*, 32 (3/4): 279–304.

Fasuri (1975) Company newsletter of Fazer Confectionery, no. 1.

Freidson, Eliot (1986) *Professional Powers*. Chicago: University of Chicago Press.

Gummesson, Evert (1993) 'Marketing according to textbooks: six objections', in D. Brownlie, M. Saren, R. Wensley and R. Whittington (eds), *Rethinking Marketing*. Coventry: Warwick Business School Research Bureau. pp. 248–58.

Hajba, Sirpa (1982) 'Yritysjohdon ammatillistuminen ja valikoituminen osana yritysten institutioitumista'. Series A-5, Turku School of Economics, Turku.

Halinen, Aino and Törnroos, Jan-Åke (1998) 'The role of embeddedness in the evolution of business networks', *Scandinavian Journal of Management*, 14 (3): 187–205.

Halttunen, J. (1981) 'Aloittavat metalliteollisuusyritykset'. Series A:11, Teol-listamisrahasto Oy, Helsinki.

Hosking, Dian-Marie and Morley, Ian E. (1991) *A Social Psychology of Organizing: People, Processes and Contexts*. Harvester Wheatsheaf: Hemel Hempstead.

Karsi, Anneli (1991) 'Kluuvikadun sokerileipurit', *Kauppalehti Optio*, 7 March: 38–9.

Knights, D. and Morgan, G. (1991) 'Corporate strategy, organizations and sub-jectivity: a critique', *Organization Studies*, 12 (2): 251–73.

Laaksonen, Oiva (1962) *Suomen liike-elämän johtajisto*. Porvoo: Weilin and Göös.

Lilja, Kari and Tainio, Risto (1996) 'The nature of the typical Finnish firm', in R. Whitley and P.H. Kristensen, *The Changing European Firm*. London: Routledge. pp. 159–91.

Lilja, Kari, Räsänen, Keijo and Tainio, Risto (1992) 'A dominant business recipe: the forest sector in Finland', in R. Whitley (ed.), *European Business Systems*. London: Sage. pp. 137–54.

Luotonen, Jouni (1973) 'Sokerileipomo kansainvälistyy', *Talouselämä*, (4): 13–17.

McKenna, R. (1988) 'Marketing in an age of diversity', *Harvard Business Review*, 66: 88–94.

Morgan, Glen (1992) 'Marketing discourse and practise: a critical analysis', in M. Alvesson and H. Willmott (eds), *Critical Management Studies*. London: Sage.

Näsi, Juha (1978) 'Perinteisen organisaatiokäsityksen ja tuotepäällikköajattelun välinen koordinaatio-ongelma. Sovellutustapauksena Oy Karl Fazer Ab:n tuotepäällikkösysteemi'. Unpublished paper, University of Tampere, Tampere.

Pettigrew, Andrew (1985) *The Awakening Giant: Continuity and Change in Imperial Chemical Industries*. Oxford: Basil Blackwell.

Pettigrew, Andrew and Whipp, Richard (1991) *Managing Change for Competitive Success*. Cambridge, MA: Blackwell.

Smith, Chris (1991) 'Engineers and the labour process', in C. Smith, D. Knights and H. Willmott (eds), *White Collar Work*. London: Macmillan.

Svensson, Lennart G. (1990) 'Knowledge as a professional resource: case studies of architects and psychologists at work', in R. Torstendahl and M. Burrage (eds), *The Formation of Professions*. London: Sage. pp. 51–70.

Tainio, Risto, Räsänen, Keijo and Santalainen, Timo (1985) *Suuryritykset ja niiden johtaminen Suomessa*. Tampere: Weilin and Göös.

Thomas, Michael (1994) 'Marketing – in chaos or transition?', *European Journal of Marketing*, 28 (3): 55–62.

Torstendahl, Rolf (1990a) 'Essential properties, strategic aims and historical development: three approaches to theories of professionalism', in M. Burrage and R. Torstendahl (eds), *Professions in Theory and History*. London: Sage. pp. 44–63.

Torstendahl, Rolf (1990b) 'Introduction: promotion and strategies of knowledge-based groups', in R. Torstendahl and M. Burrage (eds), *The Formation of Professions*. London: Sage. pp. 1–10.

Vironmäki, Emma (1997) 'Marketing education in Finland'. Paper presented to the PhD tutorial of the 14th Nordic Conference on Business Studies, Bodo, 13–15 August.

Webster, Frederik E. Jr (1988) 'Rediscovering the marketing concept', *Business Horizons*, 31: 29–39.

Webster, Frederik E. Jr (1992) 'The changing role of marketing in the corporation', *Journal of Marketing*, 56: 1–17.

Whitley, Richard (1992) 'Formal knowledge and management education'. Working Paper no. 236, Manchester Business School.

Whittington, R. and Whipp, R. (1992) 'Professional ideology and marketing implementation', *European Journal of Marketing*, 26 (1): 52–63.

15 On the Idolization of Markets and the Denigration of Marketers: Some Critical Reflections on a Professional Paradox

Hugh Willmott

> By constructing an antithesis to the implicit thesis in much of what is written in our area, we are much better placed to make a reasoned assessment of what is said.
>
> (Wensley, 1987: 26)

In the consumer societies of the First World, increased importance is being placed upon the role and operation of markets in allocating resources. As established markets have become saturated and demand can no longer be taken for granted, specialists have grown in number and influence who claim to be experts *inter alia* at identifying customer needs, building brand identities, shifting consumption from generic to specialist products and developing niche markets.

In response to crises of overproduction in 'mature' markets, there has been a strong incentive to create markets for previously uncommodified goods and services – such as leisure and personal services – that were previously organized within the domestic sphere or the local community rather than provided through the more impersonal means of the market. In addition to this substitution of marketed commodities for self-organized goods and services, there has been a rapid development in markets dedicated to the creation and elaboration of images (Baudrillard, 1975) of products, services and self-identity – a development that many commentators associate with 'the postmodern' (see Brown, 1993; Firat, 1993; as well as the contributions by Brown and by Hetrick and Lozoda, Chapters 3 and 12 in this volume), but which is perhaps more plausibly represented as the hypermodern (Willmott, 1992; 1994).

A widely held and ascendant belief in markets – as superior, efficient and effective allocators of resources and satisfiers of customer needs – surely presents marketers, whether full-time or part-time (Gummesson, 1991), with 'a powerful rhetoric' for augmenting their credibility and authority as well as extending their influence. Certainly, the rhetoric of markets is currently being deployed in advanced capitalist societies 'to promote and justify all kinds of change' (1991: 55; see also Hunt, 1976; Levitt, 1960). In the private sector, companies are deploying market mechanisms, such as outsourcing and internal markets, to respond to turbulent market conditions – tactics which themselves often contribute to market turbulence and uncertainty, thereby fuelling the demand for marketing expertise to exploit and manage the opportunities and risks. And, in the public sector, market disciplines are being identified and introduced in an effort to reduce levels of expenditure that are also intended to improve the quality and responsiveness of services (see Walsh, 1993).

And yet, despite the positive valuing of markets, and the demand for the services of marketers, both practitioners and academics, there has not been an equivalent shift in their prestige or, relatedly, the credibility of marketing knowledge (Gaski and Etzel, 1986). On the contrary, as a number of contributors to this volume indicate, it would seem that the established shibboleths of marketing are coming under increasing critical scrutiny, a process that has been facilitated by the pluralistic editorial policies of a number of journals – notably, the *Journal of Consumer Research*. Whilst it may be argued that academics have a vested interest in detecting crises which they, as 'experts', then proceed to analyse and for which they prescribe remedies, it is probably also fair to say that, in academia as in industry, marketing continues to be viewed with some scepticism and suspicion, if not distaste, and has yet to achieve full respectability as an academic discipline or as a management specialism.

How have marketers – academics and practitioners – responded to this paradox of marketing? In this chapter, two strands of their response are reviewed: first, the redoubling of efforts to justify the (scientific) authority of marketing in response to those who doubt its academic respectability; and, secondly, the effort to extend the scope of the discipline to encompass (or colonize) new terrains of practice. It is recognized that these two strands form part of a thicker, loosely woven cord that has been developed by marketers to establish, develop and defend their specialism. Other strands include the formation of 'professional' associations and the awarding of qualifications, as well as the struggles with other specialists to dictate the direction of coporate agendas and strategies (Armstrong, 1986; see also Eriksson, Chapter 15 in this volume).

What the two strands to be examined here share, it will be argued, is a disinclination to reflect more critically upon the relationship between knowledge and the relations of power (e.g. patriarchy: see Knights et al., 1993) that are the object and medium of the production of (marketing) knowledge. Instead, the tendency is to reassert the value of marketing knowledge, most recently by arguing, for example, that 'what marketing needs now is a recognition of its inherent strengths in the postmodern society' where, it is claimed, there is more awareness and scope for the 'identification of market segments via the conscious use of customer images and the process of positioning the company in relation to the images of the market' (Tornroos and Ranta, 1993: 174). In respect of these strands, the response of many marketers to the paradox of marketing is comparable to the motorist who, when stuck in a muddy field, presses harder on the accelerator in preference to stepping out of the car to gain a fresh, and potentially enlightening, perspective on the predicament.

The chapter begins by relating the growth of the marketing specialism to the shift from production to consumption as a source of meaning and self-identity (du Gay and Salaman, 1992; Rose, 1990) that has accompanied the economic and social development of advanced capitalist societies. Since the visibility and influence of marketing are undoubtedly greatest in the field of consumer goods and services rather than in the industrial sector, it is this area that provides the primary focus of the discussion. The efforts of marketers to gain greater recognition for their professed expertise are then addressed. In the realm of *marketing theory*, where the academic credibility of marketing knowledge is at stake, the chapter highlights, and questions the value of, its reliance upon a scientistic philosophy of science. Secondly, in the realm of *marketing management*, where the exclusivity and general-izability of marketing practice are in question, it challenges the value of marketers' efforts to widen the relevance and applicability of marketing expertise. Each stratagem for gaining greater recognition and credibility is seen to be problematical and, in some respects, to be counterproductive. A scientistic philosophy of science inhibits an appreciation of the relationship between knowledge and power which, arguably, is important for developing a more rounded and coherent self-understanding of marketing discourse and practice; and those who seek to extend the domain of marketing expertise have not recognized the contradictory consequences of this imperialistic project.

Having opened up questions about efforts to increase the credibility and influence of marketing in respect of its knowledge claims and generic aspirations, the analysis is developed by focusing upon the conceptual foundations of marketing in exchange theory. The identification of 'market-ing as exchange' is seen to devalue and marginalize any sustained reflection upon the role of power in shaping and constraining market relationships. Moreover, by taking as given the way that market relations act to define and satisfy human needs, their commodifying and alienating consequences are naturalized. This may be helpful in aligning marketing with the demands of capitalism for the extensive commodification and marketization of goods and services whose exchange is the source of capital accumulation. But where this process conflicts with established cultural values – for example, those concerned with honesty, fairness and social justice – then it may be damaging for the reputation of marketing as a management specialism and academic discipline. And, in this respect, the tensions and paradoxes present in marketing theory and practice are more a symptom of the contradictory dynamics of capitalist development than they are a failure of marketers to act as 'high priests of the marketplace' (Whittington and Whipp, 1992: 60). In conclusion, it is suggested that a more modest, reflective orientation to the development of marketing theory and practice would help clarify its condi-tions, temper its claims and ambitions, and reduce antagonism to its development. To address the paradox of marketing, marketers must be more willing to reflect critically upon the historical conditions of marketing knowledge and its application, and actively work towards a transformation of these conditions.

Modernity and marketing

In modernity, there has been a shift in the ascription of social value from production to consumption; and from community to self-identity. How income is spent becomes as important, and perhaps more salient, for a sense of meaning and purpose, than how it is earned. This shift has been distinguished and explored recently by Giddens who observes how, in what he terms 'the post-traditional era',

> the question 'How shall I live?' has to be answered in day-to-day decisions about how to behave, what to wear and what to eat – and many other things – as well as interpreted within the temporal unfolding of self-identity. (1991: 216)

Self-identity is increasingly derived from consumption of goods and services (Douglas and Isherwood, 1980; Fox and Lears, 1983). Through the medium of popular culture and advertising, commodities are ascribed a symbolic value that promise to enhance self-identity in addition to providing more mundane forms of use value (e.g. reducing effort or increasing convenience). As Featherstone has noted, in the modern era of mass consumption, commodities

> take on a wide range of cultural associations and illusions. Advertising in particular is able to exploit this and attach images of romance, exotica, desire, beauty, fulfilment, communality, scientific progress and the good life to mundane consumer goods such as soap, washing machines, motor cars and alcoholic drinks. (1990: 7)

Of the management specialisms, it is marketing that takes the leading role in promoting and facilitating consumerism as it enables modern individuals to identify with particular images and lifestyles that they fulfil through their identity-work as consumers. Marketers have become key cultural inter-mediaries (Bourdieu, 1984) who educate the masses in the pleasures of consumption, their customers in the added value provided by their goods and services, and their fellow managers in the value of a marketing orientation (Hooley et al., 1990; Keith, 1960). Not only do marketers seek to represent and enhance the symbolic and identity value of commodities but, through the medium of internal marketing, they may seek to persuade other organiza-tional members of the importance and effectiveness of appraising all cor-porate activities in terms of the needs of customers and the operation of markets. By identifying markets as the most important and effective media of exchange, marketing discourses and practices simultaneously promote dehomogenization and turbulence as markets are presented as the most relevant and effective means of addressing 'problems' of saturation. In the process, people are encouraged to equate satisfaction with consumption. There is a progressive 'monetization and commodification of social relations' as marketers construct, open up and promote new media of capital accumulation. In this world,

> marketing can tell us the 'price of everything, but the value of nothing'. Anything can be marketed. It does not have to be the more obvious goods and services; it can be 'good causes', 'political parties', 'ideas'. The world is a market and we are consumers in a gigantic candy store. Just sit back and enjoy it! (Morgan, 1992: 143–4)

And yet, as the role of markets and marketing has expanded, marketers have experienced frustration and anxiety regarding the credibility, status and power of their specialism. The growing influence of a marketing orientation in organizations and society is reflected neither in the status ascribed to *marketing knowledge* nor in the social and organizational position of those responsible for *marketing management*. Paradoxically, the increasingly central role of exchange and consumption in advanced capitalist societies has been accompanied more by resentment and self-doubt than by self-assurance and conviction (Thomas, 1993).

The struggle for recognition

Marketers' efforts to gain greater recognition, respectability and influence manifest themselves in a variety of ways that are also paralleled by other management specialisms with whom they compete for resources and, more specifically, for control over the discourse and practice of strategic management. Stratagems for raising the profile and credibility of these specialisms include the formation of 'professional' associations and associated effort to establish monopolies of expertise that, if deemed to be legitimate, serve to enhance their symbolic value as well as to raise their exchange value (Willmott, 1986; Willmott et al., 1993). In the following analysis, attention is focused upon two strands of what is a complex and interconnected array of stratagems developed by management specialists to convince others – fellow specialists as well as other specialists and, ultimately, those responsible for determining and resourcing corporate strategy – of the credibility and importance of marketing expertise for diverse areas of management decision-making.

The *first strand* is concerned with the authority of *marketing knowledge*. This strand is concerned with the issue of how to secure and justify the reliability or *depth* of knowledge. The most widely favoured way of addressing this concern has been to strive to make marketing knowledge comply with what common sense takes to be the conventions of science. The *second strand* is less concerned with marketing knowledge *per se* than with the *breadth* of terrain in which *marketing management* presides or exerts a significant influence. One important tactic for achieving its expansion, which will provide the focus of the following discussion, is to convince others that marketing knowledge resides at the centre of most, if not all, forms of social interaction, including strategic management decision-making.

To repeat, these strands and tactics are intertwined with other efforts to raise the credibility, status and influence of marketing. Thus, a capacity to convince others of the relevance of marketing will in part, depend upon their confidence in marketing knowledge. Likewise the credibility of marketing knowledge will depend, in part, upon whether the influence of marketers expands to the point at which they shape conceptions of credibility and/or steer human behaviour in ways that contrive to make their claims self-fulfilling. And, of course, the formation of professional associations is accompanied by efforts to define and elaborate the distinctive expertise of the membership whilst continuously extending the terrain of application. The dynamic affinities (and tensions) between these strands suggest a challenging agenda for future research in this field. However, the following discussion will be restricted to the less ambitious task of considering, in turn, the 'depth' and 'breadth' approaches to raising the prestige and authority of marketing discourse and practice.

Discourse on Depth

When vying for credibility against the claims of other, more established management disciplines (e.g. accounting, operations research), marketers – practitioners as well as academics – have tended to rely very heavily upon what I will term a scientistic philosophy and associated methodology of knowledge generation (see Hunt, 1983; Jones and Monieson, 1990; Ozanne and Hudson, 1989). Since the term 'scientism' is often used in a rather loose way, it is necessary to say what I mean by it: namely, an orientation to the production of knowledge in which it is assumed that disputes about whether information is reliable or factual are settled epistemologically – for example, by ensuring that scientific method has been properly applied.

In effect, this approach to knowledge generation limits self-reflection to questions of methodology. The assumptions that underpin scientific method are either disregarded or uncritically accepted. Little or no attention is paid to the question of how the social objects of scientific study (e.g. consumer needs) are themselves constituted historically and culturally. Any questioning of these restrictions is deemed to be irrational or anti-scientific as an embargo is placed upon reflecting critically upon what Habermas has termed 'the ontological illusion of pure theory' (1972: 307). To put this another way, scientism disregards the way power relations in society are implicated both in the production of the social phenomena that are the objects of its investigation *and* in the methodology that is advocated to study these phenomena.

Although differences between traditions of research can be exaggerated (Heath, 1992), much market(ing) research remains staunchly scientistic in the sense that it incorporates minimal appreciation of the historical and political construction of its research 'objects', or of the way that the construction and application of scientific method is itself a socially organized process. Market research and the leading marketing journals are heavily engaged in the application and legitimation of scientism. Their overriding concern has been to refine instruments with which to measure the ever increasing number of variables that supposedly enable them to predict human behaviour. This project is reinforced by the understanding that, by following what are commonsensically understood to be the protocols of natural science, levels of prediction and control over human behaviour comparable to those established over nature will eventually be achieved.

Both academic and practising marketers have expended much energy in developing and perfecting methods of enquiry that understand 'objects' in the social world to be ontologically continuous with objects in the natural world. The fundamental weakness of such methods is that they take insufficient account of how human behaviour and attitudes are mediated by socially constructed meanings and relations of power. Approaches – such as Hunt's (1990; 1992a; 1993) well-informed and eloquent advocacy and defence of 'scientific realism' – are no less scientistic in their studied refusal to acknowledge and explore the relationship between knowledge and power. They denigrate and marginalize the claims of other more dialectical methodologies (e.g. symbolic interactionism and various kinds of critical social theory) that could, potentially, remedy the scientific myopia of so much marketing knowledge. Despite some signs of disillusionment with, and departures from, the positivist paradigm of marketing knowledge (e.g. Anderson, 1983; 1986; Dholakia and Arndt, 1985; Firat et al., 1987; Hudson and Ozanne, 1988; Muncy and Fisk, 1987; Peter, 1992; Peter and Olson, 1983; Rogers, 1987; Zinkham and Hirschheim, 1992; for a comprehensive overview of these departures in the field of consumer research, see Sherry, 1991), there is little reason to believe that these alternatives have yet had much impact upon marketing theory and research.

From within its closed-loop perspective, the products of scientism appear more neutral and objective than seemingly less rigorous, reflective and often non-quantitative modes of inquiry. Potentially, the latter methods of inquiry could be deployed to indicate the limitations, and to challenge the assumptions, of scientism. Currently, however, they are routinely dismissed by, or occasionally incorporated within, and subordinated to, the production of objectivistic research programmes – for example, by using ethnographic data selectively to supplement other more 'objective' forms of information rather than to doubt the assumptions that secure the latter's credibility. As a consequence, the scientistic self-understanding of marketing research has remained comparatively undisturbed. As Desmond has observed,

Until recently the conventional wisdom in marketing has not seen fit to question the conditions within which its discourse is produced. Such questions are undoubtedly circumscribed by the prior assumption that the production of scientific marketing knowledge is logical, neutral and objective. (1993: 262)

The contemporary apologists and guardians of marketing expertise, such as Hunt (1983, 1990, 1992a, 1992b, 1993), rely upon some variety of scientism to brace the credibility of marketing knowledge. However, marginalizing the importance of meaning and power in the formation and investigation of social phenomena carries with it the penalty of being unable to grasp the historical and political construction of these 'objects'. Practically, contradictions arise when findings are discovered to be useless or misleading because they do not disclose the cultural complexity or the organizational dynamics of social life. As Arndt (1985a; 1985b) amongst others has observed, the findings of established methodologies are too often trivial, conservative and unilluminating. They also leave marketers ill equipped to understand and address how the status and influence of marketing are socially constructed and negotiated within asymmetrical relations of power. Finally, marketing research is rendered ethically contentious in respect of its representation and treatment of human, reflexive subjects as inert, malleable objects. In each of these respects, marketing is not dramatically different from other management specialisms, although it could be argued that reflection upon the relationship between power and knowledge is considerably more developed elsewhere, even in the more quantitative fields of accounting (Power and Laughlin, 1992) and operational research (Mingers, 1992).

Discourse on Breadth

The second strand of activity through which concerns to improve the credibility, status and influence of marketing are articulated is the endeavour to extend its field of relevance and application. Established definitions of marketing are reconstructed or stretched to encompass wider fields of human behaviour. For example, it is increasingly being argued that marketing has as much relevance in the public and voluntary sectors as it has in the private sector. The attempt to extend its domain is clearly evident in Kotler's formulation of 'the generic concept of marketing' where, imperialistically, he argues that

marketing is a general function of universal applicability. It is the discipline of exchange behaviour, and it deals with the problems related to this behaviour. (1972: 39)

Or, as Kotler earlier formulated the generic concept of marketing:

Marketing applies to an organization's attempts to *relate to all of its publics*, not just its consuming public. (1972: 55; emphasis added)

The marketer is a specialist at understanding human wants and values and *knows what it takes for someone to act.* (cited in Morgan, 1992: 142; emphasis added)

Of course, marketers are hardly unique am
pushing for the extension of their province
1992). Other management specialisms have
press their credentials when making rival cla
specialization for guiding strategic decisior
and Morgan, 1990). However, Kotler's ge
exceptional in representing marketers as expe
conceivable kind of transaction within org
organizations and their diverse stakeholders.

Those who accept and support Kotler's vi
concept believe that organizations and their p
every manager and employee were effectivel
key ideas and concepts (or, others might say, its dogmas and ideologies).
One obvious contradiction in this proposal is that the proposed universal-
izing of marketing *knowledge* threatens the position of marketing *specialists*
who profess or aspire to be its monopoly providers. That talk of markets and
their discipline has recently proved to be a powerful resource for promoting
and legitimizing social and organizational change (Piercy, 1990; Piercy and
Morgan, 1990) (to be discussed further below) is not in dispute. But it is not
self-evident that the idea of marketing as a generic activity will be beneficial
for the credibility or influence of marketing specialists.

In defence of the generic concept of marketing, Baker (1987: 9) has
suggested that the reduced need for marketing specialists in a marketing-
oriented organization should disarm the resistance of other functional
specialists to this orientation. However, this is likely to occur only when the
generic concept of marketing is perceived to be congruent with, if not
identical to, the orientations of the other specialisms. A logic for internal
marketing is more likely to be acceptable, as Brownlie and Saren (1992)
have observed, if it is attentive to the orientations of potential users instead
of being preoccupied with repackaging the traditional marketing concept
(Webster, 1992). The problem is that instead of seeking an accommodation
with other specialists – as TQM, for example, has contrived to do by appro-
priating a common managerial ideology that claims to be concerned with the
quality of its specialist contributions (Bank, 1992) – the generic concept of
marketing directly questions the relevance, competence and effectiveness of
the other forms of specialist expertise which it aspires to supplant.

When marketers advocate a generic concept of marketing, they are likely
to find themselves in direct conflict with the efforts of other specialists –
such as accountants and human resource managers – who do not necessarily
fully understand, share or endorse the 'marketing concept', its professed
'orientation', its alleged understanding of human wants and values, or its
view of how organizations should be managed (Kohli and Jaworski, 1990).
As Whittington and Whipp have observed, if marketers are 'to be effective
in marketing implementation they will have to become shrewd organizational operators who are sensitive to a variety of approaches and cautious in
their expectations' (1992: 60). Unhappily for those who harbour or support

...listic ambitions, its devotion to scientism inhibits an ...he politics of human behaviour, including the politics of ... learning. The commitment to scientism marginalizes the ...of forms of knowledge that, potentially, could provide insights ... meaning-imbued and politically charged nature of organizational ...sion-making. Assuming its claims to be self-evidently authoritative, ...arketing either fails to acknowledge, or underestimates, the capacity of other specialisms to disregard or challenge its claims, and thereby frustrate its colonizing ambitions.

The discourse of exchange

So far, the chapter has addressed the credibility of marketing in terms of its knowledge claims and its generic aspirations. The weakness as well as the strength of marketing knowledge and management, it has been argued, resides in its neglect of the meaningful and power-invested quality of human behaviour. This weakness is perhaps most clearly evident in its understanding of what is, arguably, the central concept of marketing: exchange.

In presenting itself as 'the discipline of exchange behaviour' (Bagozzi, 1975: 78) or as 'the behavioural science that seeks to explain exchange relationships' (Giddens, 1979: 308), marketing excludes consideration of how 'exchanges' are mediated by, and reproductive of, asymmetrical relations of power. In identifying exchange as its central concept, marketing provides what appears to be a comprehensive and compelling means of understanding the complexities of human interaction. However, it is a formulation that distracts attention from how 'exchange behaviour' is a medium and outcome of systems of domination and exploitation. As Giddens (1979: 272, footnote 83) has observed, the basic deficiency of exchange theory is that it 'does not incorporate power . . . and tends to remain tied to a framework of utilitarian individualism'. In other words, parties in an exchange relationship are represented as separate 'atoms' with their own unique schedule of preferences and capacities that seek fulfilment. What this formulation *disregards* is, first, the way that the richness of human relationships – even those directly concerned with the exchange of goods and services – is reduced to a calculation of economic costs and benefits; secondly, the way that the behaviour of parties to such a relationship is conditioned by their positioning within structures of power that pattern their access to resources and make them more or less dependent upon each other; and, thirdly, the way that the actual (e.g. market) mechanism of exchanging goods and services itself articulates and sustains the preferences of those whose position in society is secured by the sense of freedom and equality that it produces.

In defence of the concept of 'marketing as exchange', Bagozzi (1975) claims that the individualism present in the formulations of exchange theory developed by Blau (1974) and Homans (1964) can be avoided by drawing upon the work of Lévi-Strauss where greater attention is given to generalized and complex exchanges involving more than two-party reciprocal relationships. However, Bagozzi's defence is quite limited. For the critique of the individualism of exchange theory is concerned not with the number of parties engaged in the 'exchange' but with the way that their relationship is theorized (see also Houston and Gassheimer, 1987). Marketing's formulation of exchange relations is deeply 'individualistic' not just in the sense that its focus tends to be upon individual consumers or aggregates of individual exchanges but, more fundamentally, in the sense that the 'needs' of those engaged in 'exchange relationships' are routinely abstracted from the construction of those needs within political and cultural media of self-identity formation.

The discourse of exchange is so beguiling because it suggests that each individual is a customer who is free to pick and choose in the marketplace. The discourse of exchange appeals to a common-sense humanism and voluntarism that inflates the individual's sense of autonomy and provides a central plank in marketing's professional ideology (Willmott, 1998). Its promise is to recognize and expand, through the medium of market relations, the individual's sense of autonomy and freedom. However, it is questionable whether, in its theory and its practice, marketing facilitates consumer sovereignty or promotes corporate monopoly (Dickenson et al., 1988; Perrow, 1988). For what it consistently fails to acknowledge and address are the *social* relations of inequality that either privilege or exclude participation in *marketized* transactions.

Of course, all relationships, including those that are most personal and intimate, can be represented in the language of exchange. And, in so far as these relationships are increasingly shaped and represented by marketing practices which take it for granted that exchange forms the core phenomenon for study in marketing (Morgan, 1992), they may indeed come to conform more closely to the 'truths' that such knowledge conveys (Foucault, 1977). As this happens, the plausibility of marketing's claims is enhanced. However, as Foucault (1977) has also argued, wherever there is disciplinary power, such as the power of marketing to constitute and satisfy consumer need (see Knights and Odih, Chapter 9 in this volume), there is a potential for transgression. An unintended consequence of treating social relationships as media of exchange is a tendency for individuals to feel, existentially, empty and anomic rather than more autonomous or fulfilled (Alvesson and Willmott, 1995; Smith, 1987). Although this feeling can simply fuel further consumption in an effort to fill the emptiness, it can also prompt a search for alternative lifestyles and politico-economic systems.

When people feel that they are being treated as objects who are 'targeted' by those (e.g. marketers) who design the delivery of services as well as the features of products, they may feel more (ab)used than served. In responding to the desire for more 'personalized' forms of exchange relationship, the efforts of marketers to 'customize' their operations – for example, through relationship marketing that aspires to move from 'the manipulation of the customer to genuine customer involvement; from telling and selling to communicating and sharing knowledge' (McKenna, 1991, cited in Thomas, 1993: 116) – are likely to have the effect of further depersonalizing relationships by introducing contrived forms of personalization and communication rather than supporting the development of a structure of social relationships in which a more genuine and attentive orientation arises without their faked informalization or customization. In this respect, attempts to reform marketing by distancing its practices from what are considered to be an outmoded and discredited 'marketing concept' may be received as an exemplification and extension of marketing hype rather than as a radical departure from it. As Pine, a leading advocate of mass customization, has acknowledged, proliferating variety tends to be accompanied by feelings of 'intimidation, oppression, being overwhelmed by choices, and believing that a science degree is necessary to make intelligent choices' (1993: 247).

It is therefore conceivable that the hyperconsumerism of hypermodernity will generate a backlash against the commodifying processes of exchange and consumptionism – of which the Great Refusal of the late 1960s and early 1970s may be identified as a precursor, and of which the New Puritanism and 'downshifting' amongst segments of the educated middle class in North America may be its contemporary symptom (see, for example, Varadarajan and Thirunarayana, 1990). With this backlash it can be anticipated that a preoccupation with the contents and mechanics of 'having' will be replaced by a growing concern with the nature and process of 'being' (Fromm, 1962; 1979). Instead of interacting through, and within, a discourse of exchange where it is assumed that human desires can be satisfied through the (market) provision of goods and services, it is possible to contemplate an alternative discourse of mutuality in which the overcoming of alienation from nature, self and others is identified as an alternative, less existentially and ecologically contradictory path to human fulfilment (Taft, 1998). Whilst acknowledging that an appreciation of the indivisibility of knowledge and power (Foucault, 1977) would counsel caution when making claims about the possibilities of freedom, it can be anticipated that such a shift would at least move us a little closer to the ideal of a society in which 'individuals would freely determine their needs and desires and would resist being moulded by institutions which mainly wish to manipulate and exploit them' (Harms and Kellner, 1991: 65).

Discussion

As an economic system, capitalism requires that demand is continuously stimulated by encouraging consumers to identify with, and possess, goods and services for which, in the absence of messages and pressures most closely identified with the expertise of marketing specialists, they would have little or no need or use. The introduction of 'customer care' programmes, for example, which are now invading both public and private sectors, does not enable potential consumers to reflect critically upon the discourses that identify their 'needs', and then to act upon this evaluation – perhaps by declining the opportunity to consume, if not by radically questioning the social construction of needs and consumption. Rather, the individual intent and aggregated outcome of such programmes is to shape or reinforce the understanding that these needs are identified and fulfilled by choices made by sovereign consumers. More generally, what Foucault would term the dominant 'truth effect' of marketing's emphasis upon exchange and customer orientation is to inhibit reflection upon the seeming self-evidentness of needs and the capacity of goods and services to fulfil them.

Capitalism has an insatiable appetite for profitable growth which it pursues through the creation and penetration of new markets. Emergent within this politico-economic context, marketing's rapacious orientation to customer needs is more plausibly attributed to the dynamics of capitalism than it is to any innate quality of marketing theory or practice. Nonetheless, marketing routinely endorses and promotes discourse and practice that are psychologically deleterious and socially divisive; and the comparatively low status of marketing as an occupation and management specialism, which is directly associated with these effects, is compounded rather than alleviated by efforts to conceal this predicament with the fig leaf of scientific objectivity and generic social value.

It is extraordinarily naive or perhaps depressingly cynical to suggest, as Hunt (1992b: 306) has recently done, that 'the ultimate client for a truly professional discipline is always society and its needs . . . for high quality products and services that are reasonably priced, responsibly promoted and conveniently available'. The problem with such proclamations is not, of course, the espousal of such ideals, with which few people would quarrel. Rather, the problem lies in the institutionalized failure of marketing discourse to reflect critically upon the questions of how these needs, prices, responsibilities and access to markets are all socially defined within relations of power, and its failure to recognize the role of marketing in contributing to their definition as well as their fulfilment (Leiss, 1976). As a commentator on Hunt's (1992b) paper 'Marketing is . . .' has cogently observed, its view of marketing not only is 'too simplistic' but offers an idealized characterization of ' "good", "proper", or "profitable" marketing, not marketing's functions in society' (Albaum, 1992: 314). Presently, the rhetoric of markets and marketing is being used (in First World economies) to drive through changes – notably, in the financing and organization of public sector goods and services – that are critical for restoring processes of capital accumulation but are of uncertain or even dubious benefit to the 'customer' (du Gay and Salaman, 1992; Keat, 1990; Morgan, 1992).

Summary and conclusion

This chapter has sought to illuminate and diagnose a central paradox of marketing: it exerts a growing influence upon processes of production and consumption in advanced capitalist societies, yet it is ascribed a comparatively low social and organizational status. This condition, it has been argued, is associated with, but is not reducible to, a reliance upon scientism and imperialism to support its authority and extend its domain.

A major impediment to achieving wider recognition and credibility is the effort to build respectability upon claims, fuelled by the demands of capitalism for the expansion and differentiation of markets, that are as implausible as they are arrogant. A recognition of the limitations of scientism and an appreciation of the socio-political organization of marketing theory and practice are therefore both relevant for unravelling the paradox. As an academic and applied discipline, marketing will continue to be viewed with suspicion, and to lack social status and influence concurrent with its expanding role in shaping the organization of production and consumption, so long as it is widely deemed to be implicated, deeply and uncritically, in processes of hype and manipulation that are stimulated by the relentless quest for sources of capital accumulation where markets for basic goods and services are saturated and competition is intense. For all its insistence that it serves the customer, marketing theory and practice tend to be uncritically subordinated to the service of corporate values and priorities.

The effects of marketing may not be entirely transparent to consumers or theorized by them. Yet, the relationship of consumers to marketers is widely sensed, or suspected, to be more often one of institutionalized subordination and exploitation than one of mutuality or unconditional reciprocity. An open recognition and admission of the inadequacy of its fig leaves, and with it a commitment to a more self-critical understanding of marketing expertise and its effects, would seem to be an obvious first step in improving the credibility and status of marketing theory and practice. To this end, marketing academics and practitioners could usefully draw upon critical and hermeneutic methodologies that are capable of appreciating how transactions are mediated by relations of meaning and power (e.g. Hudson and Ozanne, 1988; Murray and Ozanne, 1991; and various contributions to this volume).

Note

This is a revised version of a paper prepared for the Rethinking Marketing Symposium held at Warwick University, 2 July 1993. I would like to thank David Knights, Dale Littler, Pam Odih, Peter Simcock and Richard Whittington for comments and suggestions on earlier notes and drafts.

References

Albaum, G. (1992) 'What is marketing? A comment on "Marketing Is . . ."', *Journal of the Academy of Marketing Science*, 20 (4): 313–16.
Alvesson, M. and Willmott, H.C. (1995) *Making Sense of Management: a Critical Exploration*. London: Sage.

Anderson, P.F. (1983) 'Marketing, scientific progress and scientific method', *Journal of Marketing*, 46: 18–31.

Anderson, P.F. (1986) 'On method in consumer research: a critical relativist perspective', *Journal of Consumer Research*, 13: 155–73.

Armstrong, P. (1986) 'Management control strategies and inter-professional competition: the cases of accountancy and personnel management', in D. Knights and H.C. Willmott (eds), *Managing the Labour Process*. London: Macmillan.

Arndt, J. (1985a) 'On making marketing science more scientific: role of orientations, paradigms, metaphors, and puzzle solving', *Journal of Marketing*, 49: 11–23.

Arndt, J. (1985b) 'The tyranny of paradigms: the case for paradigmatic pluralism in marketing', in H. Dholakia and J. Arndt (eds), *Changing the Course of Marketing: Alternative Paradigms for Widening Marketing Theory*. Greenwich, CT: JAI Press.

Bagozzi, R.P. (1975) 'Marketing as exchange', *Journal of Marketing*, 39: 32–9.

Baker, M. (1987) 'One more time – what is marketing?', in M. Baker (ed.), *The Marketing Book*. London: Heinemann with the Institute of Marketing.

Bank, J. (1992) *The Essence of Total Quality Management*. London: Prentice-Hall.

Baudrillard, J. (1975) *The Mirror of Production*. St Louis: Telos.

Blau, P. (1974) *Exchange and Power in Social Life*. New York: Wiley.

Bourdieu, P. (1984) *Distinction: a Social Critique of the Judgement of Taste*. London: Routledge & Kegan Paul.

Brown, S. (1993) 'Postmodern marketing?', *European Journal of Marketing*, 27 (4): 19–34.

Brownlie, D. and Saren, M. (1992) 'The four Ps of the marketing concept: prescriptive, polemical, permanent and problematical', *European Journal of Marketing*, 26 (4): 34–47.

Day, G.S. and Wensley, R. (1992) 'Marketing theory with a strategic orientation', *Journal of Marketing*, 47: 79–89.

Desmond, J. (1993) 'Marketing: the split subject', in D. Brownlie, M. Saren and R. Whittington (eds), *Proceedings of Rethinking Marketing: New Perspectives on the Discipline and Profession*. Coventry: Warwick Business School.

Dholakia, N. and Arndt, J. (1985) *Changing the Course of Marketing: Alternative Paradigms for Widening Marketing Theory in Research in Marketing*, Supplement 2. Greenwich, CT: JAI Press.

Dickenson, R., Herbst, A. and O'Shaughnessy, J. (1988) 'The marketing concept and customer orientation', *European Journal of Marketing*, 20 (10): 18–23.

Douglas, M. and Isherwood, B. (1980) *The World of Goods*. Harmondsworth: Penguin.

du Gay, P. and Salaman, G. (1992) 'The cult(ure) of the customer', *Journal of Management Studies*, 29 (5): 615–33.

Featherstone, M. (1990) 'Perspectives on consumer culture', *Sociology*, 24 (1): 5–22.

Firat, A.F. (1993) 'Postmodern marketing: concept or culture?' in D. Brownlie, M. Saren and R. Whittington (eds), *Proceedings of Rethinking Marketing: New Perspectives on the Discipline and Profession*. Coventry: Warwick Business School.

Firat, A.F., Dholakia, N. and Bagozzi, R.P. (eds) (1987) *Philosophical and Radical Thought in Marketing*. Lexington, MA: D.C. Heath.

Foucault, M. (1977) *Power/Knowledge: Selected Interviews and Other Writings, 1972–1977*. Brighton: Harvester.

Fox, R.W. and Lears, T.J. (1983) *The Culture of Consumption*. New York: Pantheon.

Foxall, G.R. (1984) *Corporate Innovation: Marketing and Strategy*. London: Croom Helm.

Fromm, E. (1962) *The Sane Society*. New York: Rinehart.

Fromm, E. (1979) *To Have or To Be?* London: Abacus.

Gaski, J.F. and Etzel, M.J. (1986) 'The index of consumer sentiment towards marketing', *Journal of Marketing*, July.

Giddens, A. (1974) *Positivism and Sociology*. London: Heinemann.

Giddens, A. (1979) *Central Problems in Social Theory*. London: Macmillan.

Giddens, A. (1991) *Modernity and Self-Identity: Self and Society in the Late Modern Age*. Cambridge: Polity.

Gummesson, E. (1991) 'Marketing-orientation revisited: the crucial role of the part-time marketer', *European Journal of Marketing*, 25 (2): 60–75.

Habermas, J. (1972) *Knowledge and Human Interests*. London: Heinemann.

Harms, J. and Kellner, D. (1991) 'Critical theory and advertising', in B. Agger (ed.), *Current Perspectives in Social Theory*, Vol. 11. Greenwich, CT: JAI Press. pp. 41–67.

Heath, T.B. (1992) 'The reconciliation of humanism and positivism in the practice of consumer research: a view from the trenches', *Journal of the Academy of Marketing Science*, 20 (2): 107–18.

Homans, G.C. (1964) *Social Behaviour: Its Elementary Forms*, rev. edn. New York: Harcourt Brace Jovanovich.

Hooley, G.J., Lynch, J.E. and Shepherd, J. (1990) 'The marketing concept: putting the theory into practice', *European Journal of Marketing*, 24 (9): 7–23.

Houston, F.S. and Gassheimer, J.B. (1987) 'Marketing and exchange', *Journal of Marketing*, 51: 3–18.

Hudson, L.A. and Ozanne, J.L. (1988) 'Alternative ways of seeking knowledge in consumer research', *Journal of Consumer Behaviour*, 14: 508–21.

Hunt, S.D. (1976) 'The nature and scope of marketing', *Journal of Marketing*, 40: 17–28.

Hunt, S.D. (1983) *Marketing Theory: the Philosophy of Marketing Science*. Homewood, IL: Irwin.

Hunt, S.D. (1990) 'Truth in marketing theory and research', *Journal of Marketing*, 54: 1–15.

Hunt, S.D. (1992a) 'For reason and realism in marketing', *Journal of Marketing*, 56: 89–102.

Hunt, S.D. (1992b) 'Marketing is . . .', *Journal of the Academy of Marketing Science*, 20 (4): 301–11.

Hunt, S.D. (1993) 'Objectivity in marketing theory and research', *Journal of Marketing*, 57 (2): 76–91.

Jones, D.G. and Monieson, D.D. (1990) 'Early development of the philosophy of marketing thought', *Journal of Marketing*, 54: 102–13.

Keat, R. (1990) 'Introduction', in R. Keat and N. Abercrombie (eds), *Enterprise Culture*. London: Routledge.

Keith, R.J. (1960) 'The marketing revolution', *Journal of Marketing*, 24: 35–8.

Knights, D., Morgan, G. and Sturdy, A. (1993) 'The consumer rules? The rhetoric and "reality" of marketing in financial services', in D. Brownlie, M. Saren and R. Whittington (eds), *Proceedings of Rethinking Marketing: New Perspectives on the Discipline and Profession*. Coventry: Warwick Business School.

Kohli, A.K. and Jaworski, B.J. (1990) 'Market orientation: the construct, research propositions and managerial implications', *Journal of Marketing*, 54: 1–18.

Kotler, P. (1972) 'A generic concept of marketing', *Journal of Marketing*, 36: 46–54.

Leiss, W. (1976) *The Limits to Satisfaction: an Essay on the Problem of Needs and Commodities*. Toronto: University of Toronto Press.

Levitt, T. (1960) 'Marketing myopia', *Harvard Business Review*, July–August: 45–60.

McKenna, R. (1991) *Relationship Marketing: Successful Strategies in the Age of the Customer*. Reading, MA: Addison-Wesley.

Mingers, J. (1992) 'Technical, practical and critical OR – past, present and future?', in M. Alvesson and H.C. Willmott (eds), *Critical Management Studies*. London: Sage.

Morgan, G. (1992) 'Marketing discourse and practice: towards a critical analysis', in M. Alvesson and H.C. Willmott (eds), *Critical Management Studies*. London: Sage.

Muncy, J.A. and Fisk, R.P. (1987) 'Cognitive relativism and the practice of marketing science', *Journal of Marketing*, 51: 20–33.

Murray, J.B. and Ozanne, J.L. (1991) 'The critical imagination: emancipatory interests in consumer research', *Journal of Consumer Research*, 18: 129–44.

Ozanne, J.L. and Hudson, L.A. (1989) 'Exploring diversity in consumer research', in E. Hirschman (ed.), *Interpretive Consumer Research*. Provo, UT: Association of Consumer Research.

Perrow, C. (1988) 'Markets, hierarchies and hegemony', in T.K. McCraw (ed.), *The Essential Alfred Chandler: Essays towards a Historical Theory of Big Business*. Boston, MA: Harvard Business School.

Peter, J.P. (1992) 'Realism and relativism for marketing theory and research: a comment on Hunt's scientific realism', *Journal of Marketing*, 56: 72–9.

Peter, J.P. and Olson, J.C. (1983) 'Is science marketing?', *Journal of Marketing*, 47: 111–25.

Piercy, N. (1990) 'Marketing concepts and action: implementing marketing-led strategic change', *European Journal of Marketing*, 24 (2): 24–42.

Piercy, N. and Morgan, N. (1990) 'Internal marketing: making marketing happen', *Marketing Intelligence and Planning*, 8 (1).

Pine, B.J. (1993) *Mass Customization: the New Frontier in Business Competition*. Boston: Harvard Business School Press.

Power, M. and Laughlin, R. (1992) 'Critical theory and accounting', in M. Alvesson and H.C. Willmott (eds), *Critical Management Studies*. London: Sage.

Rogers, E.M. (1987) 'The critical school and consumer research', in M. Wallendorf and P. Anderson (eds), *Advances in Consumer Research*, 14: 7–11.

Rose, N. (1990) *Governing the Soul*. London: Routledge.

Sherry, J.F. (1991) 'Postmodern alternatives: the interpretive turn in consumer research', in T.S. Robertson and H.H. Kssarjian (eds), *Handbook of Consumer Research*. Englewood Cliffs, NJ: Prentice-Hall.

Smith, N.C. (1987) 'Consumers' boycotts and consumer sovereignty', *European Journal of Marketing*, 21 (5): 7–19.

Taft, K. (1998) 'Power and narrative in day-to-day consuming', PhD thesis, University of Warwick.

Thomas, M.J. (1993) 'Marketing – in chaos or transition?', in D. Brownlie, M. Saren and R. Whittington (eds), *Proceedings of Rethinking Marketing: New Perspectives on the Discipline and Profession*. Coventry: Warwick Business School.

Tornroos, J.-A. and Ranta, T. (1993) 'Marketing as image management – a postmodern reformulation of the marketing concept', in D. Brownlie, M. Saren and R. Whittington (eds), *Proceedings of Rethinking Marketing: New Perspectives on the Discipline and Profession*. Coventry: Warwick Business School.

Varadarajan, P.R. and Thirunarayana, P.N. (1990) 'Consumers' attitudes towards marketing practices, consumerism and government regulations: cross-national perspectives', *European Journal of Marketing*, 24 (6).

Walsh, K. (1993) 'Marketing and the new public sector management', in D. Brownlie, M. Saren and R. Whittington (eds), *Proceedings of Rethinking Marketing: New Perspectives on the Discipline and Profession*. Coventry: Warwick Business School.

Webster, F.E. (1992) 'The changing role of marketing in the corporation', *Journal of Marketing*, 56: 1–17.

Wensley, R. (1987) 'Strategic management: avoiding economic errors and managerial myths', *Business and Economics Review*, 2 (Winter): 21–6.

Whittington, R. and Whipp, R. (1992) 'Professional ideology and marketing implementation', *European Journal of Marketing*, 26 (1): 52–63.

Willmott, H.C. (1986) 'Organizing the profession: a theoretical and historical examination of the development of the major accountancy bodies in the UK', *Accountancy, Organizations and Society*, 11 (6): 555–80.

Willmott, H.C. (1992) 'Postmodernism and excellence: the de-differentiation of economy and culture', *Journal of Organizational Change Management*, 5 (1): 58–68.

Willmott, H.C. (1994) 'Theorizing agency: power and subjectivity in organization studies', in M. Parker and J. Hassard (eds), *Towards a New Theory of Organizations*. London: Routledge.

Willmott, H.C. (1998) 'Towards new ethics? The contributions of posthumanism and poststructuralism', in M. Parker (ed.), *Ethics and Organizations*. London: Sage.

Willmott, H.C., Cooper, D., Lowe, E.A. and Puxty, A.G. (1993) 'Making "interests coincide": an examination of discourses of governance in the ICAEW', *Accounting, Auditing and Accountability Journal*, 6 (4): 68–93.

Zinkham, G.M. and Hirschheim, R. (1992) 'Truth in marketing theory and research: an alternative perspective', *Journal of Marketing*, 56: 80–8.

16　Commentary

Michael Thomas

The two chapters in this part raise important issues facing both the marketing profession and the discipline of marketing.

The reader of this commentary should be warned that the commentator comes to this task having recently been Chairman of the Chartered Institute of Marketing (which represents the marketing profession), having more recently been resident in Finland, and having publicly professed to a Swedish audience that he is a postmodernist. These collective sins may disqualify him from saying anything that will be taken seriously.

Päivi Eriksson's chapter is a valuable contribution to a very thin literature. She pleads for more research geared toward more organizationally based process studies in order to understand 'what the role of marketing really is within different types of organizations, and how and why the role of marketing changes over time'. She also asks that 'research should pay more attention to the various national and business contexts instead of focusing on the development of universal marketing models'.

A brief comment on both pleas. The second is almost postmodern in tone. She asks that the search for universal verities be superseded by attention to detail – to cultural, social and economic context, and to individual business sector analysis. 'Beware generalization' is her plea. However, her own case report exposes some of the problems in taking that line, and must influence one's response to her first plea.

In following the contest for dominance in a family-owned business (a Finnish business owned by Swedish-speaking Finns) of engineers and marketers, she exposes a methodological problem. Is it possible to generalize about the results of her analysis? I would argue that what the case study reveals is that the context of the contest was unique, and that what was observed was in a degree predictable. The firm was production-oriented until the mid-1980s. Until that time, marketing people were bound to face a difficult task (as in so many companies with family ownership and moderate size).

Their task was compounded by unenlightened marketing leadership. In 1975 product managers in the company did not have access to sales data! Market research know-how did not exist in the mid-1970s. And the company hired fast-track Finnish product managers who never stayed long enough to understand the business. I also note with interest that the production engineers themselves, who allegedly knew the business, were influenced by 'success stories' associated with automation and continuous production and that this development almost bankrupted the company and the industry which resulted in an industry agreement to limit capacity which was unfavourable to the company. At that time the company was ripe for takeover by one of the Nestlés of this world. After that, who would doubt that marketing know-how would have prevailed?

I conclude that this case study fails to prove that skilled marketing professionals cannot compete with production engineers; the case illustrates why the marketing function did not operate effectively in this company during a particular period of its history. There is a general lesson, however. If marketing and production fail to cooperate, if they compete for dominance, then trouble develops. The case reveals the problems of an adversarial relationship between professions and professionals.

Hugh Willmott's chapter must be taken very seriously indeed. It contains an attack, coolly vitriolic, on the values of the marketing discipline and on the marketing profession. He raises issues of principle: 'the tensions and paradoxes present in marketing theory and practice are more a symptom of the contradictory dynamics of capitalist development than they are a failure of marketers to act as "high priests of the marketplace"'; he attacks marketers for encouraging 'people to equate satisfaction with consumption in which there is a progressive "monetization and commodification of social relations"'; he attacks the research methodology of the marketing discipline by attacking scientism; he attacks market research because 'market research and the leading marketing journals are heavily engaged in the application and legitimation of scientism'; he states that marketers are 'ill equipped to understand and address how the status and influence of marketing are socially constructed and negotiated within asymmetrical relations of power'; he attacks market research (again) for its treatment of consumers as 'inert, malleable objects'; he attacks Kotler for being an imperialist; and most vehemently he states that compared with other specialisms (management disciplines) 'marketing is at the forefront of manipulation and hype' and, 'for all its insistence that it serves the customer, marketing theory and practice tend to be uncritically subordinated to the service of corporate values and priorities'.

As those who bother to read me will know, I share most of these prejudices, though I am bound to say that I am a little more customer-oriented in the way I state them (Thomas, 1996b, 1996c, 1996d)!

Willmott's chapter is refreshing in part because he is not one of us, i.e. a marketer, and this brings an objectivity to his analysis, the objectivity of the outsider. It must be said however, that this chapter is a polemic directed at capitalism rather than at marketing *per se*.

Capitalism has an insatiable appetite for profitable growth which it pursues through the creation and penetration of new markets . . . marketing's rapacious orientation to customer needs is more plausibly attributed to the dynamics of capitalism than it is to any innate quality of marketing theory or practice. Nevertheless, marketing routinely endorses and promotes discourse and practice that are psychologically deleterious and socially divisive.

If you accept the hypothesis, then it is not hard to accept the criticisms that follow. Accepting the hypothesis is hard if you have lived in the real world since 1989. We have no real ideological alternative to capitalism to contemplate and, until we do (perhaps Willmottism will replace Marxism), we need to ask profound questions about capitalism and how it might perform more altruistically than it has done historically. That is why we need to explore the concept of the social market economy; that is why relationship marketing (born in the most civilized part of the capitalist world – Scandinavia) offers real insights.

Marketers and the marketing profession need to be able to face the types of criticism offered by Willmott. He however approves neither of marketers and their values, nor more importantly of capitalism, whose values, as he himself observes, marketers serve. In his chapter he offers no alternative model. In concluding this commentary, let me suggest one line of enquiry which will I believe bear fruit.

Regis McKenna (Thomas, 1996a) suggests that a new agenda for marketing exists. Knowledge-based marketing should integrate customers 'into the design process to guarantee a product that is tailored not only to customers' needs and desires but also to customers' strategies', and also develop 'the infrastructure of suppliers, vendors, partners and users whose relations help sustain the company's reputation and technological edge' (1996a: 195–6). The last point is vital since I believe that First World capitalism will only be sustainable if that world remains the source of true technological innovation.

Experience-based marketing, marketing's other paradigm, emphasizes interactivity, connectivity, and creativity. As McKenna argues, this will bring about 'a fundamental shift in the role and purpose of marketing: from manipulation of the customer to genuine customer involvement; from telling and selling to communicating and sharing knowledge; from last-in-line function to corporate credibility champion' (McKenna, 1991: 4). That is the promise of relationship marketing, and relationship marketing makes explicit the need to understand power relationships; to benefit from the richness of human relations, rather than to exploit them; and to recognize that freedom and equality are the last best guarantee that the system will continue to function effectively. As I have recently written:

> we [the marketing profession] must recognize that, in addition to high standards of objectivity, integrity and technical competence, we must, in responding to the changing environment, demonstrate that we can and will serve society in general. This requires a clear and articulate demonstration of our ability to be relevant in the political sense . . . if we remain tied to the forces of manipulation and hype, if we are seen merely to be servants of our capitalist masters, we will remain marginal and untrustworthy. If we can demonstrate that we have the keys to the knowledge base that will benefit society as a whole then we may prosper. (Thomas, 1996a: 203–4)

References

Groonroos, C. (1994) 'From marketing mix to relationship marketing: towards a paradigm shift in marketing', *Management Decision*, 32 (2): 4–20.

Gummesson, Evert (1995) 'Relationship marketing', in M.J. Thomas (ed.), *Gower Handbook of Marketing*, 4th edn. Aldershot: Gower. pp. 113–30.

McKenna, R. (1991) *Relationship Marketing*. Reading, MA: Addison-Wesley.

Thomas, M.J. (1994) 'Marketing – in chaos or transition?', *European Journal of Marketing*, 28 (3): 55–62.

Thomas, M.J. (1996a) 'The changing nature of the marketing profession and implications for requirements in marketing education', in S.A. Shaw and N. Hood (eds), *Marketing in Evolution*. London: Macmillan. pp. 190–205.

Thomas, M.J. (1996b) 'After capitalism?', *Perspectives in Higher Education*, 28–34.

Thomas, M.J. (1996c) 'Post modernism for dummies'. Occasional paper 96/4, Department of Marketing, University of Strathclyde.

Thomas, M.J. (1996d) 'Marketing adidimus', in S. Brown (ed.), *Marketing Apocalypse*. London: Routledge, pp. 189–205.

Part VI

MARKETING PEDAGOGY

We recognize that a key element in the overall description of the nature of marketing is one based on what we teach. However, some academics in marketing would feel distinctly uneasy if the state of knowledge in our field was judged against the criterion of the quality and content of our textbooks. Indeed such a particular observation was made strongly by some participants at the original symposium.

To deny our textbooks, as opposed to being critical of them, runs the risk of denying the codification of marketing knowledge which must be an essential part of our claim to be a 'discipline'. The chapters in this final part address in rather different ways the underlying problematic in both how we articulate the nature of our knowledge and how marketing itself is taught.

Laurent and Pras address the issue primarily in terms of the nature of the research that we should undertake to inform our knowledge more effectively and thence what is taught. Their basic proposition is that both better data and alternative theoretical bases and assumptions allow us as marketing academics to put more focus on real problems. What is the nature of these so-called 'real' problems? Their answer essentially is a reality defined by the needs of business and commerce. They give weight, for instance, to Simon (1994) in his argument that firms are not practising marketing as it is taught in courses and textbooks. They note that:

> One of the striking conclusions of a survey of marketing dissertation topics in France . . . was the lack of fit between dissertation topics and problem's of importance to companies. For example, the topic that is most popular with practitioners, on the basis of the number of books published, is salesforce management, on which few dissertations are written. At the opposite end, consumer behaviour is studied in almost half of all dissertations, while books indicate a very limited interest by practitioners.

Leaving aside some of the concerns we might have with the method proposed as one of reliably gauging the nature of business priorities, Laurent and Pras develop their analysis further by arguing that with much improved data it is possible to link consumer behaviour research much more directly to marketing actions:

> 'Experiments become feasible in which real consumers, in a real setting, are confronted with real alternatives'.

This general principle underlies much of what they then suggest in terms of new and interesting directions for marketing research alongside the proposal that marketing researchers themselves should be more multi-disciplinary and multinational in their approaches.

Dibb and Stern, on the other hand, use the example of our understanding, researching and teaching in the area of market segmentation as a way of illustrating their analysis of the central relationship between researcher, teacher and practitioner. Their conclusion is clearly stated:

> Textbooks . . . stress process issues such as segment base selection and steps and pay little attention to the underlying theory or application issues. Researchers concentrate on application issues such as quantitative techniques and models. Practitioners see the theoretical value of segmentation but find problems with process and application.

Their conclusion leads on to two further arguments. First, marketing instructors need to address the existence of contrasts and overlaps between what is researched, what is reported in textbooks and what is practised. Secondly, it is also the responsibility of the instructor to evaluate the contributions from research, textbooks and practitioners, in the light of what they term 'market evidence'. It is the latter assertion which raises some questions about the privileging of academic discourse. Not surprisingly Dibb and Stern revert to an assertion that there is a higher criterion of validity based on empirical evidence: it is more important that it is true, rather than it works!

Underlying the Dibb and Stern analysis is the almost inevitable linear model, just as with Laurent and Pras, who see the process as one of research leading to increased knowledge and thence to what we teach: their approach is from theory to process to application. The two analyses share the implicit assumption that neither what is taught nor what is applied can develop further without either theory or research. The difficulty underlying both of these chapters, in terms of the broader issues raised in this book, is the extent to which directly or indirectly the concerns of marketing practice are simultaneously privileged within what might be described as the discourse of the academic. Indeed if we were to adopt a perspective on the notion of a discipline more aligned with the writings of Foucault (1979) and others, we might note that unlike, say accounting,[1] marketing lacks many of the bases of power of a discipline such as statutory responsibilities and restrictions. In this sense, even to treat marketing as a discipline itself, as we have suggested above, may be to overestimate both its power and certainly the influence of its codified knowledge base.

In his commentary, Gerry Zaltman develops some of these issues but from a rather different perspective. Indeed he returns to some of the issues raised in our discussion of Shelby Hunt's symposium paper at the start of this volume (Chapter 2) with his concern that we should not be restrictive in our definition of the nature of marketing knowledge and theory. He argues that almost inevitably in the inherently social nature of marketing phenomena, there will be more of relevance to be found outside our 'field' than inside it. He also suggests strongly that we must be both reflexive about our own, as he terms it, 'habits of mind' as well as encouraging others, including managers, to be so in our role as instructor. One could reasonably argue that Zaltman achieves closure with his notion of the centrality of 'habits of mind', or perhaps in more traditional terms, his emphasis on cognitive routines, whilst both Laurent and Pras and Dibb and Stern, in their different ways, end with an emphasis on the nature of objective truth in terms of empirical evidence.

In the process of rethinking marketing, it is undoubtedly true that issues of cognition (thinking) and empirical evidence must be critically addressed. But it may well be that the relationship between marketing academe and practice remains even more problematic than any of these three groups of authors suggest. In particular we may need to go rather further than Zaltman, and indeed beyond just a rather restricted notion of the cognitive, to undertake a more critical analysis of the role of the academic and academe within this social arena that we call marketing.

Note

1   For an interesting analysis of these issues in the context of the shift from accounting to accountability see Roberts (1996).

References

Foucault, M. (1979) *Discipline and Punish*. Harmondsworth: Penguin.
Roberts, J. (1996) 'From discipline to dialogue', in R. Munro and J. Mouritsen (eds), *Accountability: Power, Ethos and the Technologies of Managing*. London: International Thomson.
Simon, H. (1994) 'Marketing science's pilgrimage to the ivory tower', in G. Laurent, G.L. Lillien and B. Pras (eds), *Research Traditions in Marketing*. Boston: Kluwer.

17 Research, Rhetoric and Reality: Marketing's Trifid

Sally Dibb and Philip Stern

Trifid: split or divided into three by deep clefts or notches.

(*Oxford English Dictionary*)

Marketing instructors operate with a set of widely agreed fundamental marketing principles which are influenced in three ways (see Figure 17.1). First, researchers report conceptual and applied research findings at conferences and in academic journals. Secondly, teachers present the simple mechanics of each area of the theory in an array of pedagogical tools such as textbooks. The third key influence comes from practitioners and their experiences of implementing the principles. When presenting marketing concepts, instructors need to take account of the overlaps and contradictions between all three influences. Having taken account of these aspects, a decision about the appropriate balance between them must be taken. It is entirely possible that this balance may change according to the nature of the audience. Furthermore, it is likely that the difficulties associated with achieving this balance will apply to many areas of marketing theory.

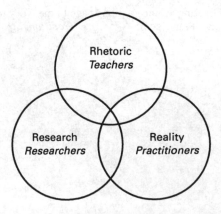

Figure 17.1 *The three key influencing factors: research, teaching and practice*

The key resource for the majority of marketing instructors is the textbook, yet it is unclear that this source provides an adequate balance among the three influencing factors. Little has been published about the lag between material in academic journals and its appearance in mainstream marketing textbooks. However, it seems that two key constraints may be broadly responsible for the nature and scope of marketing texts: heterogeneity in courses and students, and academic need for economies of scale. Most colleges and universities do not have a sufficiently large student body to warrant a customized text, so they will use those available; these, owing to the nature of the market, are standardized offerings. In order to cater for this broad readership and usage on many different types of courses, texts have a tendency to be encyclopaedic in character. Most cover a large number of topics, sometimes in relatively little depth. This tendency towards the encyclopaedic is supported by academics wishing to recommend just one text, and by students who may lack the resources to purchase more than one book. The ability of students using a particular text may be quite diverse, and so there is a tendency for key concepts to be simplified. In situations where more intellectually challenging material is appropriate, it seems that instructors are not always proactive in providing it.

Research and administration pressures cause faculty members to try and develop scale economies in the courses they teach. It is not necessarily in the instructor's own interest to frequently change how courses are taught; as a result, course content, style and textbooks may change relatively slowly. The result of this is that texts which stray away from the accepted format (structure and content) are likely to meet with limited success. Faculty members are particularly under pressure to publish in learned journals, especially since formal appraisal of this form of output has increased in the UK and the USA, causing this to take precedence over the writing of text-books. The sheer volume of research published also means that only a small proportion could practically be included. For these reasons, ground-breaking research very rarely appears first (or at all) in textbooks. Marketing instructors accept that texts cannot cover all relevant up-to-date research details and therefore develop reading lists of articles to accompany their courses. Although many texts include some appropriate references to further reading, this cannot adequately replace the efforts of individual academics in identifying and consolidating the most up-to-date and relevant journal publications.

The difficulties which instructors face in achieving a balance in what they teach are compounded by concerns about the profession's credibility. Whittington and Whipp (1992) identify what they term the 'chronic weakness of British and American manufacturers at marketing' and suggest that the influence of the discipline relies on its ability to refine its techniques and develop its professional ideology. In this respect, research indicates that marketing has fallen behind accounting and finance in the professional credibility stakes (Armstrong, 1985; Richardson, 1988). According to Elliott (1973), the accountants' success is linked to their ability to build a 'professional ideology', supported by a system of examination and professional control. Walker and Child (1979) argue that marketing is still only a 'quasi-profession' which has not properly developed its area of expertise or properly legitimized its resources. More fundamental concerns about the credibility of marketing principles complicate the situation further. Wong (1993) reviews the debate about the role of marketing and the effect of market orientation on business profitability (Deshpande and Webster, 1989; Kohli and Jaworski, 1990; Webster, 1988). In this sense, Wong (1993) apparently agrees with the concerns of Whittington and Whipp (1992) about the 'technological effectiveness' of marketing. She goes on to identify a corporate-wide lack of confidence in marketing as a function, which she attributes to the discipline's lack of professionalism. It is beyond the scope of this chapter to fully examine anxieties about the professionalism and effectiveness of the marketing discipline. However, these concerns help to put the discussion of balance between the contributions of researchers, instructors and practitioners into context and add an additional dimension to the debate which will be revisited later.

This chapter uses the market segmentation concept to illustrate the contradictions which exist in the subject matter presented by researchers, instructors and practitioners through journals, textbooks and practical evidence, and examines the teaching difficulties which result. The term 'trifid' has been adopted to refer to these three areas of influence. Market segmentation is chosen because it is a widely understood and accepted marketing principle which is usually taught in a mechanical way, has an established research tradition, but in practice can prove difficult to implement. By examining the marketing trifid, this chapter aims to show how the balance between the activities of the researcher, instructor and practitioner can be better understood. The chapter also raises concerns about professionalism in marketing and questions whether the lack of a professional ideology and anxieties about the performance of marketing further complicate the instructors' task.

Elements of the trifid

This chapter is structured around two dimensions, each comprising three aspects. The first dimension relates to the activities of the researcher, teacher and practitioner. The second dimension is concerned with providing a structure for organizing these activities. These dimensions can be summarized using an example from the market segmentation literature. According to Wind (1978a) companies which adopt a market segmentation strategy can enjoy increased profitability. In presenting this assertion to students, the academic who teaches market segmentation theory might wish to consider the contributions which have been made to the debate by the researcher, teacher and practitioner. This corresponds with the first of the two dimensions:

Table 17.1 *The contrasts and overlaps framework*

	Theory Underlying assumptions	Process Modelling the assumptions	Application Testing the assumptions
Research Is it true?			
Rhetoric Does it make sense?			
Reality Does it work?			

- The *researcher* would be concerned with the question: 'Is it true?'
- The *teacher* would probably ask: 'Does it make sense?'
- The *practitioner* would be interested in: 'Does it work?'

These appear to be straightforward questions. However, they can and do generate a very large body of information. By adding a second dimension it is possible to present a more organized overview of the evidence which might arise. This second dimension is concerned with the following aspects:

- *Theory*   What are the underlying assumptions or rationales for the assertion?
- *Process*   What guidelines or rules might help in modelling the assertion?
- *Application*   In what ways can the assertion be tested?

These dimensions can be used to construct a framework for describing the contrasts and overlaps between the influencing factors which impact on marketing teaching. The elements of the trifid are examined in relation to the three evidential aspects of the framework as illustrated in Table 17.1.

Researcher

Market segmentation has an extensive literature which provides a convenient way of examining the research agenda in order to see how it relates to the areas of teaching and marketing practice.

Theory   There is remarkably little published research which debates the fundamentals of market segmentation, although there is a wider literature which debates the issues of product differentation. Claycamp and Massy (1968), Mahajan and Jain (1978), Smith (1956) and Tollefson and Parker Lessig (1978) provide a variety of normative approaches which assume markets are segmented at the *product* level. The genesis of this stream of research lies in economic theory typified by Robinson (1954) and then developed by marketing theorists such as Alderson (1957).

Process As Wind (1978a) commented 20 years ago, 'The majority part of publishable segmentation research still is devoted to the search for bases for segmentation.' Beane and Ennis (1987) provide a review of these issues focused on consumer markets and Plank (1985) looks at industrial applications. Here, many researchers use a qualitative framework supported by case study example, while some use quantitative consumer attitude data to empirically validate the specific approach. The main problems with these quantitative approaches are that the interpretation of the output of the process may not be managerially meaningful (Lilien and Kotler, 1971), and that customer attitudes may not be useful predictors of actual behaviour (Wind and Lerner, 1979).

The research literature tends to concentrate on the segmentation process itself (even when referring to a stepwise approach, e.g. Plank, 1985) and largely ignores segment selection and resulting marketing mix issues.

Application Research into the tools for, and applications of, market segmentation is reviewed by Wind (1978b) and Beane and Ennis (1987). With some notable exceptions (e.g. Blattberg et al., 1978) most of this research examines market segmentation at the *brand* level, with two widely quoted examples being Johnson (1971) and Haley (1968).

Application research uses either preference data (see the previous section for one problem with this approach) or actual choice data to determine segments (e.g. Doyle and Saunders, 1985; Kamakura and Russell, 1989; Moriarty and Reibstein, 1986). The use of choice data still leaves a number of problems such as stability of segments (Calantone and Sawyer, 1978), the context specificity of the results (Ehrenberg, 1992) and practical use. As noted by Wind (1978a), 'Very little is known about how results of segmentation research actually are used by management.'

In addition there has been little published research overtly critical of the brand segmentation concept, despite extensive research in the field of buyer behaviour which questions the reality of brand segmentation in an empirical (Ehrenberg, 1992) as well as a theoretical sense (Ehrenberg, 1988; Jeuland et al., 1980).

If established empirical knowledge is accepted as the only basis for validating the segmentation concept, then its use becomes questionable and its popularity amongst most teachers and practitioners requires some explanation. There is no doubt that it is a construct which is widely believed and so it is valid for those believers. Further, if there are no significant costs associated with the concept (i.e. the economic impact of following a segmented rather than a mass market approach is negligible) then in practice the issue of validity is irrelevant. Thirdly, if segmentation is only a marginal activity in the overall scheme of marketing, again its validity is unlikely to be a major concern, and so its omnipresence warrants attention.

Instructor

The viewpoint of the instructor can be reviewed by considering the components of market segmentation and its coverage in key marketing texts. The selection used for this review includes some of the most popular books which are adopted at all teaching levels.

Theory The underlying rationale for market segmentation is twofold. Customers vary in their needs and wants, requiring different combinations of product and service offerings. Companies which supply these customer needs have limited resources and are unable to offer precisely the right mix of benefits for each consumer or buying organization in every situation. These companies can improve their chances of competing effectively by choosing to serve only part of a market. Segmenting markets – aggregating customers with homogeneous needs into groups – allows companies to choose attractive areas in which to compete, while ensuring that diverse customer needs are identified and satisfied. All texts selected define and explain the reasons for market segmentation using a mix of these ideas.

Overall, the texts acknowledge that the application of market segmentation offers a range of managerial and research benefits. The identification of marketing opportunities (McCarthy and Perreault, 1990), clearer understanding of customers and competitors (Dibb et al., 1991; Kotler, 1991), better marketing programmes (Baker, 1992) and more efficient focusing of resources (Dibb et al., 1991; Kotler, 1991; Lilien and Kotler, 1971) are all cited as convincing reasons for adopting a segmented view of the market. These segmentation benefits are expanded further by Dibb et al. (1991) and McCarthy and Perreault (1990), who focus on the market penetration, product development, market development and diversification opportunities which effective segmentation can present.

Process Many texts recommend a step-by-step routine for segmenting markets. The most well known (Kotler, 1991) proposes three simple steps: *segmentation*, deciding how to group customers; *targeting*, choosing segments on which to focus marketing effort; and *positioning* (STP), designing a marketing programme to position the firm's product concept in the mind of the customer (Dibb et al., 1991; Kotler, 1991). Although not all texts formally review this particular model, some implicitly highlight the different aspects (Baker, 1992). The mechanics of the process are then further discussed within the context of these three steps. At the segmentation stage the discussion focuses on the choice of base variables (those by which the market is segmented). Usually this debate is subdivided to consider consumer and industrial markets. For example, in consumer markets, segmentation bases are split into consumer characteristic variables (such as demographics or psychographics) and those relating to how consumers buy and use products (such as methods of usage and product attitudes: Cannon, 1992). Many texts examine the characteristics and possible application of these variables and move on to consider the use of descriptor variables in segment profiling.

At the targeting stage, most texts review the criteria which should be considered when selecting segments and examine the broad choices of undifferentiated, differentiated and concentrated marketing. When considering positioning, the emphasis falls on understanding the steps in the process, using positioning maps and communicating the results.

A smaller number of texts consider the research and analysis mechanics undertaken by companies wishing to segment or resegment markets. Kotler (1991), for example, reviews a *survey, analysis* and *profiling* approach to the problem. McCarthy and Perreault (1990) adopt a different view, choosing to conceptualize the segmentation process as narrowing down from generic to product markets.

Application It is less common for texts to dwell upon the quantitative segmentation techniques available to the researcher. Discussion of these issues is confined to more research-oriented texts, such as Lilien and Kotler (1971), which have the individual techniques as the focus and use market segmentation as an illustration of how the techniques can be used. Table 17.2 illustrates the areas covered by the selected texts.

Practitioner

The practitioner's view of market segmentation is the most difficult of the trifid to evaluate. Successful applications are reported descriptively as case studies in textbooks while research often uses single sets of data to validate specific models, and so the practitioner has a less generalizable basis for examining segmentation than either the researcher or the instructor.

Theory Segmentation advocates the grouping of customers into homogeneous segments, as the ultimate goal of marketing is more profitably satisfied customers. Practitioner-oriented publications (e.g. see Hlavacek and Ames, 1986; Plank, 1985; Winter, 1984) place particular emphasis upon the opportunities which market segmentation presents, but urge caution when applying the technique.

In practice virtually all markets are characterized by relatively similar competitive offerings. In consumer markets the focus of competition tends to be at the brand level; and in most industrial markets, business units with similar capabilities tend to compete for customer purchases. The main problem for consumer marketeers is that segmentation theory is grounded at the level of the product and it is unclear how the theory can be extended to the brand level where it would have real economic impact.

Process In industrial sectors, market segmentation models have been developed which allow the gap between the theoretical segmentation concept and practical use to be bridged. The macro–micro model (Wind and Cardozo, 1974) suggests that managers should use existing market structuring as the starting point for the analysis. While this *a priori* approach has a certain intrinsic appeal, it is partly at odds with research which implies the need to

Table 17.2 *Market segmentation issues covered by key texts*

Issues	Ba	Ca	Di	Ko	Mc	LK
Market segmentation as a three-step process: segmentation, targeting and positioning			X	X		
Pursuing opportunities through market segmentation	X		X		X	X
Mass marketing, product variety marketing and target marketing				X		
Narrowing down to target markets: contrasts between generic and product markets and market segments	X				X	X
Segmentation as aggregation	X		X		X	
Market preference patterns: homogeneous, diffused and clustered				X		
Market segmentation procedure: survey stage, analysis stage and profiling stage				X		
Quantitative techniques for segmentation	X			X	X	X
Segmentation bases for consumer markets	X	X	X	X	X	X
Segmentation bases for organizational markets	X	X	X	X	X	X
Profiling the customer segments	X	X	X	X	X	X
Requirements for effective segmentation	X			X	X	X
Marketing targeting: evaluating the market segments	X		X	X		
Selecting market segments: undifferentiated, differentiated, concentrated			X	X	X	
The relationships between segments, supersegments and segment-by-segment invasion plans				X		X
Defining and explaining the need for positioning	X		X	X		
Positioning as a means of differentiation	X	X	X	X	X	
Step-by-step guide to positioning	X		X			
Deciding which product/company/service attributes should form the basis of the positioning	X		X	X	X	
Communicating the company positioning				X	X	
Use of positioning maps	X		X	X	X	

Key to texts: Ba (Baker, 1992), Ca (Cannon, 1992), Di (Dibb et al., 1991), Ko (Kotler, 1991), Mc (McCarthy and Perreault, 1990), LK (Lilien and Kotler, 1971).

take a fresh view of segmentation analysis. The nested approach (Shapiro and Bonoma, 1984) centres on the ease and expense of implementing a range of alternative segmentation bases.

Application The managerial usefulness of solutions and the ease with which they can be implemented are important (Blattberg et al., 1978). These implementation issues usually hinge on the resource implications of identifying segments and allocating marketing programmes to them. Sometimes the restructuring of resources and changes to the sales and distribution organization which are prescribed by a segmentation exercise cannot realistically be achieved. Application problems of this type stem from giving too much attention to the segmentation techniques and not enough to the relevance of the approach (Garda, 1981; Johnson and Flodhammer, 1980).

Evidence from industrial marketing indicates that companies frequently adopt a more *ad hoc* and intuitive approach to market segmentation than prescribed in theory (Winter, 1984). This may be stimulated by direct customer requests which are satisfied by modifications to the product and marketing programme.

Summary of the imbalances

The review of the theory, process and application elements used by researchers, instructors and practitioners suggests that there are imbalances in how each addresses the different aspects. Textbooks, for example, stress process issues such as segment base selection and steps and pay little attention to the underlying theory or application issues. Researchers concentrate on application issues such as quantitative techniques and models. Practitioners see the theoretical value of segmentation but find problems with process and application.

Wind (1978b) suggests there is a discrepancy between segmentation research and its application in reality. He indicates the need to re-evaluate traditional segmentation studies taking academic design and analysis ideas into consideration. Lilien and Kotler (1971) emphasize this point in a different way: 'The discrepancy between management needs and normative developments can be attributed, at least partially, to difficulties in measurement and in the implementation of the theory.'

Discussion: the trifid overlap

There has been some prior research examining the nature of marketing teaching, but most considers either the philosophical bases of 'marketing knowledge' (see, for example, Cavanagh, 1993 who draws on the well-established Hunt–Anderson debate) or some aspect of the technology of courses such as structure (Cox, 1992), learning methods (Foreman, 1992) or support (Mitchell, 1989). One of the exceptions is Law and Wensley (1979) who propose that the main objective of marketing teachers is to help marketers do their job better. They examine the role of the instructor in terms of expert, engineer and counsellor and suggest a reappraisal of the traditional profile towards that of counsellor. Perhaps the continued cultural dominance of the US academic community, and the primacy of scholarly research which subjugates practical help to marketers, go some way to explaining the apparent lack of progress along the counselling dimension in the intervening period.

Hansen et al. (1988) would agree, claiming that in practice academics compete for the attention of colleagues because so few managers read the relevant journals. They believe that marketing teaching has become too abstract and lost touch with the reality of markets and that the solution is to develop the use of expert systems in teaching the subject. This approach could, however, obfuscate the issues associated with instructors helping their classes to address open-ended problems of the type typically faced by the practising marketer. Thus the focus might move away from deriving good versus bad solutions towards right versus wrong answers. More recently Fayerweather (1994) provides a detailed history of the teaching, research and professional developments in international business since the post-war period, but the detail is intentionally descriptive.

While accepting Law and Wensley's principle, most marketing instructors are rarely (if ever) faced with classes consisting solely of experienced marketers. Other writers do not provide a framework to help the instructor create a balance between the sources of knowledge which are available in a general and specific sense, and this overlap is now considered.

Theory overlap

Textbooks, like research, spend relatively little time reviewing the rationale and economic bases for segmentation. The key contrast between research and textbooks is in the debate about opportunities presented by segmentation. Research tends to focus on the product class which is the appropriate unit of analysis when trying to understand how patterns of consumption vary across identifiable groups of customers. On the other hand, textbooks tend to expand the analysis to the brand level, as this is where students of marketing either operate or hope to operate. From this practice point of view, it is mainly segmentation opportunities which come to the fore. This suggests that any parallels between the rhetoric and research stem more from the underlying reasons for adopting a segmentation view than from the opportunities which it provides. Links between teaching and practice are found in the potential benefits and rewards which a segmentation strategy offers, over and above a mass marketing approach.

Interestingly, the relatively recent adoption of 'category management' by practitioners may indicate a stronger current overlap with the researcher than the instructor (Zenor, 1994), something which textbook authors might be keen to address.

Process overlap

Researchers and textbooks both focus on the identification of segment bases using either *a priori* or cluster-based approaches and simple step-by-step models of the process. However, discussion of positioning and marketing mix issues is found mainly in textbooks. Practitioners frequently apply the simpler textbook models but their search for an appropriate process is driven by the need to make sense of current market situations. Practitioners attempting to use the more complex models such as two-dimensional perceptual mapping encounter a variety of procedural difficulties, for example, interpreting the axes from the consumers' rather than the researchers' perspective.

These findings identify some common ground between processes adopted by researchers, instructors and practitioners. The models in textbooks tend to be simplified versions taken from research. In some circumstances practitioners may simplify these textbook models, while other more sophisticated users may have to refer back to and adapt the original research.

Application overlap

Textbooks, in general, devote little space to discussing the tools available to operationalize market segmentation. This means that some of the methodological pitfalls are at best left to references in the relevant research literature and at worst ignored. But it is precisely these issues which are of fundamental relevance to the practitioner. Returning to the example of two-dimensional perceptual mapping, once the procedure has been determined and the axes labelled, the logic of representing brand positionings as defined points rather than as averages with variance should be questioned. An important and related issue is the absence of discussion about the temporal stability of market segments which is reviewed in the research literature. Both research and textbooks use brand-specific case studies rather than an empirical evaluation of the competing brands. This means that practitioners' needs are not fully addressed in the textbooks.

Teaching implications and conclusions

This chapter has looked at the issues faced by instructors in balancing the activities of researchers, teachers and practitioners in relation to how they present market segmentation. The research literature highlights base selection, quantitative methods and the use of preference and choice data. Additionally, there is some discussion of normative segmentation and economic theory. Textbooks focus on segmentation rationale and the opportunities which it presents. There is little discussion of quantitative techniques, but marketing programme issues are explored. For practitioners, the emphasis is on segmentation opportunities and the use of simple *post hoc* models in order to justify or modify existing marketing programmes. This is summarized in Table 17.3.

These findings suggest that marketing instructors need to address the existence of contrasts and overlaps between what is researched, reported in textbooks and practised. Having understood the nature of these similarities and differences the next step is to devise appropriate combinations of the trifid elements when designing courses. Although there is no obvious reason why the teaching stance should vary according to audience, the exact balance of material from each element may vary. In most cases, irrespective of the nature of the course, a textbook will rarely provide sufficient coverage and insight into all elements of the trifid.

A further responsibility of the instructor is to evaluate the contributions from research, textbooks and practitioners in light of market evidence. For example, it seems that some practitioners may attempt to segment their

Table 17.3 *Understanding the contrasts and overlaps between segmentation research teaching and practice*

	Theory Underlying assumptions	Process Modelling the assumptions	Application Testing the assumptions
Research Is it true?	• Demand analysis • Normative segmentation • Economic theory	• Base selection	• Preference data • Choice data • Product level
Rhetoric Does it make sense?	• Segmentation rationale • Segmentation opportunities	• Segment bases • Process models	• Little discussion of quantitative techniques • Positioning and mix issues
Reality Does it work?	• Segmentation opportunities	• Simple *post hoc* models	• Ease of use • *Ad hoc* modifying of marketing programmes

markets at the brand level but with little success. The study of such markets shows that brands tend to attract similar levels of loyalty, with the biggest brands attracting the highest levels. They achieve this position by attracting the largest number of buyers, i.e. appealing to the majority of consumers. This is illustrated by large brands like Kit-Kat, Coca-Cola, McDonald's and Marks and Spencer. Finally, once the balance has been assessed, the instructor must recognize the limitations inherent in the subjective nature of marketing issues. There are three points to consider here. First, decision-makers must be aware of the problems arising from attempts to develop and operationalize marketing decision models. For example, Little (1970) developed decision calculus, a stepwise process for building marketing decision models, but despite the intrinsic appeal of the approach, a number of criticisms have been made. According to Chakravarti et al. (1981) most decision calculus models rely partly on managers' abilities to specify key variables and explain the relationship between them. There may therefore be situations where models are incorrectly specified or oversimplified and have poor predictive power (Chakravarti et al., 1977; Tversky and Kahneman, 1974). In a series of experiments to assess the effectiveness of models, Chakravarti et al. (1981) also found that improvements in decision-making are more likely to be linked to managers being required to process information and consider alternative scenarios, rather than because they learned much about the market response to input variables. Chakravarti et al. concluded that

it may not be advisable to use judgement based models to determine the optimal level of the decision variables. Instead model usage might be restricted to assessing the marginal effects of small changes to the decision variables. Effort then would be directed at obtaining a more efficient rather than the optimal deployment of the firm's resources.

These issues are important to this chapter because having accepted brand segmentation as a valid construct, it is necessary to be clear about the bases which determine the resulting segments, especially as prior assumptions will highlight certain problems and not others. Secondly, appropriate validation techniques should be employed to test the robustness of the analysis (Dibb and Stern, 1991), as it is clear that the often quoted 'common-sense' check (e.g. of segment membership) is inevitably influenced by preconceptions. Additionally, the purpose of any analysis is to provide insight and is valuable only when it contributes to understanding.

In conclusion, this discussion has started to unravel the complexities faced by marketing instructors when developing their courses. Dealing with these complexities requires the instructor to consider exactly what is taught and how to balance material from different sources. The question of what is taught is linked to concerns about the lack of professional ideology (Whittington and Whipp, 1992) and involves the instructor using available evidence to question the effectiveness of the principles being delivered. This endorsement of marketing's practices and tools can then be transferred to practitioners so that they become both knowledgeable and proficient in applying basic marketing tools (Wong, 1993). In transferring this knowledge the instructor must then consider the balance between the three areas of the marketing trifid, the contribution of researchers, teachers and practitioners.

Although this discussion has used segmentation to illustrate contrasts between research, teaching and practice the instructor is faced with similar problems when teaching other marketing principles. A number of theoretical areas, such as marketing orientation and buyer behaviour, have already been evaluated; more are under consideration. The contribution of the marketing trifid to this analysis is that it identifies the areas of influence which must be considered and shows where contrasts and overlaps may occur. In this sense, the purpose of this chapter has not been to identify good or bad teaching practice, but to highlight the breadth and variety of information with which instructors must deal.

References

Alderson, W. (1957) *Marketing Behaviour and Executive Action*. Homewood, IL: Irwin.
Armstrong, P. (1985) 'Changing management control strategies: the role of competition between accounting and other organizational professions', *Accounting, Organizations and Society*, 10 (2): 129–48.
Baker, M.J. (1992) *Marketing Strategy and Management*. London: Macmillan.
Beane, T.P. and Ennis, D.M. (1987) 'Market segmentation: a review', *European Journal of Marketing*, 21 (5): 20–42.
Blattberg, R., Buesing, T., Peacock, P. and Sen, S. (1978) 'Identifying the deal prone segment', *Journal of Marketing Research*, XV (August): 369–77.

Calantone, R.J. and Sawyer, A.G. (1978) 'The stability of benefit segments', *Journal of Marketing Research*, XV (August): 395–404.

Cannon, T. (1992) *Basic Marketing: Principles and Practice*. London: Cassell.

Cavanagh, D. (1993) 'Hunt v Anderson round 16', in D. Brownlie, M. Saren, R. Wensley and R. Whittington (eds), *Rethinking Marketing: New Perspectives on the Discipline and Profession*. Warwick: Warwick Business School Research Bureau. pp. 36–49.

Chakravarti, D., Mitchell, M. and Staelin, R. (1977) 'A cognitive approach to model building and evaluation', in B. Greenberg and D. Bellenger (eds), *Contemporary Marketing Thought, 1977 Educator's Proceedings*. Chicago: American Marketing Association. pp. 213–18.

Chakravarti, D., Mitchell, M. and Staelin, R. (1981) 'Judgement based marketing decisions', *Journal of Marketing*, 45 (3): 13–23.

Claycamp, H.J. and Massy, W.F. (1968) 'A theory of market segmentation', *Journal of Marketing Research*, V (November): 388–94.

Cox, A. (1992) 'The needs of marketing education in the 1990s', in *Marketing Education Group Conference Proceedings*, University of Salford. pp. 174–85.

Deshpande, R. and Webster, F.E. Jr (1989) 'Organizational culture and marketing: defining the research agenda', *Journal of Marketing*, 53 (January): 3–15.

Dibb, S. and Stern, P. (1991) 'Reality or myth: do market segments exist?', in K.D. Frankenberger, H.H. Larsen, F. Hansen, M. Friestad and G.S. Albaum (eds), *Proceedings of the Fifth Bi-annual International Conference of the Academy of Marketing Science*. International Conference Series, Vol. V. pp. 84–190.

Dibb, S., Simkin, L., Pride, W. and Ferrell, O.C. (1991) *Marketing Concepts and Strategies*. Boston: Houghton Mifflin.

Doyle, P. and Saunders, J. (1985) 'Market segmentation and positioning in specialized industrial markets', *Journal of Marketing*, 49 (Spring): 24–32.

Ehrenberg, A.S.C. (1988) *Repeat Buying*. London: Charles Griffin.

Ehrenberg, A.S.C. (1992) 'Theory or well-based results: which comes first?' Working Paper, London Business School.

Elliott, P. (1973) 'Professional ideology and social situation', *Sociological Review*, 21: 211–28.

Fayerweather, J. (1994) 'A personal odyssey through the early evolution of international business pedagogy, research and professional organization', *Journal of International Business Studies*, 25 (1): 1–44.

Foreman, S.K. (1992) 'Taking the distance out of distance learning', in *Marketing Education Group Conference Proceedings*, University of Salford. pp. 186–97.

Garda, R.A. (1981) 'Strategic segmentation: how to carve niches for growth in industrial markets', *Management Review*, 70 (8): 15–22.

Haley, R.I. (1968) 'Benefit segmentation: a decision orientated research tool', *Journal of Marketing*, 32 (July): 30–5.

Hansen, S.-O., Carlsson, C. and Walden, P. (1988) 'Marketing education: present needs and future challenges', *European Journal of Marketing*, 22 (3): 48–60.

Hlavacek, J.D. and Ames, B.C. (1986) 'Segmenting industrial and high tech markets', *Journal of Business Strategy*, 7 (2): 39–50.

Jeuland, A.P., Bass, F. and Wright, G.P. (1980) 'A multibrand stochastic model compounding heterogeneous Erlang timing and multinomial choice processes', *Operations Research*, 28: 255–77.

Johnson, H.G. and Flodhammer, A. (1980) 'Some factors in industrial market segmentation', *Industrial Marketing Management*, 9: 201–5.

Johnson, R.M. (1971) 'Market segmentation: a strategic management tool', *Journal of Marketing Research*, VIII (February): 13–19.

Kamakura, W.A. and Russell, G.J. (1989) 'A probabilistic choice model for market segmentation and elasticity structure', *Journal of Marketing Research*, XXVI (November): 379–90.

Kohli, A.K. and Jaworski, B.J. (1990) 'Market orientation: the construct, research propositions and managerial implications', *Journal of Marketing*, 54 (2): 1–18.

Kotler, P. (1991) *Marketing Management: Analysis, Planning, Implementation and Control*. Englewood Cliffs, NJ: Prentice-Hall.

Law, P. and Wensley, R. (1979) 'Marketing teaching', *European Journal of Marketing*, 13 (1): 15–26.

Lilien, G.L. and Kotler, P. (1971) *Marketing Decision Making: a Model-Building Approach*. New York: Harper and Row.

Little, J.D.C. (1970) 'Models and managers: the concept of a decision calculus', *Management Science*, 16 (April): B466–B485.

Mahajan, V. and Jain, A.K. (1978) 'An approach to normative segmentation', *Journal of Marketing Research*, XV (August): 338–45.

McCarthy, E.J. and Perreault, W.D. (1990) *Basic Marketing*. Boston: Irwin.

Mitchell, I.C. (1989) 'Computers in marketing education', in *Marketing Education Group Conference Proceedings*. Glasgow Business School. pp. 727–39.

Moriarty, R.T. and Reibstein, D.J. (1986) 'Benefit segmentation in industrial markets', *Journal of Business Research*, 14 (6): 463–86.

Plank, R.E. (1985) 'A critical review of industrial market segmentation', *Industrial Marketing Management*, 14: 79–91.

Richardson, A.J. (1988) 'Accounting knowledge and professional privilege', *Accounting, Organizations and Society*, 13 (14): 381–96.

Robinson, J. (1954) *The Economics of Imperfect Competition*. London: Macmillan. pp. 179–88.

Shapiro, B.P. and Bonoma, T.V. (1984) 'How to segment industrial markets', *Harvard Business Review*, May–June: 104–10.

Smith, W.R. (1956) 'Product differentiation and market segmentation as alternative marketing strategies', *Journal of Marketing*, 21 (July): 3–8.

Tollefson, J.O. and Parker Lessig, V. (1978) 'Aggregation criteria in normative market segmentation theory', *Journal of Marketing Research*, August: 346–83.

Tversky, A. and Kahneman, D. (1974) 'Judgments under uncertainty: heuristics and biases', *Science*, 185 (September): 1124–31.

Walker, D.S. and Child, J. (1979) 'The development of professionalism as an issue in British marketing', *European Journal of Marketing*, 13 (1): 27–54.

Webster, F.E. Jr (1988) 'Rediscovering the marketing concept', *Business Horizons*, 31 (May–June): 29–39.

Whittington, R. and Whipp, R. (1992) 'Professional ideology and marketing implementation', *European Journal of Marketing*, 26 (1): 52–63.

Wind, Y. (1978a) 'Introduction to special section on market segmentation research', *Journal of Marketing Research*, XV (August): 315–16.

Wind, Y. (1978b) 'Issues and advances in segmentation research', *Journal of Marketing Research*, XV (August): 317–37.

Wind, Y. and Cardozo, R. (1974) 'Industrial market segmentation', *Industrial Marketing Management*, 3: 153–66.

Wind, Y. and Lerner, D. (1979) 'On the measurement of purchase data: surveys versus purchase diaries', *Journal of Marketing Research*, XVI (February): 395–45.

Winter, F.W. (1984) 'Market segmentation: a tactical approach', *Business Horizons*, January–February: 57–63.

Wong, V. (1993) 'Marketing's ascendancy and transcendance: is this what it takes for businesses to succeed?', in D. Brownlie, M. Saren, R. Wensley and R. Whittington (eds), *Rethinking Marketing: New Perspectives on the Discipline and Profession*. Coventry: Warwick Business School Research Bureau.

Zenor, M.J. (1994) 'The profit benefits of category management', *Journal of Marketing Research*, XXXI (May): 202–13.

18 Research in Marketing: Some Trends, Some Recommendations

Gilles Laurent and Bernard Pras

This chapter outlines some key trends in marketing research and their implications for the future. While it is based on the recent book *Research Traditions in Marketing*, edited by ourselves and Gary Lilien (1994), it does not describe the state of the art in marketing research or provide a comprehensive review of the literature covering all research traditions. Rather, it gives the authors' viewpoint on selected topics.

Three main changes, in the last 10 years, have been (1) a more realistic view of consumers and markets, (2) more focus on real problems, and (3) a broader conception of marketing research.

A more realistic view of consumers and markets

In other parts of this book, it is argued that the behaviour of consumers may be changing in many different ways. In this section, we develop a slightly different argument, namely that, even if that behaviour does not change, research in marketing has changed, and will change, in depth. This results from two main causes: better data, and alternative approaches (alternative theoretical bases and assumptions).

Better data

We are in the midst of an information revolution, in which more and better data become available. These data describe the behaviour of individual consumers, aggregate consumer behaviour, causes of both, as well as actions taken by manufacturers and retailers. Similar tendencies are at work for industrial marketing data.

There are three main trends. First, scanner data are becoming available in more and more countries. Be they at the store or at the household level, they give a much more precise view of real purchase behaviour and, perhaps more importantly, of many causes of that behaviour. Secondly, there is a long-term tendency towards direct marketing, towards the development of extensive databases on individual customers which allow a firm or retailer to have a full perspective on each customer's history, rather than a one-shot view of a single transaction. Thirdly, the trend according to which a growing part of the economy comes from services, and a decreasing part from products, leads naturally to a longer-term view of customer relationships, and therefore to the accumulation of better data on each customer.

This has several consequences, not only for marketing research, but also for marketing management.

These databases allow for a better analysis of the cause-and-effect relationships at work in consumer behaviour (Blattberg and Neslin, 1990). We now see clearly that, in the purchase history of a household, or of a consumer, a number of explanatory variables have a very strong predictive power. Promotions are the prime example of marketing actions that trigger very strong behavioural consumer reactions. Moreover, these explanatory variables themselves are most often better measured. For example, features and dispays at work in specific stores can be precisely identified. As a consequence, many marketing decisions can now be precisely related to their consequences for retailer and consumer behaviour.

A likely consequence is that actions that lead to strong and instantaneous results, such as promotions, could command more management attention and higher budgets than actions whose consequences are more difficult to track, such as advertising. This could lead to an *effet pervers*, as useful long-term investments in brand image, through advertising and other means, may end up being excessively neglected. On the other hand, one could perhaps argue that it is normal for marketing managers to be results oriented.

Another consequence could have to do with the style, or rather content, of the marketing management profession. May we borrow from a practitioner (Romain Durand) the following parallel with the art of war? It used to be that artillery consisted of firing *bombardes* that were imprecise, required a long time to load, and generated a lot of smoke, jeopardizing the observation of the results, which were transmitted by courageous pedestrian observers located in the field, near to the target. That could be compared to the use of massive marketing tools, reaching indistinctively many persons, with little opportunity to measure exactly who gets reached and what is the ensuing behaviour, and with only delayed reports (four or six times per year) on aggregate consequences. This can be contrasted with the new marketing world, relying on databases, scanner data, and very focused, if not individualized, marketing actions – a marketing world that could be paralleled to war using laser-guided missiles. Can we expect, as a consequence, to see some changes in the profile of marketing managers? The caricature of a marketing manager may switch from a seat-of-the-pants, energetic decision-maker, with a strong ability to 'feel the situation' in the middle of a smoking battlefield, and to decide intuitively on the right next move, to a more methodical, quantitative person, developing finely customized plans on the basis of in-depth analyses of extensive databases, and after trying a number of simulated plans using advanced software tools.

Somewhat paradoxically, this increased precision in identifying cause-and-effect relationships is deeply correlated with the emergence of a more stochastic view of consumer behaviour. As soon as one looks at precise behavioural data at the level of individual households, one realizes that even the strongest causal relationships do not lead to 100 per cent prediction. It is impossible to predict with certainty what a consumer will do in a given period and situation, except perhaps if he or she is dead. What can be done is to evaluate the probability that she or he will behave in a certain manner. This is of course deeply linked to the availability of microscopic data on specific situations and atomistic components of behaviour, as well as to current developments in hardware and software.

Among explanatory variables, individualized variables, such as 'brand loyalty', have a special status, stemming from their strong predictive power. Consumer 'loyalty', as defined by Guadagni and Little (1983), is a weighted average of a consumer's recent purchase behaviour, and it is a very good predictor of the forthcoming behaviour of that consumer. This holds on many dimensions: brand loyalty, size loyalty, flavour loyalty, store loyalty, etc. It is similar to explanatory variables used by mail order companies such as recency, frequency and quantity. From a research perspective, this shows that the best predictors may be individualized variables, taking a specific value for each consumer, rather than 'common' variables describing massive marketing actions and taking the same value for many different consumers, or for all of them. This also shows that a fine description of past behaviour is quite often the best prediction of future behaviour. In managerial terms, those results stress how pertinent is the orientation championed for many years by colleagues from direct marketing (with their wise old maxim 'Our best clients are our clients') and from many colleagues from the Scandinavian school (working on long-term buyer–supplier relationships: Johansson and Mattsson, 1994; Möller, 1994).

This leads to four major consequences, from both a managerial and a market research perspective.

First, a major substantive question remains open. Why is it that 'loyalty' variables are such strong predictors? Is it because they are a simple, efficient way of measuring individual differences across consumers, past behaviour being a simple and good proxy for unobservable underlying differences in preferences? With this interpretation, each consumer would have constant preferences. Is it rather because there is a real positive feedback effect on each consumer following her or his purchases? With this interpretation, when a consumer purchases brand X, this increases her or his personal probability of buying brand X again on the next occasion. This positive feedback effect could be explained in different terms: the consumer indeed derives satisfaction from product usage, hence the increase in probability; the recent purchase may simply make the brand more salient in the consumer memory; etc. This substantive question has important practical consequences in terms of promotion efficiency. After a purchase on promotion, does the consumer keep (for the next purchase) her or his usual purchase probabilities for each brand? Or is there a change in these future purchase probabilities to the benefit of the brand purchased on promotion, owing to positive feedback? The evaluation of a promotion's profitability changes a lot depending on the answer. If there is feedback, one could think in terms of the 'lifetime' value of the consumer. If not, one could concentrate on short-run results.

Secondly, what is the best way of defining individual variables for a given consumer? Should we describe a consumer through constant variables (i.e. constant for each person)? Should we rather use some kind of conceptual template, consisting of a fixed formula (the same for all consumers) applied to a set of constantly updated individual data? For example, Guadagni and Little (1983) compute 'brand loyalty' as an exponential smoothing of recent purchases. The smoothing formula is the same for everyone, but the data on recent purchases differ from person to person, and also differ over time for the same person. In direct marketing, the classic recency–frequency–amount analysis leads, for a given person, to constantly changing values of the explanatory variables over time. The underlying view of consumers and consumer research is quite different.

Thirdly, for a given consumer, should we really try to define 'general' variables, that can later be applied to predict or explain different aspects of that consumer's behaviour? Or should we rather develop specific variables for each aspect of the consumer's behaviour? Take a banking example. Should a bank develop a careful and complete general typology of its consumers, and then use it to predict all aspects of their behaviour? Or should it rather perform specific analyses on each aspect of behaviour?

Fourthly, the marketing profession may soon be running into strong econometric problems: simultaneous equations, specification errors. Given the increase in micro-marketing (individualized actions directed at specific persons), it is likely that potentially more responsive persons will be the target of more marketing actions. When a promotion is offered indistinctively to all consumers of a store, one can analyse the global impact of the promotion, in comparison with the no-promotion results of the previous week, or maybe of another store. If the promotion, thanks to some data-based targeting of the promotion, is offered only to heavy consumers of the category (or of the brand), it may become more and more difficult, or impossible, to assess the impact of the promotion by comparing the behaviour of persons who have received the promotion with the behaviour of those who have not received it, since those persons were different in the first place.

Alternative theoretical bases and assumptions

In a completely unrelated manner, a more realistic view of consumers and markets comes from alternative, more realistic theoretical bases and assumptions. We mention briefly five examples.

The role of affective variables in consumer behaviour had been neglected for a long time, with marked exceptions. Conversely, excessive assumptions about the ability or motivation of consumers to collect and process data may have led to an excessive reliance on rational models of consumer decision-making. This is changing on both counts.

Behavioural decision theory (Kahneman et al., 1982) has evidenced and analysed a wealth of effects, according to which a person's perceptions and decisions are affected by a large number of heuristics and biases that are in contradiction with simple assumptions of rational decision-making. This applies, for example, to choices under uncertainty, to choices between outcomes allocated over time, to context effects, to attraction effects, to the role of 'phantom products', etc. Applications to marketing phenomena have begun, but many more developments can be expected in the future.

Several basic disciplines from the behavioural sciences are providing new conceptual frameworks that may be applied to marketing. Rejuvenation for our discipline is likely to come from better knowledge and use of these new theoretical approaches. To take a single example from cognitive psychology, the numerous theoretical studies on typicality within a category can be applied to consumer perceptions. What is the most typical brand in a product category? Conversely, what is the most typical product for a multi-product umbrella brand?

Similarly, social psychology may provide more realistic assumptions on influence processes at work among consumers. For example, the patterns of imitation between innovators, early buyers of a new product, and later buyers of the product, may be described in a more realistic fashion on the basis of the underlying social network. More realistic assumptions may lead to better models of the diffusion of innovations (Steyer, 1993).

Several colleagues have shown the importance of situational influences on consumer behaviour. A consumer can no longer be analysed as a relatively simple being, answering to a given stimulus (a brand, for example) in a consistent manner. The same person will behave very differently depending on the setting, be it defined by the presence or absence of other persons, by different goals or different moods, by a festive occasion, etc. Such behaviour can be described as that of a 'chameleon consumer'. This jeopardizes many traditional approaches in which a person's behaviour is explained only in terms of permanent traits, be they socio-demographics, involvement, life-styles, values, etc.

Finally, consumers, and industrial customers, are likely to be better described and analysed in a long-term framework. Individuals, and purchasing organizations, may be better understood in a dynamic setting. One purchasing act cannot be legitimately separated from past and future acts. Furthermore, relationships between suppliers and customers are built over time.

More focus on real problems

Two main factors should lead marketing academics to put more focus on real problems. A number of elements increase the pressure to study problems of importance to companies. In addition, methodological developments may lead to a better empirical assessment of marketing phenomena. On this basis, we discuss selected directions for future research.

Reality breeds research problems

In the last decade, another important trend observed in many large companies is the change of attitude towards research, and specially towards research in marketing. Companies open more widely their databases for research purposes, be they market research companies, large consulting firms, or service or industrial companies. Similarly, Wells (1993) states that 'government and industry inputs have expanded, enriched, and enlivened academic consumer research'. There are at least three reasons for that. First, a cultural change has occurred and research on management is better accepted than 10 or 20 years ago. Secondly, the environment is increasingly competitive, and companies are in urgent need of reliable analysis and decision tools; flexibility and innovation in methods are more necessary than ever. Thirdly, academic research centres can combine credibility and relatively low costs.

The environment of companies and organizations is evolving very quickly, and this brings forward new marketing problems to be tackled. Let us simply mention, for example, a few recent French cases: the deregulation of prices; the move from state monopoly to competition in airline transportation, or for tobacco; errors that can be made by companies with little background in competitive marketing, such as the French Railways for pricing; the change in mindset for many companies that used to think in terms of 'users' and now have to think in terms of clients; organizational changes deriving from this, such as new organizational forms for marketing activities, the problems of inculcating a marketing culture or philosophy in companies which saw themselves as public services (Lambin, 1993); etc. Relatedly, the current crisis leads to more attempts to evaluate marketing productivity (Parsons, 1994), or an organization's marketing orientation (several dissertations on this topic were presented at the 1995 Doctoral Colloquium of the European Marketing Academy).

Simon (1994) argues that we, marketing academics, should get into closer contact with real, successful companies; we may have a natural tendency to concentrate on topics that are of interest to us, to retreat, as he states bluntly, to the ivory tower. Two ideas put forward by him need to be pondered. They also agree with arguments developed by McGuire (1982). First, Simon argues that we are mainly studying a restricted part of the marketing domain: consumer products, sold in supermarkets. Not enough work on services, not enough work on industrial goods, not enough work on exports. For example, academics do not study enough the sectors that have been the basis of Germany's world commercial success, such as industrial machinery. We would certainly agree with this criticism. Note, as a corollary, that this also suggests that we devote too much work to short-run effects, not enough to long-run actions. Secondly, Simon argues that we might well be teaching inaccurate principles. He made an empirical study of a number of small German firms which were very successful in international markets, world leaders. He came, perhaps with some slight exaggeration for pedagogical purposes, to the conclusion that these firms were not at all practising marketing as we teach it in our courses and textbooks. We are not going into details here, but Simon's argument is worth reading.

Relatedly, one of the striking conclusions of a survey of marketing dissertation topics in France (Laurent and Gregory, 1992) was the lack of fit between dissertation topics and problems of importance to companies. For example, the topic that is most popular with practitioners, on the basis of the number of books published, is salesforce management, on which very few dissertations are written. At the opposite end, consumer behaviour is studied in almost half of all dissertations, while books indicate a very limited interest by practitioners. We are certainly not advocating here the selection of dissertation topics on the basis of short-term industry needs, but we should take more account of what's going on out there.

In another direction, the most important development in consumer behaviour, these days, could be that we are at last really studying consumer behaviour. Over many years we have seen, under the umbrella of 'consumer behaviour', a large number of studies which dealt neither with behaviour, nor with consumers. Behaviour was replaced by attitudes, or other non-behavioural variables, by a researcher's personal perceptions, remembrances or interpretations. This does not imply that such variables are of no interest. For example, consumer involvement is an important domain of study. But variables such as consumer involvement have often been studied totally apart from real consumer behaviour. There are three ways, at least, of doing so. First, produce sweeping statements about what highly involved persons and low-involved persons should be doing, but do not bother to check these statements empirically (textbooks are full of this). Secondly, study the relationship of consumer involvement with other psychographic variables, but not with behaviour. Thirdly, use semi-related measures of behaviour, such as intentions, self-reports, answers to hypothetical scenarios, behaviour in artificial experiments, etc. These are ways not to study real behaviour. Equally, we too often do not study real consumers. Let us denounce once more here the use of students, very often students taking a marketing course, in lieu of consumers. Conducting research on more realistic samples should lead to gains in managerial relevance.

Fortunately, today, it becomes increasingly feasible to study how real consumers behave in real situations. As indicated above, data are becoming available, with great reliability, covering more variables, descriptive or exploratory, over longer time periods, for larger samples, in very diverse categories. There are scanner data for frequently purchased goods, as discussed before, but also data on banking behaviour, on insurance, on telephone usage, on medical expenses, on going to the opera, on travelling behaviour, etc. Thanks to payment by card, hypermarkets may now have as much information on their customers as mail order companies have had for a long time. On the basis of such data, many predictive studies are feasible, but also many explicative analyses. Consumer behaviour can be better linked to marketing actions. Experiments become feasible in which real consumers, in a real setting, are confronted with real alternatives. Long-term phenomena can be studied. In addition, it is often possible to ask attitudinal questions from the same persons whose behaviour is known.

One implication of this is specially motivating. It is possible first to discover phenomena, empirical regularities, and then to try to model and explain them. This has been advocated for a long time by Ehrenberg (1994) for the analysis of brand penetration and repeat purchasing over time. Another good example is the consumer loyalty variables introduced by Guadagni and Little (1983), and described earlier. In practice, such variables have a high predictive power, and are therefore very useful for companies. At the same time, we assert that they will be the basis of important development in academic consumer research, not only because they resolve important problems, but also because they pose important problems. Once one has found a pervasive empirical regularity, such as consumer loyalty, this creates a set of research problems. Is it true of all products, or are there exceptions, and why? Are there situations when loyalty becomes reduced, or increased? As discussed earlier, is it rather due to a positive purchase feedback, or to consumer heterogeneity? Through this example, we illustrate a more general contention. By allowing us to better observe what's going on in the market, the new data collection methods are bound to identify important phenomena begging for an explanation, and thus to open new avenues for consumer research.

Wells (1993), who is both a researcher and a practitioner, has given strongly worded advice to American academics, with four recommendations which should be required reading for researchers and for doctoral students: leave home, reach out, start small and stay real, and research backward (i.e. starting from the results you want to obtain). Andreasen (1985) also proposed that research be conducted backward: start from the implementation, determine what the final report should be, specify the analysis necessary, and scan the available (or necessary) data. Actually, this is also useful when starting a research project on the basis of a real problem identified in a company. A fifth heading in Wells's recommendations, forsake mythology, has more to do with methodology. But the methodological problems posed by Wells are likely to lead us, if we ignore them, to major substantive problems: if we forget about real customers to concentrate on students, if we study phenomena in artificial rather than real settings, if we content ourselves with explaining 3 per cent of the variance, provided it is 'significant', if we imply causation when we find correlation, if we think that merely describing validity problems in a footnote will solve these problems.

For years, a number of colleagues (Johansson and Mattsson, 1994; Möller, 1994), most often from Scandinavia, have reminded us that we have too short-sighted a view of marketing. Concentrating on individual transactions, on a single purchase, is wrong. Rather, we should study long-term relationships: how links develop, over the long run, between a company and its clients; how more complex networks are established between multiple actors, at different stages of the product or service conception, manufacturing, delivery and consumption. As Lambin (1993) puts it, 'Firms should shift the emphasis from the product to the consumer; the objective becomes to provide solutions to the buyer's problems, not simply products; this implies long lasting relationships rather than pure transactional marketing.' Scandinavian colleagues have mainly studied industrial marketing, and have complained, with good reason, that too much attention is being paid to consumer marketing. According to Möller (1994), there are four conceptual approaches for research on interorganizational marketing exchange: the transaction cost approach, the political economy approach, the interaction approach, and the network approach. Möller advocates more integration between these four approaches. As Frazier (1993) puts it, 'A key challenge is to better understand the variety of different research approaches and frameworks applied to the channels area.'

Methods that are appropriate for the study of one-shot purchases, such as surveys or laboratory experiments, may be totally inadequate to deal with such long-run relationships. A number of alternative methodological approaches consider marketing phenomena in a longer perspective. They are more pertinent and will become more important. For example, Johansson and Mattsson (1994) describe the Swedish tradition as 'less quantitative and more qualitative, less deductive and more inductive, less theory testing and more theory developing, less specifically oriented to marketing management and more holistic, less prescriptive and more descriptive'. Other examples are quasi-experimental designs tracking, over a long period, a major change in a market; retrospective studies that use historical, or quasi-historical, methods; the study of decision processes over time, especially when the decision is not a split-second event that takes place in front of the shelf, but rather an extended sequence of phenomena over several weeks or months, involving multiple persons and organizations; in-depth case studies analysing strategic marketing phenomena such as the development or demise of alliances. This does not exclude quantitative analyses, for example, using databases to study long-run loyalty to an organization.

Finally, methodological considerations, in addition to being important by themselves, lead to a constant reassessment of substantive concepts and relationships. Failures to measure a variable or to statistically support a hypothesis are likely to lead to a better understanding of the underlying phenomenon. Structural equation methods, such as LISREL or PLS, are a good protection against unsupported sweeping statements. International comparative studies, international replications, are an excellent, but still too rare, way to test the reliability and validity of theories and instruments designed in a single country. Means–end analysis can lead to an in-depth redefinition of the concepts and hypotheses relevant to a problem. Equally, methodological considerations for case research (Yin, 1992) will generate substantive progress.

Selected topics

We now suggest several directions for future research. They belong to classical domains of marketing (product policy, branding, retailers, sales promotion, distribution, customized marketing, consumer behaviour). We believe that 'rethinking marketing' can largely be done by going further in such classical domains.

Product policy had for decades been a neglected element of the so-called marketing mix. We must thank our academic friends from production management, and our friends from industry, who have reminded us, in practice, of the importance of a clever and innovative product policy. Quality, of course, has become essential, everywhere. Quality should be studied in relation to client satisfaction, be it in industrial or consumer settings, for services and for goods. Satisfaction is certainly a major cause of client loyalty, a central phenomenon in today's marketing thinking, as everyone comes to understand that keeping a consumer is easier, and more profitable, than recruiting a new one. In addition to quality management, we should do more research on questions such as standardization versus adaptation (or how to combine standardization and adaptation), quick reactions to demand, services added to the product (or should we say incorporated into the product), the optimal rhythm of product replacement, etc. Let us stress, finally, how important product and production policies are for services. Take a single example, dealing with a very old service: restaurants. The owner of the Bistro de la Gare, in Paris, has managed, by introducing dozens of innovative elements in the organization of his restaurant chain, to offer his customers good quality meals at very reasonable prices. This has led him to fast growth, and to make a fortune. Many elements of his service production policy could be extended to other sectors.

Branding will remain a major topic for research in marketing. It is as interesting from the client-customer end as from the manufacturer end. Several topics are of high interest, beyond those related to brand extensions, which are currently heavily researched. 'Brand equity' is mentioned everywhere, but we have not yet reached the final word on it. The monetary evaluation of brands permits joint studies with colleagues from law, finance and accounting. How many different brands should one have in a market, in order to occupy store shelves, consumer minds and market shares? Should a company move towards unified brands in different European countries? What should brands do against 'low-price' products that are invading many markets?

Retailers have emerged recently as major disruptive players in the quieter game that used to be played between consumers and manufacturers. This is true for pricing, with manufacturers sometimes unable to implement the pricing policies they had designed. This is true for promotions, which are strongly controlled, or disturbed, by retailers. This is true in some sense for advertising, where a major advertising campaign makes sense only if it is supported by good shelf space, to be decided by retailers. This is true for branding. Retailers develop a control over national brands. They can take, so to speak, major brands as hostages, through their control of assortment and shelf space. As an illustration, Colgate managed to be ejected for six months from the shelves of one of the leading retailers in France. Angelmar (1986) indicated that the power structure was simple: Colgate represented 1 per cent of the retailer's sales, and the retailer represented 12 per cent of Colgate's sales. Retailers can also create retailer-controlled brands of comparable quality and stature, direct competitors to national brands. With the stronger retailer power, marketing is no longer a two-person game, it is at least a three-person game, and all our analyses should be revised accordingly. What we call in French 'trade marketing' has become a major preoccupation of manufacturers. In a related vein, the power of intermediaries had been growing enormously in advertising markets. Organizations that were buying advertising space *en masse*, and later selling it to individual manufacturers, developed an enormous, prominent power. Recent legislative action seems to be changing this in our country, but the phenomenon would need to be studied.

Sales promotion has had ever increasing importance in recent years. This is so obvious it only needs to be mentioned briefly. Budgets have grown quickly everywhere. In France, a price war between car manufacturers is going on, that apparently started in the form of temporary and limited price promotions. More and more research will be devoted to sales promotion. Many topics are important, dealing with consumer behaviour in response to promotions, of course, but also with manufacturer and retailer decisions, and the game-like relationships between these two. We refer the reader to two articles describing directions for future in this domain (Blattberg et al., 1994; Neslin et al., 1994).

Customized marketing is another direction. Let us illustrate the next point with a personal anecdote. Five or six times over the last winter, one of us took a plane from Paris to London, once or twice on British Airways, the rest of the time on Air France. On both companies, he was flying to the same London airport, Heathrow, where the two companies are competing. One day, he received a letter from British Airways, explaining that another London airport, Gatwick, was more conveniently connected to London by train, and that he should try it. BA offered a promotion to encourage trial: a free train ticket from Gatwick to London, and a coupon for £10, to be spent in the duty-free shop. The trial took place, and the traveller became convinced of the convenience of Gatwick, where British Airways had a monopoly on the Paris–London route. This illustrates nicely several aspects of the new marketing we are thinking about. Changing behaviour may be easier than changing attitudes: the traveller still thinks highly of Air France, but is flying British Airways. Promotions may have long-lasting effects: with one coupon, BA will sell many flights in the future. A company should aim at very precise targets: business people and consultants who want to get quickly into London. For this, they need to rely on well-organized databases. We enter the era of 'mass customization', to use the title of a book by Pine (1993). Lastly, a company should manage its long-term relation to its clients. Companies with a detailed knowledge of their clients can develop highly tailored treatments. Examples will multiply. In a sense, this development has an ironic twist. We discussed the network, long-term view of marketing held by colleagues from Scandinavia, speaking mainly of industrial marketing. Many persons working on consumer marketing, either practitioners or academics, are just rediscovering the arguments put forward long ago by these colleagues.

Finally, take consumer behaviour. We briefly mention three new topics. The first is role dissociation: one person chooses a product or service, another pays for it, a third one uses it. This has of course been studied empirically, within the family, or for organizational decision-making (Bon and Pras, 1984). But role dissociation is becoming particularly important from a public policy viewpoint. In future years, there may not be enough public financing to pay for health care, education, social or cultural activities that traditionally were used by certain persons, decided by others, and funded by anonymous taxpayers. The second is time: In addition to research on time budgets and time constraints, one can study the time orientation (past, present, future) of individuals and its impact on their behaviour (Bergadaà, 1990). The third is interpersonal influences, especially those that are not based on a rational transfer of objective information. This includes rumours (Brodin and Roux, 1990; Kapferer, 1989), but also non-verbal influences, such as those created by symbols.

Broadening marketing also implies a more international view, too much work having been done within national boundaries. Douglas et al. (1994) describe several neglected themes for international consumer research: the role of societal factors, such as social norms, social stratification and social status; the dynamics of changes in lifestyle, consumption and behavioural patterns; the diffusion of innovations, ideas and information across countries; comparative studies of consumption values and attitudes, of cognitive processes and decision-making, of purchasing and consumption behaviour. Also, of course, the need for reliable and valid cross-national research instruments remains strong, and cannot be solved only by translating American instruments into other languages. Underlying research traditions in comparative sociology, comparative political science, comparative management, we find two schools of thoughts: the emic approach (no comparison across cultures and societal contexts is possible since each event is unique), and the etic approach (it is possible to identify universal and culture-free theories). Both approaches have been used in the key areas of cross-national consumer research.

A broader conception of marketing research

Marketing research should become broader from two points of view: extending the limits of marketing, to include more strategic problems; and forming relationships with a larger set of colleagues.

An extended set of problems

Whom are we competing against? This major and ancient problem will continue to be researched, as it is more and more difficult to define precisely one's own competitive universe for different reasons. First, the environment is changing quickly (deregulation, for example, and strong uncertainty). Secondly, these changes attract newcomers from unexpected horizons (distributors or retailers, companies from other sectors). A great diversity of approaches is feasible, from more synthetic and qualitative strategic analyses to panel-based diagnostics (Aurier, 1993), and to econometric studies, such as those discussed by Leeflang and Wittink (1994).

Alliances, vertical or horizontal, between complementary companies or between competitors, are studied in strategy and marketing with a variety of approaches. The distinction between qualitative and quantitative research makes less and less sense here, as in consumer behaviour, marketing and management research in general. It is customary to first study alliance processes in qualitative detail, to focus next on a few variables analysed by quantitative methods. Sometimes a qualitative probe of a few cases may complement quantitative outputs and help understand them. We should often use both inductive and deductive processes, qualitative and quantitative approaches.

Order of entry and pioneering effects are important. Will the first entrant build an enduring advantage? Will it shape preferences for the future by permanently influencing consumer perceptions, or through more objective economic effects? Relatedly, one can look for reductions in new product development delays, for a capacity to react quickly to changes in the national and international environment, to shifts in demand. Should one attempt to follow a 'Japanese' strategy and launch a new product simultaneously on as many markets as possible? The timing to be followed for the introduction of successive generations of a product or service is yet another topic. In all these cases, clearly, considerations of marketing strategy are deeply intertwined with R&D, operations management and logistics.

The development, and measurement, of a marketing orientation in companies is increasingly studied. In many European countries, a number of companies and organizations are moving from the public to the private sector. This is a unique opportunity to study how a large, established organization can change itself to acquire a marketing orientation and culture. Can this be decided from the top? Does one need to feel the first crushing blows from competitors to become convinced of the need for a marketing orientation? Some interesting cases can be observed in France these days, for public transportation, for post offices, for the national cigarette company, for example. Relatedly, economic pressure leads to better attempts to evaluate marketing productivity (Parsons, 1994). Loyalty and satisfaction will remain key issues for companies in the actual environment. Measurement problems are important on this matter.

We refer the reader to Webster (1992), who analyses the changing role of marketing in the corporation (see also Nevett, 1991; Powell, 1990; Simon, 1994). The first part is devoted to 'types of relationships and alliances: markets and transactions; repeated transactions; long-term relationships; mutual, total-dependence buyer–seller partnerships; strategic alliances; joint-ventures; networks'. The second part 'redefin(es) marketing's role: at the corporate level, market structure analysis, customer orientation and advocacy, positioning the firm in the value chain; at the SBU level, market segmentation and targeting, positioning the product, deciding when and how to partner; at the operating level, redefining the marketing mix, managing customer and reseller relationships'. This is at both the national and international levels. More generally, we should be monitoring more closely the changes taking place in marketing activities and strategies, and use this more frequently to identify new research avenues.

Research on international strategic marketing remains obviously essential. Many topics remain important: for example, 'global versus local'. One could argue that this classical alternative is no longer relevant, as one should think globally and act locally. A main point for companies is to retain flexibility. Grey exports are another challenge to standardization, especially with growing retailer power. Yet another problem is to adapt the organization to this global–local strategy while maintaining the motivation within the company, and without losing market share. Besides, one may wonder, like Bauman (1992), a sociologist, whether 'postmodernity is fit for globalization. Postmodernity is a culture of the privileged part of the world. It cannot be simply made into everybody's way of life.'

An extended discipline

We do not rely enough on basic disciplines. Douglas et al. (1994) underline that, for research in international marketing, colleagues have increasingly adopted approaches common in experimental and cognitive psychology, and more recently, in ethnography and semiotics. Leong (1989) and Wells (1993) have analysed the patterns of cross-disciplinary citations in the *Journal of Consumer Research*. But more needs to be done. In general, we advocate doing more research in collaboration with colleagues from underlying disciplines such as economics, sociology, psychology, statistics, engineering, etc. At a more fundamental level, a strong training in one or two underlying disciplines would give doctoral students richer perspectives on marketing problems, equip them with other conceptual and methodological tools. After they become marketing professors, they should keep contacts with colleagues from this other discipline, keep reading other journals and attending other conferences. Very rich results can be expected from such cross-fertilization. A doctoral education limited to the domain of marketing, as currently defined, may be too narrow. Changes in rules and curricula would be necessary in some European and maybe American universities.

The list of underlying disciplines given above could be extended to history, semiotics, linguistics, rhetoric, geography, ethnography, etc. (for example, see Cochoy, 1994; Van den Bulte, 1994). An interesting model is provided by semiotics, with the double special issue of the *International Journal of Research in Marketing* edited by Pinson (1988). It showed that semiotics research has been quite active, both in academia and among European practitioners. Work is going on, for example, on the five senses: the role of atmosphere in retail stores, the impact of smell on consumer behaviour (such as the role of odours in the Paris subway), the impact of colours. An important element is the consistency between these sensorial elements and the image of the product or service. Studying each sensorial element separately, without reference to the brand image, may lead to erroneous conclusions.

We do not have enough contacts between marketing scholars across borders. In the USA, one sees colleagues moving from one university to another after their dissertation, and often on several occasions during their careers. In Europe, we have mostly colleagues who have been educated in one country, and who teach in the same country, often in the same university where they had been educated. When generations of young colleagues have been educated by the same colleagues, with the same problems, same concepts, same methodological approaches, this is asking for trouble. This should change. New thinking will emerge from contacts with foreign colleagues with varied backgrounds, interests, conceptual and methodological orientations, when researchers are confronted with problems, environments, consumers, manufacturers, retailers different from those they have been in contact with for almost all their life. Fortunately, European conferences are more eclectic than American conferences, less specialized, mixing scholars from different research traditions. But one conference a year is not enough. Let's enrich, so to speak, our genetic endowment. Some recommendations to doctoral students: attend doctoral seminars at the European level, such as those offered by the European Institute in Brussels or by the European Marketing Academy; spend at least a term, maybe a year, in another country, during the dissertation period or immediately after it; include at least one foreign professor in each dissertation committee; attend international conferences. It could be suggested, at the European level, to create a post-doctoral degree that would rely on research done in a foreign country, on a foreign topic, and require this degree from all future professors. It is an unfortunate fact that there are only a few marketing academics in each European country, compared with the US. We need therefore to let European doctoral students take advantage of all European scholars, not only those living in the same country.

Looking back over the past 20 years of marketing research, we pointed out in the book *Research Traditions in Marketing* (Laurent et al., 1994) some of the research streams and controversies existing in the field. In this chapter, on the basis of that book, we have discussed some of the trends and divergences likely to emerge in the coming years.

References

Andreasen, A.R. (1985) 'Backward market research', *Harvard Business Review*, 63 (May–June): 176.

Angelmar, R. (1986) 'Colgate-Palmolive France'. Case Study, INSEAD.

Aurier, P. (1993) 'Analyse de la structure des marchés: réflexions et propositions théoriques sur la relation entre deux alternatives de choix', *Recherche et Applications en Marketing*, 8: 77–96.

Bauman, Z. (1992) *Intimations of Post-Modernity*. London: Routledge.

Bergadaà, M. (1990) 'The role of time in the action of the consumer', *Journal of Consumer Research*, 17: 289–302.

Blattberg, R.C. and Neslin, S.A. (1990) *Sales Promotion: Concepts, Methods, and Strategies*. Englewood Cliffs, NJ: Prentice-Hall.

Blattberg, R.C., Briesch, R. and Fox, E.J. (1994) 'How promotions work'. Working Paper, Northwestern University.

Bon, J. and Pras, B. (1984) 'Dissociation of the roles of buyer, payer and consumer', *International Journal of Research in Marketing*, 1: 7–16.

Brodin, O. and Roux, E. (1990) 'Les recherches sur les rumeurs: courants, méthodes, enjeux managériaux', *Recherche et Applications en Marketing*, 5 (4): 45–70.

Cochoy, F. (1994) 'The emerging tradition of historical research in marketing: history of marketing and marketing of history', in G. Laurent, G.L. Lilien and B. Pras (eds), *Research Traditions in Marketing*. Boston: Kluwer. pp. 383–97.

Douglas, S.P., Morrin, M.A. and Craig, C.S. (1994) 'Cross-national consumer research traditions', in G. Laurent, G.L. Lilien and B. Pras (eds), *Research Traditions in Marketing*. Boston: Kluwer. pp. 289–306.

Durand, R. Personal communication.

Ehrenberg, A.S.C. (1994) 'Theory or well-based results: which comes first?', in G. Laurent, G.L. Lilien and B. Pras (eds), *Research Traditions in Marketing*. Boston: Kluwer. pp. 79–108.

Frazier, G.L. (1993) 'A perspective on interorganizational exchange in channels of distribution', in G. Laurent, G.L. Lilien and B. Pras (eds), *Research Traditions in Marketing*. Boston: Kluwer. pp. 378–82.

Guadagni, P.M. and Little, J.D.C. (1983) 'A logic model of brand choice calibrated on scanner data', *Marketing Science*, 2: 203–38.

Johansson, J. and Mattsson, L.-G. (1994) 'The markets-as-networks tradition in Sweden', in G. Laurent, G.L. Lilien and B. Pras (eds), *Research Traditions in Marketing*. Boston: Kluwer. pp. 321–42.

Kahneman, D., Slovic, P. and Tversky, A. (eds) (1982) *Judgement under Uncertainty: Heuristics and Biases*. Cambridge: Cambridge University Press.

Kapferer, J.N. (1989) 'Les disparitions de Mourmelon – origine et interprétations des rumeurs', *Revue Française de Sociologie*, 30 (1): 81–9.

Lambin, J.J. (1993) 'Priorities in marketing management practices: implications for research and for teaching', Invited Address, 22nd Conference of the European Marketing Academy, Barcelona.

Laurent, G. and Grégory, P. (1992) 'Les thèses de marketing depuis 1986', *Recherche et Applications en Marketing*, 7: 43–64.

Laurent, G., Lilien, G.L. and Pras, B. (eds) (1994) *Research Traditions in Marketing.* Boston: Kluwer.

Leeflang, P.S.H. and Wittink, D.R. (1994) 'Diagnosing competition: developments and findings', in G. Laurent, G.L. Lilien and B. Pras (eds), *Research Traditions in Marketing.* Boston: Kluwer.

Leong, Siew M. (1989) 'A citation analysis of the *Journal of Consumer Research*', *Journal of Consumer Research*, 15: 492–7.

McGuire, J.W. (1982) 'Management theory: retreat to the academy', *Business Horizons*, July–August: 31–7.

Möller, K.E. (1994) 'Interorganizational marketing exchange: metatheoretical analysis of current research approaches', in G. Laurent, G.L. Lilien and B. Pras (eds), *Research Traditions in Marketing.* Boston: Kluwer. pp. 347–72.

Neslin, S., Allenby, G., Ehrenberg, A.S.C., Hoch, S., Laurent, G., Leone, R., Little, J.D.C., Lodish, L., Shoemaker, R. and Wittink, D. (1994) 'A research agenda for making scanner data more useful to managers', *Marketing Letters*, 5: 395–411.

Nevett, T. (1991) 'Historical investigation and the practice of marketing', *Journal of Marketing*, 55 (3): 13–23.

Parsons, L.J. (1994) 'Productivity versus relative efficiency in marketing: past and future?', in G. Laurent, G.L. Lilien and B. Pras (eds), *Research Traditions in Marketing.* Boston: Kluwer. pp. 168–96. Publishers.

Pine, B.J. (1993) *Mass Customization: The New Frontier in Business Competition.* Boston: Harvard Business School Press.

Pinson, C. (1988) 'Semiotics and marketing communication research', *International Journal of research in Marketing.* Double Special Issue, 4 (3 and 4).

Powell, W.W. (1990) 'Neither market nor hierarchy: network forms of organization', *Research in Organizational Behaviour*, 12: 295–336.

Simon, H. (1994) 'Marketing science's pilgrimage to the ivory tower', in G. Laurent, G.L. Lilien and B. Pras (eds), *Research Traditions in Marketing.* Boston: Kluwer. pp. 27–43.

Steyer, A. (1993) 'La théorie des avalanches: physique sociale des phénomènes de propagation'. Doctoral dissertation, Ecole des Hautes Etudes Commerciales.

Van den Bulte, C. (1994) 'Metaphor at work', in G. Laurent, G.L. Lilien and B. Pras (eds), *Research Traditions in Marketing.* Boston: Kluwer. pp. 405–25.

Webster, F.E. Jr (1992) 'The changing role of marketing in the corporation', *Journal of Marketing*, 56 (4): 1–17.

Wells, D. William (1993) 'Discovery-oriented consumer research', *Journal of Consumer Research*, 19: 489–504.

Yin, R.K. (1992) *Case Study Research Design and Methods*, rev. edn. Newbury Park, CA: Sage.

19   Commentary

Gerald Zaltman

The chapters by Dibb and Stern and by Laurent and Pras address important issues in insightful, provocative ways. Moreover, it is difficult to conceive of two more important topics that need to be addressed in this way: how we inquire, and how the fruits of inquiry are taught or shared among students, practitioners and researchers. Each chapter is thoughtful in its identification and elaboration of a number of tensions and imperatives facing marketing professionals.

The two chapters must be read as a unit since production and dissemination processes ultimately shape one another. For example, the research-oriented chapter by Gilles Laurent and Bernard Pras raises a major instructional dilemma: 'When generations of young colleagues have been educated by the *same* colleagues, with the *same* problems, *same* concepts, *same* methodological approaches, this is asking for trouble' (italics added). While they refer to doctoral instruction, the statement applies equally to instruction at other levels and other domains such as executive education. Their concern, of course, is with the cloning of minds through sameness.

Cloned minds in instructional, management, or research activities are not conducive to the production of the new ideas or rethinking required by a changing environment. The teaching-oriented chapter by Sally Dibb and Philip Stern stresses this when they identify a goal common to both teaching and research: 'the purpose of any analysis is to provide insight and is valuable only when it contributes to understanding.' New insight and understanding, like the avoidance of cloned minds, is central to rethinking marketing.

Understanding is not the possession of knowledge

In its own way, each chapter suggests that rethinking marketing requires the acquisition of insight and understanding in teaching, practice, and research. This prompts the question: what is it we have when we have an understanding? My answer is that understanding involves the capacity to use knowledge to solve open-ended or novel problems. The mere possession of knowledge is not enough. We can know but not understand. That is, we can possess a set of 'facts' but not know how to use them when confronted with a unique problem. Acquiring 'answers' from textbooks, experience, and research doesn't help much if market phenomena are no longer posing the corresponding questions. This is the instructional dilemma in rethinking marketing: *how do we train the minds of managers, teachers, and researchers to know when and how to be led by novel questions rather than prepackaged answers?* Indeed, the concept of lifelong learning requires that teachers provide students and managers with the ability to generate their own new ideas and new ways of using existing ideas.

The four authors are sensitive to the need for wide cognitive peripheral vision in rethinking, that is the need to be open to and willing to integrate diverse sets of information. For instance, Dibb and Stern 'highlight the breadth and variety of information with which instructors must deal' in order to provide insight and understanding, and Laurent and Pras discuss the real and potential impact of 'better data, and alternative approaches (alternative theoretical bases and assumptions)' especially from other disciplines as a source of new ideas. However, I'm not sure they go quite far enough (although, consistent with the quality of good writing, the authors provide most readers with something to disagree with).

In the space remaining, I'd like to build on their thinking (my judgement, not necessarily theirs) and state some premises – positions that need to be recognized and accepted – necessary for rethinking marketing. However, alternative positions exist in marketing with respect to each premise. Different positions will result in very different strategies for rethinking how we teach, manage, or conduct research in marketing. Hopefully, by taking one particular position, I will stimulate readers to rethink and develop their own position further.

Moving from knowledge to understanding

The premises below are central to the task of moving beyond knowledge to understanding.

Premise 1 Marketing is an inherently social phenomenon.

Most explanations of marketing share a basic idea: marketing consists of activities which foster exchange relationships. Exchange relationships are irreducibly social in nature and fundamental to marketing. Thus, whatever else marketing may be, it is a social phenomenon. This simple idea encompasses an eclectic range of marketplace behaviours varying from the simple to the complex, a wide variety of market mechanisms relating to those behaviours, and diverse ways of monitoring and understanding behaviours and associated mechanisms.

There exists a division of labour within marketing appropriate to the complexity of the phenomenon. For example, some people focus their attention on improving and/or applying mathematical and statistical tools to help others monitor and understand market processes. Others focus attention on understanding the behavioural properties of markets using various conceptual frames of reference. Many people engaged in marketing orient themselves to important marketing contexts such as channels of distribution, pricing, communication, independently of methodological and conceptual orientation. This complexity in the social organization of the discipline mirrors the fact that marketing, at its core, is an inescapably human enterprise no matter what our preferred units of analyses are, why they are interesting to us, or what our methodological orientation is. This brings us to the next premise.

Premise 2 There is more marketing relevant knowledge 'outside' the field than in it.

Given the inherently social nature of marketing, the complexity and variety of its phenomena, and the diversity of its methods of inquiry, it is reasonable to ask: how much extant understanding of human behaviour at both the micro and the macro level is accounted for by marketing or even the management sciences? The answer is quite humbling, no matter how one chooses to make the calculation. We represent a small sliver of a substantial pie involving human affairs. Even if we lop off most of the pie as not being for us – which would be a mistake – a substantial meal remains. (Let me acknowledge that a major issue of how relevance is established is not addressed here.) I find this encouraging since any contribution to our understanding of human behaviour is potentially relevant to our field.

There is more of relevance to marketing issues to be found outside the field than in it if only because the human and fiscal resources devoted to common issues greatly exceed our own. The resources expended in relevant, non-marketing domains and the results achieved dwarf what we could ever hope for in our own discipline.

While extensive work in the social and biological sciences and in the humanities is very relevant to the marketing discipline, there are access barriers. First, there is much that is not relevant to marketing (also a criticism of some market research) and separating the wheat from the chaff is not always easy. Secondly, considerable start-up capital in the form of time and commitment is needed to process this work effectively. Thirdly, there are language barriers. Some of this work is not very friendly to new users. Another barrier is that the soundness of the work may be difficult to assess. Validity and reliability are implemented differently in different fields and often the methods used are unfamiliar ones.

Premise 3 Frontiers of knowledge tend to be at disciplinary borders.

Another premise is that the frontiers of knowledge are to be found more often at the perimeters of a discipline where it borders others rather than in the centre of already well-colonized disciplinary territory. For instance, it is likely that revolutionary work being done concerning mind/body/behaviour interfaces – work outside the current marketing mainstreams – will be the primary driver of rethinking in marketing. Whether this occurs sooner or later depends on a variety of factors which cannot be addressed here, with one exception noted below. If the future rethinking of marketing, indeed of the management sciences generally, is driven more by developments outside the field than in it, the real issue is: *who will lead the rethinking of marketing based on dramatic developments now occurring outside the field?*

Premise 4 'Borrowing' is a good practice but a bad metaphor.

The chapter by Gilles Laurent and Bernard Pras particularly encourages broadening cognitive peripheral vision by working with ideas and colleagues from other disciplines. Yet there is much criticism within marketing of what is interestingly called 'borrowing'. I'd like to address this further since the metaphor contains a hidden attitude which is a barrier to the development of marketing thought in our teaching and research programmes.

One of the most fundamental norms of science involves communality. In Robert K. Merton's words:

> The substantive findings of science are a product of social collaboration and are assigned to the community. They constitute a common heritage in which the equity of the individual producer is severely limited . . . Property rights in science are whittled down to a bare minimum by the rationale of the scientific ethic. (Sztompka, 1996: 271–2)

The findings of science belong in the public domain. No one discipline, much less one person or department, 'owns' an idea or research finding. Rather, what is owned is the esteem or professional recognition independently accorded the source of the concept or finding. Research in cognitive neuroscience about memory, language, and affect, or econometric research on market behaviour, are no more the property of scientists in those fields than they are of the marketing scientist, the physicist, or the anthropologist once the ideas enter the public domain of the research literature which is also where recognition is conferred.

If ideas are public property, they can't really be borrowed. The supply isn't diminished or made less available by virtue of usage. The idea of borrowing is quaintly capitalistic. It is also an impediment to the advancement of knowledge. In the marketing field we hear cautions about borrowing, the need to repay other disciplines, the need to develop our own theories (and presumably no one else's), and so on. Interestingly, I have never heard these cautions from practitioners, only from academics.

The borrowing metaphor is helpful if it alerts us to the fact that other scientists and scholars are generating ideas relevant to marketing problems. It is an unconstructive metaphor if it implies: (1) wrongdoing and the discouraging of charity (both captured in the admonition of American inventor/essayist Benjamin Franklin, adapted from *Hamlet*, 'Never a borrower nor lender be'),

(2) a need to return the 'property' unaltered and hence the discouraging of improvements, and (c) a sense of subordination (a borrower is indebted). The pejorative qualities of the metaphor also (4) encourage waste if it results in expending resources to reinvent or rediscover what is already established.

Probably the chief cost of the borrowing metaphor is its fostering of ethno-centrism ('That's not marketing!') which is a bit like condemning infants because they are not already functional adults or because their prospects for becoming such are unclear. If we see marketing science in particularistic terms, we put brakes on its progress.

Premise 5   Teaching habits of mind is at least as important as teaching codified knowledge.

What are the ultimate drivers of progress in marketing? What should be the ultimate core competence to develop among marketers? For lack of a more precise term, let me refer to these drivers as *habits of mind*. Habits of mind are the special ways we identify and structure problems and approach their solution. They include, for example, how we use existing knowledge to fashion novel ideas, whether we tend to represent information inductively or deductively, our preferred systems of metaphor, and so on. They exist within and among individuals. In fact, the latter probably have greater causal impact on the former than the reverse.

Habits of mind guide how we make meaning out of marketing data and translate this meaning into marketing action. These habits are central to the worlds of the instructor and manager alike. As much as anything else, habits of mind determine the character and rate of progress in marketing thought and practice. Let me go further, and suggest that nowhere is this more important than with regard to data involving ill-structured or open-ended problems. These are problems which are non-routine, often lacking a clear best answer or solution (perhaps even having multiple good answers), and where the exact nature of the problem may be unclear, it being certain only that there is a problem. These problems are disproportionately important in personal and professional life. It is with ill-structured problems that habits of mind have their greatest liberating or inhibiting impact.

Surprisingly little marketing literature is devoted to habits of mind, i.e. to the topic of how we think. Stimulating and useful discussions often occur about the meaning of data, their validity, or the wisdom of a corresponding course of action. But seldom do we address or explore the most essential process of all: the individual, group, and organizational mechanisms generating and/or inhibiting the creation of meaning and its translation into action. A good way to throw cold water on a heated discussion is to ask participants how they came up with their interpretations and/or how they moved from those interpretations to a recommended action. In short, people have trouble describing the process whereby they acquire understanding. What habits of mind refer to with such utterances as 'Clearly the data say . . .' or 'Obviously we must . . .' turn out to be far from clear or obvious to those sharing their insights. (Research in neural science helps explain why this is the case.)

Conclusion

One of the most reliable forecasts we can make about the future is that change never arrives as quickly as people say it will and, when it does arrive, we're never ready for it. The chapters by Sally Dibb and Philip Stern and by Gilles Laurent and Bernard Pras raise a number of ideas that, if given more attention, would hasten our rethinking of marketing (a task justified throughout this volume). To help prod this rethinking along, I have made a number of assertions arguing that marketing is an inherently social phenomenon and thus there is more of relevance to our subject matter 'outside' the discipline than in it. This is a simple consequence of resource allocation: we are outnumbered and outspent by colleagues in other fields also concerned with the human enterprise. Even if this were not the case, it makes sense to explore the interface marketing has with the social and biological sciences since that is where the frontiers of knowledge most often lie. For this reason, we need to re-examine certain attitudes toward engaging other disciplines. The borrowing metaphor, for example, might discourage the activity to which it refers. Finally, and perhaps most importantly, I have suggested that we need to give more attention to how we think. If what we think is important, then it is no less important to improve those knowledge producing factors I've called habits of mind.

Reference

Sztompka, P. (ed.) (1996) *Robert K. Merton: On Social Structure and Science.* Chicago: University of Chicago Press.

Index